Investor's Passport to Hedge Fund Profits

Investor's Passport to Hedge Fund Profits

Unique Investment Strategies for Today's Global Capital Markets

SEAN CASTERLINE

ROBERT YETMAN, JR.

WILEY

John Wiley & Sons, Inc.

Published by John Wiley & Sons, Inc., Hoboken, New Jersey.
Published simultaneously in Canada.

For general information on our other products and services or for technical support, please
contact our Customer Care Department within the United States at (800) 762-2974, outside the
United States at (317) 572-3993 or fax (317) 572-4002.

Wiley also publishes its books in a variety of electronic formats. Some content that appears in
print may not be available in electronic formats. For more information about Wiley products,
visit our Web site at www.wiley.com.

Library of Congress Cataloging-in-Publication Data:

Casterline, Sean, 1969–
    Investor's passport to hedge fund profits : unique investment strategies for today's global
capital markets / Sean Casterline and Robert Yetman, Jr.
        p. cm. – (Wiley trading series)
    Includes index.
    ISBN 978-0-470-42744-6 (cloth)
    1. Hedge funds. 2. Hedge funds–United States.   I. Yetman, Robert, 1962–   II. Title.
    HG4530.C328 2010
    332.64′5–dc22

                                                                        2009050961

Printed in the United States of America

10 9 8 7 6 5 4 3 2 1

Dedication

To my wife, Amy, who has always believed in my dreams and helped to make them a reality; and to Jonathan and Beau...my best investments.

—SEAN CASTERLINE

To my wife, Dallas, whose love and devotion were essential to making it through the long hours and late nights necessary to finish this project; to Hunter and Dalton, who have been gracious and kind to the latest additions to their family; to my terrific son, Brandon, for remaining as patient as ever with his busy dad; and, finally, to my late parents, Robert G. and Geraldine C. Yetman, whose wisdom and grace continue to both guide and inspire me to this day.

—ROBERT G. YETMAN, JR.

Contents

Introduction

For the purpose of this book, and in accordance with our outlook, we take a broader, more general view of just what makes a hedge fund a hedge fund. If you begin with the general definition that a hedge fund is a pooled investment fund that's structured in such a way so as to reduce risk, preserve capital, and maximize returns in any given market climate, you are off to a good start. In fact, that is really, in a nutshell, what a hedge fund is.

The definition of a hedge fund has become both fluid and expansive over the years, to the point where there is now a wide variety of hedge fund *styles* to meet the discerning tastes and unique goals of investors. The more purist view of a hedge fund dictates that it engage in such stereotypical hedging strategies as short selling and derivatives used to *hedge* the performance of mainstay asset classes (notably stocks) to maximize gains and limit losses to as great an extent as possible. That said, you find we are not slaves to traditional hedge fund dogma, in the sense that if you do not use derivatives often, or at all, then you are somehow not *really* prosecuting a hedge fund approach to your portfolio; we are not tied to the idea that the *ex*clusion or *in*clusion of select strategies makes or breaks you as a hedge fund manager. The real issue, in our view, is adherence to the aforementioned definition, and while your pursuit of realizing same may include your decision to utilize more typical hedge fund mechanisms, doing so is by no means a requirement, and focusing so single-mindedly on the use of such strategies might even cause you to lose sight of the forest for the trees. In actuality, a large number of hedge funds do not utilize derivatives instruments or leverage at all, which is not the popular conception; the popular conception is that hedge funds take massive and highly leveraged positions in a particular asset class that is very much in favor at a particular time with a given manager. Although those funds certainly exist, that is a somewhat overblown view of hedge funds. It is certainly within one's rights to look at a hedge fund as a mechanism by which to place some (somewhat) managed bets on markets or market components in order to try to make a killing, but that is not the manner in which we embrace the hedge fund concept here. We believe that the core benefit of the hedge fund approach lies in the ability to rotate weightings throughout the available asset classes (as well as countries and regions) on a basis that allows us to, overall, beat benchmark returns.

Rather than selecting a highly specific style (i.e., distressed securities, special situations, short selling) that rules the way in which our portfolio is composed and managed, we refrain from needlessly boxing ourselves into a corner and instead adopt a more blended approach to our investing. For example, we do not focus primarily on aggressive growth securities or on those that are distressed; we do not believe the use of leverage has to be a mainstay, and that if you choose against its use then you are not really applying a hedge fund perspective to your portfolio management. Our approach is to consider all key asset classes, guided chiefly by a mix of fundamental and technical analysis, with some intuitive reasoning thrown in, and utilizing more acutely aggressive options only when it seems to make real sense to do so. You are free to do what you want, and the core methodologies and concepts contained here will serve you well regardless of which specific hedge fund style you adopt, but we are comfortable with a portfolio management style that involves maintaining a capital preservation foundation from which we construct growth opportunity structures.

It is important to note that while the traditional style of hedge fund with which we might appear to have most in common—global macro—is actually a more aggressive approach traditionally, we view the term slightly more conservatively than do many who actually adopt that style. To us, a global macro view of investing speaks to our top-down approach, where we look at what worldwide market cycles are doing and decide which regions and countries are more deserving of greater weightings. It is a bit difficult, in our estimation, to engage active global investing in any way other than with a top-down approach that ultimately invites rotation and sector weightings on the basis of region and country, as well as industry and security. Global investing has to remain highly organized, simply out of deference to the breadth of available options and volume of information that must be considered and processed. The difference between our approach to global macro–type investing and that executed by fellows like George Soros is that we are less inclined to make large, top-heavy bets on anticipated movements. For example, some global macro managers were knocked around when they bet substantially that European bonds would rise in 1994 due to a belief that overseas rates would decline; when rates rose instead (following the Fed's decision to increase U.S. rates), they took a bath. Global macro may be, in one sense, an accurate two-word description of what a global hedge fund–type portfolio is all about, so it is ultimately the temperament of your trades that discerns highly aggressive global macro investing from that which we speak about here.

The hedge fund view of global investing does not require you to be a daredevil. It is, in truth, an approach that can go a long way in helping to ensure against great loss in various uncooperative world markets. The genesis of building global portfolios is both the empirical and intuitive understanding that investment opportunity is greatest globally, rather than domestically. However, that idea in and of itself does not require us to try to capitalize greatly through the use of big plays, but rather suggests that we can use it to build a sensible effort at risk-adjusted investment success through an effort that seeks to lower correlations among asset classes as much as possible. We adopt the idea that the success of a hedge fund should be gauged by its ability to preserve capital and lower overall risk to the portfolio rather than by its efforts to "hit the ball out of the park." Although no one among us would dispute the pleasure of realizing massive portfolio gains year after year, only a true seer would be able to make that happen, and so until they start making crystal balls that actually work, regular efforts to that end are going to be dangerous for individual investors who cannot afford to view their retirement plans as play money.

In the end, we do not approach global investing much differently from the way in which we approach domestic investing. The soundness of the equities securities into which we invest, ultimately, is determined by a mix of fundamental and technical analysis, just as it is when we trade domestically. Granted, the scope of the investable universe is broader, and those who might historically rely more on technical analysis must incorporate more fundamental views out of deference to the nature of the top-down approach that gets an investor from the beginning of his search for solid investments around the world to specific plays in individual countries. Still, disciplined adherence to the basic process of evaluating regions of the world down to individual companies works, and it allows you to remain focused and refrain from becoming too flustered as you begin to assemble and manage your portfolio.

A FEW FINAL, RANDOM THOUGHTS BEFORE WE BEGIN . . .

Although you find that the book is written from the standpoint of U.S. investors, the principles and methods outlined here are more than applicable to investors whose mother countries are those that Americans would regard as foreign. We hope that those of you who are kindred spirits from other investment spheres from around the world will forgive us our inherent regional bias, but we are sure you understand. In the end, the audience of this book need not be any less global than the subject matter itself, and we look forward to having as investment friends anyone who recognizes the wisdom of putting his money to work around the world.

Also, we want to mention here at the outset how we have treated the whole subject of risk within the context of this book—or, more accurately, perhaps —how we have *not* treated it. For decades now, investment offerings to individual investors on the matter of global investing have often prioritized the subject of risk to such a degree and in such a way that one might conclude that investing in foreign markets is akin to carrying around a package of high explosives. We acknowledge and respect the array of more unusual risks associated with investing internationally, but we believe that such risks are largely mitigated by maintaining an active, watchful, analytical approach to one's portfolio. For example, the idea that political risk is as dangerous to international investors today as it was decades ago when access to news was not as immediate or omnipresent is largely untenable; the active, ongoing management of your funds, combined with the tremendously high levels of access to the news worldwide, makes the threat of political risk, though certainly present, not the danger it once was. Even currency risk, historically the largest and noisiest fly in the global investing ointment, is more easily managed now with greater access to information and trading mechanisms now available to individual investors. Additionally, the acute awareness of your goals and approach to your discipline is a big help in dealing with it. For example, the inclusion of currencies as a separate, stand-alone asset class—rather than purely for use as a hedge on behalf of other asset classes—can, by itself, be a big help to addressing currency risk. Years ago, few books targeting global investing addressed the idea of trading in currencies at the individual investor level, and now currency trading is viewed by many as the latest and greatest thing to come down the pike. Furthermore, you may wish to deal with currency risk by remaining entirely unhedged, in the interest of lowering correlations among regions, countries, and sectors. The point is that once again, the evolution of information and opportunity is such that even an element as dicey as currency management can be negotiated without much downside to the manager who is involved and paying attention.

In short, our view is that the risk of global investing lies chiefly with the risk to your portfolio that arises when you *do not* invest outside of your home country. As you will see from the data contained in the book, the twenty-first-century investor who wants to enjoy a quality rate of return going forward really has little choice but to assemble a portfolio that includes a wide variety of instruments and that penetrates an array of global markets. It is the decision to refrain from doing so that is the source of real risk, in our opinion.

Lastly, we want to mention that although this book may well serve as an end unto itself for you, that need not be the case. As the title indicates, it is a *passport* to greater opportunities for your investments on the world stage, and in your pursuit of that goal, we invite you to consider tagging along with us at www.investorspassport.com to see what we have cooking; our effort there is centered on working to bring the best and most useful global investment news and opportunities to those who seek the sort of edge that can make the difference between more subdued portfolio success and that which significantly and positively impacts their standards of living.

Welcome Aboard!

CHAPTER 1

Opportunities Away from the Land of Opportunity

W e have long been fans of investing one's money, in part, outside of the United States. There are many reasons into which we delve that help to further justify forays into foreign markets, but it has always struck us as being just plain common sense to at least consider other economies as places from which to make money. Complicating the issue of looking elsewhere has long been the 800-pound gorilla sitting squarely in the middle of the room: we are Americans who live in the United States. That simple fact has, in the last several decades, afforded us the best reason to simply disregard the consideration of other markets. The reality is that we have everything we need right here. The truth is that we still do. Certainly, recent events have made even the most U.S.-centered investor wonder what better opportunities might await him or her in the other corners of Planet Earth, but in the end, most people like keeping everything here, thank you very much. It is just simpler, cleaner, easier.

Historically, when it comes to our money, we just *feel* better when our money is here in the United States (or so we perceive it to be). After all, are there not thousands upon thousands of publicly traded U.S. companies from which to choose, to say nothing of the thousands of stock mutual funds, bond mutual funds, and real estate opportunities that exist here in the United States? Indeed. We do not have to learn a new language to invest here, we know (at least anecdotally) that the best technology . . . the best platforms are here, and the financial center of the United States is still, for the most part, the financial center of the world. As a people, we love to visit other countries and exotic places, but most of us are very happy when we arrive home. It feels safe.

That intangible is largely what motivates us in everything we do—we do things because they *feel* right—even if they are wrong. We do it in interpersonal relationships, and we act accordingly in business and money relationships. To many Americans, investing our money outside of the United States just feels wrong. Historically, we have had discussions with multitudes of clients for whom foreign investment vehicles would have been an excellent fit, and yet many would exhibit a discomfort with the prospect on a level that we could not ignore. You can attack these objections with all of the left-brain logic you wish—but if it does not *feel* right—that is it.

Psychologically, many of us tend to see only the risks of such a move, rather than focus on the multitude of prospective rewards. At a root level, many people who eschew global investing do so because they feel physically more removed from their money.

It is largely the very historical success of the United States and its role, perhaps now more symbolic than real, as a world leader, that seems to have caused many to shrug off the wonderful opportunities available elsewhere. Principally, we believe that we have everything we need here, and we really do. It is historically rare that we find ourselves chasing the technology or opportunities found in other countries; instead, it has been the United States that has set the standards for trends and innovation for so long. In truth, that is changing, and has been changing for some time, but as we know, perception is reality, and the perception of so many is that the United States is still number one. We are as nationalistic as the next person when it comes to pride in one's country, but one must be careful not to permit that nationalism to blind oneself to the many glorious opportunities that exist elsewhere.

When you travel overseas, you see that the fascination with all things American remains very strong. Even many of the terrific products that are manufactured overseas, or made by companies that are otherwise based in foreign countries, and which are consumed by Americans, feel (there we go with *feeling* once again) very American.

It is our historical and cultural pride that remains perhaps our worst enemy from an investment perspective, but our relative geographical isolation plays a big part in all of that. Our role as a player on the world stage is ironic, considering how far removed we are from the rest of it. The "us versus them" mentality that permeates the thinking of so many Americans appears due, in no small way, to the fact that we have little occasion to consider other countries at all in our daily lives. Certainly we are bordered by Canada and Mexico, themselves geographically monstrous (Canada is the world's second largest country by area, while Mexico, no slouch itself, is the 14th largest by area) but more negligible in terms of corporate influences: of the 100 largest corporations in the world (as of 2008), Canada and Mexico together have a total of one between them. Compare and contrast that with Belgium, France, Germany, Italy, Netherlands, Spain, and Switzerland, which are all countries continuously surface-connected by the same land mass with adjacent, accessible borders, and which among them have 36 of the world's 100 largest corporations—five more than the mighty United States. If you want to throw in Great Britain by virtue of its channel tunnel, then forget about it; Britain's contribution of 9 of the 100 world's largest corporations brings the aforementioned total to 45.

The point in citing this is that many folks overseas, particularly those who live in or around the highly developed European continent, have a knowledge of, and relevance to, one another that we in the United States have not been able to have with anyone else. Accordingly, their acceptance of considering transborder investing is not as markedly nativistic as our own.

In our opinion, we have been done a disservice by this segregation, at a number of levels. Culturally, Americans tend to miss out on some amazing things. We often "ooh" and "aah" at the grand sights brought to us courtesy of the Travel Channel, but leave our interest behind once the credits roll. For most of us, it is just all too inaccessible. You do not have to be a wealthy person to travel from, say, France, as a resident *of* France, directly to Germany and then back to France, because you can do it all by train in much less than a day. If you are an American living in the United States, you may not have to be wealthy, per se, to travel to France or Germany, but you will likely have to spend thousands of dollars in order to enjoy any sort of meaningful trip to Europe and its neighbors. The point is that the *relevance* of other countries and people to our own, when noting it in terms of real-world experience, is largely diminished in comparison to the relevance of other countries and populations to one another.

Compounding this problem is that some of the best opportunities to make money overseas, via direct investment on the appropriate platform(s), in countries that present some of the best opportunities, will require a concerted effort to become familiar with languages, cultures, flows of information, traditions, and so forth, that remain literally foreign to most of us. Granted, that is not really true in the case of what we call the middle ground instruments of foreign investing, like mutual funds and American Depositary Receipts (ADRs), but for those who want to go all the way and take advantage of the best, most organic opportunities presented by the foreign marketplace, all of that is quite true. Staying stateside requires no such special effort or knowledge. U.S.-based companies are born, live, and breathe in a world we know and understand. Besides, there are lots of them. The number of stocks listed on the NYSE, NASDAQ, and AMEX totals about 6,000, and there are roughly 12,000 U.S. equity mutual funds at present. Our brokerages and trading platforms are highly evolved, and besides, the United States is, by history and reputation, the epicenter of the financial universe. Where else do you need to go?

Lots of places, actually. We are going to show you facts and figures a little later that illustrate how the United States is not the only game in town any longer, but you might also notice that the United States is still the biggest game in town. For example, (see Exhibits 1.1 and 1.2), of the world's 100 largest companies, those based in the United States comprise only about 30 percent percent of that list—but looked at another way, that 30 percent is far and away the largest representative, per country, of the listed companies; the next-largest percentage is attributed to Germany, at 13 percent. So it depends on how you choose to look at things: either you look at such a list and say, "70 percent of the word's largest companies are located outside of the United States," or you say, "the United States, by itself, has 30 percent of the world's largest companies contained herein; why do I need to look anywhere else to invest?" Obviously, there is a lot more to investment decision making beyond such a basic criterion, but the fact is that such a perspective is shared by even some, more sophisticated investors.

The answer to the question just asked is another question: Do you want your investing to be easy, or do you want it to be profitable? This is a big part of deciding to officially and formidably step out of the relative comfort of the United States and move into more exciting, but more challenging, realms. The truth is that from the standpoint of investment return, the United States has long been a disappointment. We discuss that more specifically throughout this chapter, but the time has come, for those who have not already accepted what the authors believe is obvious, to devote a good portion of your investment efforts to foreign-based targets.

So what are the compelling reasons for going global with one's investments? There are several, and it is likely that you are well acquainted with something between "some" and "all" of them if you have made the decision to buy this book. That said, let us take a few minutes to examine what they are—closely, for the benefit of those who are reading because they heard it was generally a good idea to go global, as well as for the benefit of those who are not certain they want to go global at all—but are nonetheless intrigued.

EXHIBIT 1.1	Fortune Magazine's List of the 100 Largest Corporations in the World (as of 2008)

Rank	Company	Revenue ($ millions)	Country
1	Wal-Mart Stores	378,799	USA
2	Exxon Mobil	372,824	USA
3	Royal Dutch Shell	355,782	Netherlands
4	BP	291,438	Britain
5	Toyota Motor	230,201	Japan
6	Chevron	210,783	USA
7	ING Group	201,516	Netherlands
8	Total	187,280	France
9	General Motors	182,347	USA
10	ConocoPhillips	178,558	USA
11	Daimler	177,167	Germany
12	General Electric	176,656	USA
13	Ford Motor	172,468	USA
14	Fortis	164,877	Belgium/Netherlands
15	AXA	162,762	France
16	Sinopec	159,260	China
17	Citigroup	159,229	USA
18	Volkswagen	149,054	Germany
19	Dexia Group	147,648	Belgium
20	HSBC Holdings	146,500	Britain
21	BNP Paribas	140,726	France
22	Allianz	140,618	Germany
23	Credit Agricole	138,155	France
24	State Grid	132,885	China
25	China National Petroleum	129,798	China
26	Deutsche Bank	122,644	Germany
27	ENI	120,565	Italy
28	Bank of America Corp.	119,190	USA
29	AT&T	118,928	USA
30	Berkshire Hathaway	118,245	USA
31	UBS	117,206	Switzerland
32	J.P. Morgan Chase & Co.	116,353	USA
33	Carrefour	115,585	France
34	Assicurazioni Generali	113,813	Italy
35	AIG	110,064	USA
36	Royal Bank of Scotland	108,392	Britain
37	Siemens	106,444	Germany
38	Samsung Electronics	106,006	South Korea
39	ArcelorMittal	105,216	Luxembourg
40	Honda Motor	105,102	Japan
41	Hewlett-Packard	104,286	USA
42	Pemex	103,960	Mexico

(Continued)

EXHIBIT 1.1 (*Continued*)

Rank	Company	Revenue ($ millions)	Country
43	Societe Generale	103,443	France
44	McKesson	101,703	USA
45	HBOS	100,267	Britain
46	IBM	98,786	USA
47	Gazprom	98,642	Russia
48	Hitachi	98,306	Japan
49	Valero Energy	96,758	USA
50	Nissan Motor	94,782	Japan
51	Tesco	94,703	Britain
52	E. ON	94,356	Germany
53	Verizon Communications	93,775	USA
54	Nippon Telegraph & Telephone	93,527	Japan
55	Deutsche Post	90,472	Germany
56	Metro	90,267	Germany
57	Nestlé	89,630	Switzerland
58	Santander Central Hispano Group	89,295	Spain
59	Statoil Hydro	89,224	Norway
60	Cardinal Health	88,364	USA
61	Goldman Sachs Group	87,968	USA
62	Morgan Stanley	87,879	USA
63	Petrobras	87,735	Brazil
64	Deutsche Telekom	85,570	Germany
65	Home Depot	84,470	USA
66	Peugeot	82,965	France
67	LG	82,096	South Korea
68	Electricite de France	81,629	France
69	Aviva	81,317	Britain
70	Barclays	80,347	Britain
71	Fiat	80,112	Italy
72	Matsushita Electric Industrial	79,412	Japan
73	BASF	79,322	Germany
74	Credit Suisse	78,206	Switzerland
75	Sony	77,682	Japan
76	Telefonica	77,254	Spain
77	UniCredit Group	77,030	Italy
78	BMW	76,675	Germany
79	Procter & Gamble	76,476	USA
80	CVS Caremark	76,330	USA
81	UnitedHealth Group	75,431	USA
82	Hyundai Motor	74,900	South Korea
83	U.S. Postal Service	74,778	USA
84	France Telecom	72,488	France
85	Vodafone	71,202	Britain
86	SK Holdings	70,717	South Korea

EXHIBIT 1.1 (*Continued*)

Rank	Company	Revenue ($ millions)	Country
87	Kroger	70,235	USA
88	Nokia	69,886	Finland
89	ThyssenKrupp	68,799	Germany
90	Lukoil	67,205	Russia
91	Toshiba	67,145	Japan
92	Repsol YPF	67,006	Spain
93	Boeing	66,387	USA
94	Prudential	66,358	Britain
95	Petronas	66,218	Malaysia
96	AmerisourceBergen	66,074	USA
97	Suez	64,982	France
98	Munich Re Group	64,774	Germany
99	Costco Wholesale	64,400	USA
100	Merrill Lynch	64,217	USA

Source: Fortune magazine.

EXHIBIT 1.2 Countries Represented in the Top 100 List (In Order of Representation)

Country	# of Top 100 Companies
United States	31
Germany	13
France	10
Britain	9
Japan	8
Italy	4
South Korea	4
China	3
Spain	3
Switzerland	3
Netherlands	2
Russia	2
Belgium	1
Belgium/Netherlands	1
Brazil	1
Finland	1
Luxembourg	1
Malaysia	1
Mexico	1
Norway	1

Source: Based on data from *Fortune* magazine.

GOING GLOBAL WITH YOUR INVESTMENTS

Reason #1. It Is the Best Opportunity Remaining to Realize Substantial Portfolio Growth Over the Long Term

In order to grow, you have to have *room* to grow, and in the United States, there just is not the amount of room there used to be. This is something that does not really require a detailed analysis to prove. Even if you chose to rely on little more than your intuition, that should be good enough. Do you know anyone who does not own a car? Do you know anyone who does not have cable or satellite television? How about appliances? Who, in your circle of friends and acquaintances, does not own a washer, or a dryer, or a refrigerator? We certainly know anecdotally that those folks are out there in the landscape of the United States, but there are not many of them. When we *do* look at the data, we see that roughly 90 percent of households own a car, about 85 percent of Americans own a cell phone, and an astounding 99 percent of American households own at least one television set, while 66 percent of those households watch cable on those sets. Refrigerators? You find those in almost 100 percent of American households; same with cooking appliances, like a stove/oven—just about 100 percent.

Now, in China, just 5 percent of families own a car. In Russia, roughly 20 percent of adults own automobiles. In the Democratic Republic of the Congo, roughly 2 percent of the population has a cell phone. In all of Africa, there are currently more than 300 million people who do not have cell phone network coverage, and in Africa there are only 35 million fixed telephone lines on behalf of almost one billion people.

This is not a scientific evaluation but rather a short, random assessment of the state of difference between the United States and much of the rest of the world. The fact is that there remains a lot of Planet Earth that does not yet have what most of us take for granted. Now, there are many complicating factors that make access to goods and services more difficult in many parts of the world. In especially poor countries, like many of those on the African continent, the matter of owning or not owning a television set is not merely a simple matter of lack of access to a Sears; it is a matter of access to money. This means that in your analysis of good countries to consider with your investment dollars, there is going to be much more to it than simply finding those places that do not have very much, and throw a lot of money at them with the blind assumption that they have to take off at some point. You will want to perform the sound research that ultimately gives you an empirical basis for pursuing a foreign market and/or industry, and those results, combined with the application of portfolio management strategies we discuss in a bit, will put you in an excellent position to reap the sorts of rewards for which hedge fund managers have become famous.

Before we continue, let us take a closer look at the principal types of markets you have to consider as a global investor. There are three fundamental terms that identify a given equity market in its growth from infant to adult: *frontier*, *emerging*, and *developed*. Let us take a moment to define and illustrate each.

Frontier   This term was first used in 1995 at the International Finance Corporation, the arm of the World Bank that procures investments on behalf of the private sector in developing countries. The term is somewhat nonspecific in scope, but it generally refers to the smallest of markets, the ones with maybe $1 billion (at most) in total market capitalization and just a handful of stock exchange listings. They generally offer the greatest risk *and* reward to investors, given their size. In terms of risk, frontier markets subject investors to exponentially greater levels of normally understood global investment risks. You can see a full list of the frontier markets indicated a little further on, but for now, think places like Bulgaria, Pakistan, and Vietnam.

From a pure return standpoint, frontier markets are the ideal targets of longer-term, growth-oriented investors. Because of their standing as relative infants on the world economic and investment stage, frontier markets have the greatest growth potential, in a general sense. Additionally, their emergence as players in the investment community typically provides a low degree of correlation to investors from developed nations seeking that feature. It is important to note that frontier markets, while sharing a broad similarity in areas like market capitalization, can actually display disparate features on a country-by-country basis. In other words, there can be several, different reasons as to why a frontier market is actually that. For example, a country may qualify as frontier because its level of development is clearly beneath that of the emerging market representatives. This is the kind of nation of which we think when we think of a frontier market. Botswana is a reasonable example of such a country. Botswana has a splendid record in certain aspects of its economic development; it demonstrated a strong record of economic growth over the last one-third of the twentieth century (roughly 9 percent per year), and is understood to have the highest credit rating in Africa. That said, Botswana has a frighteningly high HIV/AIDS infection rate, so much so that the life expectancy of the citizenry at birth has been essentially halved since 2006. Botswana's history of independence dates back only to 1966, and roughly 30 percent of the population lives below the poverty line (contrast that to other frontier nations like Estonia and Lithuania, which see only about 5 percent of their populations living below the poverty line). The quality of education continues to be an issue in Botswana, as well.

A nation may also be considered a frontier market on the basis that while it actually has achieved a high level of development, it is sufficiently small enough to be disregarded as an emerging market. An example of a country like this would be Lithuania. Lithuania has been a presence in Europe since the eleventh century, and during the fourteenth century was the largest country in Europe. A series of occupations by Russia, the Soviet Union, and Nazi Germany (notably the Soviet Union) went a long way to crushing the identity of Lithuania, which is why Lithuania has had some difficulty bolstering its standing in the world economic community. Nevertheless, Lithuania has maintained a strong democratic tradition, and has impressive national characteristics like a strong record of GDP growth among other European Union member nations, low unemployment, a modern infrastructure, a flat tax, a high literacy rate, and enjoys the highest rating of all the Baltic states by *The Economist*'s Quality of Life Index. Sound like a frontier market to you? Well, it is, on the basis of its relatively small size, but the profile of Lithuania is one that makes it attractive to investors seeking a frontier economy without many of the usual rough edges.

A third form of the frontier market nation is one that may be otherwise progressive and developed, but that has only recently loosened the investment restrictions that characterize unsophisticated investment markets. Prime examples of this type of frontier market are the component nations of the Gulf Cooperation Council: Bahrain, Kuwait, Oman, Qatar, Saudi Arabia, and the United Arab Emirates.

Emerging Markets   Emerging markets represent the middle step in the growth of a market: no longer a child, but not yet a full-fledged adult. The idea is that they will ultimately become true *developed* markets (see below), but remain in process to that end. The immaturity of the internal financial structure of an emerging market is a distinct feature, as is its evolution toward sociopolitical stability; the rise of internal political strife may not be as great as that found in a frontier market (like Namibia, for example), but it is certainly greater than that found in nations like the United States and Great Britain. Emerging markets are regarded as ideal territory for many growth-seeking global investors, precisely because they present a palatable mix of risk and reward.

There are essentially four features that characterize an emerging market. First, the emerging market nation, while not always a significant player on the global economic stage, is always one of the biggest, if not *the* biggest, factor in the region in which it resides; it may not have the singular ability to affect world economic climate (the way the United States does, for example) in any direction, but it is a market on which the other companion countries in its region are dependent; it is characterized by a vast and growing market, one supported by a large population and large amounts of resources. Second, emerging markets nations are among the world's fastest-growing economies. Third, they are markets that are characterized by progressive reforms in the area of sociopolitical and economic policy; citizens may enjoy more freedoms than they once did, businesses may enjoy less government intervention, and foreign investment enjoys greater accessibility. The overall motivation of such changes remains the hunt for greater economic viability and prosperity that history has shown is not afforded within statist regimes. Fourth, while not possessed of the ability to catalyze global economic activity on their own (individually), they *are* already players on the world political stage, and are also powerful associates in the global economy. It is principally the first and fourth characteristics cited that differentiate emerging markets from frontier markets, as many frontier markets are also characterized by transitional political and economic reform climates as well as high rates of economic growth.

Developed Markets   Developed markets are those that we readily identify as the largest on the globe and that have attained a substantial level of industrialization. From a socioeconomic standpoint, they are characterized by high levels of income and *human development*. Human development refers to the overall achievement of health and education by a nation's citizenry. It is from a narrower investment perspective that markets are strictly measured in terms of their development, and there are several criteria used in such measurement. For example, in developed markets, there is a high degree of regulation administered by formal bodies organized to that end. In developed markets, foreign investment is not dissuaded, but encouraged, and this is measured by the number and nature of rules put in place to encourage such investment; the ability of capital to flow freely across borders is always one of the strongest indicators of a nation's economic progress. Additionally, developed markets are characterized by free (nonlimited intervention by government) and modern exchange structures.

There is more. Matters of custody, clearing, and settlement are highly scrutinized, as well. Trade failure rates have to be low, and custody services have to be plentiful and up to date. Settlement must be generally three days or less.

A working derivatives market has to be in place, brokerage services have to be plentiful in number, market capitalization has to be of a certain requisite size, and liquidity cannot be an issue. There is more, but you get the picture. The developed markets are those you think they are, countries like the United States, France, Germany, and Japan. Developed markets, as a whole, present to us the classic case of stability over opportunity:

we prefer to make investments in safe economies, but we also know that those that have reached the highest levels of development have also seen a marked flattening in their growth curves.

MSCI Barra (www.mscibarra.com) is an excellent resource for investors seeking to tap into investment research, statistics, and performance analytics on behalf of their global investment goals. We turn to them now to provide a list of the countries they currently characterize as meeting the requisite standards for being frontier, emerging, or developed markets (see Exhibit 1.3).

EXHIBIT 1.3   MSCI Barra List of Developed, Emerging, and Frontier Market Nations (as of April 2009)

Developed	Emerging	Frontier
Australia	Argentina	Bahrain
Austria	Brazil	Botswana
Belgium	Chile	Bulgaria
Canada	China	Croatia
Denmark	Colombia	Estonia
Finland	Czech Republic	Ghana
France	Egypt	Jamaica
Germany	Hungary	Jordan
Greece	India	Kazakhstan
Hong Kong	Indonesia	Kenya
Ireland	Malaysia	Kuwait
Italy	Mexico	Lebanon
Israel	Morocco	Lithuania
Japan	Peru	Mauritius
Netherlands	Philippines	Nigeria
New Zealand	Poland	Oman
Norway	Russia	Pakistan
Portugal	South Africa	Qatar
Singapore	South Korea	Romania
Spain	Taiwan	Trinidad and Tobago
Sweden	Thailand	Saudi Arabia
Switzerland	Turkey	Serbia
United Kingdom	—	Slovenia
United States	—	Sri Lanka
—	—	Tunisia
—	—	Ukraine
—	—	United Arab Emirates
—	—	Vietnam

Source: MSCI Barra.

Even a casual observer can sense that the central problem with looking at the United States as a growth market is that it is highly mature and highly industrialized. Although there may be terrific growth companies that continue to open and provide grand opportunities for investors, one must eventually conclude that, as a whole, the U.S. market is not itself a good growth play. A hundred years ago? Absolutely. Now? Not so much. Opportunities still exist, of course, in the United States and in other developed markets throughout the world, but those markets, as a whole, are not as enticing, and the opportunities they *do* present require more work to discern and identify than was once required.

This is significant. Although an annualized return of 6 to 8 percent per year is something the average investor has been taught to accept as good, it is really not. In 2007, the S&P 500 index registered a total return of 5.5 percent, while South Korea's KOSPI Composite rose 32 percent. The South Korean market was by no means the best performer of 2007, but that is sort of the point in citing it; the KOSPI is but one of many that flattened the renowned U.S. markets, and it is hardly a world leader (at least that year). What may surprise many is that U.S. markets have *never* "won" the annual contest of best performing—even during heyday years like those framed in the decade of the 1990s. It does not matter what year you pick—we can find you a market that outperformed the U.S. markets.

We would wager that the idea of low-to-middle level single-digit returns being respectable investment returns stems directly from the aged idea that all investing is to take place within the United States.

What you seek now, in order to deliver to yourself a reasonable chance of seeing the regular double-digit annualized returns that so many U.S. domestic investors enjoyed in the 1990s (without having to exert much extra effort, we might add), are those modern-day versions of America 100 years ago. Not the countries that are already saturated with "stuff," but those countries that have long been the world's stepchildren in terms of wealth and economic growth, and have only recently begun to make meaningful strides toward free market economies and a concerted effort at progress and stability at all levels.

Reason #2. BRIC and the Changing Tide of Global Market Capitalization

There is a theory developed by Goldman Sachs in 2001 that serves as one of the strongest pronouncements to date in support of investors looking elsewhere to make their money. Goldman took the position that the economies of Brazil, Russia, India, and China (BRIC) are developing so rapidly that their collective rates of growth, combined with the facts that the four countries combined currently represent more than 25 percent of the world's land area and more than 40 percent of the world's population, will, by year 2050, see the combined economies of the four nations subordinate the current economies of the presently richest nations in the world. What is interesting is that while Goldman did not formally suggest that the countries of BRIC would attempt to officially create some sort of economic union, it is clear that the four *have* taken steps to at least arrange a casual alliance. To that end, it is worth noting that on June 16, 2009, Brazil president Luiz Inacio Lula da Silva, China president Hu Jintao, and India prime minister Manmohan Singh all met with Russia president Dmitry Medvedev for what was described as their first *official* summit in Yekaterinburg, Russia. Among the topics discussed was how the four nations can better work together, as well as how they can help facilitate the continued evolution of other developing nations—both topics that should at least catch the eye of the more astute investor.

The BRIC thesis has its critics. One of the principal criticisms is that BRIC is really just "C," with the "BRI" acting as nothing more than a same-syllable prefix; in other words, that the power is really wielded by China, and that Brazil, Russia, and India are just along for the ride. The critics point out that China's economy is larger than those of the other three *combined*, and that its exports and Forex holdings (reserves) are more than double those of Brazil, Russia, and India combined.

There are also other concerns, including a belief that China's admittedly impressive growth rates are not sustainable over the course of the coming decades. Brazil has been looked to for some time as a country to demonstrate some real economic power, but has only recently started to realize that potential. Will it continue? India's relationship with Pakistan is not good, and given that regional economic powers continue to thrive on the basis of cultivating relationships with neighbors, could that become an impeding economic issue at some point? Russia continues to have a difficult time inspiring confidence within the private sector with the leadership's insistence on taking direct control of companies. Should that trend continue with little abatement, it is difficult to imagine much investor confidence inspired.

Overall, as with any emerging and frontier markets countries, there's no guarantee of smooth sailing. Each of these countries still has a long way to go in terms of conquering many of the organic problems that has made each remain less than developed for so long. For one thing, while their populations may be looked to as strengths on the one hand, much of those populations remain in poverty. Widespread poverty has to be managed, and can lead to various types of "bumps in the road" during the course of this management.

Our position is that you should consider less the literal significance of BRIC, and give more weight to its role as proof of where economic growth and power is headed. For example, the use of the BRIC acronym has led to the use of similar acronyms like BRICK (the K representing South Korea), BRIMC (the M representing Mexico), and BRICA (the A representing Arab countries), and there are other variations. The point is that there is an energy that has permeated the investment thinking of those seeking more fruitful territory than that found in more developed markets, and it centers on the emerging markets.

The relevance of BRIC opens the door to a wider discussion of global economic growth as measured by *float-adjusted market capitalization* (only those outstanding shares available to the public, and not including shares held by large owners, or restricted stocks, insider holdings, etc.). It is relevant to note that although global market capitalization grew from 2001 to 2007 at an annualized rate of about 11 percent, and at an annualized rate of roughly 6 percent in the United States, it grew at a rate of about 30 percent in BRIC. Again, intuition tells us that emerging markets countries are going to be absorbing market share from the developed nations, and that indeed seems to be the case. Here are some telling statistics, courtesy of Russell Investments (www.russell.com), regarding the change in global market capitalization:

- Although overall global market capitalization *doubled* between 2001 and 2007, U.S. market cap (as a proportion of global market cap) declined during that period from 57 percent to 44 percent; the market cap of all other countries combined grew from 43 percent to 56 percent.
- Developed markets represented roughly 85 percent of the global initial public offerings in 2002, while emerging markets represented the remaining 15 percent; by 2007 that balance had shifted noticeably, with developed markets accounting for about 64 percent of the global IPOs and emerging markets increasing their share to 36 percent.
- Japan, long the "U.S." of the Asian market, saw its share of Asia's market capitalization represent 70 percent; by 2007, that representation had fallen to 50 percent.
- Analyzed by sector, the emerging markets collectively registered increases across the board: in utilities, the market cap of emerging markets rose from 5 percent in 2001 to 14 percent in 2007; in energy, the percentages over that same period went from 4 percent to 13 percent; technology, 5 percent to 12 percent; and the biggest increase was noted in materials and processing, rising from roughly 7 percent of global market cap to about 17 percent of global market cap.

There are many more telling statistics, but these should suffice. The reality is that while trends suggest that market capitalization among developed nations continues to increase, it is doing so at a much slower rate than before; conversely, the market share of emerging markets countries continues to increase. As for the effects of the Great Recession, it seems clear that these deleterious effects may be more pronounced on many of the developed markets, as we see in just a bit.

Reason #3. At Any Given Time, Another Region of the World Is Outperforming the Others in Investment Return

The reality is that from the standpoint of pure investment return, there are just too many accessible foreign markets that allow an investor to find a haven of quality performance when all around it are performing less well. Up to recently, accessing world markets was the primary impediment to capitalizing on them, but now that the problem of access has been made largely moot, we are free to roam the earth and hold the performance of world markets against one another.

2008 is both a great and horrible year to examine. On one hand, it was such an aberration that it is debatable how much weight the year and associated market performances should receive as a predictor of years to come. On the other hand, it happened, and it is possible that such a year may happen once again. The reasons may change, the severity may not be as great, but in the sense that it was universally rotten, that is an eventuality that will surely be visited on us again.

That said, was every single market simply abysmal in 2008? No, not really (see Exhibit 1.4). Depending on which index you cite, the U.S. equities market was down about 40 percent. That is bad, but there were many worse (see Exhibit 1.5) and many that were much better.

EXHIBIT 1.4 Best Performing Stock Markets of 2008

Country	Return
Tunisia	+10%
Costa Rica	−4%
Morocco	−6%
Venezuela	−9%
Botswana	−15%
Slovakia	−19%
Lebanon	−21%
Chile	−23%
Mexico	−25%
South Africa	−27%

Source: BBC World News.

EXHIBIT 1.5	Worst Performing Stock Markets of 2008

Country	Return
Iceland	−94%
Bulgaria	−80%
Ukraine	−73%
United Arab Emirates	−72%
Serbia	−71%
Lithuania	−71%
Romania	−70%
Slovenia	−68%
Vietnam	−67%
Greece	−66%

Source: BBC World News.

Reason #4. Risk Reduction

Investing globally gives one the opportunity to benefit from both sides of the diversification coin. When we think of diversification, we think of it in terms of reducing risk as well as enhancing the opportunity for growth. Putting some of our money to work outside of the United States gives us the opportunity to do both, interestingly enough. Diversification provides two unique and seemingly disparate benefits from the same action. We spoke of the benefit of growth near the outset of the chapter. Presently, we want to turn an eye to the sometimes-controversial issue of international investing as a mechanism for reducing risk.

There is a long-held school of thought that taking your investable monies outside of the United States can only *increase* one's risk. Just the other day, we were perusing an article from someone who was intent on bashing the idea of international investing. The article stood out because it focused not at all on the opportunities, but exclusively on the *risks*. Although it is certainly true that there is some risk to foreign investing, the reality is that there is risk to all investing; after all, how did *your* portfolio of U.S. stocks do in 2008?

Remember that in order to properly use the tool of diversification to reduce risk, you have to actually *diversify*. In other words, you cannot allow yourself to begin chasing the next "hot" emerging, or worse, *frontier* market, and place all of your money accordingly. To diversify means just that, and it is done properly with a portfolio of equities that represent a wide range of industries and nations.

Let us look at this from a more general and philosophical point of view, as well as with the use of some real numbers. First, all countries are not the same. We realize this (somewhat ironically) in a day and age where world economies are vastly more interconnected and directly correlated than they once were. That said, the disparity between macroeconomic trends in countless numbers of nation-states remain vast enough in a variety of areas to justify an interest in investing abroad as a means of lowering risk. In other words, while it is easy to point out the increased interrelationships between nations and say, generically, that we are all in this together, it is not quite that simple. Although there are close relationships in many respects, there remain vast differences in others. It is important to note that although there is a growing correlation among broad indexes and regions of the world (you can even see a growing correlation nowadays between emerging markets as a whole and the S&P 500), there is still a great deal of beneficial/low-correlation diversification available at the next-lowest levels of investment strata (from whole regions): the country level, and then further down at an industry level. Let us look at India for a minute. In 2007, India's benchmark BSE SENSEX climbed about 47 percent for the year —which is good, especially considering the S&P 500 index returned a whopping 3.6 percent to investors that year. Now, if you were inclined to bolster your telecom holdings in 2007 and had invested in Tata Teleservices, an Indian telecommunications company, you would have enjoyed a rather ridiculous 216 percent return, while your very American bet on AT&T that year would have yielded a solid 18 percent. Eighteen percent is nothing at which to sneeze, but we like 216 percent a bit better (as an aside, a bet on France Telecom that year would have yielded nearly 16 percent; it may be anecdotal evidence, but it is interesting that the leading telecom companies of two of the world's most developed markets returned roughly the same, while an emerging markets telecom like Tata exploded as it did). Assuming you had a principally U.S.-based, broadly constructed portfolio, but also had some key weightings in emerging markets companies like Tata, the risk you run of earning only a few percentage points of a return in 2007 is largely mitigated by owning an Indian telecommunications company that pounded out more than 200 percent that year.

Speaking of indexes, let us look at those, as a whole: If you owned the S&P for the two years of 2001 and 2002, you would have lost just more than 30 percent. If you had owned India's benchmark index, the SENSEX in 2002, you would have made only a little more than 3 percent, but if you had owned the S&P 500, you would have *lost* 23 percent. If you had owned *Pakistan's* benchmark index, the Karachi 100, you would have made 112 percent. As an example, then, if you had owned all three in roughly equal measure, your portfolio would have averaged a nice 30 percent return in a year when the good ole USA was not doing much for its native investors. Remember that risk involves concerns that are quite a bit different from the normally considered "stability of principal"; for professional investors, risk is chiefly about *the risk associated with not seeing much of a return*. There lies the true meaning of risk.

Up to this point, our discussion of risk reduction has centered on justifying it through commonsense observation, even anecdotal evidence, but it can be quantified more definitively, as well. Risk reduction for pro investors is really about *correlation*, which is, quite generally, how variables move with and against one another; *positive correlation* means that the variables move together and in the same direction; *negative correlation* means that the variables move together but in opposite directions; *noncorrelation* means that the variables do not move in a defined and related way; in other words, they behave *random* to one another.

Generally speaking, risk reduction is achieved in greater measure as the investments you own attain higher levels of negative correlation. To a neophyte investor, Microsoft and Apple may be viewed as being not positively correlated because they are two different companies, but we know that is not true. Their positive correlation comes in a few ways, chiefly because they are both in the same industry and basically doing the same thing. Now, someone might suggest that KB Home and Pfizer are at least uncorrelated, because they sample apparently unrelated industries: home building and health care. Sounds good on the surface, but is it really true? Nope. Both companies, while in different industries, are U.S.-based companies, and both are listed on the New York Stock Exchange. In other words, you see less correlation than you would between KB Home and DR Horton (another builder), or between KB Home and Home Depot (building supplies), but you cannot escape the positive correlation that exists as a result of both companies persisting as U.S.-based entities that move and shake with the domestic economy. In 2007, the year that was the "calm before the storm," KB fell about 50 percent, and Pfizer fell about 8 percent; in 2007, the S&P 500 Index was *up* for the year, 3.5 percent. Granted, 50 percent down is a lot worse than 8 percent down, but you notice that both were down, and the U.S. market as a whole was up (in fact, over the previous three years, KB and Pfizer were actually correlated to the tune of a .93 coefficient). A bet on Brazil's Bovespa Index that year, however, would have seen you make 40 percent. Even the homebuilder Gafisa, representing the industry that was in the throes of coming apart worldwide, rose 5 percent during 2007, this in a year when leading U.S. homebuilders dropped roughly 50 percent.

In order to achieve a better level of noncorrelation/negative correlation, you have to diversify outside of the United States entirely. Those of you who are yelling right now, proclaiming that 2008 is proof that there is no safe haven, are reaching, in our opinion. The global economic implosion of 2008 was unique in many respects in a modern, post–WWII environment, and to point to it as "proof" that looking overseas to reduce risk is a waste would be a dangerous conclusion at which to arrive. It is reasonable to assume that we will occasionally have highly unusual years when most, if not all, markets move the same way and to largely the same degree, but even 2008 gave us Tunisia, which was actually up 10 percent for the year, and countries like Costa Rica, which were down by so little in 2008 (−4 percent) that they could be viewed as "home runs" by most of the rest of the world for that year. The point is that even though there are years when there is widespread carnage, those periods are quite unusual, and it would be a mistake for you to invest (or *not* invest) on the basis of shorter-term, highly atypical movements. Besides, if you are investing like a pro, you should be able to sidestep a good portion of the trauma.

When evaluating correlations, we look at a range between −1 and +1; zero is the representation of noncorrelation. Move above zero to the positive, and you have positive correlation. Move to the negative-negative correlation. Although it is true that the broad market indexes of developed nations are more highly correlated these days, even (investable) emerging markets indexes are seeing greater correlation with those of developed nations; as an example, the Vanguard Emerging Markets ETF and the SPDR S&P 500 are positively correlated over the past one and three years with coefficients of .91 and .85, respectively. Even on a country basis, we are seeing higher correlations, especially among the more developed of the emerging markets countries; again, looking to investable indexes, the Powershares India portfolio, which is made up of the 50 largest companies on India's two indexes, is positively correlated over the last year with the SPDR S&P 500 with a coefficient of .83. Want to try South Africa? You might be surprised. iShares MSCI South Africa Index ETF and the SPDR S&P 500 are correlated over the last 1 and 3 years with coefficients of .84 and .91, respectively.

So, does the aforementioned tell us that the idea of diversifying across the water is really specious, as in an idea that sounds good in theory but falls apart in practice? Not at all, but it does suggest two things: that the real opportunities to diversify likely lay in frontier and small emerging markets countries more so than in foreign developed and large emerging markets countries, and that while you *can* realize some great diversification in developed and larger emerging markets countries, you oftentimes may have to find it at the individual company level (remember our example of Tata Teleservices).

Reason #5. The Existence of the Internet

We do not know if there is an official use of the abbreviations "B.I." and "A.I." to distinguish the time *before* the Internet from the time *after* it came into being and widespread use, but maybe there should be. The Internet is simply amazing, and as relatively new as it is, it has already become unimaginable to consider the world without it. Its existence has revolutionized everything, and the realm of investing has been every bit the beneficiary of the Internet as anything else. This is particularly true with regard to global investing.

For U.S. investors looking to invest in U.S. companies, the process of investing in securities markets has been as developed and well formed as any. Information on companies has always been readily available and generally quite plentiful, even B.I. It is one of the benefits of living here. However, for investors seeking to move transborder, the information required to invest successfully was normally much more difficult to capture. Unless you were among the wealthiest and most sophisticated of investors, it was not possible or practical for you to realistically engage foreign markets directly. You were limited to doing your global investing in the form of mutual funds and ADRs, which are U.S. versions of foreign stocks. With the Internet, the ability to perform research, as well as facilitate brokerage activity, is becoming a breeze.

Research   Now that virtually everything and everyone now has an Internet presence, obtaining information on anything is easy. Let us say that you are impressed with the advances made by Vietnam, and recognize the government's increasing friendliness toward capitalism. You know intuitively that the emerging consumer class will have an increased need for financial services products, including insurance. Before the Internet, how realistically could you have researched Vietnam insurance companies in an expeditious fashion? Not at all. Now, all you need to do is type those very same words into a search engine and go from there. Don't like the results? Alter your word choice. By typing the words "insurance companies of Vietnam" into your Google search mechanism, you will retrieve thousands of results. The results themselves are very telling, because they seem to suggest a common denominator of *investment*. For example, the first 10 results *we* retrieved included several analyses of the insurance industry in Vietnam from an investment perspective. One of the highest-ranked results was an article titled "Vietnam Insurance Sector: Untapped Potential" found on www.researchandmarkets.com. The article itself is part of a longer report that is for sale, but even the part you can access for free had a lot of information, to include a list of insurance companies in Vietnam. From there, you just continue your research.

This is a simple example, but it illustrates the point perfectly well. This kind of access, particularly to emerging and frontier markets, was simply not available like this prior to the advent of the Internet.

Investment Activity   As we said earlier, the investment world, as a whole, has proven to be one of the Internet's biggest beneficiaries. Whether it is research, tracking data, or establishing and maintaining a formal investment account, it almost seems like the Internet was *made* to satisfy the wants and needs of investors. The process of becoming an investor has been a distinct beneficiary of the Internet. Rather than deal with the hassle of opening accounts in person (or over the phone, which is about as time-consuming), the Internet allows us the ability to take care of it all, online, in the privacy of our own homes—day or night.

Account maintenance is also a breeze, thanks to the Internet. We do not now need the U.S. mail to review statements and confirmations; it is all online.

As helpful and convenient as the Internet makes life for the average person seeking a platform at Charles Schwab, TD Ameritrade, and others, the benefit is that much more striking for the investor seeking to work off a more globally favorable brokerage, or through a country-based brokerage entirely. For example, Interactive Brokers (IB) (www.interactivebrokers. com) is a 30-odd-year-old brokerage that has been a bit ahead of the curve as far as seeking penetration of foreign markets, and has now morphed into a brokerage that is directed principally at the global-centric investor. A handful of minutes spent at IB's web site will allow you to open an account and access, through that single account, a wide array of investment vehicles available in (currently) 17 countries. Interactive Brokers is an excellent choice for the global-minded investor, and the realistic availability of direct investment options in a number of international markets would have been much more difficult without such a site.

We happen to like Interactive Brokers as a platform, and its access to direct investment in numerous worldwide markets is a terrific asset, but some of you may find that to be less than adequate. Going back to our earlier example, if you want to take advantage of the rapidly improving investment climate in Vietnam, you will not be able to do it through Interactive—but you *can* do it through Saigon Securities Inc. The Bilateral Trade Agreement signed in 2000 between the U.S. and Vietnam has propelled Vietnam into an attractive and fertile piece of investment ground—but you have to be able to access it. You can through Saigon Securities—but without the benefit of the Internet that wouldn't likely be possible. (Go to www.ssi.com.vn, and click on the icon of a British flag in the upper right-hand corner; you may still need to contact them specifically for additional help, as their application is still largely in Vietnamese.)

We speak more later on about setting up accounts that allow one to more directly target foreign markets; the point we want to leave you with here is that before the existence of a polished Internet, it was pragmatically difficult to access any aspect of foreign trading directly in an expeditious manner. That is now all in the past.

Reason #6. Other Regions of the World Are Not Plagued by a "Wealth-Guilt" Complex

One of the consequences to being an investor in twenty-first-century America is dealing with an increasingly growing self-consciousness associated with wealth accumulation. The recent election of President Barack Obama in the United States is indicative of many things, one of which is a sense that the perceived "have nots" have had quite enough of the "haves." Interestingly, it may be true that even some of the "haves" have had enough of *themselves*: polls show that Obama did very well on Election Day with both the highest and lowest wealth demographics. There is plenty of anecdotal evidence, at least, that suggests more than a bit of a backlash against the unbridled accumulation of wealth and its representations (material stuff), and this philosophical change is working in concert with the not-so-philosophical issue that buying things is much more difficult than it once was, given the persistent credit contraction that has found its way to the consumer level.

Americans, for better or worse, have long been concerned with how they are perceived by the rest of the world. By contrast, the rest of the world is not nearly as obsessed with that perception of selves. The significance here is great. If "wealth guilt" is a natural consequence of serving as a *land of plenty* for decades, those nations that have yet to enjoy that status for very long have not had a chance for that guilt to set in; for that matter, there is no assurance that it ever will. A 2007 survey by the *Economic Times* concluded that India's luxury market could grow to roughly 10 times its current size by 2015, fueled largely by a perceived cultural respect for the idea of wealth accumulation. Although the size of the Indian luxury market might be small in comparison to that of other nations, there is ample room for growth, and a long-term inclination to guilt-free accumulation in India and throughout many other countries around the world may help to present some nice prospects to extra-national investors.

The truth is that political correctness is largely a feature of nations that have had it good for a long time; success often breeds self-consciousness, and the United States, in comparison to many other nations, has been successful for a long time. There remains a wide variety of other countries that have yet to face the guilt that prosperity brings, and so will remain great consumer bases on which for global investors to focus for some time.

Reason #7. The U.S. Is Highly Overleveraged

The use of leverage, be it on a micro or macro scale, can be a tricky thing. In the short term, unchecked use of leverage can rapidly elevate consumption of goods and services, but in periods of substantial *deleveraging* (like that which helped to bring about the 2008 global economic crisis), those nations that are up to their necks in debt end up much like the odd man out in a game of musical chairs. Quite obviously, you can count the United States and its consumers as examples of the last man standing.

Other nations are not nearly as hamstrung, and it is those countries to which a smart investor will look for direct investment. As with other features of developed markets, leverage is partly a function of years of prosperity. Until that time fully arrives for them, frontier and emerging markets will simply not come to possess a mentality of lending. This is why although many of these markets have suffered from the economic downturn, those less leveraged are in a position to recover far more quickly. We see evidence of this already as the world slowly—very slowly—begins to recover from the Great Recession. Two of the world's darlings in the realm of emerging markets, India and China, have resumed their pre–Great Recession growth trend; both India and China were expected to grow at between 5 percent and 10 percent in 2009 (China retail sales climbed about 15 percent in Q1/09), while the debt-laden United States, Europe, and Japan all contracted substantially in Q1/09.

It is worth postulating that the low levels of savings in the United States are tied to an entitlement mentality that may be unique to America. The now-abandoned concept of purchasing a good or service only when you have the money to pay for it is alive and well in many other nations, but seems to be woefully missing here in the United States, as well as within other developed nations.

There are just too many good debt scenarios in too many other countries to take the United States seriously as a growth player in that regard. China and Brazil have plenty of room to lower interest rates, if necessary, and China has an enormous reserve (the largest on the planet at about $2 trillion), although there are other, once-"backward" countries that can also brag about maintaining large reserves (Russia is at about $400 billion). The idea of the United States having a reserve of any kind is laughable.

As for levels of personal household debt, the story is no better, and is actually worse: U.S. households are leveraged at an unbelievable average figure of just more than 100 percent of GDP.

In the end, countries that deal with massive debt on all levels simply cannot grow (see Exhibit 1.6). Three of the four component countries of BRIC (Brazil, Russia, and China) each have debt levels of 41 percent, 7 percent, and 16 percent (of GDP) respectively. Compared to the United States, these are countries that can breathe, plain and simple. What is more, many frontier and emerging markets nations, particularly Asia, seem to have an outright cultural aversion to carrying significant amounts of debt. Although it will be interesting to see how that behavior trends as prosperity continues to grow in these countries, for investors, these underleveraged parts of

EXHIBIT 1.6 Countries with 60 Percent or Greater Public Debt-as-Percentage of GDP

Country	% of GDP	Market
Zimbabwe	241	(undesignated)
Japan	170	Developed
Lebanon	163	Frontier
Jamaica	124	Frontier
Singapore	114	Developed
Italy	93	Developed
Seychelles	93	(undesignated)
Greece	90	Developed
Sudan	86	(undesignated)
Egypt	85	Emerging
Bhutan	81	(undesignated)
Belgium	81	Developed
Sri Lanka	78	Frontier
India	78	Emerging
Israel	76	Developed
Hungary	74	Emerging
France	67	Developed
Ghana	66	Frontier
Portugal	64	Developed
Germany	63	Developed
Canada	62	Developed
United States	61*	Developed
Morocco	60	Emerging

Source: CIA World Factbook.

*Note: Recent unofficial data suggests the U.S. figure may be closer to 80 percent in the wake of recent stimulus spending.

the world are going to be important considerations as recipients of direct investment for the foreseeable future (see Exhibit 1.7).

Reason #8. Other Economies of the World Have Been Crushed Worse Than Ours—and Thus Remain Poised for a Bigger Turnaround

In a general sense, we recognize that the lower you go, the more opportunity there exists on the way up. Markets and indexes that are pounded can become very intriguing places for us to look, with rare exception (an aside: the NASDAQ Composite may be one of those exceptions; in 2000, the index hit its peak close of 5,048, and subsequently fell 78 percent over the next two years; more than nine years later, the index is still 63 percent

EXHIBIT 1.7	Countries with 15 Percent or Less Public Debt as Percentage of GDP	
Country	**% of GDP**	**Market**
Oman	2	Frontier
Libya	4	(undesignated)
Estonia	4	Frontier
Chile	4	Emerging
Botswana	5	Frontier
Azerbaijan	5	(undesignated)
Wallis and Futuna	6	(undesignated)
Qatar	6	Frontier
Russia	7	Emerging
Luxembourg	7	(undesignated)
Kuwait	7	Frontier
Angola	9	(undesignated)
Kazakhstan	9	Frontier
Equatorial Guinea	9	(undesignated)
Ukraine	10	Frontier
Lithuania	12	Frontier
Cameroon	12	(undesignated)
Nigeria	12	Frontier
Saudi Arabia	13	Frontier
Uzbekistan	14	(undesignated)
Algeria	14	(undesignated)
Romania	14	Frontier
Hong Kong	14	Developed

Source: CIA World Factbook.

down from that same high). In comparison to the U.S.'s benchmark S&P 500 index, many nations whose markets were creamed much worse than the United States have already demonstrated great resiliency and a willingness to get back to making money.

As an example, look at two of the United States's biggest and baddest indexes: the S&P 500, the favorite index of fund managers, as well as the Dow Jones Industrial Average. The difference between the two is much like the difference between an actor and a movie star, but regardless, both have their own unique gravitas in the investment universe. For the calendar year of 2008, the S&P 500 fell 38 percent, and has returned, during the first half of 2009, a whopping 2 percent. As for the Dow, it backslid a relatively modest 33 percent in 2008, and has "recovered," if you can call what it is doing a recovery, in the first half of 2009 by posting a −4 percent return during that period. There are a variety of other factors to consider when evaluating to what degree a national market is poised for a big turnaround, and we address why the United States has a longer road to travel than others, but as we see, from the narrow terms of equity markets recovery, other nations have done much better after more solid poundings of their own.

Take China, for example. The Chinese equities market might have been the most overheated stock market of the last several years. Come 2008, it all ended—at least for a little while. The Hang Seng's return in 2008 was −48 percent, which is considerably worse than the S&P 500. This year? The Hang Seng has roared back during the first half of 2009, up 28 percent during that period.

Look at India. Same thing. If we look at the Bombay Stock Exchange Sensitive Index, or BSE SENSEX, which is India's version of the Dow 30, we see a benchmark that was crushed in 2008 to the tune of a −52 percent return. That said, the BSE SENSEX also roared back in the first half of 2009, up 50 percent during the first six months of 2009.

There are plenty of other examples. Russia is another good one. The RTSI, or Russian Trading System Index, is a 50-stock composite of the RTS Stock Exchange, and 2008 saw *it* hammered down by 72 percent! The news in 2009? Halfway through the year it had gained 56 percent from where it ended 2008.

Pakistan? Why not? The Karachi dropped 58 percent in 2008, and has bounced back up 22 percent halfway into 2009.

Compare and contrast the numbers associated with these countries to those of the more-developed nations. For example, a look at the top five countries represented in the *Fortune* magazine's list of top 100 corporations in the world gives us the United States, Germany, France, Britain, and Japan, in that order. Their respective benchmark index performances follow in Exhibit 1.8.

As a general observation, it is fair to say that more developed economies were not hurt as badly by the Great Recession, and neither have they had rip-roaring performances in 2009. The simple truth is that

EXHIBIT 1.8   Top Five Countries and Their Index Performance

Country	Index	2008 Return	Return (First Six Months of 2009)
United States	S&P 500	−38%	+2%
Germany	DAX	−39%	−.04%
France	CAC 40	−42%	−2%
Britain	FTSE 100	−31%	−4%
Japan	Nikkei 225	−39%	+12%

Source: Based on data from *Fortune* magazine.

younger countries, those truly emerging or frontier, are excellent candidates to watch for money-remaking opportunities when those that are most solid historically face strong headwinds.

The list goes on, and there is a lot of room left in many of these various national markets for a big upside to come. As we have said, there is a variety of other factors to consider besides mere "crush factor" when evaluating the potential of a national economy and its associated securities markets to rebound solidly in the near-term future, but seeing especially beaten markets is a good place to start. The psychological component is such that the market "knows" it has scaled lofty heights before, and is therefore not looking at all-time highs with quite the same sort of wishful thinking it did when it had yet to reach them the first time (we accept, again, that the NASDAQ Composite from the beginning of this century may be a notable exception).

The countries that have responded particularly well in 2009, in addition to benefiting from having nowhere to go but up,and have other fundamentals well suited to their success, so this element cannot be disregarded in favor of focusing purely on the degree of "beat-down." For example, China, which has come back quite strongly in 2009, is characterized at present by a reasonably stable rate of inflation. The upshot is that, if needed, China can make aggressive rate cuts, as it has lots of room to do so. Additionally, there is the rate of savings among China's populace, the highest in the world by some measures. India presents much of the same promise to investors, in addition to its market tumble; in India, you have the combination of 50 percent of the population under 25, a rate of savings comparable to China's, and lots of needed infrastructure upgrades. These features are why it is badly hit *emerging* economies that tend to rebound well; the culture and profile of the country is such that it is primed to keep moving, whereas highly developed nations no longer benefit from the endemic need to move inexorably forward, even during difficult global times.

Reason #9. The Condition of the U.S. Economy for Years to Come Makes Looking Elsewhere a Smart Idea

Some will suggest that the very fact a market has been beaten down is the reason to look to that same market as an opportunity. It makes sense intuitively, and it is oftentimes a fair assumption. However, a severely beaten down market simply means that it is worth perhaps undergoing an examination. The *results* of that examination, one that includes consideration of factors well beyond the simple scope of market performance, will help to determine the weighting we choose to give to a national economy. For us, the overall prospective condition of the U.S. economy in the near term is something that causes us to have an even greater interest in looking to other national markets for investment relief.

Trade Deficit　The United States continues to manage a huge trade deficit, and although the U.S. trade deficit improved by about $50 billion from 2006 to 2007, and again from 2007 to 2008, to rest at $677 billion, it is still enormous. There are theoretical debates about the importance of the trade deficit to the national economy, but it is not really a matter of theory that spending more than one makes cannot persist interminably. There are those who will allege that ultimately paying is not a problem, because the United States can print as much money as it wants to, which is true, but most of us are aware that the result of such an approach is a devaluation of U.S. currency. A devaluation of our currency naturally results in a strengthening of overseas currencies, and thus a further strengthening of the positions of those who own foreign assets (be they foreigners or U.S.-based global investors). In other words, the typically considered "currency risk" that has been pointed to as problematic for so many investors would become fairly riskless, overall.

Aging Population　The population of the United States is not what it once was, to be sure. We are getting older. It is estimated that those of us who are at least 45 years old will go from representing about 39 percent of the population in 2010 to representing 43 percent of the population in 2040. The significant effects of the 2008 financial crisis aside, we were already heading toward becoming a consumer base intent on contracting its spending. According to a 2005 Harris Interactive study, roughly 70 percent of people in their fifties who plan to move on behalf of retirement will do so principally to live out their remaining years in something more affordable. Studies have shown that the standard life-cycle model that illustrates that savings rates increase during working years but decline in retirement remains intact. However, it is reasonable to assume that the depletion of savings in retirement is by no means an indication of an increase in discretionary spending, but rather spending on essential goods and services. In other words, an aging population with lower savings rates does *not* suggest a populace that is going to buy lots of goods and services. This phenomenon (aging) is something that we will see in a number of developed, industrialized nations over the course of the coming decades, which is no real surprise. The further developed a nation becomes, the slower its birth rate, for a variety of reasons.

　　The matter of a decrease in discretionary spending is by no means limited to "stuff." Also in decline will be investments in just about everything. With fewer funds being channeled into investments of any type, the momentum effect that rarely fails to cause an appreciation in asset values would be missing. Goods and services, then, as well as financial market products, will likely be seen as less of a repository of the population's money in the United States over time.

An associated problem is that Baby Boomers, given their sharply growing representation of the population, will be tapping Social Security and other publicly funded resources at a rate not seen before. The resulting strain on the system, made worse by a shrinking worker base, and one that will likely be dealing with higher rates of unemployment going forward, should prove to be an ever-present drag on the United States's growth for many years.

Labor Costs/Outsourcing   It is no secret that jobs in the United States are being shipped overseas with increasing frequency. It is likely that if called the customer service department on behalf of any of the goods you own, you found yourself speaking with someone from India, which has become a favorite whipping boy regarding the matter of outsourced U.S. jobs. There are two parts to this outsourcing. One part is that it is U.S. companies doing the outsourcing, so it is these same companies that are shoring up their own bottom lines and making themselves more attractive to investors; fair enough (after all, we're not saying you should be avoiding U.S.-based equities). The other part is the resulting accumulation of greater wealth and opportunities by populations in the countries to which more of this labor is being outsourced. We know that manufacturing jobs have been disappearing for decades. Now, we are seeing the *service* jobs that we thought would always remain on U.S. shores moving away, as well. Your authors could go off on a rant at this point about the unfortunate effects of what is taking place in the U.S. economy, but we will instead merely point out that what you see is more the basis for looking overseas with your investment dollars.

There is an even broader issue, beyond the simple matter of the United States. The question can be asked more generally if developed markets are not just a worse option right now, anyway. The Great Recession has pounded the daylights out of developed markets. There are many components to the headwind that the United States will be facing for years to come, beyond those mentioned earlier. Right now, individual states are in major financial trouble; California, by itself the world's eighth-largest economy (estimated), faces a $24 billion-plus deficit, which represents about a quarter of the state's general fund. Britain has seen the outlook on its sovereign debt lowered from "stable" to "negative" by Standard & Poor's. France, with rising unemployment and collapsing growth, is currently in much the same position as the United States.

These troubles throughout developed nations prompt us to consider if, in fact, there is not an increased risk by *focusing* on the United States and other developed markets. Although some developed markets appear to be successfully burrowing their way out of the underground (supposedly the United States is one of those), they have a long, long way to go. Even once they successfully extricate themselves from the primary and secondary effects of the financial disaster, the question is beckoned, "what then?" As we have seen from our discussions earlier, many of the frontier and emerging markets have acquitted themselves nicely in the earliest stages of the recovery, while the developed markets will continue to be slow moving. For example, China's stimulus package, announced in the fall of 2008, totaling roughly $600 billion, is targeted at housing, infrastructure, transport networks, and technical innovation. The cool thing is that while it is not sure from which source(s) China will find the money, it is worth noting that even if China borrowed all of it . . . which is highly unlikely . . . their national debt-to-GDP ratio would still come in at around 30 percent, while the United States's is around 75 percent. In other words, China is much better prepared to start throwing money around than the United States, Japan, and a host of other developed markets.

GLOBAL INVESTING IS MORE THAN A FAD

We grant you that an entire book could likely be written on just why it is a good idea to become a truly global investor. The reasons we present here are the ones we think are perhaps among the more compelling, but what you should take from this chapter is that global investing will be much more than a fad; that given the long-term and perhaps permanent changes that are taking place demographically, politically, and economically in the world, that a global-centric portfolio will be the only reliable way that an investor can access, going forward, the kinds of returns we took for granted in the 1990s.

CHAPTER 2

Accurately Reading the World's Economies

An Intermarket Primer

A t any given point in time, money flows to some pocket in the world. When the global economy went into recession and equities subsequently fell into a bear market from 2000 to 2003, money poured out of most equity markets around the world. However, that money did *not* disappear, nor did investors completely detach and move their money out of the capital markets as a whole. Savvy investors moved their money into countries like China, whose stock market was blossoming into a raging bull market. Most investors did not know anything about the Chinese market until years later, when all the newspapers were raving about the bull market. The point to take from this is that if you are able to follow the intermediate- to long-term flows of capital from market to market, you will remain ahead of the curve and enjoy exceptional returns. The point of this chapter is not to necessarily tell you in which country to invest. It is, however, meant to serve as a tool to tell you which areas of the global market you should be targeting. For example, if the expectation is for a global economic slowdown and lower commodity prices, you will come to understand that the best place to invest is within the realm of fixed-income vehicles. Armed with this information, you can search the globe for the best yields and for the country from which they come (we give you that tool in a later chapter). This is a chapter that, although it appears at the beginning of the book, is really meant to bring all the areas of global investing together. The book is meant to help you understand what markets are available to you and how to invest in them. The purpose of this chapter is to enlighten you to the markets within markets as it applies to global investing.

Most investors have something we like to call "tunnel-vision syndrome." These investors tend to focus on one market and absolutely analyze it to death. We cannot tell you how many investors e-mailed or called us in the midst of the earlier-mentioned global bear market asking what stocks they should buy. Their scope is so narrow that they tend to miss the forest for the trees. Our typical answer to these folks was, "Buy bonds." That sounds like an easy answer because of the potential for a flight to quality—but that was not our motivation. Fixed-income was the asset class that was making people money as global equities fell, and as a result, the fall in stocks created a raging bull market for bonds. One of the economic side effects of the bear market was a massive lowering of interest rates by the Federal Reserve and their counterparts around the world. As we mentioned earlier, there is a factual relationship with fixed-income investments because prices run inversely to rates. If rates are coming down, bond prices are going up. In the end, if you had the foresight to invest in one of the most boring asset classes (bonds) during this time frame you would have received the interest payments as normal, and would have also received a nice capital gains kicker that was driven by turmoil in another asset class. The truth is that investors who focus on the bigger picture portrayed through *all* the markets tend to be the ones who enjoy better performance. When the industrialized countries are mired in recession, most economies and most equity markets will head lower. There will always be a stock market in some country moving higher. But, they are fewer and further between. Thus, investors should look not only for the hottest equity markets around the world, but search as well for the most profitable asset classes in any type of economy.

ASSET CLASSES

There are four main asset classes we analyze in our investment universe: stocks, bonds, commodities, and currencies. There are also the extensions to any one of those categories. For example, a normal extension of stocks would be stock options. That aside, the majority of capital market investments can be categorized in one of these four areas. Many traditional investors would have you believe there are only three, but we feel these four classes, taken together, create a good picture of what is happening in any given economy and, more generally, the global economy.

Narrowly focused investors simply do not know that these four asset classes all tell stories about each other and in many ways work to forecast one another. For example, in 2008, the global markets came under heavy pressure because of rising commodity prices. Oil and various building commodities were rocketing higher. One of the biggest drivers of these inflationary prices was the demand coming out of China. China was devouring any natural resources on which they could get their hands because of a huge infrastructure build-out effort. Rising commodity prices caused the United States and many other global economies to slow; it seems pretty obvious that higher oil prices will cause individuals to use less gas and curb their discretionary spending to make up for the higher prices they face at the pump. Do not forget, too, that airlines are going to charge a lot more money for tickets if they are paying $135 a barrel for oil as opposed to $65 a barrel. The totality of such microeconomic reactions pointed to slower growth. A natural response by the Federal Reserve was to try and stave off recession by lowering interest rates, as lower interest rates typically act as a catalyst for economic growth. As you can see from our brief example, all these markets work in tangent and have predictive powers for investors. Commodity prices went up, which predicted a bad economy and a bad environment for stocks. Lower stocks predicated lower interest rates. From the standpoint of investors, there were two or three trades being set up in the stock market by what we were experiencing in other markets. Remember, too, that it is not always the absolute level of prices in these classes that is important, but the *trend*. It took years for the price of oil to get to $150 a barrel. The rising trend of oil was the biggest concern, and it warned of a worse trend on the horizon.

A truly diversified investment approach should include investments and research in these four major asset classes: stocks, bonds, commodities, and currencies. Further, a diversified portfolio should not limit its dollars to one country, but include holdings in a number of markets around the world. By following multiple markets, an investor gets the "big picture" and is able to see significant market and economic changes earlier than investors with a single-market focus. The multiple market investors can then move portfolio holdings from one sector or market to another with greater ease as conditions change. That said, if your investment dollars are focused in one area, say as an equity trader, the wisdom of intermarket analysis is not lost on you. Analyzing all four markets as a whole can certainly help you to discern the sectors on which you should be focused, and even whether to hold more or less cash.

Now that you understand the importance of intermarket analysis and understand the basics, let us take a look at some simple rules to look for as it relates to these four asset classes. Keep in mind that investing is never a zero-sum game. If you have any experience in investing, you understand that it is not black and white. Accordingly, these rules we are giving you are not meant to be set in stone. If you see interest rates going down in a particular country, it does not mean it is time to jump into that country's stock market with both feet. Again, it is the longer-term trends in all these asset classes that we are looking for, not short-term anomalies. There is a great deal of ebb and flow in any capital market with which you need to familiarize yourself. Additionally, movements in any one of these four areas may be affecting countries and economies worldwide. For example, if a major oil patch is discovered in Russia, the news may well begin to drive down the price of oil globally, not just within Russia itself.

Before we look at how these four classes work, let us take a brief step back and define them.

Commodities

A commodity is anything for which there is demand, but which is supplied without qualitative differentiation across different markets. In other words, copper is copper, corn is corn, and oil is oil, regardless of what country you are trading in. Levi's, on the other hand, come in many varieties of quality. Consumers consider them to be distinct from jeans sold by other firms and the better the jeans, the higher the price consumers will pay, whereas the price of oil is universal, and fluctuates daily based on global supply and demand.

One of the characteristics of a commodity is that its price is determined as a function of its market as a whole. Well-established physical commodities have actively traded spot and derivative markets. Generally, these are basic resources and agricultural products such as coal, crude oil, ethanol, iron ore, sugar, coffee beans, soybeans, aluminum, rice, wheat, gold, and silver. When we are analyzing commodities as a whole, you can analyze the prices of individual commodities such as gold, or you can analyze them as a basket. There are multiple indexes you can look at like the Goldman Commodity Spot Index or the Reuters CRB Price Index. It is our preference to look at the CRB index, but indexes typically all run in tangent.

As a side note, keep in the back of your mind that commodities typically rise and fall on a global scale. For example, if you see that corn prices are rising in the United States, they are more than likely rising globally, and it is not a trend unique to just that particular country. As we see later, there is a big difference in intermarket relationships as it applies to countries that import commodities versus countries that primarily export commodities. However, this is the one intermarket area that tends to swing on a global basis.

Bonds

Bonds are pretty simple to understand. A company sells a bond to an investor and then pays that investor interest over a period of time. At the end, the issuer pays the bondholder back the principal at what is called "par value" or the issue price.

There are numerous types of bonds that pay interest (i.e., governments, municipalities, and corporations). So which interest rate do we look to for our analysis? The interest rate that we typically follow as a proxy for interest rates in the United States is the yield on the U.S. Treasuries 10-year note, and most governments around the world issue similar types of bonds, which investors can use as proxies. One caveat to this rule is that credit markets change and you may find, down the road, that market participants are using a new proxy. You may even come to find that relevant rates in one country are not relevant rates in another. Therefore, although it is perfectly fine to start by targeting the government yields we discussed, keep an open mind to changes as you move from country to country.

Most countries have entities like the U.S. Federal Reserve; the European Central Bank would be an equivalent "across the pond," and these governing bodies set interest rates that affect their respective economic regions in the same way the Fed's actions do so here. The truth, though, is that when the Fed raises or lowers interest rates, it is simply symbolic to the markets. There have been numerous times throughout history where the Fed lowered interest rates and the yield on the 10-year note was rising. The reason is because the yield on the 10-year note, and similar rates in other countries, are driven by supply and demand. Thus, investors in these types of bonds are typically looking forward. In many ways, central banks around the world are typically behind real market rates. Therefore, do not put as much weight in governing body interest rate announcements around the world, as the only rates that truly matter are the ones governed by supply and demand.

Stocks

We do not go too deep into definitions here except to say that stocks are an ownership interest in a company. As well, a stock index is a composite of stocks. There are numerous websites, like http://finance.yahoo.com/intlindices?e=europe where you can go to find out the index prices/charts for countries.

Currencies

A currency is a unit of exchange, facilitating the transfer of goods or services. It is one form of money, where money is anything that serves as a medium of exchange. Most countries have their own currency and it is the relationship of this currency to other classes that makes an important mark.

THE IRREGULAR ECONOMY EXCEPTION

Let us preface the following breakdown of the four classes by telling you that the rules are applicable to a *normalized economy*. A normalized economy is one that is showing signs of growth, although remember that recessions can also be part of a normal economy. A normalized economy is also showing signs of inflation that is under control. Typical inflation in a normal economy is between 1.5 and 3 percent. The economy does not have to be booming, and inflation does not have to be excessively low, but both need to be in an acceptable range for an economy to be considered normal.

On the flip side of the normalized economy we just described are two animals called *stagflation* and *deflation*. Both are types of abnormal economies that cause the normal relationship between the asset classes to be forced out of whack.

Stagflation is the "kiss of death" for an economy/stock market and is defined as a period of inflation combined with stagnation (i.e., slow economic growth and rising unemployment), to include recessionary characteristics. By the way, the term *stagflation* is generally attributed to British Chancellor of the Exchequer Ian Macleod, who coined the term in a speech to Parliament in 1965.

There are two principal contributing causes of stagflation. First, stagflation can result when an economy is slowed by an unfavorable supply shock, such as an increase in the price of oil within an oil importing country. This supply shock raises prices at the same time that it slows the economy by making production less profitable. All of this was taking place throughout most of the global economy from 2007 to 2008. Second, both stagnation and inflation can result from misguided macroeconomic policies. Central banks can cause inflation by permitting excessive growth of the money supply. When combined, the presence of both these factors is more than sufficient to launch an era of stagflation. For example, policies that promote growth in the money supply to allow consumers to afford higher priced oil contribute to runaway inflation. The global stagflation of the 1970s is often blamed on both causes: it began with a huge rise in oil prices, but then continued as central banks used excessively stimulative monetary policy to try to avoid the resulting recession and stagnation, causing a runaway wage-price spiral.

Deflation is defined as a general decline in prices, which is often caused by a decrease in the supply of money or credit. Deflation can also be caused by a decrease in government, personal, or investment spending. The opposite of inflation, deflation has the side effect of increased unemployment, as there is a lower level of demand in the economy (which can lead to an economic depression).

One of the best-known cases of deflation was witnessed in Japan from 1985 to 2000. Prices spiraled downward during this time frame, and to counteract this trend, the Japanese government continued to lower interest rates in an effort to raise demand and, by consequence, prices. However, the Japanese consumer would not come off the sideline and spend his hard-earned money. It took a massive cultural and economic shift to finally bring the economy out of its multiyear deflationary spiral.

The Japanese example is a good one to mark to see why intermarket analysis is less effective in a deflationary economy. The Bank of Japan, which is Japan's central bank and policy setter, did everything in its power to reinflate prices. Typically, lower rates promote borrowing and economic activity. However, because deflation had taken hold of the country, typical intermarket relationships did not hold. In a deflationary environment, we typically see bond prices rise and stock prices fall. As you will see, in a normal economy, rising bond prices equate to lower interest rates and thus *higher* stock prices.

Although most people had difficulty recognizing the signals, the capital markets were expecting a deflationary circumstance to arise during the global bear market from 2000 to 2003. Exhibit 2.1 shows the S&P 500, along

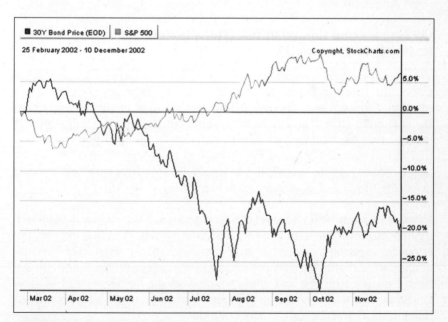

EXHIBIT 2.1 Performance of Bond Market (30-year note) and S&P 500, 2/2002 to 12/2002
Source: Stockcharts.com.

with the bond price action for the 30-year note. We are jumping ahead in the chapter a bit by telling you that bond prices and stock prices normally trend in the same general direction; in a deflationary economy, that reverses. Bond prices will move up while stock prices drop. We did not actually see deflationary numbers from 2000 to 2003, as gauged by the Consumer Price Index (CPI), but the markets were pricing it in and expecting prices to fall. Take a look at Exhibit 2.1 and you see that the bond market was moving higher while the stock market tumbled. In a normal economy, stocks and bonds move in the same general direction. Again, what you realize with intermarket analysis, and investing in general, is that it is not always the numbers that matter. It is the numbers the capital markets are *expecting* that matter. If you do not have fresh batteries in your crystal ball, now is the time to get some.

Deflation and stagflation are not conditions we see often. Thus, to say the following relationships are applicable in *most* markets around the world is fair. As we mentioned earlier, the following are trends that need to be analyzed on a long-term basis. Trends in these four asset classes do not change overnight, so we want to focus on long-term pivot points on which we can capitalize. Here are some general guidelines you need to be aware of as they pertain to the four asset classes.

Currencies and Commodities Typically Run Inversely to One Another

This section should be subtitled "A Tale of Two Countries." There is a big distinction that comes into play any time you are comparing commodities to other asset classes. The distinction lies in whether the thrust behind the economic growth and prosperity of the country you are analyzing lies in exporting its commodities. If you went down the line, you would find that most countries do some importing and some exporting of commodities. However, the distinction lies in whether a country's entire economy is driven by the export of one or two commodities.

Primary Commodity Exporters   Let us look at the emerging commodity export powerhouse of Brazil. As of this writing, Brazilian exports are booming, creating a new generation of tycoons. Major export products include coffee, soybean, iron ore, orange juice, stell, ethanol, and corned beef. Further, iron ore and steel, which account for 15 percent of total Brazilian exports, were seeing unlimited demand out of China because of that country's huge infrastructure build-out.

As you can see from Exhibit 2.2, the consistent and steady rise in commodity prices also created a huge demand for the Brazilian stock market, the Bovespa. The country's currency, the Real, also made marked

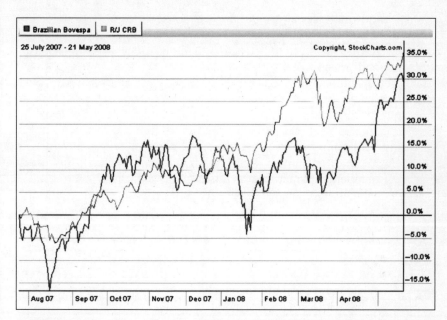

EXHIBIT 2.2 Performance of Brazilian Stock Market (Bovespa) Versus R/J Commodities Research Bureau (CRB) Commodity Index, 07/2007 to 05/2008
Source: Stockcharts.com.

positive strides. The currency rose because there was significant demand for Brazilian commodities and investors/buyers had to convert their home currency to the Real to make purchases. Investors across the globe were eating up any commodities that came out of Brazil and the rise in commodity prices acted as a slingshot for Brazilian profits. Exhibit 2.2 bears this out and shows how the two were moving in lockstep during this time frame. If you were investing during this time, you would have made a lot of money in the Bovespa. Also, if you could even somewhat make out the general level at which commodity prices would ultimately top out, you could make money shorting the currency or the market itself.

You can see another example of a primary exporting company in Exhibit 2.3. Russia has the world's largest natural gas reserves, the second largest coal reserves, and the eighth largest oil reserves. It is the world's leading natural gas exporter and the second-leading oil exporter. Oil, natural gas, metals, and timber account for more than 80 percent of Russian exports. You can see a strong similarity in appearance between the exhibits for Brazil and Russia. As commodity prices have risen, Russian stocks have also appreciated substantially.

EXHIBIT 2.3 Performance of Russian Stock Market Versus R/J CRB Commodity Index, 07/2007 to 05/2008
Source: Stockcharts.com.

EVERYONE ELSE—THE "NORMAL" ECONOMIES

All economies import and export goods. But, there is a definite distinction between a country like Brazil and a country like Germany. Germany is the world's largest exporter with $1.133 trillion exported in 2006. But, most of the country's products are in engineering, especially in automobiles, machinery, metals, and chemical goods. Germany is also the leading producer of wind turbines and solar power technology in the world. That said, take a look at the Exhibit 2.4 and you see a difference between Brazil and Germany in a time frame when commodity prices were booming. Germany is a huge exporter of finished products, but because of the types of exports they manufacture, they are a major *importer* of commodities. Thus, when commodity prices spiked higher in 2007–2008, it sent the German market plummeting. In reality, higher commodity prices meant higher input prices for manufacturing companies.

Exhibit 2.4 shows you how higher commodity prices affected a country like Germany. Germany tends to be an extreme example because of the amount of natural resources and commodities that they import. However,

EXHIBIT 2.4 Performance of German Stock Market Versus R/J CRB Commodity Index, 07/2007 to 05/2008
Source: Stockcharts.com.

the exhibit proves a point because a country like Germany can weather, for a time, a rise in commodity prices. Nevertheless, at some point, that relationship detaches and ultimately causes economic problems for the Germans, who, on whole, are importers of its inputs.

Australia gives us another example of an economy that is a primary importer of commodities and has the world's fourth-largest current account deficit in absolute terms. Further, agriculture and natural resources numbers are on the rise for Australia, but they constitute only 3 percent and 5 percent of GDP. As Exhibit 2.5 shows, the rise in commodity prices also hamstrung investors in the Australian markets.

Bond Yields and Commodities Tend to Move in the Opposite Direction

We all know there is an inverse relationship between bonds and interest rates. Thus, when bonds are moving higher, interest rates tend to move lower and vice versa. When bonds are moving higher, and rates are turning downward, the result is usually an invigorated economy. Money becomes cheaper to borrow and it becomes more available to businesses and investors. In a healthy economy there is an abundance of demand for things like copper, oil, wood, grains, and steel. These are the inputs to a healthy

EXHIBIT 2.5 Performance of Australian Stock Market Versus R/J CRB Commodities Index, 07/2007 to 05/2008
Source: Stockcharts.com.

economy. When an economy is strong, there is more demand for cars, trucks, and houses. This strong demand for products translates into a strong demand for the commodities that are used to build those products.

Let us look at an example. Exhibit 2.6 shows the 10-year U.S. Treasury Note compared to the CRB Commodity Index. The 10-year note is considered the economic proxy for interest rates in the U.S. economy. Keep in mind that what we are analyzing here is the overall trend and not necessarily the percentage move for these indexes. During the time frame on the exhibit, the markets were moving significantly lower and the global economies were heading quickly toward recession. In an effort to counter this recession, the Fed began to quickly, and drastically, lower interest rates. This reduction sent a charge into the commodities market. Rates continued to come down globally for several years, which was one of the factors behind the raging bull market we saw in the commodities space.

Bond Prices and Equities Tend to Move in the Same Direction

There is not a much to expand on here. When interest rates are moving up, this squelches the availability of economic capital and thus the ability for

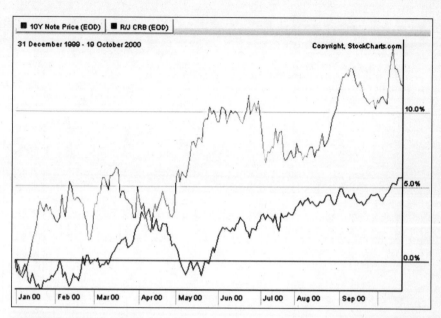

EXHIBIT 2.6 Performance of U.S. Treasury 10-Year Note Versus R/J CRB Commodities Index, 01/2000 to 10/2000
Source: Stockcharts.com.

businesses to expand. High interest rates work to curb economic growth. When rates are trending higher, borrowing costs are also trending higher and this is bad for business. If it is bad for business, it is bad for the economy, and bad for the stock market of that country or the world markets in general if the global trend of rates is moving higher.

Exhibit 2.7 illustrates this point as well. It is an exhibit for two ETFs: the SPDR International Treasury Bond portfolio (BWX) and the MSCI EAFE portfolio (EFA). The indexes represent both the global fixed-income market and the global equity markets. Although they do not track exactly, you can certainly see that the overall trend shows a high correlation. You find that in most markets, good *or* bad, these two asset classes tend to migrate in the same general direction.

Bond Prices Tend to Peak and Trough Ahead of Equities

As with most of these relationships, it makes rational sense. People rarely think about how all these markets interrelate, but when you do, the relationship is logical. Low interest rates are a major driver of economic growth. They promote lending and capital infusion. Easy access to capital is what drives growth for corporations and economies. If companies have access to capital and they are able to expand their businesses, they

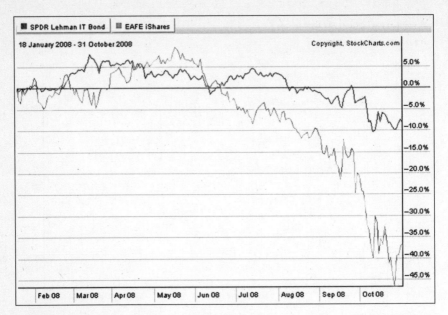

EXHIBIT 2.7 Performance of SPDR International Treasury Bond ETF (BWX) Versus iShares MSCI EAFE ETF (EFA), 01/2008 to 10/2008
Source: Stockcharts.com.

become more valuable. As they become more valuable, the value of their stocks goes up.

Take a look at Exhibit 2.8. It is an exhibit from March 2008 to December 2008 for the proxy of our global stock and bond markets. Both capital markets were in significant downtrends with the global capital markets being hurt by a severe credit crunch. But, late in 2008, the trend began to change and bonds began to turn higher. Next, several months later, stocks used lower rates as a catalyst to break from a severe downtrend to start their own run higher. What the exhibit does not show is that the global equity markets went on to hit a new low in early 2009, while the global fixed-income markets had already put in their ultimate bottom in late 2008. The moral of this story is that bonds typically bottom before equities. Therefore, it is incumbent on you, as equity investors, to carefully watch interest rates in the countries in which you are investing, and to keep an eye on the global bond markets, as a whole.

A Rising Currency Is Typically Good for Bonds and Equities

Conceptually, it makes sense. When the currency for a particular country is on the rise, it is a good sign. It means that there is demand for that

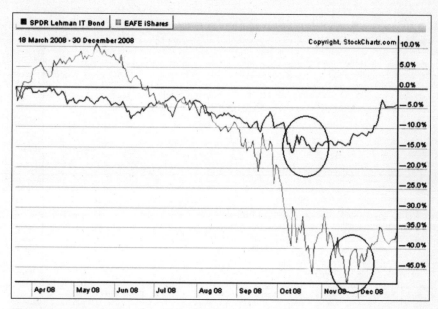

EXHIBIT 2.8　Performance of SPDR International Treasury Bond ETF (BWX) Versus iShares MSCI EAFE ETF (EFA), 03/2008 to 12/2008
Source: Stockcharts.com.

country's goods and services as foreign countries and foreign companies are exchanging their currency for the domestic currency in order to make an investment/purchase. That investment may be in the domestic company's government bonds, out of deference to attractive yields; it may come in the form of purchasing goods and services; or, it may be a foreign direct investment. In any case, it is a positive sign when a country's currency is showing strong demand.

Let us look to the Japanese Yen and the Japanese equity markets for an example. Japan experienced strong growth throughout the 1960s, 1970s, and 1980s. However, growth slowed markedly in the late 1990s, largely due to the Bank of Japan's failure to cut interest rates quickly enough to counter the effects of overzealous investment at the end of the 1980s. Because of this failure, Japan entered a liquidity trap where nominal interest rates were near zero and the central bank was unable to stimulate the economy with traditional monetary tools. To keep its economy afloat, Japan ran massive budget deficits to finance large public works programs. By 1998, these projects still could not stimulate enough demand to end the economy's stagnation. In desperation, the Japanese government undertook "structural reform" policies intended to wring speculative excesses from the stock and real estate markets. Unfortunately, these

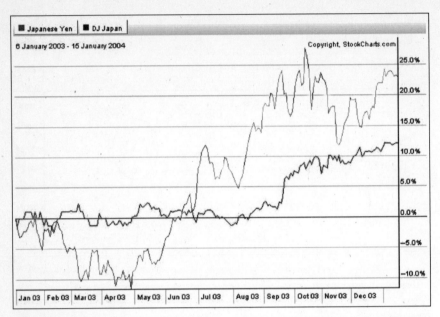

EXHIBIT 2.9 Performance of Japanese Stock Market Versus Japanese Yen, 01/2003 to 01/2004
Source: Stockcharts.com.

policies led Japan into deflation on numerous occasions between 1999 and 2004. Moving forward, the government decided to expand the money supply internally and, in the end, the ploy worked. By 2005, the economy finally began a sustained recovery driven by domestic consumption. How does this apply to our analysis? Take a look at Exhibit 2.9. Capital markets look ahead and the Japanese markets are no exception. As you can see, the Yen and the Japanese equity markets bottomed at about the same time in early 2003 and both began sustained bull markets. Investors saw that change was taking hold and began to make investments into the country.

We want to finish up this section of the chapter by relating to you that intermarket relationships are fluid and they tend to flow off investors' expectations, not just factual data. When we first discovered the world of intermarket analysis, it seemed straightforward and logical to us. We were excited to have found this tool and were anxious to apply it to our trading. However, as we integrated it into our day-to-day research, we came to find that there was more to it than meets the eye. For example, if current data is telling you that the economy is normal and growing, but the intermarket relationships are out of whack and potentially pointing you toward relationships that look more like a stagflationary economy, you need to adjust your thinking. We all know that capital markets are forward-looking and typically trade on expectation for the next six to nine months. Intermarket analysis works the same way. Thus, you cannot only garner predictive insights into the four subgroups by using this analysis, you can predict the type of economy that a country is in and invest accordingly.

A FEW TAKEAWAYS

Many investors simply do not have the time to analyze capital markets all day, so this would be a good time to give you a few simple takeaways from the information we provided. One of the best ways to look at these four subgroups is to pair them against each other to see which ones are performing better relative to the others. If you go to www.stockcharts.com, you will see a link for "SharpCharts." If you click on that link, you have the opportunity to put in a symbol. However, instead of putting in a single symbol, you can put in one symbol, a colon, and then another symbol. For example, if we wanted to compare global equities to global bonds, we would put in the symbols for the SPDR International Treasury Bond portfolio (BWX) and the MSCI EAFE portfolio (EFA) we used earlier; BWX:EFA. You can also use this tool to compare stocks against indexes or rates against prices. After adjusting the chart a bit for our personal preference, it looks like Exhibit 2.10. What you can interpret from this chart is that, because the overall trend is slowing upward, that global bonds have been outperforming global bonds since October 2007. Why is this important? See our two takeaway points that follow.

Takeaway 1

Our first takeaway is that a rising commodity/bond ratio favors inflation-type stock, including gold, energy, and basic materials stocks like metals and forest products. For our commodity index, we are going to use the Reuters/Jefferies CRB Index ($CRB) and for the bond market we will use the SPDR International Treasury Bond portfolio (BWX). If you look at Exhibit 2.11, you will see two numbered trend lines. The first line, identified as number one, is trending higher because commodity prices were outperforming bonds. In other words, the commodity/bond ratio will always be sloping higher on a chart when commodities are outperforming. During this time frame, materials, energy, and gold were all booming on the equity side of the markets.

EXHIBIT 2.10   Technical Chart Comparison of SPDR International Treasury Bond ETF (BWX) Versus iShares MSCI EAFE ETF (EFA)
Source: Stockcharts.com.

Takeaway 2

Second, a falling commodity/bond ratio favors interest rate-sensitive stocks, including consumer staples, health care companies, and utilities. In Exhibit 2.11, we have labeled the second line pointing down as number two. This time frame represents a period when bonds were performing better than commodities; therefore, the ratio is negative and the slope is down. At this time, we were entering a nasty global bear market that took down most equity groups. However, defensive stocks like health care and consumer staples most outperformed in the equity markets, which was to be expected.

One last thing: you do not necessarily have to abandon all aspects of commodities if the trend is sloping lower. In our portfolios, we still break down the groups into their individual components. During the time frame noted earlier, many investors, including ourselves, felt we were potentially facing significant inflation if and when the global economies recovered.

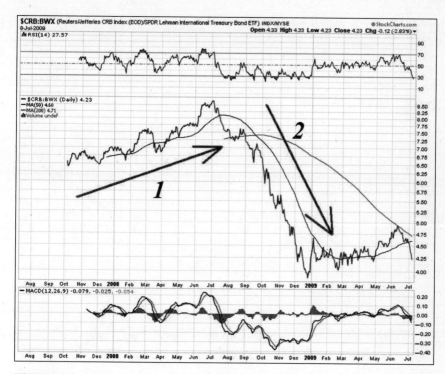

EXHIBIT 2.11　Technical Chart Comparison of R/J CRB Commodities Index ($CRB) Versus SPDR International Bond Portfolio ETF (BWX)
Source: Stockcharts.com.

That said, we thought our precious metals positions were worth holding. So, we decided to do some comparative analysis on the metals group. Exhibit 2.12 shows you that analysis.

Our first Exhibit shows a chart for the StreetTRACKS Gold ETF (GLD) versus the Reuters/Jefferies CRB Index ($CRB) basket. The GLD is not an exact proxy for the precious metals sector as a whole, but it is the one we owned and that is why we use it here. As you can see in Exhibit 2.12, the trend for gold stocks versus the commodities basket remained very positive even in a time frame when commodities had turned down. This was a positive sign if we were looking to hold our position.

The ultimate goal we have as hedge fund managers is to beat our benchmark. If manage a fixed-income hedge fund, your benchmark is not going to be the MSCI EAFE; rather, it will be some type of global fixed-income index. Accordingly, we need to have positions in our portfolio that are not only fundamentally sound, but beating the benchmark. Exhibit 2.13 was made at www.stockcharts.com by putting in the symbol GLD:EFA.

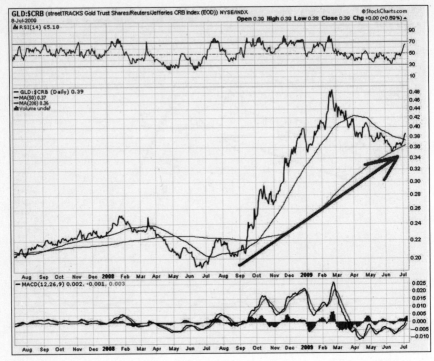

EXHIBIT 2.12 Technical Chart Comparison of StreetTracks Gold ETF (GLD) Versus R/J CRB Commodities Index ($CRB)
Source: Stockcharts.com.

It is pitting our gold ETF against our benchmark, the MSCI EAFE portfolio (EFA). What we are once again seeing is a sector that is outperforming. It is not only outperforming its group, it is outperforming our benchmark. In this case, we held the position. The commodity/bond rule is valuable and in this case, holding the GLD was more of an exception to the rule than a flaw in the rule itself. That said, you should always be willing to dig as deep as possible on any positions you own or any position you may be looking to take.

RESOURCES

Several of the resources we use in our intermarket analysis are those you may have already pulled from the chapter, but we want to give you a few

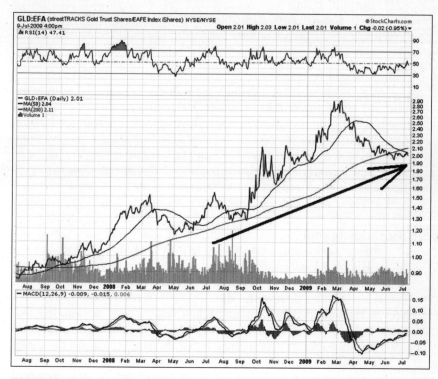

EXHIBIT 2.13 Technical Chart Comparison of StreetTRACKS Gold ETF (GLD) Versus iShares MSCI EAFE ETF (EFA)
Source: Stockcharts.com.

more specific sites and resources you can use in your day-to-day analysis. Intermarket analysis was first introduced to us by John Murphy, who wrote a book on the subject, *Intermarket Analysis: Profiting from Global Market Relationships* (Wiley, 2004). John has been on our radio show several times and he is one of the real pioneers of the technical side of investing. His site is www.stockcharts.com and can be used as a starting point for all categories. From there, you can use the following in your analysis.

Equities

There are numerous web sites around the world that will give you a ton of information and charts that pertain to equities. Equities are the component of our intermarket analysis on which you would have the least amount of difficulty procuring data. If you are Internet savvy and perform a simple

Google search, you will have more information than you can handle. Let us give you a few of our favorite sites:

- **Yahoo World Indexes**

  http://finance.yahoo.com/intlindices?e=americas—Put in this link and you see a box that gives you all the country indexes for that relevant part of the world. As you scroll across the top of this box, it allows you to change the part of the world the indexes are coming from. You can look at indexes from the Americas, Asia/Pacific, Africa/Middle East, and Europe. Another nice feature of this site is that, for many countries, it gives you the index components for that country. Thus, if you are looking for stock ideas within a country, this is an excellent starting point. We delve further into this subject in a later chapter.

- **Stockcharts.com**

  www.stockcharts.com—We are sure you will notice that we are a bit biased by the simple fact that we have used exhibits from this site in much of the book. When you go to the site, look for a small Rolodex symbol at the top right of the site. If you click on the symbol, it takes you to the site's symbol catalog. When you get into the catalog, you can search for things like "South Africa" and easily click on a chart for the Dow Jones South Africa Stock Index ($ZADOW). One of the things we like about this site is that after you find a few symbols you want to compare, you can click on the "PerfCharts" link on the top left of the site. This allows you to analyze countries against each other. As you saw earlier, it also allows you to chart currencies, commodities, interest rates, and indexes on a single chart for many countries around the world.

- **MarketWatch**

  MarketWatch is a great place to find news from different segments of the world. You can also find some commodities news on this same page. The page we use is www.marketwatch.com/markets. When you go to this page, you will see that MarketWatch does a nice job of almost creating sites within the site. If you click on the link for "Asia Markets," it will bring up a whole separate site with a ton of news on equity markets, fixed-income markets, and currencies.

Fixed Income

In most countries, the relevant rates are the freely traded government bond rates. In the United States, it is the yield on the 10-year Treasury note. In other countries, it is usually similar. Here are some of the sites we have bookmarked to use in our global fixed-income analysis.

- **FXStreet.com**

  The pertinent portion of the site can be found specifically at www.
  fxstreet.com/fundamental/interest-rates-table/. This particular part of
  the site will show you links for most countries around the world. If
  you click on the name of the country itself, you can view a chart for
  the interest rates of that country and the trends for fixed-income.

- **Standard & Poor's**

  S&P (www.standardandpoors.com) does a lot of good research.
  They are known for their equity indexes, but they also do a great job
  on the fixed-income side. You can break down the indexes and get a
  lot of good credit market data.

- **The *Economist***

  The *Economist* presents a lot of good information from the global
  business and sociopolitical perspectives. It is a good way to get a
  feel for not only what markets are doing, but what governments are
  doing that can affect the capital markets. One part of the site, www.
  economist.com/markets/rankings/displaystory.cfm?story_id=8835500,
  will actually give you country risk rankings for most countries around
  the world, which is invaluable. As of this writing, the United States
  was not in the top 10 list. It makes you think.

Commodities

Commodities research mostly comes in baskets, where you can research
the individual issues.

- **Commodities Research Bureau (CRB)**

  The Reuters/CRB index is one of the more closely followed indexes as it relates to commodities and one that we follow closely.
  The company sells research, so not everything on the site is free. However, there is a lot of good information and news from the commodities
  front. Also note that much of the site is geared to trading and traders,
  so you get a good perspective from that side. You can find them at
  www.crbtrader.com.

- **Barchart.com**

  Barchart.com is actually the parent company of the CRB. If you
  go to the site, you see a section on the left titled "Futures Overview."
  This is a site that you can use to analyze many of the subgroups that
  make up the commodity baskets. You can review prices, charts, and
  research. It is a good composite site.

- **Standard & Poor's**

  If you go to the S&P web site at www.standardandpoors.com, you
  can do a search for "S&P GSCI," which is the joint index between S&P

and Goldman Sachs. The site gives you all kinds of data on the index and also allows you to break it down into its individual components. In fact, with a little digging, the site gives you multiple links for more data such as the "Sources for World Production Data."

Currencies

Most of the sites you find around the Web are for currency trading brokers. You may or may not want to trade currencies, but the following offer some of the better charting packages we have found.

- **Forex.com (www.Forex.com)**
  Forex.com is a division of GAIN Capital Group. The firm is well capitalized and has a great web presence. Chinese, English, and Spanish are all available languages at Forex.com, and you can locate a large amount of data within the site.
- **FX Solutions (www.FxSol.com)**
  The company has been recognized as one of the United States's fastest growing private companies by *Inc.* magazine for three consecutive years. Languages available are Chinese, English, and Spanish. The site has good charts, with a real broad collection of technical indicators you can utilize. As a disclaimer, Sean Casterline has a personal currency trading account with FX Solutions.
- **Yahoo! Finance**
  Yahoo! Finance is a good source for just about anything financial, and if you follow this link, http://finance.yahoo.com/currency-investing, you will go directly to their section on currencies. This area gives you quotes, currency converters, and a good array of news.

CHAPTER 3

The Tools in Your Equity Toolbox

Although other types of investments are generally more limited in scope, that is by no means the case with international equities, and so we wanted to spend just a little time focusing on some of the key particulars of the tools by which you can do your equity investing as a globally minded personal portfolio manager. Our look at these tools includes an examination of them based on both specific investment type (mutual fund, stock, ETF, etc.) as well as the platforms from which you trade and manage your assets (U.S.-based and foreign brokerages). In the end, the decisions you make with regard to asset selection are personal; by definition, a hedge fund can basically do what it wants, and thus so can you. For that matter, the strategies you decide to employ, as well as the instruments you choose to utilize, may vary widely. That said, the key feature of a hedge fund that you always want to maintain, without regard to management style, is the constant attempt to maximize returns and limit losses in any given market climate through some combination of strategies and instruments; to that end, your equity positions, whether long or short, will likely serve as a linchpin in that effort. It is, therefore, important to understand the key benefits *and* limitations of the global equity instruments available, as well as the benefits and limitations of the available custodial brokerage opportunities through which you may elect to execute your transactions.

A lot is made of the differences between the kinds of foreign investments you can transact easily in purely U.S. terms, and those that are much better representations of a true foreign security (to include the natural foreign security itself). You know the standard "knocks" against instruments like U.S. multinationals and exchange-listed ADRs: they're too big and slow, and they're too closely correlated with both U.S. markets and U.S. investor behavior to offer the key sought-after benefits of foreign investing. That's all generally true, but that said, none of that means they do not have their roles as foreign plays. For example, a U.S. multinational like Coca-Cola, one that realizes most of its revenue from other countries, can be an attractive play during periods of dollar weakness (which we see in just a bit). We're not huge fans of exchange-listed ADRs as one of the better ways to target rich growth markets, but they certainly fill a role for the investor who wants to build a hedge fund as simply as possible. The point at which you begin to limit yourself in terms of building a properly diversified portfolio is when you decide that these kinds of vehicles should serve as the foundation of your global portfolio. Nevertheless, they are not at all without their value. Adopting the approach of a comprehensive hedge fund manager seeking global success, any one of the equities and transaction platforms listed here may have a suitable and valued role in your portfolio; just remember that any vehicles you select that are further removed from an organic foreign environment are those that will likely dilute the beneficial effects of the foreign exposure. It does not mean that they do not have value as instruments, but may represent more your domestic makeup than your foreign, depending on your analysis and how strategically you implement them as a part of your fund.

U.S. MULTINATIONALS

In our opinion, U.S. multinationals are not really ideal vehicles by which to develop an effective, global-centric investment portfolio, but they are not entirely without relevance to that end. You simply have to keep them in perspective and realize that they would be perhaps the most "Americanized" of your global investment selections. The reason for that, of course, is that U.S. multinationals *are* U.S. companies, and while many realize their revenue from around the world, their marriage to the United States and both the culture and psychology of U.S. business means that their stock prices are highly influenced by the behavior of U.S. equities markets. To be candid, the idea of turning to multinationals as a centerpiece of one's foreign investment strategy is both ineffective and, to be frank, woefully unsophisticated in this day and age, when access to true foreign investments in growth-oriented markets is easier than it has ever been before.

The support of the multinational as foreign play has never been based on much more than the simplistic notion that if a company has developed a significant presence in other countries besides the United States, that is a form of foreign investing. In our opinion, that depends on what you presume foreign investing to be. If you see foreign investing as something that is to remain subordinate to your U.S.-based investing, then the multinational may suit your purpose; if, however, you see it as the essential component by which to create a winning portfolio going forward, then they may be of little use to you. Put another way, the multinational is the ideal foreign investment vehicle for those who do not really want to invest in foreign markets.

Those who want to argue in favor of the multinational as foreign investment usually trot out Coca-Cola as their favorite son. It is easy to see why that is, because more than 70 percent of Coca-Cola's total revenue has come from overseas markets for years now. Granted, that is an impressive statistic, but there are not many Coca-Colas in the realm of the U.S. multinational. Even Boeing, which is, by many measurements, the largest manufacturer of aircraft in the world, as well as the largest exporter in the United States, sees only about 40 percent of its revenue from overseas markets. Again, that is significant in relative terms, but it is hardly a pure foreign investment play. General Electric, currently the world's largest company (source: *Forbes*), receives about 45 percent of *its* total revenue from foreign markets. For Wal-Mart, that same figure is at roughly 25 percent, as it is with Walt Disney.

Then again, say proponents of multinationals, that is precisely what you want; a way to play both sides of the water simultaneously without overexposing yourself to all of the much-ballyhooed risks of foreign investing (e.g., political uncertainty, economic instability, currency confusion) that affect the more direct investor in foreign markets. Using multinationals, then, is sort of a "one foot in the water" approach to global investing.

Again, though, you have to get back to why you are investing globally. It is principally to make money, not principally to hedge your risk (although risk management is certainly an important component), which is what a multinational-based portfolio essentially is: a more defensive approach to global investing, which will do you little good over the long term.

As we saw in Chapter 2, the U.S. markets are by no means the best-performing markets, and the S&P 500 has never been the best-performing market index in any calendar year. Again, multinationals are U.S.-*based*, so while somewhere between "a few" to "some" may have some significant measure of foreign exposure, it is not the same thing as being foreign-based; it is that simple.

One particular problem with U.S. multinationals as foreign investments is that for all of the foreign exposure of some, they generally offer little exposure to emerging and frontier markets. Most of the foreign countries in which U.S. multinationals have significant exposure are in more developed markets—about 80 percent. Even emerging markets like those that comprise BRIC have, to date, seen little direct exposure to U.S. multinational companies.

We grant you that in periods when the U.S. dollar is particularly weak, as was the case during a good portion of the time during which this book was being written, multinationals can see a bump in profit based on no more than the beneficial conversion of their foreign revenue, which is a nice feature. Coca-Cola, for example, saw revenue increase 9 percent from Q3/07 to Q3/08 but according to the company's earnings statement, two-thirds of that increase was attributable to the strength of foreign currency versus the dollar. According to Merck's earning statement for the same period, worldwide sales dropped by 2 percent... but the effect of foreign currency conversion exerted a positive impact on the figure by 4 percent; in other words, Merck's sales figure would have looked *much worse* if not for the benefit to this multinational of an especially weak dollar during this time. It is worth noting the converse, as well; the trend of a strengthening dollar going into 2009 wreaked havoc on multinationals. In Merck's case, currency-neutral revenue from Q2/08 to Q2/09 actually improved by 3 percent, but the adverse impact of the stronger dollar caused actual revenue to *fall* by 3 percent. In Coca-Cola's case, adverse currency effects over the same period brought its 4 percent increase in revenue all the way down to a loss of 10 percent.

Another problem with multinationals is that they are, by definition, large companies. That is, they are companies that have already realized the primary growth spurt that you principally seek when looking to invest for capital accumulation. Some of the biggest multinationals, in terms of amount of foreign revenue, are also the largest companies in the world: Coca-Cola, Boeing, General Electric, Wal-Mart, Walt Disney, and Caterpillar. Of the Dow 30 components, most of those are true multinationals in our book (annual overseas revenue accounting for at least 20 percent of total revenue), and really only a small handful see less than 20 percent of total revenue from foreign sales.

There is a behavioral component, as well, that affects their usefulness as foreign investments. Who typically owns U.S.-based stocks, multinational, or otherwise? Americans. Even though multinationals may see a large percentage of their revenue come from foreign sales, their shares are owned by Americans, and so they are considered in the context of the U.S. economy and U.S. market movements. This is exceedingly important to you as a prospective global investor, because the behavior of your fellow shareholders is as important as the fundamentals of the country itself. When U.S. investors turn to their U.S. brokerage accounts to sell their U.S. holdings in the wake of some dire domestic news that is screamed out over U.S. media outlets, they generally do not spare their U.S. multinationals on the basis that they have a significant presence in hundreds of other countries around the world; they just click "sell."

EXCHANGE-LISTED AMERICAN DEPOSITARY RECEIPTS

ADRs listed on U.S. exchanges are, in our opinion, the "cousin" of the U.S. multinational in terms of useful global investment vehicle—they can be legitimately considered as foreign investments, making them significantly different from multinationals in that regard, but still suffer a bit from the issue of being notably influenced by U.S. market activity. Still, they do represent an honest foreign investment play, and that, along with the ease with which they can be negotiated by U.S. investors, makes them popular and not altogether ineffective.

The simple definition of the ADR is that it is the U.S. version of a foreign stock. Technically, an ADR is not actually the share of the foreign stock, but rather a negotiable certificate that is issued with the stock as its backing, essentially, and is fully tradable just like a stock on U.S. exchanges. ADRs are issued by U.S. depository banks, and can represent anything from fractional shares, to an even whole share, to multiple shares, of the underlying foreign stock. We do not want to get too bogged down in the incidental technicalities as to structure, because that ceases rather quickly being relevant to you. If you think of ADRs as U.S. shares of foreign stock that favor U.S. investors by being denominated in U.S. dollars, paying dividends in U.S. dollars, and trading as domestic shares on U.S. exchanges, you basically know what you need to in that regard. Some of you might quarrel with the fact that that we do not get into the differences between sponsored and unsponsored ADRs, or the differences between ADRs and American Depositary Shares as well as Global Depositary Shares, but again, these are more technical distinctions that are not terribly relevant to the core discussion. Suffice it to say that all of the aforementioned are basically slightly different variations of one another.

ADRs came about precisely to combat some of the key difficulties typically associated with transborder investing. In addition to the usual impediments like currency-related issues, investing in foreign markets was always made historically more difficult on the basis of access; until the Internet age, as well as increased communications abilities all the way around, direct investment in foreign markets was always on the tedious side. The introduction of the ADR mechanism (by J.P. Morgan, by the way, on behalf of British retailer Selfridges and Co., in 1927) essentially solved these problems for the domestic investor. We might argue that the evolution of organic global trading platforms is perhaps beginning to eat away at some of the historical transactional benefits of ADRs, and consequently the inclination of investors to do without some of the biggest advantages of owning foreign shares directly within the foreign companies' home markets, but the reality is that even many serious U.S.-based investors seeking foreign portfolio exposure will opt for an element of simplicity and transactional ease in their investment efforts—so ADRs will be with us for a long time to come.

Again, the benefits to investors of using ADRs can essentially be summed up as being on the basis of transactional and administrative simplicity, which we clearly believe is not without its merits. Because ADRs are listed on domestic exchanges, they are bought and sold just like any other stock; settlement issues are also the same. The ADRs are denominated in the U.S. dollar, which means dividends are paid that way. Prospectuses and other information are all in English. In other words, from the transactional and administrative standpoint, buying the ADR of Taiwan Semiconductor is no different from buying a stock as organically American as Home Depot. Additionally, foreign companies whose shares are made available in the United States through ADRs must provide financial reports that are prepared in accordance with the accounting practice standards in the developed Western world (GAAP or IFRS).

All in all, the number of exchange-listed ADRs available is high enough to be functional; there about 500 or so spread across the NYSE, AMEX, and Nasdaq (although, in sum total, there are thousands available in the United States when you include those available throughout the OTC markets, which is something we discuss later).

For your reference, we include both lists of the biggest depositary receipt investors (Exhibits 3.1 and 3.2), as well as of the most widely held, exchange-listed depositary receipts.

In our opinion, ADRs, although better than U.S.-based multinationals in terms of serving the generally understood goals of the true global investor, suffer from some limitations that cannot be wholly disregarded. First, because ADRs are indeed "Americanized" versions of foreign stocks, they have a tendency to oftentimes behave more like American issues than foreign issues. This idea is a surprise to many who first consider it, and it is understandable; after all, ADRs are, at their root form, foreign stocks, so even though they are *available* in the United States on U.S. exchanges, they are foreign equities first and foremost, right? Well, yes—*and* no. Although it is true that ADRs generally move in the same way that the underlying foreign stock moves in its home market, that is not always the case. In our practices, there have been numerous instances where we have seen ADRs react more like domestic issues than foreign ones. The fact is that U.S. investors will react in generally the same way to economic news and

EXHIBIT 3.1 Top 10 Depositary Receipt Investors (as of July 2009)

Company	Value of DR Investments ($mm)	% of DRs in Total Equity Portfolio
Fidelity Management and Research	$20,922	5.32%
Barclays Global Investors, N.A.	$16,475	3.54%
Wellington Management Co., LLP	$12,982	6.82%
Dodge and Cox	$12,802	17.35%
Capital World Investors	$12,451	4.76%
Capital Research Global Investors	$12,204	4.14%
AllianceBernstein L.P.	$ 8,960	5.00%
Fisher Investments	$ 8,202	39.23%
Brandes Investment Partners, LP	$ 7,304	17.07%
T. Rowe Price Associates, Inc.	$ 6,842	4.17%

Source: J.P. Morgan.

market conditions; they are more inclined to view their NYSE stocks, for example, as being the same: stocks they own to be either bought or, more typically, *sold* en masse. This hearkens back to the limitations of the aforementioned U.S. multinationals, which are fundamentally U.S. issues before they are anything else. That characteristic is not as prevalent here, but it still applies.

A secondary problem with ADRs is that they tend to be representative of larger companies that start to take on the features of multinationals with high correlations to U.S. markets. Companies like Sony, BASF, and Unilever are present in hundreds of countries around the world, and

EXHIBIT 3.2 Most Widely Held, Exchange-Listed Depositary Receipts (as Measured by Ownership Value as of July 2009)

Security Name	Country	Exchange	Symbol
Teva Pharmaceutical Industries	Israel	NASDAQ	TEVA
Petroleo Brasileiro SA	Brazil	NYSE	PBR
America Movil S.A.B.	Mexico	NYSE	AMX
Petroleo Brasileiro SA (Class A)	Brazil	NYSE	PBR.A
BP p.l.c.	UK	NYSE	BP
Taiwan Semiconductor	Taiwan	NYSE	TSM
Royal Dutch Shell p.l.c.	UK	NYSE	RDS.A
Novartis AG	Switzerland	NYSE	NVS
Vale S.A.	Brazil	NYSE	VALEP
Total S.A.	France	NYSE	TOT

Source: J.P. Morgan.

the reason companies seek to sponsor ADRs is precisely because they are seeking a high degree of visibility to both investors and consumers, as well as the prestige of a U.S. exchange listing. That is all well and good if, again, you are taking a more defensive/less aggressive approach to global investing, but if you seek aggressive gains from unique, more isolated markets, ADRs may not work as well for you.

Asset management legend Louis Navellier, in his book *The Little Book That Makes You Rich* (John Wiley & Sons, 2007) states at one point that he likes that ADRs (we are presuming he is referring to exchange-listed ADRs) are representative of companies that are conservative and are often characterized by a high degree of government ownership, because those features tend to allow the global investor to sleep well at night. With all due respect to Mr. Navellier, *our* position is that global investing should be less about being defensive and more about taking advantage of acutely profitable markets—your risk, such as it is, is controlled by your active management strategies. To many investors, ourselves included, having the features of "large" and "government-owned" are more likely reasons to grant *less* consideration to a prospective investable company, not more.

FOREIGN ORDINARIES AND ADRs ON THE OTC

The Over-The-Counter (OTC) market, as represented by the OTC Bulletin Board (OTCBB), the Pink Sheets, and the Grey Market, gives global investors a unique opportunity, in comparison to multinationals and exchange-listed ADRs, to purchase foreign securities of companies that are smaller and more targeted plays of more remote economies. What further makes this particular market so attractive is that many of these securities are actually the same securities that are traded on the foreign company's native exchange, but denominated in U.S. dollars; they are the *foreign ordinaries*. ADRs are available on the OTC market as well, but most of these ADRs are not of the big, foreign-based multinationals that you find listed on exchanges; these ADRs, by and large, are representative of the smaller, more local companies in which you ideally want to invest with your foreign-earmarked monies. The bottom line is that when it comes to the OTC market, the precise form of the security, ordinary or ADR, is not as important as the market itself, where you can access securities of companies that present you with superior growth opportunities than the multinationals or exchange-listed ADRs.

Let us clarify ordinaries before we move on. Technically, ordinaries are the purest form of foreign security you can buy in the United States without having to trade those directly in a foreign market yourself. There are thousands of ordinaries available on the OTC—the land of the unregulated—and do so usually for reasons related to making life easier and less expensive: some companies want to avoid the onerous requirements of Sarbanes-Oxley, while smaller companies with lower trading volumes want to avoid the exchange listing fees ($50,000 per annum on the NYSE). More than a few foreign companies that trade OTC were once listed on U.S. exchanges, but decided they did not need the hassle. Although OTCBB companies have to be current with required SEC filings, they do not have a minimum market capitalization requirement, do not need to meet a minimum share price threshold, or really have any other requirement. Pink Sheets and Grey Market standards are actually lower, as the eligibility to be quoted in the Pink Sheets or Grey Market does not require that you really meet any useful standards at all. Although it is true that companies that trade OTC, and particularly those that trade Pink Sheets/Grey Market, are among the riskiest in which to invest, that is by no means always the case. Perfectly sound companies will often turn to the OTC market exclusively for the reason that they do not want to deal with costly and administratively onerous listing requirements.

In theory, the ordinary is the same stock as the organic version traded in the company's natural market, and it essentially is. The differences typically come down to pricing; while you buy the ordinaries through U.S. exchanges during U.S. trading hours, you pay a premium for being able to do that, to include fees to the local agent for facilitating the transaction on his end, a currency conversion fee (remember, you are buying the ordinary here in U.S. dollars), and other administrative costs related to custody and settlement.

Again, ADRs are also available on the OTC market. Some companies are represented as ordinaries, some as ADRs (and even, in a few cases, as *both*). The difference between the ADRs available OTC and those that are exchange-listed typically has to do with size; securities that trade OTC are generally smaller, which is what you want as a capital accumulation investor. The advantage of looking OTC is the opportunity to find securities—be they ordinary or ADR—that are more disconnected from, and less correlated with, the United States and its markets.

This is not to say that *all* foreign stocks that trade OTC are small unknowns. Nestlé, BASF, and Adidas are three examples of well-known companies that are happy to trade OTC, and all three do it as ADRs *and* ordinaries. The reason? These companies simply feel that the more cumbersome regulatory requirements associated with earning a more "prestigious" U.S. exchange listing is not worth it—and that their brand awareness is such that investors will find their shares no matter where they are.

For example if you like what Brazil's Natura Cosmeticos SA is accomplishing as a growing player in both Latin America and France (but not the United States) in the manufacture and distribution of cosmetics, you have to buy it as a foreign ordinary on the OTC, where it trades more specifically on the Grey Market. Alternatively, if you want to play one of Asia's largest financial services firms, DBS Bank, you can do it OTC, by way of purchases of DBS Thai Danu Bank PLC. Those are but two small examples from a whole universe of foreign securities available through the OTC market that do not have much stake in the fortunes of the United States.

There are tens of thousands of companies available as ordinaries and ADRs on the OTC Bulletin Board, Pink Sheets, and Grey Market, and one great tool in your research is the search mechanism at www.pinksheets.com. Specifically, if you go to "OTC Company Search," you can search companies and markets using a variety of screens. Ideally, this tool is probably best used in concert with your other research mechanisms. That is, as you begin to narrow down regions, countries, markets, and industries in which to invest, you can use the resources at Pink Sheets to help determine the specific companies in which you might ultimately place some money.

A few other items to note: You will likely recognize this soon enough as you start getting more familiar with the Pink Sheets site, but we wanted to mention that when you go OTC, the stock symbols for ordinaries all end in the letter "F," while the symbols for ADRs all end in the letter "Y" (here is a quick example: BASF, which trades both as an ADR and an ordinary on the OTC, has as its ADR symbol "BASFY," while its ordinary symbol is "BSASF"). That is not an earth-shaking detail, but we want you to be extra aware of it so that you pay close attention to exactly what you are buying; there can be not-insignificant price differences between the ordinaries and ADRs of the same companies, so keep them straight. Also, we are sometimes asked why anyone would bother transacting directly in overseas markets if so much of the emerging world is available OTC. There are several reasons, but the *central* reason has to do with the risks associated with liquidity, pricing, and lack of timely corporate information. Liquidity in smaller OTC issues can often be an issue, and it can *really* be an issue when it comes to little-known foreign securities. Many of these issues are thinly traded, and you may not be able to find a seller when you want to buy, or worse, a buyer when you want to sell. If you do your transacting in the security's natural market, that problem typically disappears.

As for pricing, we mentioned earlier that buying ordinaries and ADRs via OTC may cause you to pay more than it would if you buy the shares direct. That can happen frequently. Lastly, one of the more general risks associated with buying foreign shares is that your remote positioning in the United States means you may not receive information in a timely fashion (or at all) from your company's investor relations department. Our advice is that if you do decide to take positions in any such issues, you make it a habit to frequently visit the company's proprietary site just to be sure you are not missing out on some important piece of information.

COLLECTIVE INVESTMENTS

Collective investment vehicles are often sneered at by professional investors as being the tools of the less sophisticated, but we believe they most certainly have their place in an intelligently constructed portfolio that wants to play a market or region of the world without having to discern and choose among what, to many, are too little known companies *within* these markets. Additionally, collective investments relieve investors of the issue of owning an extensive selection of stocks in a particular market on a piecemeal basis—although trading individual securities in what have historically been remote markets is getting easier, it can still be a logistical pain for some people, and is certainly not without its expense issues.

This, then, is why we like funds for the more sophisticated investor: they give that person the opportunity to make his life easier within a certain portion of his portfolio, and if he pays attention to what he is doing with it, he can reliably look to his fund allocation as something that serves as a reliable performer that may rarely overwhelm him with noticeably good returns in relation to the rest of his holdings, but should not be the source of any sleepless nights, either.

Open-end mutual funds are the saviors of the average investor. Really. We do not say that because we think they are the best type of equity vehicle out there—far from it. We say that because Americans are generally happiest with those things that are heavily complemented by ease of use. In the world of investing, open-end funds satisfy that criterion perfectly. As for collective equity investments as a whole, the only alternative to open-end funds are exchange-traded vehicles, and those are not for everyone. Open-end funds give the average person access to the equities markets in easy, *relatively* cost-efficient fashion, and thus also grant them the ability to do something besides rely on paltry-paying bank savings accounts and the dubious future of Social Security in order to achieve financial independence and security by the time they will need it. We like that, and we are happy to see it.

That said, if you, or someone you love, is gravitating toward using open-end funds as the centerpiece of a global investment effort, stop.

Anyone who is seeking to develop a targeted global investment portfolio is not likely the same person whose investment efforts begin and end with his automatic biweekly contribution to his employer's 401(k), which means that if you are making extra efforts on behalf of investing, make real ones. As for open-end funds, do not misunderstand us; we think they have *a* place—we just do not think they should occupy *the* place.

If you are inclined to buy and hold, you are probably not reading this book, but if you do already have a portion of your portfolio allocated to investments that you do not want to have to think much about, they are likely open-end funds. We have already alluded to the benefits—the ease of use and the low transaction costs (assuming you are sticking with no-load and no-transaction-fee funds, which you should). The central "con" of open-end is that they are mostly actively managed. Most professional investors tend to hold actively managed funds in disfavor because they do not want to have to guess what a portfolio manager will do; it is reasonable to assume that the effective use of technical analysis by you on behalf of your managed funds may be mitigated on the basis that you have no idea what the fund manager may do. Another reason actively managed funds tend to fall into disfavor with proactive investors is because the managers so often tend to under-perform the benchmarks they track. If you defer to a money manager, you want to be sure that he is at least going to beat the standard against which he measures himself.

If you do opt for inclusion of open-end funds in your portfolio, we encourage you to subject them to the same sort of analysis to which you expose your stocks and other exchange-traded instruments. Because we are not sure how valuable that may be, you have to do your best, but you clearly want to watch them. Go to Morningstar (www.morningstar.com) to start building your open-end universe.

So much for open-ends; in pursuit of global investment success, it is really the collectives of ETFs and closed-end funds that give you a better chance of arriving at the portfolio you really want.

Let us start with closed-end funds *first*. Until the advent of exchange-traded funds (ETFs), which are really the collective of choice for pro investors seeking fund exposure, closed-end funds were the place to go. Closed-end funds, which can lay claim to only about 3 percent of the total number of assets found in open-ends, may share the name "mutual fund" with their open-end brethren, but that is about it for the similarities.

Beyond the huge disparity in assets, there are other important dissimilarities, as well. Another key difference between the two lies in the infrastructure of the portfolio assets. One of the features of open-end funds that hamper managers is the same one that provides such mass appeal of the funds—the continuous offering and redemption of shares. That is great for the consumer, but an ongoing irritation for the manager who is trying to maximize performance. The open-end manager, by consequence of his circumstances, must always transact with an eye to satisfying redemption requests, while the closed-end boss knows he will not have to sell more illiquid holdings to satisfy withdrawals, which means he can get into those less liquid securities in the first place. Because of this, if you are looking for a managed fund option, closed-end funds are worth a look. The fact is that funds that target more remote global markets will always run up against opportunities that require the ability to persevere with holdings—closed-end funds, by nature of their structure, will be able to do that better than open-ends. Additionally, open-ends trade right at net asset value (NAV) (the simple, transparent valuing of share value on the basis of underlying asset value), while closed-ends do the "premium/discount-to-NAV" dance. We do not make a big deal of that distinction, other than you need to be aware of it and take it into account of your transaction decisions, as appropriate. One of the tools we like the best to get a good snapshot of closed-ends, including the premiums or discounts at which they are trading, is ETFConnect (www.etfconnect.com), which, despite its name, provides good data on closed-ends.

All of this said, though, when you are dealing with mutual funds, be they open-end or closed-end, you are dealing with actively managed portfolios. It is important to note, however, that one of the hallmark reasons touted years ago by the pro-mutual fund crowd for buying funds—the portfolio oversight by an "expert"—has been debunked in recent years. Many investors accept that while there may be years where fund managers outperform indexes, it has become apparent that there are too many years where they *under-perform* them. Many investors have since decided that although they like the idea of targeted collectives in their portfolios, they would prefer that those collectives remain essentially unmanaged; said investors will do the discerning on their own with individual stock selections, thank you very much.

ETF powerhouse iShares has published some data that speaks to the matter of "Persistence of Skill," as they term it: the ability of mutual fund managers to outperform their benchmarks in consecutive years. According to the data published in their report *Challenging Conventional Wisdom—Do Active Managers Perform Better in Inefficient Markets?*, the report indicates that in a year when 43 percent of S&P 500 managers outperformed their benchmark, that year was followed by a rate the next year of 23 percent, and then down to 12 percent in the third year. MSCI Emerging Markets managers had, relatively speaking, higher percentages, but the numbers were not *much* better. For the MSCI, a year that saw roughly 56 percent of managers come out ahead of their benchmark was followed by a year that saw roughly 32 percent of managers beat the index, and a third consecutive year when just 19 percent bested it. This data suggests not only that even in "good" years do barely 50 percent of managers beat their benchmark index, but even more tellingly that even that limited success can be difficult to maintain by managers, as a group.

This brings us to exchange-traded funds, or ETFs. ETFs are perhaps the final stage in the natural evolution of collectives. ETFs, to many, offer the best of open- and closed-end funds. Like open-end funds, ETFs transact at NAV, but like closed-end funds, they trade throughout the market day and allow for the standard specialized transactions like limit and stop orders; they can also be shorted like closed-ends. Best of all, they are generally unmanaged. There are a growing number of *managed* ETFs that have taken root, but their arrival on the scene is still recent. Assuming the matters of transparency, tax efficiency, and liquidity do not change, the deciding factor in using actively managed ETFs over their unmanaged counterparts will simply be the ability of the manager to beat his benchmark index, as well as the individual investor's desire to compete against the fund manager in his own analytical capacity.

If you want to be technical, note that many ETFs trade at premiums/discounts to NAV, as well, but mostly do so to the tune of less than 1 percent deviation from NAV, so the issue is negligible.

Once again, if you want to get a good comprehensive look at the unmanaged ETFs you might be considering, go to ETFConnect (www.etfconnect.com), which is a useful site.

Ultimately, you have to decide what role you want collectives to play in your hedge fund portfolio. If you want to include funds where the management team is going above and beyond in seeking to find some unique way to bolster performance, perhaps a closed-end, or maybe even a particular open-end, is good for you. If you are happy using collectives as more of a noncontroversial, reliable, low-maintenance component, then an unmanaged ETF is likely the way to go. None of these collectives really deprive you of the ability to apply solid analytical methods to each, but the effectiveness of same may be more mitigated in some circumstances, particularly as it is applied to managed collectives.

INTERNATIONAL INVESTING FROM U.S.-BASED BROKERAGE PLATFORMS

Once as seemingly impotent in their ability to facilitate international transactions as the U.S. investor himself (years ago, that is), U.S. brokerages are beginning to look genuinely appealing to many global-minded investors in the United States as they improve all aspects of their operations to make the pursuit of foreign opportunities through their respective entities more worthwhile. Recognition of the recent but obvious trend toward globalization has prompted more brokerages to make global access a significant priority, to include seeking deeper and wider penetration of foreign markets and improving *better*, as well as *more*, transactional-based relationships with local markets around the world. In the end, one of the most important tools in your toolbox will be a formal relationship with a U.S.-based brokerage, which you have or want *anyway*, that gives you the opportunity to do at least a reasonable amount of transacting directly in foreign securities.

One of the advantages of buying the foreign stock on its home market is the matter of liquidity, which is an issue that we touched on when we discussed buying ordinaries via OTC; if you recall, we said that one of the problems with the ordinaries is that the market may be so small that you never know when the next transaction will take place, no matter how much you want it to. Having the ability to transact directly on the various foreign markets gives you the opportunity to transact with investment fluidity, which is ideally what you always want. The only sure ways to do that are with a U.S. brokerage account that gives you direct access to your market of choice, or by having brokerage accounts opened in individual target countries or associated regions of the world (which we discuss later). In the end, you probably need/want to have both, as U.S.-based brokerages, while gaining increased direct market exposure for their clients, do not generally have transactional access to some of the more remote markets on the globe; for those kinds of reaches, you may find yourself wanting to set up accounts in other countries. Like we said in the beginning of this chapter, you want an *array* of tools to help you assemble the best, most efficient global investing machine possible.

On that note, let us take a look at three of the more effective U.S.-based brokerage opportunities available to you. We invite you to do your own research on each before opening an account, which is prudent because this kind of information runs the perpetual risk of becoming outdated rather quickly, but more importantly, because we fully expect the processes of advancement and expansion on behalf of the global investor to continue throughout the industry as foreign investment becomes increasingly recognized as the key to investment success in the coming decades. That said, it is also reasonable to assume that the firms that have established themselves as superior candidates for your foreign-earmarked monies presently will likely be intent on keeping those positions in the future, as well, so we expect that the companies profiled here will remain useful to you. Oddly, there are some well-known firms with generally solid reputations that are still curiously far behind the curve when it comes to granting timely and useful access to global markets. For example, while Charles Schwab and Co. has a perfectly decent global desk, the level and type of access they provide is oddly pedestrian considering we are almost a full decade into the twenty-first century and they are, well, *Charles Schwab*. For example, all of their global trading is done via broker assistance, and their prices are not terribly competitive. One clue is the relative dearth of information on global investing through any of Schwab's online sites, while the three firms we mention next each present a great deal of information for you to consider before you even contact them for further information. In short, it is clear that Schwab and some other big names like TD Ameritrade have yet to fully commit to the global investor, which is certainly their prerogative but will undoubtedly lead to a loss of market share as global investing becomes much more mainstream. As for the bevy of firms that fashion themselves as cutting-edge international access firms when, in reality, they are just market makers for the ADRs and ordinaries traded OTC, we did not want to mislead you by featuring those as direct-access U.S. brokerages. There is nothing wrong with what they do, but the sample firms we want to specifically mention here are those that offer the kind of direct foreign market access that allows you to trade directly in a foreign market through the native currency.

EverTrade Direct Brokerage

EverTrade Direct Brokerage (www.evertrade.com) is a part of the Ever-Bank family of companies, a Jacksonville, Florida-based financial services firm. EverTrade recognized years ago that a market for foreign investment options existed and would only grow in the future, given worldwide economic trends. To meet that need, EverTrade has introduced a terrific degree of direct access to foreign markets through its brokerage. The key particulars are that you can trade foreign equities for $50 per trade, but the trades have to be transacted over the telephone with an EverTrade broker. In addition to providing direct market access to the majority of the world's developed markets, EverTrade currently provides access to equities markets in the emerging markets countries of Mexico, Russia, South Africa, and Thailand.

E*TRADE

With E*TRADE's Global Trading platform (www.etrade.com), you can access six of the world's *developed* foreign markets *online*, in local currencies: Canada, France, Germany, Hong Kong, Japan, and the United Kingdom. The online access is significant, because until fairly recently, brokerages offering direct foreign market access did so *only* through broker-assisted trades. E*TRADE has done a good job designing an integrated online account page that clearly shows you both your United States and global accounts on a single-view page. You can view your global securities values in U.S. dollars. Within this single-view page is an option to manage your global portfolio that allows you to place trades, exchange currency, and transfer funds, among other things. Per E*TRADE's global trading desk, you can also access a wide variety of other markets directly via broker-assisted trades

Interactive Brokers

If you are seeking a consolidated brokerage in the United States that will allow you to trade the full array of financial instruments directly in a (fairly) sizable number of markets both home and abroad, Interactive Brokers (IB) (www.interactivebrokers.com) may be the place for you. With IB, you presently gain electronic access to stocks in 14 foreign countries, options in 14 countries, and futures in 17 foreign countries. Through IB's benchmark account product, the Universal Account, you can manage all of your global trading activities with great convenience from a single account. When you open a Universal Account, you select a "base currency," which is the currency through which the value of your holdings is expressed and the currency through which margin requirements are determined. The way in which you trade instruments denominated in another currency is by a loan that's created against your base currency in order to fund your given transactional currency. IB seems keen on capturing as many U.S. global-centric investors as possible, but as with all U.S.-based brokers, has a long way to go to establishing direct access in smaller markets for the benefit of its clients; of the 14 foreign countries in which you can transact stock directly, 11 are in developed markets. Still, in relative terms, Interactive Brokers is far ahead of the curve when it comes to U.S. brokerages and functional global access to securities, and seems dedicated to developing tools and technology that allows for an effective reach to markets around the world.

SETTING UP ACCOUNTS IN FOREIGN COUNTRIES

Up to this point, we have touched on every way—except one—that you can trade foreign securities. We have looked at some of the least exciting methods, like open-end mutual funds, and gone from there. The truth is that if you stopped right now, and added no more tools to your toolbox, you would probably do just fine as a global investor in equities. From exchange-traded funds, to exchange-listed ADRs, to open-end mutual funds, to all of the securities available OTC, along with all of the resources available from some of the more progressive U.S. brokerages like E*TRADE and Interactive Brokers—you might well have all you need, and then some, to succeed as a global investor. Still, it may not be *quite* enough.

EXHIBIT 3.3	Emerging Markets Countries That Allow Direct Access by U.S. Investors	
Brazil	China	Czech Republic
Egypt	Hungary	Indonesia
Malaysia	Mexico	Morocco
Peru	Philippines	Poland
Russia	South Africa	South Korea
Taiwan	Thailand	Turkey

As for setting up brokerage accounts directly in foreign countries, we would love to be able to tell you that the process is such that it is a simple, turn-key system—one that would allow you to visit a central web site that contains listings of all U.S. investor-friendly brokerages in all countries that allow investment by U.S. investors, and that you simply go from there. Unfortunately, that is not the case. The reality is that things, while obviously much, much better than they were even 10 years ago, are not that smooth and simple just yet. Not only are there several interesting (from an investment standpoint) countries that do not allow foreigners to set up accounts within them—even in countries where it *is* allowed, some *firms* either do not allow it or simply do not want to be bothered with it. As a result, finding a firm with which to open a brokerage account in a foreign country you find appealing usually comes down to some old fashion elbow grease. It begins with Google, and probably a notebook and pen, and involves you doing things like plugging in search words and phrases such as, for example, "Poland stock exchange," "Poland stock brokers," along with any and all associated variations, to come up with a list of Poland-based brokerages that you can then query on an individual basis. Now, even though the countries noted in the list (see Exhibits 3.3 through 3.6) that follows *theoretically* allow you to invest with them, all is not always what it seems; in some nations, the *brokerages* will have widely differing rules regarding under what circumstances they can set up an account for you.

EXHIBIT 3.4	Frontier Markets Countries That Allow Direct Access by U.S. Investors	
Bahrain	Botswana	Croatia
Estonia	Jordan	Kazakhstan
Kuwait	Lebanon	Lithuania
Oman	Qatar	Romania
Sri Lanka	Tunisia	Ukraine
United Arab Emirates	Vietnam	

EXHIBIT 3.5 Emerging Markets Sample

Country	Brokerage Name	Brokerage Website
Brazil	Agora	www.agorainvest.com.br
China	Boom Securities	www.boom.com
Czech Republic	Global Brokers a.s.	www.globalbrokers.cz
Hungary	Concorde Securities	www.concordesecurities.hu
Malaysia	Kenanga Investment Bank	www.kenwealth.com
Poland	Dom Maklerski	www.dmbzwbk.pl
South Africa	BoE Securities	www.boe.co.za
Thailand	KGI Securities	www.kgieworld.co.th

[1]This list is not intended as, nor should be construed as, a recommendation for any of the listed brokerages. The future availability of, and/or access to, any of the following is in no way guaranteed.

One of your goals as a pro trader should be to try to find *regional* firms that provide you with direct access in multiple desired markets through one account. For example, a single account at Hong Kong's Boom Securities (www.boom.com) gives you direct access to Australia, China, Hong Kong, Indonesia, Japan, Malaysia, Singapore, South Korea, Philippines, Taiwan, and Thailand; Orion Securities (www.orion.lt), with offices in Sweden, Norway, and Lithuania, gives you direct access to those three markets, as well as to Latvia and Estonia; so, if you set up accounts at, for example, E*TRADE, Boom, and Orion, you would have direct access to 20 countries outside of the United States, including seven emerging

EXHIBIT 3.6 Frontier Markets Sample

Country	Brokerage Name	Brokerage Website
Botswana	Stockbrokers Botswana	www.stockbrokers-botswana.com
Croatia	Abacus Brokers	www.abacus-brokeri.hr
Estonia	Orion Securities	www.orion.lt
Kazakhstan	Visor Capital	www.visocap.com
Lithuania	Orion Securities	www.orion.lt
Oman	Al Madina Financial	www.almadina.com
Qatar	Qatar Securities	www.qatar-securities.com
Romania	Tradeville	www.tradeville.eu
Sri Lanka	Asha Phillip Securities	www.ashaphillip.net
Ukraine	Dragon Capital	www.dragon-capital.com
United Arab Emirates	MAC Sharaf Securities	www.mac-sharaf.com
Vietnam	Saigon Securities Inc.	ssi.com.vn

markets and two frontier markets. Not bad—but your consolidation can go even one step better. You can set up an account with Gibraltar's Investors Europe (www.investorseurope.com) and trade, either online or by phone, 24 European markets, 1 African market, and 8 Asian markets, with case-by-case availability to other markets, as well; now that is access.

To as realistic an extent as possible, securing a more regional foreign brokerage account should be your goal; rather than narrowly focusing on single firms operating within a single country and its associated principal exchange, do your research to uncover those firms that recognize the global push and which seek to be more regional in makeup, have seats on several key exchanges throughout a region of the world. That way, the oversight of your global investment portfolio, while admittedly more involved than that required by a single domestic account containing only U.S. securities, is far more manageable. As for the single-country accounts you consider opening in addition to the regional ones—your inclination to set those up will be determined by just how compelling you view that given opportunity to be.

Although online access rules the day, and will do so with much-increasing frequency, using the old-fashioned telephone to procure help in setting up your overseas accounts is not a bad idea. It is tempting to stick with e-mail, and most of us, if we are honest, as busy professionals, prefer e-mail to live phone contact. That said, when it comes to operating in more remote markets, it is not a bad idea to personalize your relationship with a brokerage as much as possible. We do that on this end, and the human relationships we have established have been great helps to us when problems arise, as they invariably do when you are trading in foreign markets from the United States.

One thing to note: other parts of the world will often have different and sometimes somewhat unusual requirements for when you invest in their respective countries or regions. For example, to invest in Sri Lanka's stock exchange, the Colombo Bourse, you must do so through Share Investment External Rupee Accounts (SIERA), which have to be established through commercial banks. The brokerage, knowing that you are a foreign national, will undoubtedly know to tell you of this major requirement, but the point is that you should take nothing for granted, and *ask*. There are a number of other interesting markets that have their "special" requirements, and it is up to you to know what those are. In the frontier market of Croatia, a condition of opening an account there is that you have to open a custodial account with the Croatian Central Depository Agency (www.sda.hr). Again, the brokerage will likely inform you of the requirement, and we can tell you that the requirement is clearly indicated on the account opening paperwork we reviewed on behalf of a Croatian stock brokerage, but the point is that whenever you seek to break into a new market—always ask a representative if there is *anything* else you need to know.

We did not want to beat your brains out with a bunch of minutiae regarding the different equity options available to you, but we did want to present a nuts-and-bolts overview of the central instruments and platforms you will likely use. It is an important topic; as we said at the outset, while your hedge fund may include a variety of other instruments, it is safe to assume that stocks, either or both in individual and packaged forms, will be the general constant in your portfolio. Having said that, using a hedge fund style, we seek not to build static portfolios, but rather those in which the investments will be readily transacted in both directions. By consequence, you should not endeavor to "marry" any one of these security types or brokerage options, but rather force yourself, if necessary, to maintain a constant variety. The important thing is to emerge from here with a better idea of the instruments and infrastructure available to you as we now head into the strategic applications that you can apply to your chosen equities. In the end, it is the applications of fundamental and technical analysis to your foreign securities, as well as the use of effective portfolio management techniques on same, that will serve as the more important tools in your effort to build a high-functioning hedge fund machine.

CHAPTER 4

Key Strategies for Realizing Winning Returns in Foreign Equities

For the novice investor, the idea of analyzing a multinational company basically consists of going to Yahoo!, examining the P/E ratio, and making a determination on that basis as to whether they like the stock. For the hedge fund manager, it is a much more involved process. Not only do you have to consider the economic and company-specific data, you have to make a determination about the political and cultural differences within those countries. You do not have to commit to being a full-time money manager in order to effectively apply the lessons in this book, but it does take more time to set up quality systems and properly analyze a stock, particularly from a global perspective, than the average investor is willing to give.

To begin your research, you need to first decide the type of analytical methodology on which you will principally focus. There are two distinct schools of study in stock selection from a global perspective: bottom-up analysis and top-down analysis.

Bottom-up analysis is an investment approach that puts less weight on the significance of economic and market cycles, and more emphasis on the analysis of individual stocks. In bottom-up investing, the investor focuses his attention on a specific company, rather than on the industry in which that company operates or on the economy as a whole. The bottom-up approach assumes that individual companies can do well even within an industry that is not performing soundly. Making sound decisions based on a bottom-up investing strategy entails a thorough review of the company in question, and includes gaining familiarity with the company's products and services, its financial stability, and its research reports.

Top-down analysis is an investment approach that involves looking at the big picture in the global economy, and then breaking the components down into finer details. After looking at the broader conditions around the world, countries and industrial sectors are analyzed in order to select those that are forecasted to outperform the markets. From this point, the stocks of specific companies are further analyzed and the "cream of the crop" is chosen for your hedge fund. Although there is some debate as to whether the top-down approach is better than the bottom-up approach, many investors have found the top-down approach useful in determining what countries, and sectors *within* those countries, are superior.

As you may suspect, bottom-up investing is not the type of analysis on which we will focus in this book. Certainly, it has its merits, but if you want to be a global investor, you first have to analyze the world on a macro scale in an effort to find economies and markets that are outperforming the rest of the world. From there, you will go deeper to find the industries and sectors within the countries that are expanding most rapidly, and finally, you will descend to the root level to perform the kind of analysis that will help you identify the best companies in those sectors to target for investment. It is this methodology through which we are about to lead you.

Note that at the end of this chapter, we are going to delve into some technical analysis. Much of the chart analysis we do is translatable from one section of our top-down analysis to the next, but regardless, it is important to have an education on the technical side of investing; as a hedge fund manager, if you are looking only at earnings and ratios, you are missing an important, much bigger picture. If you are able to gain mastery of both fundamental *and* technical analysis, your chances for above-average returns rise dramatically.

THE GLOBAL ECONOMY

The first step in digging down to your ultimate stock positions is to look at the global economy as a whole. In reality, you will have pockets of countries around the world that will be running contrary to the rest of the global economy but, on the whole, world economies tend to run in congruency. Never was this more evident than at the start of 2008. The American stock market was falling as investors felt the American economy was going into a recession. They were right, and as the money flowed away from the U.S. market, it went into various international funds, stocks, and countries. Investors truly believed the world economies had developed enough and become strong enough to hold their own without the assistance of a strong U.S. economy. So, instead of taking their money out of stocks as a whole, they simply moved their monies to new economies around the world. By mid-2008, investors who embraced that reallocation strategy came to the realization that they could not have been more wrong. The U.S. recession was, in fact, a *global* slowdown, and it spread rapidly around the world. Indeed, many of the global equity markets fell far faster than did the U.S. stock market. The point is that global economic analysis does not necessarily involve analyzing each country individually; it begins with the analysis of the global marketplace as a unified economy.

We could break down our economic analysis into a million different indicators, but when it is all said and done, there are three primary indicators we need to analyze in order to get a grasp on the global economy: projected growth, inflation, and interest rates. Most other indicators tend to exist as collateral components of one of these three areas.

Growth

As economies grow, they create positive earnings momentum for companies within their markets. Earnings drive equity markets, so it is critical that you start your analysis with a view of how the world is growing. Keep in mind that this portion of your analysis is driven on a macro scale by industrialized countries; if you are trying to get a feel for what the global economy is doing, focus on the larger and more economically established nations. You can do a Google search and find a number of sites that will give you projections on global growth, but here are a few on which we rely with our analysis:

> ***The Organisation for Economic Co-operation and Development***   The group produces the OECD Economic Analysis, which you can find by following this link: www.oecd.org/oecdEconomic Outlook. This report gives you a lot of useful information, including some global economic projections. Also, while you are on this page, you will see a link for "Macroeconomic Links" on the top right of the page. Click on it and bookmark it, because it gives you a lot of excellent information on individual nations, which will be helpful as you begin to analyze individual countries.
>
> ***Federal Reserve Bank of New York***   The web site is at www. NewYorkFed.org. When you get to the site, click "Research" at the top; when you get to the next page, click on the link for "Global Economy" on the top left; from there, click on the link for "Global Economic Indicators" below the "Global Economy" link. This site does not provide you with economic analysis as a whole, but it will break down the world into large subsets. It segments the world into big enough chunks for you to be able to put the picture together.

The International Monetary Fund (IMF)   The web site can be
found at www.IMF.org. One of the unique features of this site is
that the IMF produces a report called the World Economic Outlook. If you click on "Data and Statistics" at the top right of the
front page, you can find both current and historical World Economic Outlook reports. Also, if you want to look more closely at
a specific country, follow this link: http://www.imf.org/external/
country/. When you get to a specific country, you can see their projected growth rates listed on the top left side under "Projected %
Change."

Two other sites we use are www.DismalScientist.com and www.
WorldBank.org. Both are definitely worth bookmarking, and have their
own unique information to bring to your analysis. Also, we would be re-
miss if we did not give you our site at www.InvestorsPassport.com. Our
site and our subscription services are geared toward tying together all the
information you will find in our book, but we provide a lot of economic
research, as well.

When you are analyzing the world as a whole, do not get too hung up
on what specific countries are doing. First, attempt to get a grip on whether
the world economy as a whole is moving forward or backward and what
the overall direction, or trend, looks like. The sites we have given you in
this section will basically do the analysis for you. Again, at this point, you
are not doing too much critical thinking, but attempting to get a feel for
global growth.

Inflation

Inflation is a rise in the general level of prices of goods and services in
an economy over a period of time. Inflation has been characterized as a
wholly negative feature as applied to modern economics, but a controlled
low level of inflation is, in fact, normal in a growing economy and should
not necessarily be construed as completely negative. Hyperinflation is bad,
because it erodes the real value of assets and economies. For example, if
you lived in Spain and you paid one euro for a loaf of bread in 2008, but
paid two euros for that same loaf in 2009 (i.e., 100% inflation), you would
have a big problem, especially if your income only went up 3 percent. In a
real-life example, from 1986 to 1994, the base currency unit in Brazil was
shifted three times to adjust for inflation in the final years of the Brazilian
military dictatorship era. A 1967 *cruzeiro* was, in 1994, worth less than
one trillionth of a U.S. cent, after adjusting for multiple devaluations and
note changes. A new currency called the *real* was adopted in 1994, and
hyperinflation was eventually brought under control. Interestingly, the *real*

was also the currency in use from 1690 to 1942; one present-day real is the equivalent of 2,750,000,000,000,000,000 of those old reals. That is a scary thought, and it is a great example of why governments around the world work so feverishly to contain inflation (again, they do not want to kill it entirely, but they do want to keep it in a reasonable range). When inflation is under control, its presence can be a sign of stable economic growth. Depending on the country, inflation can be considered "normal" when it is in a 2 percent to 4 percent range in terms of growth.

In doing your analysis, you will hear people talk about a "real" rate of growth in an economy. A real rate of growth for a country is simply the GDP growth minus the rate of inflation. The GDP rate without removing the inflation rate is termed the "nominal" rate of growth. For example, if the Japanese economy was growing at 5 percent per year and inflation was at 3 percent, Japan would have a 2 percent real GDP growth rate, as the growth in the economy is outstripping the growth in prices of goods and services by 2 percent. In the same example, if the inflation rate was 8 percent, the real growth rate would be −3 percent. This is a bad situation because the economy is not growing fast enough to cover the rise in costs of goods and services, and so the nation and its consumers are becoming poorer in real terms.

The easiest way to find global inflation rates is at www.CIA.gov. We know that it seems like an odd place to find economic data, but it actually is home to a lot of useful information for global investors. When you go to the site, click on the link on the top right part of the page that reads *World Factbook*. Halfway down the next page on the left, you see a link for *Search World Factbook*. On the next page in the *search term* box, you type in "inflation rates." Click on the first link it gives you, and you see a listing of inflation rates for most countries around the world. Much like we did with growth rates, you are looking for the larger industrialized countries and attempting to get a feel for what the global flow of inflation looks like.

Inflation is closely tied to economic growth. In normal economies, slower economic growth will translate into slower inflation. Therefore, if you see that economic growth is falling off a cliff (like we saw in late 2008), you may need to adjust your inflation projections down prior to actually seeing slower inflation numbers.

Interest Rates

Interest rates are one of the key drivers of global growth on several levels. First, a stable interest rate promotes a healthy economy and that, in turn, attracts outside investment into a country. The *level* of interest rates is also important. If government bonds in the United States are yielding 3 percent, and the equivalent government bonds in Australia are yielding 6 percent, money will flow toward Australian bonds, all else being equal. This flow into Australian bonds will also strengthen their currency, but we will say more about that later on in our fixed-income chapter, Chapter 5. Also, there is an obvious correlation between interest rates and economic growth. When interest rates are high or rising, borrowing costs go up, which inhibits lending. This, in turn, slows economic growth. When interest rates are low, we see the opposite effect. Companies are able to get their hands on affordable funds to grow their business and make capital investments. We showed you how this relationship has worked in the capital markets in Chapter 2 on intermarket analysis.

In the overall scheme of things, you will find that the *trend* in interest rates is more important than the level of rates themselves. For example, if rates in Country Z were around 8 percent, but you believed rates would come down drastically in the coming years, this may be a positive investment opportunity. At 8 percent, rates are not low, but if rates decline as you forecast, this will help spur economic growth and more than likely spur both the equity and fixed-income markets. Interest rate trends will have a more direct effect on bonds, but will influence both stocks and bonds significantly as the trend persists.

There are several free sources we use to track interest rate trends around the world. A couple of them are listed here:

www.FXStreet.com: This is a site geared toward currency trading. However, as we mentioned in Chapter 2 on intermarket analysis, these economic factors are all intertwined. Specifically, if you go to www.fxstreet.com/fundamental/interest-rates-table/, you will see a list of more than 20 countries and their associated current interest rate levels. If you click on the name of the country, it will expand that section into a chart for the trend in interest rates in that country. Keep in mind that these are not free market interest rates; these are the rates set by that country's governing body.

The Organisation for Economic Co-operation and Development: The OECD's statistics and data site is comprehensive and useful. When you land on the site, insert "interest rates" into the search box on the left just above *General Statistics*. When you click the double arrow, it will expand the subsection of *Finance* and highlight the term "interest rates." Click on "interest rates" and it will take you to a table that has a country-by-country breakdown of current rates. You will see links that allow you to download data into Excel, as well as a link that brings up a chart on interest rate trends for multiple countries.

In the overall scheme of things, these three indicators are intertwined, and one will have a great deal of influence on the other two. For example, if inflation is high in Brazil, the probability is high that the government would raise interest rates in an effort to slow economic growth and thus curb inflation. If the Canadian economy is in a recession, the government will likely lower interest rates as a catalyst for economic growth. Again, keep in mind that these three indicators should be analyzed more in the context of their *trends* as opposed to their absolute levels. If you were simply looking at levels in 2000, you would have thought it was a great time to invest. However, time would "bear" (pun intended) out that the trends were foretelling investors of some bad weather to come—some very bad weather, indeed.

COUNTRY ANALYSIS

There are times when one or two countries catch fire when others are just smoldering; this circumstance is why country analysis is such an important component of your research. Take a look at the following exhibit. The period referenced was a stretch of time when most countries around the world were experiencing a drawn-out recession. In the United States, the bear market chewed away 50 percent of investors' wealth from 2000 to 2003, and most individual stocks suffered a far worse fate. The downtrending line on the exhibit represents the S&P 500; the line jumping higher represents the China Fund (CHN), an exchange-traded fund (ETF) proxy for the Chinese equity markets. As you can see, at a time when most global equity markets realized substantial losses, the Chinese market *rose* more than 60 percent. The Chinese economy was expanding rapidly and experiencing a huge infrastructure build-out, one that was propelling their economic freight train forward at full speed (and this at a time when most economies were contracting). The fruits of the Chinese economy stemmed from reforms the government launched in 1978 in an effort to reform the economy away from central planning and government ownership. In-depth global and country research on your part will help your hedge fund identify these types of diamonds in the rough. They do not come around often but, when they do, you will be ready (see Exhibit 4.1).

There are numerous fundamental factors you have to assess when you are analyzing countries, but from a macro point of view, the most important are the given country's economic environment, cultural environment, and political/legal environment. When you find countries whose climates are positive and stable on all three fronts, you have likely corralled a good investment opportunity.

EXHIBIT 4.1 Comparative Look at the Performance of U.S. and China Equities Markets from the Mid-1990s to 2003
Source: esignal.com.

Economic Environment

One of the first things we want to mention is that it is not safe to assume uniformity across the world as it applies to the *wealth* of a country. We were speaking recently to a client regarding prospects for several countries around the world, and during the course of the conversation we realized that he was assuming the countries about which we were speaking were more or less on the same level in terms of wealth, which is a drastic mistake. At the time, we were discussing the investment merits of a country like Canada versus a country like India. His contention was that the sheer strength of population of India would make it a far better investment than Canada. We suggested to him that a country-to-country comparison on the singular basis of population strength is flawed analysis. Yes, India has a massive population; however, India is a lower-middle income economy and Canada is a high-income economy as measured by per capita GDP. This does not mean that Canada is a better investment than India, as a national economy; indeed, as we know, there is much to like about India's increasing economic *gravitas* as an aggressively growing emerging market country. However, two economically potent nations may possess different wealth characteristics. If you have a huge population with low income, what is the driver for the economy? There can be several drivers, such as a relatively manageable debt ratio in comparison to more prosperous economies that are basically maxed out in their use of credit, but the point is that you cannot decide that one nation is a more or less fertile plain for investment unless you are willing to subject each to rigorous evaluation utilizing multiple and standardized measurements.

The Analysis

Let us start with a broad overview of how we analyze a country. In our analysis, we look at countries just as we do individual equities. Countries, like stocks, have fundamental data available for analysis, so it follows that you can use those facts and figures to compare and contrast a given country to *other* countries, as well as against itself in historical time frames. We evaluate countries using five primary methods: price to earnings, price to book, beta, dividend yield, and projected growth. We compare the current measurement for each metric with its 10-year average. If a country is at a large markdown to its 10-year average, then it ranks well. If it trades well above its 10-year average, it ranks poorly and may even be a good short candidate. We go through a numerical example shortly, but in the end, we are attempting to discern which countries rank the best and compare their valuations against the MSCI EAFE (Morgan Stanley Capital International Europe Australasia and Far East). For comparative purposes, you can analyze the iShares MSCI EAFE exchange-traded fund from both the fundamental and technical side; it trades under the symbol EFA. Once we have found our fundamental gems, we go to the charts. We attempt to determine which countries are outperforming the global markets, as gauged by the iShares MSCI EAFE, on a *relative* basis. Let us say, for example, our research leaves us 10 countries that appear to offer our hedge fund good value from the ratios we described earlier. We can then take those countries and compare them to the overall global market, as well as to each other, on our charts to determine which are outperforming and have positive momentum. Reality tells us that it is not enough to simply discover value in a country. If the rest of the investing world does not also see some value, the buyers will not bid those countries up and you simply will not make money. This is why technical analysis is so important.

The easiest way to analyze a country from the perspective of our five indicators is to analyze country exchange-traded funds, or ETFs. In the case of a country ETF, it would hold positions in an array of companies based within that country. For example, the ETF representing Germany trades under the symbol EWG. If you look within the fund, it has holdings in companies like Siemens, Bayer, Deutsche Telecom, and Volkswagen. Because it trades as a proxy for this country, we can analyze the ETF much like we would an individual stock. The valuations at which we arrive will not be perfect substitutes for analyzing every stock on Germany's DAX index, but it will serve as a good proxy and it is a lot easier to work with; you must always be open to methods of achieving "reasonable expediency" when you are faced with performing a lot of analysis.

Let us analyze the iShares MSCI Germany ETF (EWG) as an example, and head over to www.Ishares.com. iShares is owned by Barclays Global Investors and is one of the biggest issuers of country ETFs in the entire ETF universe, so they are a good source of data. Once at the site, type "EWG" in the search box at the top left of the page. This will bring up information for the iShares MSCI Germany ETF. On the left side of the page, you will see a .pdf link for Fund Fact Sheet. Click on this link and it will bring up the information on the fund. We reproduce here portions of the fact sheets for the EWG and the EFA (our MSCI EAFE proxy). Using EWG as a proxy, we can see that Germany trades at a P/E ratio of 14.91, a P/Book ratio of 1.69 and a Beta of 1.41. On the site portion, they also list the yield on the EWG at about 1 percent and the yield on the EFA at about 3 percent. The EFA shows a P/E of 12.69, a P/Book of 2.06 and a Beta of 1.18. Quick analysis tells us that Germany is probably not the best country for us to focus on for our investment dollars. Its P/E ratio is higher than that of the MSCI EAFE, the yield is lower, and the beta, which is a measure of volatility and risk, is higher. The Price/Book is slightly lower. But, when all is said and done, the EWG is not as attractive as the EFA. Further, when we evaluate projected growth figures, the EWG becomes that much more unattractive. Currently, German growth is expected to be flat, whereas the MSCI EAFE is projected to grow between 2 and 3 percent. Therefore, Germany is not a country in which we would want to hold a position at this point in time. There are certainly worse countries in which we could invest, but we only want the best of the best for our hedge funds. Also, note that if we look at Germany from a 10-year historical comparison against where its valuations have been, it looks *somewhat* attractive, but the global markets are down and there are more attractive alternatives even from this perspective (see Exhibit 4.2).

Keep in mind that you are rarely going to find countries that show each of our valuation measures trading more attractively than the MSCI EAFE *and* offer higher growth and dividends. However, what you are looking for are countries that trade at *comparable* or *better* valuations than the MSCI EAFE, and which offer better growth prospects. For example, India and China are currently trading close to the MSCI EAFE as far as valuations go, but both are offering substantially higher growth prospects than the rest of the world. Thus, India and China would be on our list for further analysis, which we start further on.

We want to make a few more points about evaluating the growth of a country. Projections for growth rates are vital to your analysis, and the easiest place to find projections will be at the World Bank site

EXHIBIT 4.2	Portions of iShares Fact Sheets on MSCI Germany Index Fund (EWG) and MSCI EAFE Index Fund (EFA)

Ticker	EWG	Ticker	EFA
Inception Date	3/12/96	Inception Date	8/14/01
Expense Ratio	0.52%	Expense Ratio	0.34%
Stock Exchange	NYSE	Stock Exchange	NYSE
Net Assets	$334 Million	Net Assets	$32 Billion
P/E Ratio	14.91	**P/E Ratio**	12.69
P/Book Ratio	1.69	**P/Book Ratio**	2.09
# of Holdings	52	# of Holdings	830
Beta vs. S&P 500	1.41	Beta vs. S&P 500	1.18

Source: www.iShares.com.

(www.WorldBank.org). For example, the World Bank projects the growth of the high-income countries to be around 1.2 percent, whereas developing countries are projected to grow GDP at a clip of around 5 percent. Further, the World Bank is projecting a growth rate in the East Asia and Pacific Rim area to be around 7 percent. If growth was the only factor we were considering, we would obviously focus our research on the higher-growth developing countries within East Asia and the Pacific Rim. Within the East Asia and Pacific Rim space, we find that China is projected to grow GNP around 8.5 percent and Indonesia is projected to grow around 5.5 percent. Quickly and easily we have done a quick top-down analysis to arrive at these two countries. If you perform a Google search for "World Bank Forecast Summary," you will see a link that will give you all the projections for these areas of the world and many of the countries within those regions.

When we are researching countries, growth rates are certainly important, but the *volatility* surrounding those growth numbers is equally as important. In other words, we have to analyze the numbers and take into consideration the chances that the actual growth could ultimately prove to be vastly different from that estimated in our projections; we would rather take a position in Country A growing at 4 percent than Country B growing at 6 percent if we are more confident that Country A will hit its numbers by virtue of lower indicated volatility. Obviously we prefer the anticipated returns of B, but higher volatility in that country may suggest the possible implosion of our entire portfolio with an errant investment.

Other Factors

After we have "kicked the tires" with our fundamental analysis, we have to consider a few additional factors within our countries. As we bore down to our best possible country options, we have to consider country-specific factors like inflation, deficits/surpluses, monetary policy, and debt. All these factors are intertwined and together can give you a good picture of a country's investability. Let us break each of them down individually to give you an idea of what to look for in your analysis.

Inflation   As we noted previously, inflation is a rise in the general level of prices of goods and services in an economy over a period of time. Inflation itself is not always bad, even though you typically hear it spoken of in a negative light. In a normal growing economy, you always have some level of inflation, but when the general price level rises, each unit of a country's currency buys fewer goods and services; therefore, inflation can exert adverse effects on the economy if it is above normal. For example, uncertainty about future inflation may discourage investment and savings. High inflation can also lead to shortages of goods if consumers begin hoarding out of concern that prices will increase in the future.

Inflation is a dimension of a country's economy that really acts as the linchpin for its many other facets. It affects interest rates, exchange rates, the cost of living, and the rest of the world's confidence in a country's political and economic well-being. In fact, it is such an integral part of most countries' economic profile that the *constitutional charge* of the Bundesbank, the central bank of Germany, is to control inflation. After the fall of the Berlin Wall in 1989, inflation rose to 2.7 percent in 1990 and a high of 4.1 percent in 1993. The Bundesbank raised interest rates in an effort to rein inflation back in (see Exhibit 4.3).

High inflation tends to force interest rates up when it reaches an uncomfortable level, and there are two reasons for this phenomenon. First,

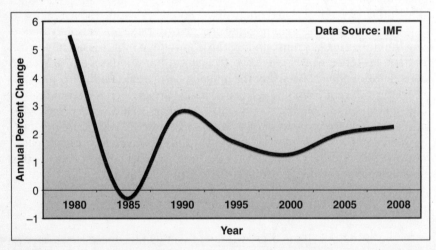

EXHIBIT 4.3   Germany: Inflation, Average Consumer Prices
Source: IMF.

interest rates must be higher than inflation so that they can reflect a *real return* on interest-bearing assets. Real interest rates are simply calculated as the nominal or quoted rate minus inflation. Therefore, if rates were 4 percent in Germany and inflation was at 5 percent, the *real* rate of return on that asset would be −1 percent; no one, of course, would want to purchase an investment that would pay them −*1 percent* if they knew about it up front. Second, monetary authorities around the world tend to use high interest rates as their main weapon to bring down inflation. Knowing this, investors must watch the governments of high-inflation countries to determine what economic policies might be used to balance inflation; economic growth could slow down, causing the market to be a less attractive place to do business.

In our last section on economic growth, we discussed the potential for same in China. As you can see in Exhibit 4.4, however, the monkey wrench in the engine for China at this writing may be the trend of rising inflation. If inflation continues to grow, the People's Bank of China (China's Central Bank), will be forced to raise rates, which will slow the economy. Suddenly, the 8.5 percent GNP growth rate our research originally indicated to us could change to 4 percent, which would, in turn, cause the Chinese market to become a less attractive place in which to do business (see Exhibit 4.4).

Inflation can also be a major force behind political destabilization. If the government tries to control inflation by regulating wages, the real income of the population falls and frustration sets in; if the government takes a "wait and see" approach, the economy may deteriorate to the point where

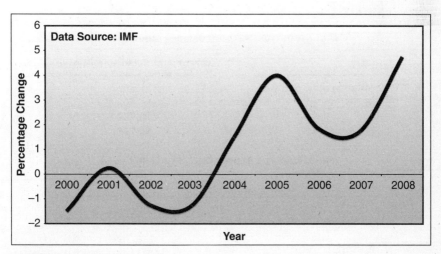

EXHIBIT 4.4   China: Inflation
Source: IMF.

real incomes fall anyway. Additionally, instituting tighter financial controls when the government is already in a fragile state can be devastating. It is for these reasons that global governments do so much to try to keep rising prices from becoming uncontrollable inflation.

Deficits/Surpluses   The *balance of payments* of a country includes the transactions between the residents of one country and all other countries around the world. Each of these transactions constitutes either an export or an import. The major balance of all these transactions is called the *current account balance*.

A country's surplus or deficit does not have a direct effect on that country, but the data that comprises the balance-of-payments data does influence exchange rates, which would obviously flow over to influence corporate plans. The size of a country's deficit is typically measured as a percentage of GDP, but it can also be measured in absolute terms. Exhibit 4.5 shows the four largest current account surpluses and four largest deficits, measured in millions of U.S. dollars. In Exhibit 4.6, you can see the trends of the balance of payments.

The only two ways to solve a current account deficit are to restrict imports, or to slow down economic growth through *higher interest rates* so that demand for imports slows. Neither of these is a particularly attractive course of action from an investment standpoint, as both make your country

EXHIBIT 4.5   Current Account Balances of Select Economies

Highest Current Account Balance (2007 est.)

Country	Current Acct Balance (millions)
People's Republic of China	371,800
Germany	254,500
Japan	210,500
Saudi Arabia	86,720

Lowest Current Account Balance (2007 est.)

Country	Current Acct Balance (millions)
Italy	−57,940
United Kingdom	−111,000
Spain	−126,300
United States	−731,200

Source: IMF.

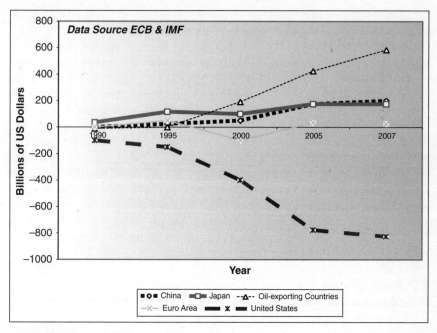

EXHIBIT 4.6 Balance of Payments Trends
Source: ECB and IMF.

less appealing to investors. For example, Country A may look attractive with a healthy 5 percent GDP growth rate and low inflation at 2 percent; however, the markets are always looking forward, and if the government plans on reducing its current account deficit by raising interest rates, it could change the economic landscape of Country A, thus making it a less attractive investment choice. As a hedge fund manager, you need to do your due diligence and not only look at the static picture of where a country is presently, but also mind the trend of where it seems to be heading.

Monetary Policy   Monetary policy is the process by which the government, central bank, or monetary authority of a country controls the supply of money, the availability of money and the cost of money, as well as the rate of interest. The government controls these factors in an effort to attain a set of objectives oriented toward the growth and stability of the economy.

A policy is considered *contractionary* if it reduces the size of the money supply or raises the interest rate. An *expansionary* policy increases the size of the money supply, or decreases the interest rate. Monetary policies can also be described as follows: *accommodative,* if the interest rate set by the central monetary authority is intended to create economic growth; *neutral*, if it is intended neither to create growth nor combat inflation; or *tight*, if intended to reduce inflation.

Keep in mind that a country's governing body can significantly hinder an economy if its decisions to sway the economy in one direction or another counteract the natural forces at work through supply and demand. For example, in 1997, the Japanese Diet hiked the country's consumption tax just as the economy was emerging from recession, because it was concerned that growing budget deficits would fuel future inflation. Ironically, not only did they wind up stalling a nascent recovery in the Japanese economy, they pushed the country into deflation.

A similar mistake was made in the United States during the Great Depression. After the United States abandoned the gold standard, GDP growth rose at a double-digit pace between 1934 and 1937 and the unemployment rate dropped close to 10 percentage points, down to 15 percent. However, the U.S. economy was still in a precarious position, and a self-sustaining recovery had not fully taken hold. Nevertheless, taxes were increased with the establishment of the Social Security Program in 1935. To add insult to injury, the Federal Reserve doubled its reserve requirements that year, fearing the return of inflation. The result was a deep recession over the course of the next two years.

The confusing part about monetary policy is that not all countries have the same target goal for their policies. The difference between types of monetary policy lies primarily with the set of instruments and target variables that are used by the monetary authority to achieve their goals. Exhibit 4.7 summarizes the types of policies currently in place.

Debt   A country's external debt is that part of the total debt in a country that is owed to creditors outside the country. The debtors can be corporations, governments, or private households. One consequence of the rise in oil costs during the 1970s was the equally rapid increase in many countries' external debt. This mountain of debt resulted as developing countries sought help from foreign governments to finance oil imports and other products necessary for development. Large debt loads present the same inherent problems for countries as they do for individuals and companies.

There are four ways to measure a country's external debt, but we will only focus on two as we believe they are the most relevant: percentage of GDP and debt-service ratio.

The percentage of GDP allows us to take a country's external debt and compare it to countries in other parts of the world, as well as to that country's capacity to hold debt. The pure size of a country's external debt may look massive by itself, but may look much more contained when compared to its economy and the rest of the world. Take a look at the following

EXHIBIT 4.7   Principal Monetary Policies, with Associated Variables and Goals

Monetary Policy	Target Market Variable	Long-term Objective
Inflation Targeting	Interest rate on overnight debt	A given rate of change in the CPI
Price Level Targeting	Interest rate on overnight debt	A specific CPI number
Monetary Aggregates	The growth in money supply	A given rate of change in the CPI
Fixed Exchange Rate	The spot price of the currency	The spot price of the currency
Gold Standard	The spot price of gold	Low inflation as measured by the gold price
Mixed Policy	Usually interest rates	Usually unemployment plus CPI change

Source: Federal Reserve Board.

exhibit and you see both the absolute and percentage of GDP for the world's top national debt loads. The external debt load for the United States is massive, but as a percentage, it is much more reasonable than that of the rest of the countries indicated. On average, countries in Asia and the Pacific Rim tend to have lower external debt levels; Japan is around 35 percent and China (not indicated here) is, amazingly, still in single digits (see Exhibit 4.8).

The debt-service ratio is the ratio of interest payments, plus principal amortization, to exports. Many countries around the world spend more

EXHIBIT 4.8   Top Global Debt Loads, by Nation, Both Absolute and as a Percentage of GDP

	Relative Debt Loads (2007–2008)		
Country	External Debt (millions)	External Debt Per Capita	External Debt (% of GDP)
United States	$13,703,567	$42,343	99.95%
United Kingdom	$10,450,000	$189,855	376.82%
Germany	$4,489,000	$54,604	159.92%
Ireland	$1,841,000	$448,032	960.86%
Japan	$1,492,000	$45,287	34.93%
Switzerland	$1,340,000	$509,529	441.95%

Source: CIA World Factbook.

EXHIBIT 4.9 Bolivia Debt Service Ratio

Year	Value	Change	Cumulative Change
1996	25.2	−0.40%	−24.78%
1997	23.3	−7.54%	−30.45%
1998	28.6	22.75%	−14.63%
1999	19	−33.57%	−43.28%
2000	18.3	−3.68%	−45.37%
2001	17.1	−6.56%	−48.96%
2002	17.6	2.92%	−47.96%
2003	20	13.64%	−40.30%
2004	12.6	−37.00%	−62.39%

Source: Indexmundi.com.

than a quarter of their export earnings simply to service their debt load. That really hampers economic stimulation and growth. On the flip side, some countries are in the process of trending their debt loads down. Take a look at the debt service ratios for Bolivia in Exhibit 4.9. The percentages were not dropping every year, but the overall trend was toward a lower debt level for their country. If debt-service ratio was the only factor with which we were concerned, perhaps Bolivia would be a good investment candidate for our hedge fund (see Exhibit 4.9).

In the end, a country's debt is not, in and of itself, a negative feature of the country. In fact, a country's use of debt can be a sign of strength. However, unserviceable debt levels can create an environment that is politically and economically unstable. Additionally, in such an environment, governments may be forced to institute a variety of measures to control their debt levels, including slowing down economic growth.

Cultural Environment

Culture consists of particular learned norms based on attitudes, principles, and beliefs, all of which live in every society. The cultural element is, as you can imagine, pretty subjective. We even debated whether to put a section on this topic in the book, simply because of the inability to quantify the cultural component in any helpful way. However, it is an important subset to analyzing a country and its business practices or management styles. When you are analyzing a company in a different part of the world, you should first determine whether a business practice that is normal to you is also common to that foreign country. If the practice differs in a material way, you must decide what, if anything, needs to be adjusted in your analysis.

Let us consider an example. In the not-too-distant past, it was not unusual for a Japanese bank to make loan to a company and not receive payment of interest. In lieu of interest payments, the bank would take back shares of stock in the company to which it made the loan. Now, Japan is a nationalistic country, and they employed this practice as a way of supporting their companies and simultaneously benefiting when the companies used their loans to enhance their profitability. The fatal flaw with this practice? When the stock market collapsed, the banks basically became insolvent; instead of cash reserves, they had huge portfolios of stock. A great many investors lost a lot of money as a result of this circumstance—and it was predicated on a culturally based business practice.

If you dig deep, you will find groups of countries that are relatively similar to one another. We see this common thread because they share many attributes that help mold their cultures, such as language, religion, geographical location, ethnicity, and level of economic development. The following exhibit gives you a few examples of how countries are grouped by attitudes and ideals based on data obtained from a large number of cross-cultural studies. As a global hedge fund manager, you can expect to make investment decisions, at times, on the basis that fewer cultural differences exist when moving within a geographically and culturally connected region (see Exhibit 4.10).

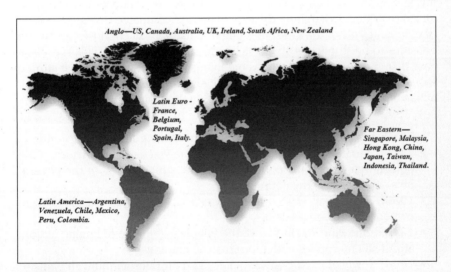

EXHIBIT 4.10 Regional View of World Based on Cultural Similarities

Political/Legal Environment

The global political landscape is actually rather simple to assess from a broad view. The two extremes, in a theoretical sense, are *democracy* and *totalitarianism*, and it is from these two broad classifications that most other forms of government derive. Many governments that were once restrictive and constraining of the populace fully embrace both freedom, in general, and free markets, in particular, and that trend of transition continues as more nations welcome both the beneficial concept and reality of wealth. In addition to the more obvious benefits that accrue to the global investor when countries embrace capitalism in one form or another, less obvious, but still important, benefits are realized, as well; for example, democratic governments are almost always more forthcoming with the key information and data that you need to perform proper analyses, while governments based around a totalitarian government tend to be more closed off.

Also, it behooves you to note that intragovernmental action is not always consistent. For example, in the United States, at least three government agencies share the duty of regulating nonagricultural exports: the State Department, the Department of Defense, and the Department of Commerce—and yet, each of these agencies has a primary focus that is different from the others, which means that each agency has a different viewpoint from the others on how to regulate exports.

One important aspect to evaluating government behavior as a global investor is to maintain a close watch on those governments that seem inclined to taking ownership positions in private companies. Nationalization of companies is not always something that happens in countries we would consider to be "the usual suspects." Indeed, in America in 2009, there is a case that can be made that some companies from a few of our most storied industries are on the verge of true nationalization. Let us take a quick look at some of the better-known cases of nationalization in modern history:

- **1947:** Australia nationalized Quantas, the leading airline in the country.
- **1975:** The Canadian Province of Saskatchewan nationalized part of the potash industry. Many potash producers agreed to sell to the government instead of being nationalized.
- **1959:** The Cuban Castro regime gradually expropriated all foreign-owned private companies.
- **1946:** Following World War II, the People's Republic of Poland nationalized all enterprises with more than 50 employees.
- **2006:** Newly elected Bolivian leader Evo Morales announced plans to nationalize the country's natural gas industry; foreign-based companies were given six months to renegotiate their existing contracts.

- **2008–2009:** Countless banks and financial institutions around the world were partially or fully nationalized to prevent collapse, including Fannie Mae and Freddie Mac in the United States.

A major concern for a hedge fund manager investing in international markets is that the political climate will change in such a way that their investment position will deteriorate or even disappear, regardless of company fundamentals. Although there is no mathematical formula that one can apply to determine the likelihood or effect of these kinds of changes, it is imperative that your ongoing analysis includes maintaining a close watch on global events and political machinations. You simply cannot be a successful global investor without including intensive, daily attention to world news as a part of your analytical regimen.

TECHNICAL ANALYSIS—COUNTRIES

Next, let us flip over to the technical side of analysis and look at some charts. As we mentioned previously, we use *both* fundamental and technical analysis in evaluating countries, industries, and individual stocks. Note that for the examples that follow, we are using the MSCI EAFE index as our benchmark against which we compare the movements of individual countries in which we might consider investing.

Take a look at Exhibit 4.11. It was created at www.StockCharts.com and is reflecting how India, using the iPath MSCI India ETF (INP), is performing compared to the rest of the world, as measured by the MSCI EAFE ETF (EFA). To create this exhibit, we entered the symbol "INP:EFA" under the Sharpcharts section of the site. It is clearly evident, as indicated by the upward trending arrow, that India is outperforming the rest of the world, as gauged by our benchmark EFA.

Next, take a look at Exhibit 4.12. It is a simple stock chart that shows how Japan is performing, using the iShares Japan ETF (EWJ) as a proxy. On the surface, the exhibit is positive; the ETF is trending higher, both moving averages are pointing up, and the MACD gave a recent positive cross. What is not to like? Here is where a simple exhibit will fool you. There is no doubting that the exhibit is positive, but this is also a time frame when global markets were recovering, so just about every country was trending higher. The question you have to ask yourself, as a world-class hedge fund manager, is whether you should invest your fund dollars into this country; the answer comes by analyzing Exhibit 4.12.

Contrast Exhibit 4.12 to Exhibit 4.13. Exhibit 4.13 is a representation of Japan, as gauged by the iShares Japan ETF (EWJ), versus the MSCI EAFE.

EXHIBIT 4.11 Performance of Indian Equities Markets Versus Performance of Broad Global Equities Markets During First Half of 2009
Source: StockCharts.com.

EXHIBIT 4.12 Performance of Japanese Equities Markets During First Half of 2009
Source: StockCharts.com.

EXHIBIT 4.13　Performance of Japanese Equities Markets Versus Performance of Broad Global Equities Markets During First Half of 2009
Source: StockCharts.com.

The symbol we used for this exhibit is "EWJ:EFA." As you can see from the downtrending arrow, Japan is not a country we would use in our portfolio because it simply is not keeping up with our benchmark. If we invest in the EWJ, we are not investing in the best possible parts of the world, and there is an opportunity cost associated with investing in Japan versus a country like India. Again, this is where a simple exhibit will fool you. By not comparing the *relative* performance of these countries, you can miss the bigger picture.

Sector/Industry Analysis

The sector analysis you do as your own hedge fund manager is also important, and some hedge fund managers would argue it is *more important* than your global or country research. If you surmise that the software sector is primed for a big move and you are correct, you do not have to necessarily be the best stock picker to make big profits in the group. The fortunes of an individual stock are closely intertwined with those of the sector in which it operates. In fact, historical research has shown that as much as 65 to 70 percent of a particular stock's movement can be traced back to the performance of the industry represented by the stock. If that number maintains its veracity in the future, and you are adept at picking strong industry groups, you stand a great chance of being a premier hedge fund manager, regardless of the type of global market in which we find ourselves at any given time.

Again, for edification, a sector is a group of companies that generate revenue in similar ways, and tend to rise and fall at the same time in the economic cycle; "industry" is the term we normally use to describe the next-smaller subset of sectors. The sectors tracked by Standard & Poor's are Basic Industries, Financials, Technology, Industrials, Energy, Consumer Staples, Consumer Services, Utilities, and Transport/Cyclicals.

The industries and stocks that are leading the global equities markets today are probably not going to be the leaders a few years down the road. For example, a Japanese electronics manufacturer, Akai Electric Corp., was founded in 1929 and for decades was one of the world's greatest electronics manufacturers. In some of its most profitable years, its products included reel-to-reel audiotape recorders, tuners, audio cassette decks, amplifiers, video recorders, and loudspeakers. Akai is also generally regarded to have built the best 8-track players during the 1970s. Perhaps you can see where we are going with this. If you were a hedge fund manager back in the 1970s, you most certainly would have considered Akai as a play in the technology sector. If we then fast forward to 2004, you would see Akai being bought out of bankruptcy by Hong Kong's Grande Group, primarily for the name. The point is that sectors and industries change, and the cogs that drive these industries changes.

One of the behavioral flaws we often see within investors is that they always have the desire to go "back to the well"; they always want to try to buy the stocks from which they have made money in the past. It is an understandable aspect of human nature, a comfort mechanism, if you will, for investors to go back and buy stocks that have made them money previously—but to do so without reanalyzing the industry is fraught with risk. If you had given in to this instinct with Akai in, say, the late 1990s, you would have lost your shirt.

We are going to look at our industries from the standpoint of both fundamental and technical analysis. One of the less-considered but still important reasons we believe you should incorporate technical analysis into your research is that countries, companies, and industry gurus *lie*. As we know all too well, there are people operating in the various spheres of the investment world who are less-than-ethical, and they will actually lie to investors about any (or perhaps all) of a wide variety of fundamentals. Do we really need to look past WorldCom or Enron for proof of how corrupt and downright deceitful the management of a company can be? On that note, take a look at the exhibit of Enron. The scary part about the exhibit is that, if you were only using fundamental analysis, you probably would have been

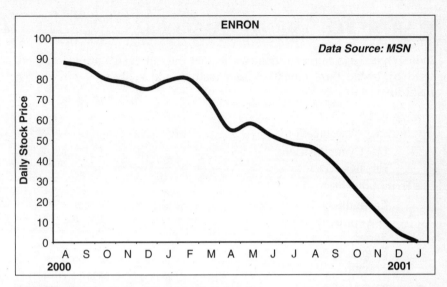

EXHIBIT 4.14   Chart of Enron in Its Dying Days
Source: MSN Encarta.

buying Enron stock all the way down to the low single digits. Management was lying to investors and putting out illegitimate numbers; however, when fundamental analysis was telling you to buy the stock, technical analysis was telling you something was wrong (Exhibit 4.14).

Now, if you think companies can be deceitful, wait until you start taking information from countries and cartels. For the longest time, the Chinese government told the world, "our economy is growing at 8 percent," without giving out any additional information. They simply would not divulge any information about their economy. How can you analyze a country when the government will not allow a flow of information? Years later, the Chinese government put out numbers that showed an increase in manufacturing activity, but they do not actually publish the numbers; you have to take their word for it. However, something was not adding up in our research. Chinese capacity utilization numbers, which *are* published, were declining. When the Chinese discovered the conflict in their two numbers, they *stopped publishing* the capacity utilization numbers. Problem solved! Furthermore, how can you analyze world oil supply when you are dealing with a cartel like OPEC? They set their quota levels, and then all the member countries cheat on those quotas.

The solution to problems such as these is to use both schools of analysis together in order to gain a more complete view of what is happening. Our industry analysis will start from the fundamental perspective and then progress to the technical aspect.

FUNDAMENTAL INDUSTRY ANALYSIS

Industry analysis can take many forms, but the following outline is widely used by hedge fund managers and institutional analysts (source: CFA Institute):

- Industry Classification
  - Life Cycle Position
  - Business Cycle
- External Factors
  - Technology
  - Government
  - Social
  - Demographic
  - Foreign
- Demand Analysis
- Profitability
- International Competition and Markets

Industry Classification

Industries are typically classified in terms of their life cycles, as well as their business cycles. Life cycle refers to the organic life span, from birth to death (if applicable) of an industry, while discussions about the business cycle pertain to the industry's relationship and reaction to macroeconomic influences. Below we take a closer look at each.

By Industrial Life Cycle Position   In a general sense, industries are defined by the products they produce or the services they provide. Banks, insurance companies, and brokerage firms all fall under the sector heading of financial services, but each are representative of the financial services subsectors, or industries; an industry is simply a deeper breakdown of the sector as a whole. Book, newspaper, and magazine publishers are all components of the broad publishing sector, but each of those falls into a specific industry within the publishing sector. As an investor, you certainly rely on broad categorical affiliations, but further segment these sectors by certain economic characteristics in the course of preparing and performing your analysis.

You can pick up any corporate finance book and find that the most widely used segmentation tool is the *industrial life cycle*, which outlines four phases that mark the birth-to-death life span of an industry: pioneer, growth, mature, and decline.

1. **Pioneer:** The pioneer phase is the riskiest point of an industry's existence. At this point, the industry is struggling to establish a niche for its product and future leaders are attempting to position themselves for what they believe will be exponential growth. The potential for huge upside attracts investors, but as an investor, you would be wise to remember that 7 out of 10 start-up businesses fail to survive.

2. **Growth:** This is the most exciting stage and the one where an investor typically stands to make the big money. In this stage, the industry's product is accepted, roll out begins, and growth accelerates. Unfortunately, as an investor/analyst, there is little comparison for future demand for the products. The big question before you, then, is how far and how fast the industry can run. In most cases, growth companies prosper independent of the business cycle. What does that tell you? That if you are an astute student of the global industry game, you can make money in almost any global economic climate.

3. **Mature:** In this stage, industry trends begin to more closely mimic the growth trends of the global economies. If the economy grows by 2.5 percent, the industry's sales will increase by 2.5 percent. You can still find a few growth companies within the mature industry, but they are few and far between; a company can reflect growth characteristics at this stage in either of two ways: First, it can create the "better mousetrap"; the company can produce a product that is superior to that which is being produced by its competitors. We have seen this for years in the automobile industry; while Ford and General Motors basically grew earnings on par with the economy, Toyota and Honda saw strong demand for their products. Also, a company can experience a material growth spurt in a mature industry by acquiring competitors.

4. **Decline:** In this stage, shifting preferences or technologies have overtaken the industry and demand for its products is steadily decreasing. As demand dries up for the companies in these industries, many individual companies fail. The companies that survive are the ones that can take their previously earned cash flow and invest it into other, more promising industries. In today's markets, many of these companies will go across borders to initiate these types of investments. This stage, and what it ultimately means, is the primary motivation for why many multinational firms decide to open their own investment banking arms—they want the means to intelligently invest their excess dollars. As it happens, companies like Disney, Intel, and Microsoft all have their own investment banking operations.

By Business Cycle   In addition to the industry life cycle, the global investment community characterizes industries by the way they react to the normal economic, or business, cycle. The business cycle is defined as the recurring and fluctuating levels of economic activity that an economy experiences over a long period of time. The five stages of the business cycle are the growth (expansion), peak, recession (contraction), trough, and recovery stages. As we all know, global economies do not grow in a straight line in perpetuity. A typical economic cycle will typically run between 5 and 10 years. In most cases, the global markets will go through the stages of an economic cycle together, particularly those that are developed. On that note, the cornerstone of the global economies remains the U.S. economy, and most foreign economies continue to follow it in its capacity as the most powerful and fluid economy in the world (at this time).

Take a look at Exhibit 4.15, and you get an idea of where we are headed with this. The first thing we would point out is that the equity markets are always going to lead the economic cycle by at least six months. The exhibit's middle hump representing the equity market cycle is always going to be sitting to the left of the hump on the right, which represents the economic cycle. That makes intuitive sense, as market participants are not focused on where the economy has been, but rather where it is headed.

At any given point in the economic cycle some specific industry or sector will be leading the global marketplace. As you can see from the exhibit,

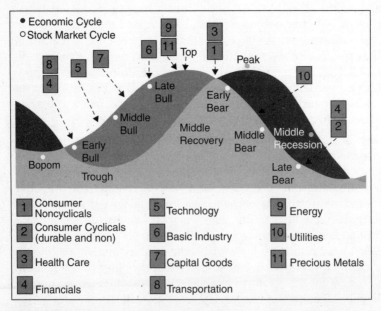

EXHIBIT 4.15   Relationship of Stock Market and Economic Cycles
Source: Standard & Poor's.

the best place to be during the early stages of a bear market is in consumer noncyclicals, or consumer staples, and health care. Given that, if your investment opinion is that the economies are headed into a global recession, you may want to begin researching healthcare stocks like Johnson & Johnson (U.S.), Bayer (Germany), or Takeda Pharma (Japan). Additionally, you may want to consider consumer staples like Nestlé (Switzerland), InBev (Belgium), or Kimberly Clark (U.S.). If you happen to be more risk averse, you have the option of using an ETF position for either of these industry groups, perhaps something like the Vanguard Consumer Staples Fund (VDC).

A common error made in the analysis of a sector occurs when the investor paints the entire global industry with a broad brush; a *bigger* error made is when the analyst paints the entire industry with a broad brush *across borders*. For example during the late 1990s and early twenty-first century, wireless companies saturated the U.S. market, as well as the markets of most of the industrialized countries around the world. Service providers like Sprint, AT&T Wireless, and Verizon made piles of money, running up huge double-digit gains in revenues and earnings during this time frame. However, the market ultimately became *over*saturated and price wars ensued. The companies had seen their best days; the industry had matured. That said, as of 2009, many of the emerging market countries around the world were just starting *their* growth cycles. Take a look at the following comparison. Companies like China Mobile (CHL) and Mexico's American Movil (AMX) both saw their earnings more than quadruple from 2001 to 2007. In the same time frame, Verizon and the newly combined company of SprintNextel managed to see *their* earnings go *backward* (see Exhibit 4.16).

As Exhibit 4.17 reflects, leading wireless services providers in many of the emerging markets around the world saw substantial gains in their stock prices, while companies like SprintNextel and Verizon actually lost money for their shareholders.

You may be able to look at yesterday's trends in industrialized countries and extrapolate them forward to emerging markets; what has been a high-growth industry in the United States may be tomorrow's big moneymaker elsewhere around the globe. In any case, you do not want to discount an industry globally simply because it may not be right in a particular country; a mature industry in one nation or region can easily be seen as a high-growth industry in another.

External Factors

No industry operates in a vacuum. All industries are subject to numerous outside influences that can significantly influence the day-to-day operations

EXHIBIT 4.16 Comparative Look at China Mobil, American Movil, Sprint Nextel, and Verizon from July 2006 to April 2007
Source: Fxaccucharts.com.

of a company (and, by consequence, their earnings). External issues fall into the five primary categories listed here.

1. ***Technology***: Your primary focus on the technology issue is survival. Simply because a company has a leading product or service does not necessarily mean that technology is going to stay on the cutting edge forever. An obvious example is how the record player industry became obsolete with the advent of the CD player.

CHL				AMX				S				VZ		
Year	EPS ($)	Price ($) High Low		Year (Dec)	EPS ($)	Price ($) High Low		Year (Dec)	EPS ($)	Price ($) High Low		Year (Dec)	EPS ($)	Price ($) High Low
2001	0.91	33	13	2001	0.12	7	3	2001	1.05	26	16	2001	3.14	55	41
2002	1.03	18	11	2002	0.33	6	3	2002	0.40	18	6	2002	3.08	48	24
2003	1.09	15	9	2003	0.72	9	4	2003	0.63	15	9	2003	2.58	42	29
2004	1.28	18	12	2004	0.75	17	9	2004	0.94	23	14	2004	2.51	40	32
2005	1.65	26	14	2005	1.61	31	15	2005	0.95	24	19	2005	2.07	39	27
2006	2.08	45	22	2006	2.15	46	26	2006	1.18	24	15	2006	2.06	37	28
2007	2.85	104	40	2007	3.00	69	41	2007	0.88	23	12	2007	2.36	46	35

www.InvestorsPassport.com

EXHIBIT 4.17 Comparative Look at Stock Prices for China Mobil, American Movil, Sprint Nextel, and Verizon from 2001 to 2007
Source: www.StockCharts.com.

2. ***Government***: Government taxes, laws, and regulations impact every industry across the world, and the *level* of government involvement varies drastically from country to country. It is, therefore, critically important that you understand not only a given government's current level of involvement in an industry, but also the *culture* of the countries in which you are investing, as the government's level of "meddling" could drastically change. You do not see rash changes in levels of involvement in countries like Britain and the United States; however, in places like Russia, things are different. In 2003, the Russian government seized one of the largest oil companies in the country, Yukos Oil Company. The company's CEO, billionaire Mikhail Khodorkovsky, was subsequently sent to jail and the company's assets were distributed. In August 2006, a Russian court declared the company bankrupt. How would you have felt as a debt holder of a company in a country like that, given the demonstrated propensity for government "access?"

3. ***Social Changes***: Social factors boil down to two classifications: lifestyle and fashion changes. Of the two, fashion changes are the less predictable, and you need to be careful not to make the mistake of categorizing a short-term fashion cycle for a long-term trend. Lifestyle changes, by contrast, take place over long periods of time but still yield noticeable economic impact. For example, over the past 10 years, we have seen a significant global shift toward health consciousness; this movement has sparked a per capita decline in hard liquor consumption.

4. ***Demographics***: Demography is the statistical study of all populations. How does the consideration of this factor influence change the investment landscape? Well, demographics told us that as of a few years ago in Malaysia, about 50 percent of the population was under the age of 21; accordingly, one of the areas on which you may have focused your investment dollars in Malaysia is the *alcohol* industry, in anticipation of a surge in the beer/wine/liquor population. Also, courtesy of demographic studies, we know that per capita incomes are steadily on the rise in many emerging markets countries. A natural focus of your investment consideration, therefore, might be the rising demand for electric appliances, as well as the future growth of local utilities. These are two simple examples, to be sure, but they illustrate the point. Note that demographic trends unfold over long periods of time, so they can be easy to identify prospectively.

5. ***Foreign Influences***: As global trade expands, and economies become more fluid across the globe, industries become more sensitive to foreign influences. For example, in its current state, the U.S. economy is obviously heavily dependent on imported oil. As oil prices rose

dramatically in 2007 and 2008, the U.S. economy was slowed significantly. This was only part of the reason for the grand recession that commenced in 2007, but it was nevertheless a significant factor, and one that could not be positively influenced by the U.S. government.

Demand Analysis

If you have ever analyzed stocks, you understand that earnings drive a company and its associated share prices. If you want to make money in a stock, you need to understand the demand drivers behind their products or services. There are three primary ways to analyze demand:

1. *Top-Down Demand Analysis*: With top-down analysis, we are looking for specific macroeconomic variables that show a strong correlation to an industry's demand numbers. For example, demand growth for cement in Mexico is historically 1.7 × GDP growth. Therefore, if you were analyzing Cemex, the world's third-largest cement producer based out of Mexico, you could use a GDP growth forecast to help you forecast the company's demand numbers.

2. *Industry Life Cycle*: We previously discussed an industry's life cycle and defined each component stage. In this case, we can use the positioning of the industry within that cycle to project demand. As an example, the food industry in France is certainly a mature industry. Therefore, we would expect it to grow at about the same rate as GDP. If we expect French GDP to grow 3 percent per year, the food industry should do about the same, and we can use that in our demand analysis.

3. *External Factors*: Many industries are fairly consistent and fairly stable. Thus, the impacts for most external factors are predictable. In other industries, the external factors tend to be a bit unpredictable, and can wreak havoc on your demand numbers.

Profitability and Pricing

As a hedge fund manager, you want to focus your efforts on profitable industries. In reality, why would you invest in companies with strong sales growth if their profitability was declining? Profitability is the main driver behind any company or industry's ability to grow. Additionally, the trend of profitability is as important as the level itself. If a given industry is expected to sell more units this year, but profitability has been falling, that industry is not as valuable as the simple revenue numbers may indicate. An industry's pricing power is an integral cog to its profitability.

International Factors

International industry analysis must evaluate the effects of not only world supply, demand, profitability, and cost components on behalf of an industry, but also different valuation levels due to accounting conventions and, finally, the impact of exchange rates on the industry as a whole, as well as on its component firms.

From the standpoint of commerce and general economic interaction, the world is fast becoming completely borderless. This reality has long been evident in such industries as oil, metals, and foods, but is also pronounced in a variety of other highly influential sectors, like textiles, chemicals, and technology. In fact, a little more than 40 percent of the earnings for the companies in the S&P 500 can be traced back to international business operations, and that number will only grow in the years to come.

The key to successfully investing in industries across borders is having in-depth knowledge of the industries themselves, first and foremost. You need to be intimately familiar with any industry into which you put the resources of your hedge fund, but the need for a high level of familiarity becomes even more crucial as you target these industries from the standpoint of their various foreign market penetrations. To that end, the quality of your industry resource materials is crucial. Next, we tell you a few of the resources we use to research global industries for the benefit of our managed accounts.

Industry Publications

Standard & Poor's Industry Survey: This is a two-volume reference work, divided into 34 segments and dealing with 69 major industries.

Standard & Poor's Analysts Handbook: The handbook contains selected income account and balance sheet items, along with related financial ratios. With this tool, it is possible to compare the major factors bearing on industry movements.

Value Line Industry Survey: The survey contains summary statistics on assets and earnings for 91 industries, and also highlights other important and highly usable ratios. The survey also provides an industry stock price index, as well as a table that offers up comparative data for all of the individual companies within a given industry, and ranks them on the bases of timeliness, safety, and financial strength. The discussions consider the pertinent factors affecting the given industry, and finish with an overall recommendation for the investor.

Industry Magazines   Magazines seem to strike some as being almost too casual a type of resource, but they are actually wonderful sources of data and timely information. Many industries are represented by multiple, high-profile periodicals, and magazines like *Computers*, *Real Estate Today*, and *Automotive News* serve as essential information lifelines for active investors in the computer, real estate, and automotive industries, respectively.

Trade Associations   Trade associations are organizations set up by those intrinsically involved in some way with an industry in order to provide information to practitioners on behalf of such topics as education, problem solving, and lobbying. In the pursuit of these goals, the associations typically gather extensive statistics, and it is these statistics that can be very useful in your research. A quick Google search will locate for you an association for the benefit of just about any industry. We are always accessing as much trade association information as we can, as diligent effort to that end has often yielded to us valuable nuggets about what is happening next within a given industry, particularly in terms of global direction.

TECHNICAL INDUSTRY ANALYSIS

Our main goal from the technical perspective is to visually identify industries and sectors around the world that are currently leading the global markets or rolling into favor for future leadership. Note that our technical lessons are somewhat universal because you are able to utilize them regardless of whether you are analyzing countries, industries/sectors, or individual stocks. In fact, most of the patterns we go over in Chapter 6 on currency trading are also relevant to individual stocks; we simply did not want to rehash the same technical ideas throughout the book—many of these technical lessons are universal in their application to differing types of investments. On that note, the relative performance analysis we went over when we were analyzing our countries is something we revisit here, so you can get an idea of how it looks in your sector global analysis. There are two primary ways we analyze our sectors from the technical side: trend analysis and relative analysis.

Trend Analysis

As with most types of trading methods, there is more than one way to "skin a cat." However, we have one method for discerning trend analysis that we think is exceptional, and it involves one *primary* technical tool, combined with several confirmatory indicators. Let us take a look at these mechanisms individually.

Trendline Analysis: Our methodology begins with trendline analysis. An evaluation of any chart quickly reveals that prices usually move in trends. Often, a series of ascending bottoms in a rising market can be joined together by a straight line, and so, as well, can the tops off a descending series of rally peaks be joined the same way. These lines, known as trendlines, are a simple but useful way to discover rotations around the world from country to country or from industry to industry. In fact, trendlines are the foundation of our analytical approach. A proper trendline has to connect two or more peaks or troughs. Frequently, we see people constructing lines that touch only one point. This is a fundamentally significant flaw, because whenever you draw or interpret a trendline, you cannot forget that a true trendline is a graphic way of representing the underlying trend. Consequently, if it touches only one point, it is not a true trendline. Further, the more times a trendline is hit and supported, the more powerful that trendline becomes. You see evidence of that indicated in the next exhibit.

Take a look at Exhibit 4.18 for the iShares Global Energy ETF (IXC). At the time, we were experiencing a five-year bull market in the global energy sector. In this particular case, the trendline was set up five different times, which makes it a very important long-term trendline. When the IXC finally *broke* this trendline, we knew it was an important leadership change in the markets from the 2003 lows. Up to this break, energy stocks had led all global sectors. This was a clear sector rotation *out* of the energy issues, and it proved to be the precursor to a rotation out of commodities as a whole. Keep in mind, as well, that the fundamentals for the group never looked better than when this trendline was broken. However, savvy investors knew there were dark clouds on the horizon, and that a global recession would cause a precipitous drop in oil prices. Also, although it is a bit hard to see on the longer-term chart, after the IXC broke its trendline, it consolidated in that area for some time further. As a hedge fund manager, you can use this type of consolidation to build your position, which in this case would be to the short side. After analyzing countless numbers of charts, we think it is accurate to say that 80 percent to 85 percent of stocks, sectors, and markets that break a trendline come back at some point to *retest* that line. Given that, you do not have to be overly aggressive in trying to force your way into a position; you can build your position using these retests and consolidations. See Figure 4.18.

The next couple of indicators we use in our strategy are confirmatory indicators. They confirm what we are observing with our trendlines. The chart/trend of the group is the main thrust with our other indicators confirming whether or not the rotation has real backing.

On-Balance Volume: On-Balance Volume (OBV) is one of the best confirmatory indicators for individual stocks in the entire market. It was developed by Joseph Granville in 1963 and was revealed inside

EXHIBIT 4.18 Chart of iShares Global Energy ETF (IXC) Reflecting Years of Strength Followed by Acute Technical Weakness
Source: Esignal.com.

the pages of his book, *Granville's New Key to Stock Market Profits* (Prentice-Hall, 1963).

OBV is a momentum indicator that measures positive and negative volume flow. In reading the theories surrounding OBV, it is apparent that Granville felt volume to be the driving force behind the markets. The indicator was designed to project when major moves in stocks and markets would occur, and described the increase or decrease of his indicator, setting new highs or lows, as "a tightly wound spring." He went on to explain his theory by stating that when volume increased or decreased dramatically, and the underlying issue's price did not change significantly, then at some point the price would shoot upward or downward. We see something interesting in this theory that seems to have a lot of merit. It appears that as the institutions begin to buy into an issue that the retail investors are still selling, the volume is increasing as the price is still slightly falling or leveling out. Over a period of time, the volume begins to drive the price upward and the converse then begins to take over as the institutions start to sell their positions while the retail investors begin to accumulate *their* positions again. As institutions are buying the stock or ETF of the average investor at the bottom, and then selling it back to him at or near the top, we see a living example of the concept of "smart money." You can also see how the OBV indicator can suggest major trendline turnarounds.

Let us take a look at an example of how OBV can give you an early signal as to the next price direction for a group. The exhibit below is one of our global industry ETFs, the iShares Global Financial (IXG). As you can see from the exhibit, the IXG had been moving higher for many years. In fact, the global financial services sector had been one of the biggest winners after the bear market that began in 2000. The OBV line was holding up quite nicely and confirming the uptrend for the IXG in textbook fashion, until early to mid-2007. At that point, the IXG began to look as though it was topping, and the OBV was confirming that point prior to the big sell-off. Notice that the IXG hit a new high in April 2007, around $95, and the OBV was confirming that high. Toward the end of the year, the IXG came back to retest that high, but the OBV was not even *close* to confirming that new high. In this case, the OBV was telling you that institutional investors around the world were quietly unloading their shares to the novice investors because they knew things were about to turn negative in the sector. The next chart demonstrates how devastating the carnage was in the global financial industry (Exhibits 4.19 and 4.20).

The basic assumption regarding OBV analysis is that OBV changes *precede* price changes. The theory is that smart money (institutional money) can be seen flowing into or out of a group by a rising or falling OBV. When the public then moves into the group, both the group and the OBV

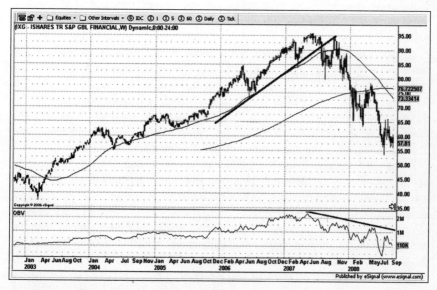

EXHIBIT 4.19 Chart Indicating Price Action and On-Balance Volume of iShares Global Financial ETF (IXG), 2003 to 2008
Source: esignal.com.

EXHIBIT 4.20   Chart Indicating Price Action and On-Balance Volume of iShares Global Financial ETF (IXG) Through the Beginning of 2009
Source: esignal.com.

will surge ahead; if the group's price movement precedes OBV movement, a "nonconfirmation" has occurred and investors should proceed with caution.

Relative Strength Index: In a broad-based rally, most sectors are advancing. However, as traders, our investment dollars only deserve the "best of the best." When talking about defining these "best" groups, few indicators work better than the Relative Strength Index (RSI). The RSI is a comparison between the days that a stock/index finishes *up* against the days it finishes *down*. It is a reasonably simple model that anyone can use, and most software packages provide it for you as an indicator.

The RSI ranges from 0 to 100. An issue is considered overbought around or above the 70 level. This number is not written in stone, and in a bull run some believe that 80 is a better level to indicate an overbought stock, since stocks often trade at higher valuations during bull markets. Likewise, if the RSI approaches 30, a stock is considered oversold and you should consider buying (make the adjustment to 20 in a bear market, as most stocks tend to get significantly oversold). Also, as with many indicators, trendlines form on the RSI line itself, which can be used to determine the "direction of the strength" for the issue or group.

Take a look at Exhibit 4.21. It is for the iShares S&P Global Information Technology ETF (IXN). You can see that the technology industry was

EXHIBIT 4.21   Chart Indicating Price Action and Relative Strength (RSI) of iShares Global Information Technology ETF (IXN) from Mid-2007 to Mid-2009
Source: StockCharts.com.

suffering in the global downturn, and the group was also suffering relative to the overall market. The trend was characterized by a series of lower highs and lower lows. However, take a look at the RSI line below the chart. It was telling you that the IXN was ready to take over leadership and that rotation was coming into the group. If you look below, you can see the downtrend in the RSI line that preceded the turn with the breakout of the RSI line coming at the circle. Once the rotation began, it led to significantly higher prices and strong profits for anyone who was able to "read the writing on the wall."

Sector rotation is not something that is new to trading. However, it is something that is exceptionally important to trading success. After years of research, we can honestly tell you that the great investors of our time (be they technical or fundamental in orientation) all had one thing in common: they were masters at rotation. The system we have laid out for you grants you a foundation for identifying global industry and sector rotations, and gives you a few indicators that will lend confirmation to your findings. Remember that in trading, it is not about who you are—but *where* you are.

Comparative/Relative Analysis

Most institutional investors' primary goal is to beat a benchmark. If you are managing an international growth-based hedge fund, your goal would be to beat the performance of the MSCI EAFE index (Morgan Stanley Capital International Europe Australasia and Far East). If you are managing a global precious metals fund, the index you are trying to outperform may be the S&P Global Gold Index. The point is that, as an investor of your own personal hedge fund, you need to establish a proxy for your returns. How else will you know if you have performed well?

Another reason to benchmark your style is in an effort to run *comparative/relative technical analysis*. As investors, we always want to have positions in our portfolios that are outperforming our target benchmark. Take a look at the following exhibit. We created this exhibit at www.StockCharts.com. It is a comparative performance chart for the iShares S&P Global Health Care ETF (IXJ) versus the iShares MSCI EAFE (EFA). It is essentially the IXJ divided by the EFA, and was run using the symbol "IXJ:EFA." If we are managing a global growth hedge fund, our benchmark is the MSCI EAFE Index. Therefore, from the technical side, we want only to invest in industries that are performing better than our benchmark. The downtrending arrow on the left half of the chart shows a time frame wherein the MSCI EAFE Index was performing better than the global health care sector; accordingly, we wanted to have minimal exposure to that industry in this time frame. In early 2008, things changed. You can see how the comparative chart broke into an uptrend and then began to trek higher. The ascending arrow on the right represents the time frame where you would have wanted to have a more significant weighting in the health care group. As a side note, it is not a coincidence that the normally defensive health care group was outperforming the rest of the world during this time frame. We had just entered into a global economic slump, and investors were pulling in their horns in favor of more recession-friendly groups (Exhibit 4.22).

Let us take a look at another example. Look at Exhibit 4.23, the iShares Global Financials ETF (IXG) versus the iShares MSCI EAFE (EFA). The global bear market that started in the fall of 2007 was driven by a credit crunch, the likes of which most of us have never seen before. As you would expect, the global financial services group was slaughtered. The relative performance of the group was following the fundamental earnings trends that banks and brokers were experiencing. At some point, the financials will bounce back, will they not (maybe you are one who does not believe

EXHIBIT 4.22 Comparative Performance Chart of iShares S&P Global Health Care ETF (IXJ) Versus iShares MSCI EAFE ETF (EFA) from Mid-2006 to Mid-2009
Source: StockCharts.com.

EXHIBIT 4.23 Comparative Performance Chart of iShares S&P Global Financials ETF (IXG) Versus iShares MSCI EAFE ETF (EFA) from early 01/2006 to 01/2009
Source: StockCharts.com.

that is so)? If you believe they *will* come back, there is no reason to try to grab a falling knife. Why attempt to pick the bottom when relative analysis will tell you when to buy? In this case, you want to wait for the relative performance of the industry, versus your benchmark, to start "acting right."

Industries and sectors do not change direction overnight. It takes months, quarters, and sometimes years for a trend to change in a group. Use the volatility to your advantage and *work into* your positions. The last thing you need to do is make some sweaty-palmed buying decision when running your own hedge fund.

Here, by the way, are the indexes we use for relative performance analysis:

- **iShares Global Consumer Discretionary (RXI)**
- **iShares Global Consumer Staples (KXI)**
- **iShares Global Energy (IXC)**
- **iShares Global Financials (IXG)**
- **iShares Global Healthcare (IXJ)**
- **iShares Global Industrials (EXI)**
- **iShares Global Materials (MXI)**
- **iShares Global Technology (IXN)**
- **iShares Global Telecommunications (IXP)**
- **iShares Global Utilities (JXI)**

Also, if you would like to see a more comprehensive list of ETFs available in the market today, simply go to http://news.morningstar.com/etf/Lists/ETFReturns.html. When you get there, be sure to click on Show Complete List to get a complete inventory.

COMPANY ANALYSIS

Financial academia would argue that the markets are efficient. The *efficient-market hypothesis* (EMH) asserts that financial markets are "informationally efficient," or that price on assets like stocks and bonds already reflect all known information. The efficient-market hypothesis states that it is impossible to consistently outperform the market by using any information that the market already knows, except through luck. In the case of the U.S. markets, we see that the case for the argument because the majority of money managers are not able to consistently beat the benchmarks.

The exciting news is that *international* markets do not appear to act efficiently. Andrew Williams, CFA, co-authored a book called *Equity Analysis Issues, Lessons and Techniques* (CFA Institute, 2004). As a component to the book, Williams performed research on the efficiency of the international markets as measured by the MSCI EAFE Index. Williams broke down the MSCI EAFE Index along the lines of baseline EAFE, EAFE value, and EAFE growth. For the 28-year period beginning December 31, 1974, and ending September 30, 2003, he found the EAFE produced an annualized return of about 12 percent. The less-expensively valued stocks in the MSCI EAFE Value Index returned an annualized rate of around 14 percent, and the Growth Index came in just over 9.5 percent per annum. From this information, he concluded that international markets provide a good opportunity for active management. They are clearly inefficient, which contrasts sharply with historical research on the U.S. markets.

Williams also found similar results in another study that analyzed rolling 12-month returns of the value versus growth components of the MSCI EAFE. The median excess return earned by the value index over the growth index was 4.3 percent. Further, value stocks outperformed growth stocks 73 percent of the time. As hedge fund managers, we like this research. It tells us that we are able, through research, to outperform the international markets and achieve above-average returns.

We always have to be especially careful in our analysis of foreign companies, and one of the biggest reasons for this due care is that accounting standards in other countries and regions are often quite different; you may well end up analyzing numbers that are not giving you a true picture of the companies you are comparing. For example, the utilization of German Generally Accepted Accounting Principles is not the same as evaluating with U.S. GAAP. During the first nine months of 1993, Daimler lost $105 million according to German accounting standards, but according to U.S. GAAP the company lost $1.19 billion. That said, the cash flow numbers were the same, which is why the majority of analysis we will do for individual stocks will be analyzing cash numbers for companies as opposed to earnings numbers. It is important, as a function of your analysis, to be able to overcome the occasionally obfuscating differences in pure accounting data by quantifying company fundamentals on the basis of certain telling valuation metrics.

Take a look at Exhibit 4.24. Researchers tracked the performance of multiple valuation measures for companies in the EAFE Index September 1991 through September 2003. For each metric, the average monthly excess return produced by the top stocks versus the average stock was determined. For the dividend yield category, the researchers compared the stocks with the best dividend yields in the EAFE Index to the average issues in the index; for the P/E category, they took the stocks in the EAFE Index with the lowest ratios and compared them to the average P/E issues in the index. Dividend yield, with a monthly excess return of .73 percent, was found to be the best stand-alone factor. Note that dividend yield,

EXHIBIT 4.24	Valuation Measures for Companies in the EAFE Index from 09/1991 to 09/2003		
Measure	**Average Excess Return**	**Standard Deviation**	**Return/Risk**
Dividend Yield	0.73%	2.43%	0.30
Price to Earnings	0.63%	2.70%	0.23
Price to Book	0.66%	3.22%	0.21
Price to Cash Flow	0.65%	2.43%	0.27
Price to Sales	0.40%	2.25%	0.18
EV/EBITDA	0.46%	2.07%	0.22
EAFE Equal Weighted	0.82%	2.41%	0.34

Source: Based on data from PIA Investment Research & FactSet.

price-to-book, and price-to-cash flow seem to work the best because they are *the factors least distorted by differences in accounting conventions around the world.* Additionally, take a look at the bottom of the exhibit: the last category listed is the equal weighted composite of the metrics. The composite score outperforms all of the individual pieces, which suggests that in assessing companies on the international front, using a multifactor approach is much better than relying on any single valuation metric alone.

The application of this multifactor approach maintains its usefulness regardless of the country in which it is applied, which means that you will have a consistent way to overcome accounting discrepancies predicated on different methodologies. It is worth noting that researchers found, through the process of evaluation through multiple factors, that different individual valuation metrics worked better in different countries; while high dividend-yielding stocks may have been the best performers in Canada, low price-to-sales stocks added the most value in France, and low price-to-earnings multiples work the best in Great Britain. In the end, using a multifactor approach is always going to be more valuable, because it is through that practice that you may determine the single best metric measurement for a given country.

Since you are now a hedge fund manager and might be considering your own long/short fund, it may also interest you to know that the same research held true for shorts. If investors short stocks that rank at the bottom on cash flow-to-price (lowest quintile versus average), they will typically fare pretty well; once again, a multifactor approach outperforms all individual measures, this time to the short side.

Now that we have established the fact that we can add value to our international hedge fund by using a multiple metric approach, let us break things down a bit further and look at the individual measures that were tested earlier.

Dividend Yield

A company's dividend yield is a financial ratio that shows how much a company pays out in dividends each year relative to its share price. It is a way to measure how much cash flow you are getting for each dollar invested in an equity position. If a hedge fund manager is looking for a stream of cash flow from his investment portfolio, he can secure this cash flow by investing in stocks that meet that dividend yield requirement. Keep in mind that companies that pay strong and consistent dividends tend to experience less price volatility.

It seems pretty logical that companies paying higher dividends will be more attractive. However, beyond simple payout, there is a second relevant issue with regard to dividends that is important, and that is *stability*. Secure dividends signal steadiness in the underlying cash flow of the company, and this stability translates into a lower level of uncertainty and business risk. If a company's dividend is erratic and unpredictable, it will increase the fluctuation of cash flows in the hands of shareholders and then *they* become more unpredictable; we could go out today and find companies throughout the world that are paying 12 percent dividend yields, but would also likely find that half of those companies are on the verge of cutting their dividends and thereby engendering shareholder instability (indeed, many high-yielding dividend payers aren't always the most stable companies, anyway). In the end, be sure to analyze the other ratios we are giving you to get a "big picture" view of the company, and do not simply invest on the basis of dividend yield.

One of the places we start looking for companies with high and stable yields is within Standard & Poor's (S&P) Indexes. In particular, S&P has four indexes that we search: the S&P Dividend Aristocrats Index, the S&P High Yield Dividend Aristocrats, the S&P Europe 350 Dividend Aristocrats and the S&P/TSX Canadian Dividend Aristocrats. Each of the indexes lists stocks that have consistently increased dividends every year for at least 25 consecutive years. Historical research shows that the indexes have fairly consistently beaten their benchmarks since 1989. As an example, the S&P Dividend Aristocrats Index has beaten the S&P 500 by about 1.3 percent annually since 1989. If you want to look inside these indexes, you can go to the www.StandardandPoors.com site, or simply do a Google search for "S&P Aristocrat Indexes." A few of the stronger dividend players we have considered recently have been: Telecom Italia (Italy) at 7.99 percent, Insurance Australia Group (Australia) at 7.95 percent, Eniro AB (Sweden) at 9.82 percent, and Manitoba Telecom Services (Canada) at 6.54 percent. Obviously, names on the list will change regularly, but these dividends show you how attractive the payouts can be around the world.

Price-to-Earnings (P/E) Ratio

The price-to-earnings (P/E) ratio is an easy number to calculate. We simply take the current price of the stock and divide it by the full year earnings for that company. Different analysts use different numbers for the earnings piece, but we prefer to use trailing 12-month earnings as opposed to calendar year earnings. In a contracting economy, the trailing 12-month earnings component gives you a better picture than the previous year's calendar earnings because it is adjusting down with the economy.

P/E ratios can be a tricky animal to compare across borders for several reasons. As we mentioned, not every country is under the same accounting standards, so the earnings number in one country, like China, may not equate to the same earnings number in another country, such as Sweden, without some serious work being done to adjust for accounting differences. Moving forward, many countries around the world are working toward a unified accounting standard to allow better comparison around the globe; in fact, 2008 saw the U.S. Securities and Exchange Commission move to allow some large U.S. companies to begin using international accounting standards for 2009, and is additionally moving to require *all* American companies to do so by 2016. While complete global standardization of accounting standards is still some time way, it is getting much closer than it once was. Additionally, it should be noted that foreign companies listed on American stock exchanges as ADRs are required to report their earnings under U.S. GAAP, so, of course, comparisons of P/E ratios in that case are legitimate.

It is misleading to compare P/E ratios across different markets without controlling for the differences in several underlying variables. With historical research as our benchmark, two particular factors come to mind: short-term interest rates and expected growth rates. History shows us that there is a highly negative correlation between short-term interest rates and the P/E ratios of a country, and even without the empirical evidence, it makes sense intuitively: High short-term interest rates make borrowing costs higher and thus cause a drag on economic growth; slower growth *should* equate to lower P/E ratios. Historical evidence also shows us that there is a highly *positive* correlation between expected growth rates in GDP and P/E ratios; again, even without the evidence it makes sense: If a country is experiencing healthy growth in its GDP, you would *expect* P/E ratios to be higher.

Let us take a look at an example of how this might look. Exhibit 4.25 is a list of three global pharmaceutical companies, accompanied by a few pertinent factors (this is a simplistic example for illustrative purposes, as we are not incorporating any of our other indicators). Looking at our example, the best investment would be Eli Lilly out of the United States. If

EXHIBIT 4.25	List of Pharmaceutical Companies Novartis, Glaxo Smithkline, and Eli Lilly, with Illustrative Fundamental Data

Company	Country	Expected 2-Year Growth	Yield	P/E Ratio	Country Short-Term Rates	Country Expected GDP Growth
Novartis	Switzerland	1%	3.8%	10	0.50%	1.15%
Glaxo Smithline	UK	8%	5.9%	13	1.00%	1.30%
Eli Lilly	United States	12%	6.4%	12	9.25%	1.25%

Sources: IMF.org.

we used the P/E ratio as our only factor, Novartis would be the most valuable company because it has the lowest P/E. However, Eli Lilly has a better growth rate, the U.S. economy has the lowest interest rates, and the U.S. economy has about the same expected GDP growth rate as Switzerland. If we also include the dividend yield in our simple analysis, Eli Lilly makes even more sense than do the other two. In the end, the P/E ratio by itself is not enough to analyze a series of companies, but it is an integral part of our overall fundamental matrix with our other indicators.

Next, we want to take our P/E analysis to another level. There is a way we can take the fundamental information from a company and use the earnings information to estimate what a company's P/E ratio *should* be. We call this the *fundamental P/E ratio* because we are constructing it from the company's fundamental data. After we create this number, we can compare it to the P/E ratio in the open market to find out if that company is undervalued or overvalued. We will spare you the academic derivation of the formula, but the end equation looks like this:

P/E = Dividend Payout Ratio(1 + growth rate in dividends (forever))/ required rate of return − growth rate in dividends forever)

Some of the required information is easy to find and some of the information takes a bit more digging to locate, but let us take a look at an example. Telefonica (TEF) is one of the largest companies in Spain and provides telecommunications services in the Spanish- and Portuguese-speaking world. As of 2007, the company traded at a P/E multiple of 9 in the open market. Additionally, the company showed a payout ratio of about 27 percent, a long-term growth rate in dividends of about 7 percent, and a required rate of return of 9.50 percent. Before we move forward with the calculation, we want to mention that we found all of the needed information by doing nothing more than performing Google searches. We searched for "Telefonica WACC" to find the required rate of return; the WACC for a company is the Weighted Average Cost of Capital. It is, simply, the overall required return from stock and bondholders of the firm and, as such, is often used internally by company directors to determine the economic feasibility of expansionary opportunities and mergers. Also, note that variables like the payout ratio can be found by checking the research portion of the website for the broker with which you are trading.

Moving forward, the "fundamental" P/E of Telefonica should be:

$$P/E = .27(1.07)/(.0950 - .07) = 11.55$$

Telefonica is currently trading in the open market at a P/E of 9, but the fundamentals of the company are telling us that the company's P/E should be trading closer to 11.55, so it is presently undervalued. Using this method becomes even more valuable when you evaluate multiple companies in the same industry. The fundamental P/E ratio is essentially a "second look" at what the P/E multiple is telling you, and as such is a very valuable tool.

Price-to-Sales (P/S) Ratio

The price-to-sales (P/S) Ratio is relatively easy to calculate. It is calculated as the price of the stock divided by its sales per share number for the year. This particular ratio has its own set of pluses. First, unlike the P/E ratio and the price-to-book value ratios, which can become negative and meaningless, the P/S multiple is available even for the most troubled companies. Also, the price to sales ratio is not as influenced by the "voodoo" accounting we sometimes see in many companies. Revenues can be manipulated, but it is much harder to manipulate revenues than it is earnings when earnings have such determinant factors as depreciation, inventory, and extraordinary charges as components that can easily sway earnings numbers to one side or the other. Additionally, the P/S ratio is not nearly as volatile as the P/E ratio. For cyclical companies, the swings from cycle to cycle can make the P/E ratio virtually meaningless. With P/S ratios, we still see fluctuations, but they are not nearly as drastic.

Like the P/E ratio, we can calculate a *fundamental P/S ratio* to compare to the actual market ratio. Again, we will not go through the derivations, but the fundamental P/S ratio formula for a stable firm looks like this:

P/S = 1 Profit Margin * Payout Ratio
      * (1 + growth rate in dividends (forever))
      (required rate of return − growth rate in dividends (forever))

Let us apply this ratio to Delhaize (DEG), a Belgian food retailer, which operates in seven countries and on three continents. In the open market, DEG was trading at a P/S ratio of about .32. After a quick search on the

Internet, we located the following values: a payout ratio of 23 percent, a profit margin of 2.4 percent, growth rate in dividends of 3 percent, and a required rate of return (or WACC) of 4.67 percent. Therefore, the P/S ratio, justified by the fundamentals, is:

$$P/S = .024 * .23 * 1.03/(.0467 - .03) = .0057/.0167 = .34$$

In this case, the markets have it right. Again, no multiple by itself proves value, as that is ultimately determined by comparisons, so we need to run this number against other similar companies in the industry group; conversely, we could compare the ratio to DEG's historical ratios to see if the company has value at this point in the economic cycle.

Let us mention one last caveat to the P/S ratio: Historical research has shown the P/S ratio is not as effective at predicting value for a company as the P/E ratio. That said, the addition of profit margins to the equation make it *much more* valuable. Accordingly, if you found a group of low P/S ratio stocks you are considering for your hedge fund, you can further narrow your numbers by analyzing the profit margins for those companies. *Low P/S Ratio stocks with high profit margins* makes for a very potent research tool.

Price-to-Book (P/B) Ratio

The book value of a company's equity is simply the difference between the book value of assets and the book value of liabilities. The P/B ratio is one of the metrics we use that can be significantly influenced by accounting standards. In the United States, the book value is calculated on the original price paid for the assets, reduced by any allowable depreciation, but this may differ around the world; as a result, you are better off reserving the use of the P/B ratio for the comparison of companies with like accounting standards.

The P/B ratio is easy to calculate, as it is simply the price per share of the stock *divided* by the book value per share of the company. You can find this ratio on thousands of sites around the world, but we also have ability to run a *fundamental P/B ratio*. Notwithstanding the derivation, the equation looks like this:

$$P/B = ROE * \text{Payout Ratio} * (1 + \text{growth rate in dividends (forever)})/$$
$$(\text{required rate of return} - \text{growth rate in dividends (forever)})$$

Let us look at an example. Embraer Brasileira (ERJ) is a Brazilian defense contractor that develops and produces aircraft for the Brazilian Air Force as well as for commercial contractors. A quick web search shows us the current P/B ratio on ERJ is .90. The company has a payout ratio of 31 percent, a ROE of 23.7 percent, growth rate in dividends estimated to be 4 percent, and required rate of return (WACC) of 7 percent. Our P/B ratio would therefore look like this:

$$P/B = (.237 * .31 * 1.05)/(.07 - .04) = 2.57$$

From our analysis, we can assume that ERJ is undervalued, as the current market P/B is .90, but the company's fundamentals justify a P/B of 2.57. Again, this is only one of our indicators, but this particular measurement tells us that ERJ has a great deal of value.

In the last section, we told you that the effectiveness of the P/S ratio was heightened when considered alongside profit margins. The P/B ratio also has an enhancer, and it is the Return on Equity (ROE). Historical research has shown us that companies with low P/B ratios and high ROE levels offer value to an investor. A simple way to compare companies in a group is to divide the P/B ratio by the ROE; the lower the number, the more valuable the company is in comparison to its peers.

Price-to-Cash Flow (P/CF) Ratio

A stock's price-to-cash-flow ratio is similar to the P/E ratio; however, rather than comparing a stock's price with earnings, you are comparing it with a company's *operating* cash flow, which is net income plus depreciation, amortization, and other noncash charges. Cash flow is a popular way to see how well a company is performing, excluding distortions caused by accounting. The P/CF ratio is probably the most valuable metric we can use across borders, as it does not rely as heavily on a unified accounting standard to be effective—the P/CF ratio standard should be the same from one company to another, *regardless* of the country in which a given company is doing business, because, in the end, cash is cash. The calculation for the P/CF ratio is simply the stock price *divided* by the operating cash flow per share, but there are thousands of web sites across the globe that will give you this information for free. A Google search of "China Mobile price to cash flow ratio" told us that the P/CF for CHL is 7.8. We did not even have to click the link to get the ratio.

Enterprise Value (EV) to EBITDA Ratio

The EV/EBITDA (Enterprise Value/Earnings Before Interest, Taxes, Depreciation and Amortization) ratio is a multiple that is often used in parallel with, or as an alternative to, the P/E ratio. It compares the value of a debt-free business to earnings before interest, taxes, and so forth. The EV component includes the cost of paying off debt, while EBITDA measures profits before interest and before the non-cash costs of depreciation or amortization.

EV/EBITDA is more difficult to calculate, but you do not necessarily need to calculate the ratio because you can readily find it for free across the Internet. Another quick Google search shows us that Vodafone (VOD) has an EV/EBITDA multiple of 7.53. Once again, this ratio is of little value in a vacuum, and needs to be compared against those of competitors, as well as that of its own history, to have real value.

The main advantage of EV/EBITDA over the P/E ratio is that it is unaffected by a company's capital structure. Consider what happens if a company issues shares and uses the money it raises to pay off its debt: usually, the earnings fall and the P/E looks higher (i.e., the shares look more expensive). However, in this same scenario, the EV/EBITDA should remain unchanged. Ultimately, the EV/EBITDA ratio allows for the ideal circumstance of a fair comparison of companies with different capital structures.

Technical Company Analysis There is not much to expand on here with respect to individual stocks, versus the country and industry analysis we gave you earlier in the chapter. All of the same lessons you learned in the previous lessons also apply to individual stocks. You can identify trends in stocks the same way you would with industries; relative analysis is every bit as important here, and is formulated the same way. Additionally, the price patterns you learn about in Chapter 6 on currency trading also apply to individual stocks, as well as to the indices themselves.

At this time, we want to readdress relative analysis with you to show you how it applies to individual stocks. There are really two ways you can compare a company on performance. One way is to compare it to its own industry, while the other is to compare it to other companies in the group. Let us run through an example. Say you have performed your entire top-down analysis and have come to the conclusion that the global economies are going to be slowing, and decide that you want to be less aggressive in your hedge fund; you further believe the defensive nature of the grocery industry means that it is a good place to invest right now anyway, and you have narrowed down your potential investment targets to two companies: Delhaize Group (DEG) out of Belgium, and Kroger Corp (KR) out of the United States. We are also going to assume that you have done your fundamental research and determined that both companies are comparable. Therefore, your ultimate decision as to which company to invest in will hinge on the results of your application of technical analysis. Let us go to the exhibits.

Exhibit 4.26 is a relative performance chart that displays DEG versus the Dow Jones Food Retailers and Wholesalers Index (you can look up the symbols for these stocks and issues at www.StockCharts.com). As you can see from the right side of the chart, DEG is outperforming the index, which tells us it is a good candidate for investment. We know we want to be in the grocery sector, and have identified a company in DEG that is performing better than the sector as a whole. Although the stock was not performing well for the first half of the chart, the trend has turned and DEG is now resolutely outperforming its index.

Exhibit 4.27 shows the relative performance of KR versus the same Dow index. As you can see, the long-term trend is very positive for KR versus the index, but in the near term, KR has been tapering off against its benchmark.

Finally, let us compare DEG versus KR to see which of the two is outperforming the other. To do this, we insert the symbol "DEG:KR" into the

EXHIBIT 4.26 Relative Performance Chart of Belgium's Delhaize Group (DEG) Versus Dow Jones Food Retailers and Wholesalers Index from August 2006 to August 2009
Source: StockCharts.com.

EXHIBIT 4.27   Relative Performance Chart of Kroger Corp (KR) Versus Dow Jones Food Retailers and Wholesalers Index from August 2006 to August 2009
Source: StockCharts.com.

Sharpchart portion of the site. As you can see in Exhibit 4.28, DEG was lagging KR for the first portion of the chart, as indicated by the down arrow, but the recent trend has changed and we would select DEG for our hedge fund over KR. We made this decision because, on a relative basis, DEG is much stronger than KR, as evidenced by the sharply trending *up* arrow on the right side of the exhibit.

As to the oversight of a global portfolio through comprehensive analysis, the use of same allows us to manage many of the risks so frequently cited as representing problems for foreign investors. Certainly, onerous tax requirements and the risks of adverse currency exchange fall outside the realm of effective mitigation through equity issue analysis, but in terms of the broad investment evaluation of regions, nations, sectors, and companies, the intelligent and consistent application of the methodologies and specific techniques described herein afford one the ability to successfully transcend cultural, informational, and accounting risks to a large degree. It is precisely because we spend so much time on these techniques that we

EXHIBIT 4.28 Relative Performance Chart of Delhaize Group (DEG) Versus Kroger Corp (KR) from August 2006 to August 2009
Source: StockCharts.com.

do not dwell inordinately on separate, extended discussions of risk management. It is your adherence to the daily review of your global portfolio using key metrics and technical analysis, all against a personal backdrop of global economic and sociopolitical awareness that will standardize your portfolio management, regardless of which global markets you choose to focus on.

CHAPTER 5

Global Fixed-Income Investment Concepts

A s manager of your own hedge fund, you have a wide variety of instruments to consider for inclusion in your portfolio. Although it is likely that equities will serve as your primary tools, you should be able to find a useful role for bonds, as well. Many who have invested exclusively through equities do not know much about bonds, except for the basics. Our outlook has always remained that an instrument that is perfectly investable and accessible by the individual investor is an instrument worth considering.

To most, fixed-income securities are not nearly as exciting as equities because they do not offer the same potential for supersonic returns, but that is a bit deceiving. In terms of an asset class that can achieve equity-competitive returns in the right climate, bonds are an excellent complement to the other asset classes that compose your hedge fund. For example, at this writing, there are excellent opportunities brewing globally in the investment-grade corporate bond sector; we are talking about senior debt of terrific quality that is proving to be the beneficiary of improving valuations throughout a variety of industries and companies around the world; this circumstance is accompanied by a marked increase in the issuance of global government bonds, which in turn is laying the foundation for investors to move out of government debt and into high-yield corporates that have an increasingly appealing level of creditworthiness. As a matter of fact, the spreads in investment-grade debt are ideal as we speak, and we are looking at reliable yields on corporates in the neighborhood of 8 percent, which, as we suggested earlier, is going to be competitive with equity returns for the foreseeable future. We want you to draw two conclusions from this part of the discussion: (1) that bonds can indeed outperform stocks at various times in the broad economic cycle; (2) but also that bonds are a perfect representation of a hedge fund-appropriate investment, particularly when you remember that the overall investment purpose of a hedge fund is to limit risk, preserve capital, and maximize returns under any and all given market conditions.

WHAT MAKES GLOBAL BONDS THE PERFECT HEDGE FUND INVESTMENT?

Maybe "perfect" is not the word we really mean to use; maybe it is "perfectly typical." The point is that when you look at what a hedge fund is supposed to do—as we said earlier, keep volatility and overall risk limited, while also prioritizing capital preservation and realizing not just excess returns but *positive* returns in any given market condition—the inherent profile of a global bond's investment advantages shows the asset class to be hedge fund appropriate. Bonds offer the fund manager an opportunity to realize three essential benefits that speak directly to satisfying the goals of a hedge fund: the benefit of diversification that is so important in the manager's efforts to control portfolio risk; the benefit of income that helps to improve the portfolio's total return; and the benefit of broad protection in poor economies that impact the investor in terms of the manager's portfolio as well as in his or her standing as a participant in the overall economy.

Diversification

Diversification is so important to investing, and a feature that receives so much emphasis, we sometimes forget that ultimately we are supposed to be investing for *return*; the concentration on diversification has gained so much gravitas that we occasionally think we are supposed to assemble portfolios just to see in how disparate a fashion the assembled asset classes can move, and nothing more. The reality is that achieving excess (and, hopefully, *positive*) returns in any given market climate *is* largely a function of diversification, and vice versa. The inherent diversification element to a bond is that it moves in a largely countercyclical fashion to other portfolio elements, particularly equities. Bonds have a solid history of noncorrelative relationships with equities, to include *negatively* correlated relationships. The continued expansion of the global bond markets (global bonds comprise more than 50 percent of the total fixed-income marketplace), to include rapid growth of fixed-income opportunities in the emerging markets countries, only enhances the opportunities to maximize

EXHIBIT 5.1	Correlation to Key Indexes of Citigroup WGBI, ex-U.S., from 9/30/04 to 9/30/07

	Citigroup WGBI Non-$ (unhedged US$)
S&P 500	.03
LB U.S. Aggregate	.38
MSCI EAFE (US $)	.33
MSCI Emerging Markets (US $)	.21
Dow Jones Wilshire REIT	.04
Dow Jones-AIG Commodity	.28
LB High-Yield Corporate	.16

Source: Morningstar Principia.

diversification throughout the world; the component countries and regions, at their respective levels, will frequently find themselves in the midst of differing market cycles, which give the global bond investor both a lot of homework—but also a lot of opportunity. Exhibit 5.1 provides one illustration of the low correlation; the data presented shows the correlation of key indexes with that of the Citigroup World Government Bond Index, ex-U.S. (no U.S. representation).

Income

Bonds are the quintessential income investment, which means that if you wish to include a reliable income stream as a part of your total return efforts, you cannot likely get far without them. Investing for income is something that always falls out of fashion during times of breathless climbs by equities, but the hedge fund approach, thankfully, demands that you adhere to a portfolio discipline that will ensure you do not ever completely stray from this benefit. As with diversification, the income feature has been greatly enhanced with the accessibility to more remote opportunities around the world. Weakness in income streams from certain markets can be compensated by stronger income streams in others. Some investors eschew bonds as income sources, opting instead for dividend stocks (and succumbing to their equity biases), but in terms of relying on the income stream as a source of total return, the fund manager needs to include bonds; although we have always known, and sometimes seen, suspension of dividend payments historically, the Great Recession of 2008–2009 has reminded us that the threat does exist. Aside from companies that have not eliminated dividends outright, there is a large number that have cut them; at this writing, dividend payments in 2009 are expected to decline by 22.6 percent in the course of the calendar year (source: S&P). The point is, if you want income, you need true income investments, and the long-standing record of foreign bonds to generate quality income where U.S. Treasuries cannot is one excellent reason to look overseas *for* that income.

Insulation from General Economic Weakness

We mentioned earlier the havoc that has been wreaked on divided stocks during the Great Recession—that is but one of the many forms of pounding that equities take in a weak economy. The bottom line is that when stocks are weak, there is both a lower income stream as well as lower share price overall, which means that stocks become more diminished as sources of money for strapped investors; the bond income remains, however. Broad weakness is evidenced at other levels, and bond investments can be reliable backstops in those spots, as well. For example, the lower rates of inflation and even deflationary pressures that result from weakness translate into greater appeal for bond income as its buying power increases. For those who have maintained a portfolio of bonds, the additional insulation comes in the form of an appreciation in bond value as the slowdown leads to stimulative interest rate cuts. As with the benefits of diversification and income, the general benefit outlined here becomes more accessible when viewed through the prism of the international fixed-income investor, who has multiple markets to penetrate for beneficial yield opportunities

Exhibit 5.2 indicates measurements of return, with associated measurements of volatility, on behalf of key, recognizable indexes. You can notice the relatively favorable numbers reflected for both global government bonds in calendar year 2008, and for both emerging markets bonds and global government bonds during the indicated 10-year period. On the basis of *risk-adjusted* return (per the Sharpe Ratio; more about that later), the global government bond index cited here offered the best return for calendar year 2008, while the emerging markets bond index noted offered the best return for the 10-year period; to boot, the global government bond index was the only one that yielded positive returns in both periods cited.

One of the features that can make or break your portfolio is your willingness to establish benchmarks and, by association, risk limits in all applicable asset classes, and that is probably more important with regard to your international bond component as it is to anything else. Global bonds, as Exhibit 5.2 indicates, have the potential to serve as a highly rewarding part of your holdings, but they require great attention to detail to account for the variety of influential exposures—large enough when looking simply *intra*-country—that can conspire to limit returns on an asset class not predisposed to capital accumulation. For example, currency management can be an important determinant of global bond return, and how you decide to implement it is a significant consideration. While your hedge fund

EXHIBIT 5.2	Returns and Volatility for Key Indexes for Calendar Year 2008 as well as 12/31/1998–12/31/2008

| | **2008** | | **10-Year Period** |
	Returns	**Volatility**	**Returns**	**Volatility**
Global Government Bonds	12.00%	9.61%	5.95%	7.91%
Emerging Markets Bonds	−10.91%	15.00%	10.17%	10.56%
High-Yield Bonds	−25.91%	11.51%	2.19%	10.43%
Commodities	−42.80%	40.97%	10.13%	24.80%
REITs	−37.57%	76.00%	7.73%	20.32%
MSCI World	−41.85%	32.66%	0.23%	15.77%
S&P 500	−37.00%	41.29%	−1.38%	15.15%

Source: Bloomberg LP.
Note: Global government bonds represented by the J.P. Morgan Global Government Bond Index; emerging markets bonds represented by the J.P. Morgan Emerging Markets Bond Index (Global); high-yield bonds are represented by the Citigroup High Yield Index; commodities represented by the S&P Goldman Sachs Commodity Index; REITs are represented by the Dow Jones Equity REIT Index; MSCI World is represented by the MSCI All Country World Free Index.

style means that you will likely include currencies as a stand-alone asset class anyway, and therefore limit, to some degree, your need to hedge your foreign bond exposures, that does not mean you can abandon the idea altogether, as your separate currency plays may well stand outside of the purview of your bond holdings, and so you will need to decide how to manage that volatility *specifically*.

Before we expand this discussion, we want to note a few things at the outset. Given the scope of the subject matter in general, we had to decide how we wanted to present the material. A thorough treatment of bonds would result in a chapter that is the size of a book, and we are not afforded that time and space latitude here. Accordingly, we had to decide on an approach, and have chosen to emphasize broad concepts of portfolio assembly and management that can serve as a compass to assist you in selecting and monitoring your best fixed-income options. On that note, the ideas outlined here are perhaps most relevant to investors in individual bonds, but they are also highly relevant to those who will access global fixed-income opportunities via the wealth of mutual funds, ETFs, and other collective schemes that exist. The principles differ not at all, but the way in which you access your bonds may alter, to a degree, the level of application. One of the convenient aspects of examining the particulars of global bond index and closed-end ETFs, for example, is that you can see what management is doing at present and conveniently access the info from the snapshots provided by the fund profiles. Once again, we often utilize sites like Morningstar (www.morningstar.com) and ETFConnect (www.etfconnect.com), which allow us the ability to augment our own analysis by providing easy ways to see what others are doing, and thus provide us with another view of the global bond from the perspective of fund managers.

DETERMINING THE PURPOSE OF YOUR FOREIGN BOND COMPONENT

One of the most important determinations you have to make at the outset of assembling your global bond portfolio is deciding on the specific purpose, or role, of your allocation to foreign bonds. You have two choices, and they are the usual ones: diversification or return. We know as investors that the two are not only *not* mutually exclusive, but are actually largely functions of one another. The issue is not that someone seeking diversification is not also in demand of a good return, and vice versa; the issue is that with the array of available global fixed-income options, as well as the different bond management styles that can be implemented, ascertaining on which goal you place the greater priority *first* will then determine how your portfolio is formulated.

If you are more interested in adding diversification to your hedge fund and lowering the overall volatility, you will be more inclined to open positions that mirror one of the key global bond benchmark indexes and hold those positions for longer periods of time. If, on the other hand, you are more interested in return, you may be okay with shorter-term positions that fall, at times, outside of the parameters of your selected benchmark index. In the end, this is largely a question of risk tolerance, where the more risk-averse hedge fund manager is going to want to opt to "stay within the lines" of his or her benchmark more rigorously than the return-oriented investor, who will want the flexibility necessary to chase returns on the basis of instrument or alternative investment style. In the end, many money managers (ourselves included) opt for a mix within the foreign bond portfolio that presents some tactical, return-oriented plays against the broader backdrop of a more benchmark-oriented strategic allocation. We discuss this in greater detail later on.

Discipline

Global bond investing is replete with volatility, and as such you need to have a good investment discipline in place as you approach it. We talk about investment discipline frequently, in one form or fashion, throughout this chapter, and one of the areas where it is so important is when you *begin*, as you have to select your parameters and investigate the wide variety of choices you have to make in several key areas. There are several component areas for which you have to establish your investment parameters as a global bond investor, including the countries/regions you are open to considering, the kinds of fixed-income securities into which you will invest, how you plan to handle currency risk, and over what sort of time frame you expect to evaluate your bond portfolio.

Selecting a Global Fixed-Income Benchmark

Professional investors do not simply invest—they target benchmarks and then work on achieving returns *in excess* of the benchmark's returns. One of the hallmarks of investment discipline, therefore, is centering on the benchmark. The selection of the benchmark is one of the most important decisions an investor makes, because it serves as the basis for his decisions in portfolio composition and management. The benchmark is particularly useful for the hedge fund–type manager or other money manager who seeks to be more active, because benchmark indexes, by their very natures, are indicative of a more passive, buy-and-hold approach to investing. The active manager seeks to exceed the returns of selected benchmarks through various strategic and tactical management styles. In the world of global fixed income, there are two benchmark indexes that are used more frequently than any others. They are the Barclays Global Aggregate Bond Index, and the Citigroup World Government Bond Index. The Barclays Index was formerly known as the Lehman Global Aggregate, and is one of the most widely accepted and tracked benchmarks throughout the global bond universe, while the Citigroup WGBI is composed of the most relevant and most liquid government bond markets in the world that also offer, at a minimum, an investment-grade rating. Although these two indexes are among the most broadly quoted and tracked by global bond professionals, the world of international bond indexes continues to expand as the size of a global bond's investable universe expands. For example, the rapid expansion and demonstrated resilience of many emerging markets has beckoned investor interest in their debt securities. To that end, J.P. Morgan has created several emerging markets bond indexes: their standard index, EMBI, which includes only Brady bonds, as well as EMBI+, which gauges Bradys, Eurobonds, and other sovereign debt instruments. J.P. Morgan has several other EM bond indexes, including the Corporate Emerging Markets Bond Index, which tracks U.S.-denominated corporate bonds that are issued by emerging markets countries.

The beautiful thing for fixed-income investors is that index development appears to be sufficiently keeping pace with the desire for global market expansion, so it is unlikely that you will be unable to find a target benchmark for use with your fund.

Specific Considerations in Selecting the Most Appropriate Benchmark

As we said, you have many indexes from which to choose, and that number will only grow as more nations aggressively seek to be the recipients of more foreign investment. For you as the fund manager, there are several reasons why proper selection is so important. For one thing, some benchmarks are more appropriate to basic investment objectives than others. Benchmarks that are made up of higher credit quality instruments with shorter durations are not going to be good for the more tactical investor principally seeking higher returns and willing to accept a higher level of volatility. On that note, the benchmark you select should match your broader risk/return objectives. Efforts at achieving excess returns, whether you are speaking of equities or bonds, are functions of establishing the right comfort zones at the outset. This is why the Barclays Global and Citigroup World indexes referenced earlier are so universally tracked by managers. The portfolio makeup of each, which is larger, more developed markets throughout the world, allow enough room for managers to add value with more tactical strategies and positions that are not too risky. Tracking a corporate emerging markets index would not afford you the same opportunities relative to the baseline. Also, you have to pay some attention to the consequences of a capitalization-weighted index; you may find yourself tracking a benchmark that has a stronger weighting in a market that causes you to violate your diversification parameters and/or exhibits subpar performance, like Japan, with its historically low yields; as an alternative, you might opt for the Pimco Global Advantage Bond Index, rolled out in 2009, which is a GDP-weighted index, and favors newer markets in the midst of rapid development but for which the growth in the size of their capital markets and market capitalizations have not kept pace. Also, note that benchmarks come in all styles as far as hedging is concerned, and it will be your chosen emphasis on diversification, total return, or some of both that will guide you to whatever determination you make on that basis, as well.

There are also a variety of other considerations. For example, what about liquidity requirements? If you want to maintain high liquidity in the foreign bond portion of your portfolio, you will surely want to use a shorter-term (duration) benchmark. Conversely, if you have little interest in liquidity and are seeking higher returns, you can opt for benchmarks that reflect that style. If you have inflation concerns, or simply wish to track a benchmark that is composed of inflation-indexed bonds, then your benchmark selection will have to take *that* into account. Inflation-indexed bonds are now issued by a fairly wide number of markets, including France, Germany, Italy, Japan, and Sweden, to name just a few; you can choose from several, including the Barclays World Government Inflation-Linked Index, and even the Barclays Emerging Market Government Inflation-Linked Bond Index, which opens up the inflation-linked world to emerging markets debt investors who would like to target countries like Argentina, Brazil, Poland, South Korea, and Turkey. The wider availability of inflation-linked debt is directly attributable to those managers who place a premium on diversification, many of whom can be found managing pension funds and thus interested principally in wealth preservation.

In the end, there are several characteristics that compose a good benchmark, including:

Low Turnover Rate—As we said earlier, benchmark indexes are usually more representative of passively managed, buy-and-hold types of investment styles. This is what you want. Not only is it difficult to track a benchmark where the investments change frequently, but it makes your effort at achieving excess returns more difficult.

Investability—The selected index must be composed of instruments that you as a fund manager can actually access in some form or fashion.

The additional significant characteristics are related, one way or another, to the issue of transparency and ready access to key information. For example, a useful benchmark has to be one for which the underlying components and characteristics can be readily accessed and viewed—the securities in the benchmark, to include weightings and other important features, must be clear. Data on the benchmark should be readily accessible and should include a history of daily prices as well as a wealth of historical returns that make it functional to you.

In the end, your best sources for bond benchmarks are going to be your own personal Internet searches; that is what we do. The truth is that there is not really a great, comprehensive resource of global bond benchmarks that gives you everything you want in one place. Index Universe (www.indexuniverse.com) is not bad, but you will likely use a variety of resources to obtain the most up-to-date information on the most current and useful indexes. Most places that offer more detailed information do so for their own proprietary indexes, like Morningstar (www.morningstar.com) and FTSE Group (www.ftse.com). Our homework on this front involves regularly searching for markets in which we have a preliminary investment interest, based on our initial evaluation of macroeconomic fundamentals, and going from there. You should also keep a close watch on new developments in the ETF markets, as occasionally we see a new ETF unveiled on behalf of an index of which we were not previously aware. In the world of bonds, you find that your homework is never really finished.

CURRENCY MANAGEMENT

Investing outside of home markets always results in exposures to foreign currencies, to be sure, but the matter of currency exposure to bond investors is particularly important. Although a fund manager nowadays will look to currencies as a separate instrument and thereby mitigate, to some degree, the need for specific currency management of bond positions (for those inclined to hedge), the nature of bond investing is such that many managers still have to make ongoing determinations about whether, or how much, to hedge the foreign bonds in the portfolio. The reality is that the volatility in foreign exchange markets is such that it actually dwarfs the inherent volatility that occurs naturally in bond markets, so it remains a significant dynamic of global bond investment returns, regardless of how it is treated by the manager.

In an "all or nothing" world, if you wish to manage your global bonds with an eye to enhancing total returns, you will likely prefer to remain unhedged more often than not so as to capitalize on the favorable exchange movements among currencies. On the other hand, if you prefer to prioritize the benefit of risk reduction within your portfolio, you will certainly lean toward hedging, although, at first glance, a hedged foreign bond portfolio is going to be more highly correlated to the U.S. bond market than an unhedged portfolio; it is the *lower standard deviation* realized from the hedged portfolio (in comparison to the exclusively U.S. bond portfolio) that serves as the source of the diminished risk.

You also have the option of *partially hedging* your portfolio; the returns of partially hedged portfolios, analysis shows, offer solid diversification with just a minor concession in return. Let us look at some data compiled on behalf of the Citigroup WGBI from 1985 to 2002 for some insight in Exhibit 5.3. (In the interest of full disclosure, we have sampled a portion of the data provided from the original source exhibit, and not all of it, in the interest of providing an expedient illustration.)

The application of the Sharpe Ratio, which is a measurement of the risk-adjusted return of a portfolio, demonstrated in the earlier-referenced analysis that a 50 percent hedged portfolio can indeed split the difference in risk and return. By the way, let us spend a minute or two *talking* about

EXHIBIT 5.3	Hedged, 50 Percent Hedged, and Unhedged Returns from 1985 to 2002 on Behalf of Citigroup WGBI		
	WGBI (unhedged), Ex-U.S.	**WGBI (hedged), Ex-U.S.**	**50% Hedged**
Return	10.66%	8.49%	9.69%
Volatility	10.4%	3.4%	6.2%
Sharpe Ratio	0.47	0.82	0.64

Source: Exhibit 49-1 in Christopher B. Steward, J. Hank Lynch, and Frank Fabozzi, "International Bond Portfolio Management," Chapter 49 in Frank J. Fabozzi (ed.), *The Handbook of Fixed Income Securities* (McGraw-Hill, 2005).

the Sharpe Ratio, as it can be a useful tool when you go to compare and contrast the securities, both actual and considered, in your portfolio, and something of real utility when comparing performances of assets hedged to varying degrees. Simply put, it is determined by looking a portfolio's excess return over and above its risk-free rate, and *dividing* that figure by the standard deviation of the excess returns realized. A higher ratio indicates better risk-adjusted returns, but the figures are not absolute, but always relative.

$$S(x) = (rx - \text{Rf})/\text{StdDev}(x)$$

where: x is the investment
rx is the average rate of return of x
Rf is the ideal rate of return of a risk-free security
$\text{StdDev}(x)$ is the standard deviation of rx

Your choice of asset of risk-free return is up to you, but often the shortest-maturity T-bill (3-month) is what is selected as the benchmark in this case. Although this type of instrument surely has a small amount of volatility, note that a more accurate reading will likely be realized if you select an instrument of the same duration as the one to which it is being compared.

We know that the Sharpe Ratio has its problems, including the fact that it is calculated using historical returns, but it is also a largely useful tool, especially when used in conjunction with a variety of other methods of analysis.

Let's look at a quick example. If you have an unhedged portfolio that returns 15 percent with a standard deviation (SD) of 12 percent, a 50 percent hedged portfolio that returns 12 percent with an SD of 9 percent, and a fully hedged portfolio that returns 7 percent with an SD of 5 percent, you need to compare the three to see which return is better on a risk-adjusted basis. Using Sharpe, let's use a 5 percent instrument (for ease of calculation) as our risk-free instrument. Plugging in the numbers, the unhedged gives a Sharpe of .83, the 50 percent hedged yields a Sharpe of .77, and a fully hedged produces a Sharpe of .40. In our contrived example, the unhedged was the better deal (and the 50 percent hedged split the difference), but the point is that you have an ongoing way of determining the relative benefit of hedging your portfolio at different points on the time spectrum.

Awareness of Risk Limitations

Managing in terms of risk factors also involves managing in terms of return. On that note, the subjects covered here as subjects of risk control will also be discussed throughout the chapter in terms of maximizing return. There is a wealth of risk factors with which bond investors must be aware, and we want to take some time to discuss those that have a particular relevance to the *global* bond investor.

In order to manage with the appropriate discipline, you need to establish solid risk parameters with respect to the wide variety of risk issues that exist on behalf of a global bond portfolio. There are 10 risk categories we want to mention here as examples of those for which you need to account. Some of this stuff can be a little technical, and the details for some of it fall outside the scope of this chapter, but we want to mention it, anyway.

Benchmark Risk   Benchmark risk refers to the risk associated with selecting the wrong index to track and evaluate in your attempts to achieve excess returns. A simple example would be the selection of an emerging markets index comprised of corporate debt against which to compare your portfolio made up primarily of developed market government debt. Again, that is an easy example used for illustrative purposes, but note that the growing number of global bond indexes means that you have more segmented choices and more derivative indexes from a broader index; using a broader index like the Barclays Global Aggregate may not be the best choice if you are doing something more specific with your portfolio makeup, like targeting Asian corporate debt singularly, so you want to be careful that your relationship between benchmark and portfolio is a case of "like for like." When in doubt, choose as your benchmark an index that is broader in scope and focuses on higher-quality debt (like using the Citigroup WBGI), so that you have more opportunity to exceed its returns.

Interest Rate Risk   Interest rate risk is a constant in fixed-income investing, and something that is managed through the cooperative use of real return (returns after inflation) relationships and economic analysis of global and regional/country behaviors to make decisions as to duration; it is ultimately the management of duration that allows us to control this risk category. Duration is a weighted average of the income stream(s) from a bond or bond portfolio; the value-weighted duration of the underlying bonds. Put another way, duration is a measurement of how many years it takes for the price of a bond to be repaid by its internal cash flows. Duration and maturity are sometimes used interchangeably as terms, which is not correct, but in a general sense they are the same thing because as rates move up, the prices of bonds with higher durations/longer maturities will drop.

Yield Curve Risk The yield curve is a graphical representation of the relationship between yields and maturities. Normal yield curves look as the one pictured in Exhibit 5.4, as shorter maturities have lower yields while longer maturities have higher yields; generally, as seen here, the curve takes the shape of a fairly even arc, the interest rate plotted are for maturities that have some noticeable differences between them (e.g., the 3-month, 2-year, 5-year, and 30-year U.S. Treasuries, which is the most benchmarked yield curve).

Again, the yield curve in Exhibit 5.4 is typical-looking. Inverted yield curves, which move from higher to lower plots, indicate higher short-term yields and lower longer-term yields; flat yield curves indicate essentially no yield differences between shorter and longer maturities, which tells the investor there is no point in holding longer-term bonds for the same yield benefit. Inverted and flat yield curves are both bad (usually); inverted

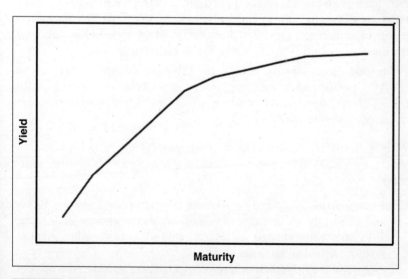

EXHIBIT 5.4 Normal Yield Curve

curves indicate that a recession is on the horizon, while flat curves, although sometimes indicative of transitions to upward slopes, usually signal a slowdown in the economy and movement toward a recession.

We discuss yield curve more fully a little later, but yield curve risk is a disadvantageous move in interest rates as reflected by the shape of the yield curve (i.e., nonparallel yield curve movements). It is another representation of interest rate risk; put another way, it is the risk that changes in interest rates will exert different influences on same-type bonds with different maturities. Yield curve risk is basically controlled in four associated ways: economic analysis, break-even analysis, partial duration analysis, and principal components analysis.

1. *Economic Analysis*: Economic analysis broadly refers to the top-down style of using global, region, and country macroeconomic information to determine possible changes to yield curve shape.

2. *Break-Even Analysis*: This analysis is performed to see at what point the returns of different instruments are the same, and deciding from there the best course to realize excess return. For example, if Bond A pays 5 percent for one year and Bond B pays 7 percent for two years, which do we choose? If our analysis of the yield curve tells us that rates will be rising, we may decide to stick with the shorter maturity and reinvest at a higher rate for the second year in order to beat, with an average, Bond B's 7 percent for two years.

3. *Partial Duration Analysis*: This analysis is performed to measure the change in a bond's, or bond portfolio's, value, when here are movements at different points on the yield curve. Using partial duration, a hedge fund manager can keep duration constant and choose bonds on the basis of an anticipated change in the yield curve.

4. *Principal Components Analysis*: Principal Components Analysis (PCA) is performed to measure movements of the yield curve on the basis of level, slope, and curvature, which are regarded as the sources of variations on returns.

What follows is a list of the more impactful types of risk associated with the yield curve, and with global fixed-income investing, more generally.

Convexity Risk: Convexity measures the curvature between prices and yields; the measurement demonstrates the change in duration as interest rates change, and is managed with option-adjusted analysis and scenario analysis.

- *Option-Adjusted Analysis (OAS)*: This measures the relative value of a bond that includes an embedded option (EO), like a call provision. EOs tend to make projected returns more difficult and make for more interest rate risk because of the chances the option will be exercised. OAS analysis attempts to evaluate the future value of a bond by taking into account the option; ultimately, it is a way of standardizing bond comparisons by accounting for the embedded feature (callable bonds have higher yields because they *are* callable).

- *Scenario Analysis*: Scenario analysis is the measurement of how valuations will change in different market climates, in consideration of factors like anticipated inflation rate, growth, and geopolitical risk. In order for scenario analysis to be of value, you want to try to account for a limited number of variables together, and to be sure the variables actually *belong* together. For example, Treasury Inflation-Protected Securities (TIPS) are bonds that would be adversely impacted in a scenario where there exists strong economic growth in a country; that nation's central bank would invoke a tight monetary policy (raise short-term rates), and yield curves would flatten a bit. The higher yields and falling inflation would not bode well for the TIPS.

Sector/Asset Risk: This represents the risk associated with your fund investing in sectors and/or assets to a different degree from that represented by the benchmark. Additionally, sector risk also refers to the inherent risks associated with investing in corporate bonds that represent the primary sectors of the economy. For example, the utilities sector, as a whole, is going to be affected by government regulation and callability; the industrial sector will be influenced by a variety of factors, including broad changes in the economic cycle; and the financial services sector will be affected by a host of factors, including interest rate movement and unemployment, where higher unemployment generally curtails demand for mortgage loans. For each country whose debt markets you are considering penetrating, evaluating sector risk in this way is important.

Credit Risk: Credit risk is principally regarded as default risk. Concerns about default risk may lead someone to include only government bonds in their hedge fund, but with the increase in general market share attributed to a growth in nongovernment debt instruments, as well as the increase in the number of emerging markets countries finding representation on the corporate debt scene, the issue is now one of greater significance to the global fixed-income investor. To combat default risk, you must engage in due diligence that analyzes the credit standing of countries and companies, and your analysis must also include an evaluation of a country's political stability.

In addition to the risk of default, credit risk also concerns itself with the relative illiquidity of riskier securities. Said illiquidity can make it more difficult for you as a fund manager to make portfolio adjustments.

Reinvestment Risk: Reinvestment risk is generally managed through call risk analysis, which involves inventorying the callable bonds in your portfolio and estimating the amount of principal you expect to see returned when rates drop.

Liquidity Risk: Liquidity risk remains a function of bonds because the market for debt securities is so much thinner than it is for equities, and that risk is naturally more pronounced when you are dealing with less mature markets around the world. Investors who plan to hold until maturity are not terribly concerned with liquidity risk, nor are investors in investment-grade government debt securities, but the more active manager who seeks to take tactically based positions that may be designed for shorter holding periods has to be concerned with liquidity risk. You can decide to address this at the outset by dealing in more limited duration instruments when you transact in riskier obligations and/or markets.

Currency Risk: We discuss currency management in other areas of this chapter, so we simply indicate it here as an element of risk that is more pronounced for global bond investors.

Political Risk: Political risk, in the context of global investing, is often more broadly characterized as *country risk*. This is because the political risk that we normally consider in terms of the United States becomes wider in scope when regarding the potential challenges of investing in foreign markets, particularly when those markets are less mature. Viewed more narrowly, political risk may involve such things as the government's adjustment of a bond's tax structure, or any of a variety of regulatory actions. As your investing goes global and pure political risk becomes supplanted by country risk, you have to consider the overall political and economic conditions within a country. These risks will demand that you look at more easily identifiable cues, such as widely reported government instability of economic difficulties, as well as more guarded information like proposed changes in laws and cultural factors.

It should be noted, as with most forms of risk, there can be another side to political risk, the *opportunity* side. For example, back some years ago, Brazil found itself in a financial crisis when they devalued the currency in 1999. What happened in Brazil would take several pages to outline, but for our purposes, suffice it to say that Brazil was in serious trouble. The financial crises that afflicted Asia and Russia in 1997 and 1998 caused a contagion atmosphere that prompted investors to begin pouring out of Brazil, as well. In response, Brazil raised rates to an attractive level to keep the money from leaving the country.

As stability eventually returned to Brazil, rates went down, but those who purchased the high-paying bonds before stabilization made a killing. We often think of country risk solely in negative terms, which is understandable, but you have to be prepared to reap the potential, associated *rewards* of risk's other persona by stepping outside the box a little, doing your homework, and putting yourself in a position to capitalize on politically motivated fund movements in foreign countries.

Risk considerations as those outlined here receive some additional clarity when considered in terms of the compatibility of trading blocs. Trading blocs result from the subdivision of the total global bond market into groups of nations that share like characteristics and are thus highly correlated. The most common trading bloc divisions are the dollar bloc (Australia, Canada, New Zealand, and the United States), the European bloc, Japan, and the emerging markets. These global regions should receive your regional attention and analysis as your global macro view begins globally and starts to work its way down.

FORMULATING A PORTFOLIO MANAGEMENT CONSTRUCT

The methods by which you actually manage your fund in pursuit of excess returns are central to your success, and nothing about your global fixed-income success in this day and age will consistently come by chance. As we said, excess returns represent those that beat the benchmark, and there are some important ways that can be achieved, some more helpful than others. The key to effective management rests with discipline. Portfolio management will not be successful if you are disinclined to adhere to your established rules and paradigms. We have already spent some time discussing this idea in Chapter 4 as it relates to equities, and the principle is no different here. You can always change the investment discipline you establish, but you should always adhere to the discipline you select. Note that the importance of discipline is more about protecting your downside than it is maximizing your upside. This is particularly important when it comes to global bonds and bond markets, where the wide variety of variables and collateral factors, to include currency matters, can cause your fixed-income plays to become losers in no time.

As for the methods by which you manage your portfolio, the bond market will demand both a top-down and bottom-up style used concurrently with one another. Principally, global investing of any kind prioritizes top-down analysis, and that is no different here; the global macroeconomic trends are what one considers first when they are pondering moving outside of the United States, and that applies regardless of the asset class in which you are seeking to invest. The reality is that the global business cycle, in coordination with global geopolitical and socioeconomic machinations, will always be the first factor you consider when looking at regions or countries to penetrate.

The top-down approach is also important because the macroeconomic trends that are considered tell the tale not just for the present day and near term, but suggest where things will be in a few years. It is the evaluation of the trends in areas like shifting political winds in countries and regions, as well as associated economic trends, with which we begin, and we use this information to narrow our options to the point of identifying countries we like (for government securities), and then going one level further down to credit and industrial sectors (for corporate bonds); once we have made it to the sector level, our bottom-up analysis will get us the rest of the way to making specific security selections. Our top-down analysis is performed in terms of analyzing factors like duration, yield curve, and credit; from the bottom-up, we consider factors such as credit quality, supply, and liquidity. Let us dig into this a little further.

One of the habits you have to adopt is constantly looking to see how global activity affects particular markets. It requires you to be a student of world affairs, but we are here to tell you that you cannot be a successful global investor without doing just that. For example, as a top-down investor, you might notice (well, you *should* notice) that, at this writing, China and others have been buying U.S. Treasuries in significant numbers; that said, we also see that they are limiting their purchases to the short end of the yield curve. They are buying Treasuries with short-term maturities, and selling those with longer maturities. Perhaps these investors (China is not the only one) are unsure of the ability of the United States to repay their debts down the road, but the point is that these foreign economies have been propping up the U.S. dollar to keep their own currencies and exports strong. That said, more of this money is now heading into corporate debt securities of other countries in order to realize higher returns. The result of this trend from Treasuries to non-U.S. corporates has been the lowering of the risk premium, which means that you do not get extra credit for putting your money into lower quality companies. You, therefore, would ideally focus on higher quality companies; why wouldn't you? Additionally, giving up on the dollar in greater numbers means that non-U.S. currencies will look better. The conclusion to which we come, at this top level, is to look elsewhere for our bonds. From here, our search takes us to other markets to see which countries and sectors we like; we listen intently when we hear Russian President Medvedev's top economic adviser, Arkady Dvorkovich, suggest that the countries of BRIC (Chapter 1) are considering buying the bonds of one another. The BRIC countries have substantial financial reserves, and this kind of incestuous transaction could be significant. In the wake of Bretton Woods II, more nations are aggressively seeking alternatives to the dollar, and these movements could have profound effects for U.S. bond investors in need of higher yields.

Once your macroeconomic analysis gets you to sectors you favor, your bottom-up analysis might have you consider the creditworthiness of the companies you like within your targeted sectors. As you look in terms of high-end investment grade choices, you can easily gauge a standard for pricing and make buy and sell decisions accordingly.

Supply and demand is also part of the bottom-up process. As we said, our bottom-analysis is implemented once we have identified sectors we like, but now we have to evaluate the sectors and companies carefully. In terms of the sector, we like to evaluate, for example, if the sector's favorability means that it may borrow to finance expansion, we want to be sure that we notice that. What about existing debt? If a sector has existing debt that is maturing soon, it will need to be refinanced. In short, the overall favorability at the sector level is largely determined on the basis of the overall debt profile and how that profile influences the supply and demand factors. The same evaluations take place at the company level, as well; is an individual company that's subject to rapid growth shortly in need of financing its expansion activities? Does *it* have existing debt maturing soon that will need to be refinanced?

As you can see, the analysis of potential global bond investments requires far-reaching analyses that principally move in a top-down direction, but which also must have bottom-up components that allow for the best evaluation.

BOND MANAGEMENT STYLES

Money management approaches remain, broadly, in the categories of fundamental and technical analysis. We have covered technical analysis elsewhere in this book, so we do not dwell on it here, but it has value to the bond investor as it has value to the equities investor. Technical trends, complemented by relative strength indicators, can be a solid tool for the bond investor. That said, we are going to focus here on fundamental analysis, because that is *our* principal method of isolating global debt securities we like. The heavy dependence of bonds (and currencies) on global economic behavior means that we prioritize the movement of the overall cycle when seeking opportunities in this asset class. As U.S.-based investors seeking foreign exposure, our world is a little tougher right from the start. We have to monitor the macroeconomic activity globally, but must also do so in terms of regions (more like bond trading blocs) and countries; this means having to keep a close eye on a large number of economic cycles occurring at multiple levels, and the movements of these cycles, to include the behavior of the bond's single greatest influence, interest rates, will often move against one another.

We find that the most helpful way to manage this activity is principally with fundamental analysis, although not exclusively. The reality is that we use a combination of three management styles on behalf of our bond portfolio, while prioritizing fundamental analysis. We also apply technical analysis, usually of shorter-term trades, and also something we call "hunch trading," which means that we rely on some intuition to help make decisions at times. Trading on intuition is not baseless, however; we process our fundamental analysis and our technical, as appropriate, and if we see a trade we like based on an exit flow from the position, we may consider it partially on that basis—a somewhat contrarian approach, if you will. In the end, though, such decisions are not made unless they have some basis in fundamental or technical veracity.

Again, we get back to *discipline*. In order for us to be successful, we have to be willing to adhere to the discipline we formulate at all levels. This includes incorporating a specific discipline with regard to trading decisions. When you invest in accordance with your selected benchmark, you need only mirror the benchmark. However, in your quest for excess returns, which we discuss shortly, you need to be willing to adhere to entry and exit points on the basis of your discipline.

Management Applications

An ideal bond portfolio is composed of two broad allocation models that exist contemporaneously. In our case, the preponderance of the overall allocation is dedicated to *strategic* allocation, where the investments selected are done so with a longer-term holding period in mind, a period of *at least* several months. The selections on behalf of this allocation are made with the classic, top-down analysis we allude to frequently throughout this chapter. Because bonds are such slaves to the economic cycle at all levels, it is this cycle to which we adhere when considering our holdings for the foreseeable future. As for our tactical allocations, we allow for more flexibility in arriving at these selection decisions. Certainly, fundamental factors play a part in tactical allocations as well, as it would be difficult—impossible, really—to consider any bond holdings in any fashion that do not align at least generally with interest rate trends and other macroeconomic activity in a given country; that said, our tactical decisions are accorded substantial considerations on the basis of things like technical analysis, which we use a lot, as well as a greater influence of bottom-up considerations.

It is also important to note that we do not spend much time trying to predict interest rates; there is little evidence that attempts at trying to accurately predict interest rates have been a source of value to global investors. Rather, we like to perform an evaluation of global markets, broken down by country, and make allocations based on a totality of factors that act as a barometer for the given market's investment climate. In order to properly gauge the potential bond investability of global markets, we have to look at those that have piqued our curiosity on a preliminary basis by looking at each country, and putting it through a rigorous process of evaluation. The process is essentially the same for all markets, and once you engage in it and establish a rank order of countries to consider, you can begin to look at specific sources of alpha, which we outline later.

As a global bond investor, you have to become a bit of an economist, at least more so than you do with other asset classes. This is entirely due to the nature of how bonds work and what makes their price components react the way they do. There are a variety of fundamental factors that you will consider as you narrow down your list of ideal countries to penetrate. Among the most relevant of the factors are broad economic indicators, monetary policy, fiscal policy, and balance of payments, as well as the political factors we outlined within the context of our section on political risk. Note that whether you actually purchase individual bonds through your foreign brokerage account or opt for something less direct, like a mutual fund, ETF, or closed-end, you should become versed in how to properly evaluate your global fixed-income targets, regardless of the specific mechanism you choose with which to negotiate them.

> ***Economic Indicators:*** Simply defined, economic indicators are statistics about a nation's economy. The ultimate purpose of these statistics is to predict future performance of the economy, with an eye to making whatever possible adjustments can be made to avoid or limit weakness that appears on the horizon. "Economic indicators" is itself a general term that can mean something slightly different depending on who is using it and in what context, but the term normally refers, in one form or fashion, to data on unemployment, industrial production, retail sales, the Consumer Price Index (CPI, a measure of inflation), GDP, valuations in equities markets, and changes in the money supply (principally M2, which

is the broadest reading of the amount of money in circulation; it is a predictor of inflation because if the supply of money outpaces its use, inflation may be on the horizon). As a global fixed-income investor, you want to become a good student of these components with respect to each region and individual country. It will be your reading of these economic indicators that will go far to helping you identify the fertile, foreign markets for your bond transactions. An excellent resource to this end is the web site of the Conference Board (www.conference-board.org), which compiles and disseminates information on leading, coincident, and lagging economic indicators, and provides detailed information on the business cycle in the following countries and regions: United States, Australia, Euro Area (those European Union countries that participate in the common currency zone), France, Germany, Japan, Korea, Spain, and the United Kingdom.

Monetary Policy: Monetary policy is the control and oversight of money supply, money availability, and *cost* of money in a national economy, as determined by a government, central bank, or some combination of the two. The fundamental dynamic of monetary policy is the relationship between interest rates and money supply, with the goal to realize beneficial climates in the areas of overall economic growth, inflation, unemployment, and currency exchange. Monetary policy is chiefly used to manage inflation, which means that most nations have as their principal policy "inflation targeting." This policy is implemented primarily by interest rate changes indicated by a given nation's Central Bank. At this writing, you can find a list of the world's Central Banks, with direct links, at www.banknotes.com. For global bond investors, the relevance of monetary policy is its pronounced influence on interest rates in each country.

Fiscal Policy: Fiscal policy is the utilization of the taxing authority and government spending to control the economy; its effects are most acutely felt in the areas of total demand for goods and services (known as *aggregate demand*), income distribution, and allocation of resources. Fiscal policy is actually derived from the ideas of British economist John Maynard Keynes, whose Keynesian economics basically states that it is government intervention in the markets and monetary policy that is the best means of ensuring stability. Ideally, fiscal policy and monetary policy are used in coordination in the effort to consistently achieve the best overall economic climate within a country. The massive stimulus packages promoted by the United States and other national governments in the midst of the Great Recession are simple and obvious illustrations of fiscal policy in action. The desired outcome of such packages is job creation and wage enhancement, which hope to "prime the pump" and restart movement toward positive growth in the economy. Expansionary fiscal policy (greater government spending) can lead to a greater supply of bonds, which, in turn, can make gains in bonds more limited. The challenge for the global bond investor is to recognize the sometimes coincident movements in monetary policy and fiscal policy within a single country—like rate cuts (monetary) and increased spending (fiscal)—during recessions, which can result in yield volatility.

Balance of Payments: The measurement of balance of payments (BOP) exists as a means of determining how much money is flowing in and out of a country. The balance of payments is actually determined by measuring exports and imports of goods and services, as well as financial capital (money used by businesses to buy what is needed to produce goods or provide services) and capital transfers (acquisition/disposal of nonfinancial assets and assets not produced). Ideally, a country's BOP should be zero, signifying a perfect balance between credits and debits, but that does not really occur in practice. The BOP measurement, therefore, reveals surpluses and deficits, and also tells us where the source of the imbalance lies. The BOP is actually composed of three categories, each of which represents a different component of the measurement: the current account, the capital account, and the financial account. The current account is a measure of inflow/outflow of goods and services, as well as investment earnings; the capital account is the measure of capital transfers; and the financial account measures inflow/outflow associated with investment in stocks, bonds, real estate, and businesses, as well as government-owned assets, private assets overseas, and FDI (foreign direct investment). A BOP surplus signifies a net inflow, which can be construed as a sign of greater stability and a stronger currency; deficits translate chiefly into an overvalued currency, which, of course, are highly relevant issues for global bond investors.

IN SEARCH OF EXCESS RETURNS

The central focus of the active fund manager is the achievement of excess returns in the portfolio. Although there are several ways to potentially outperform the benchmark, we want to mention five that are among the most useful for accomplishing that goal: currency management, duration management, bond market selection, sector rotation, and extra-index trading.

Currency Management

Of all the mechanisms available by which to realize excess returns, the use of active, effective currency management certainly ranks as one of the best. The truth is that currency movements can be more impactful than bond market movements, so there is a basis for implementing an approach of substantive currency management. In fact, currency moves can easily swallow up the yield differences between foreign bonds and U.S. bonds, so you have to maintain "currency awareness."

A fund manager like yourself basically has three options when it comes to hedging: you can remain unhedged; you can fully hedge; or you can partially hedge. Some managers never hedge, while some always hedge. A lot of the "unhedged" fans point to the greater diversification that is both implied and usually realized by remaining unhedged, while the "always hedged" crown points to the clarity that results from remaining dollar-protected. For us, there is no such thing as an all-or-nothing approach, and that sort of dogma is misplaced in this realm, anyway. Currency management, we believe, is an ongoing, active process that relies on your willingness to actively pursue the appropriate analysis in order to decide if it is better to remain unhedged, or to hedge, at a given time. In a climate of appreciating foreign currency, you would ideally remain unhedged, and vice versa. The problem with always hedging, too, is that it has a cost, and those costs can eat into returns. This is especially true when you trade tactically, which, among other things, means more frequently and for shorter terms; the costs of hedging can become downright exorbitant (although a true tactical bond trader would hopefully also be inclined to manage currency movement separately, as well). In the end, you want to hedge, as appropriate, and remain unhedged the same way; this more than likely means that you will partial hedge based on currency climates, so you need to be prepared. To us, deciding to *always* hedge a bond portfolio or *never* hedge a portfolio is a little like asking, "Should people *always* wear raincoats when they leave the house, or should they *never* wear raincoats when they leave the house?" Most people would conclude that is a silly choice, and that the decision should be predicated on the condition of the weather now, as well as the expected condition of the weather throughout the remainder of the day. To us, that is how the consideration of hedging should be treated.

The key to successful currency management lies in the ability to successfully predict future spot rates. In other words, for currency management to add value to your portfolio, you are looking to get a handle on future exchange rates, which forwards and other, more typical mechanisms do not have a great record of doing. There are things you can do to help work around this, to include overweighting in currencies with high real rates, but we want to keep this more manageable for the typical investor, so we recommend hedging with currency options or futures, which we address more expansively in Chapter 8. Also, currency movements exhibit trend-oriented behavior, so utilizing the technical analysis of currency movements that we detail in Chapter 6 is an excellent reference. Accordingly, your best hedge is going to be the active trading of currency as outlined there.

Duration/Yield Curve Management

Management of duration is another tool by which excess returns can be realized. If analysis of the economic climate tells you that interest rates are likely to fall, then you will seek to lengthen the duration of your portfolio. Changes in the shape of the yield curve will prompt changes in duration, as price sensitivity is impacted by a steepening or flattening. Positive curve duration occurs with increased exposure to the 2- to 10-year maturity portion of the curve, while a portfolio with negative curve duration (higher short-term yields) has more exposure to the longer maturities. See Exhibit 5.5, a chart that illustrates negative duration.

One opportunity available to the global investor is the ability to manipulate durations within countries as conditions dictate, and do so in a fashion that leaves the portfolio's overall duration intact. Bullet and barbell duration management strategies are effective ways of addressing changes to the yield curve; a steepening yield curve in a country will yield superior results to the bullet strategy, while a flattening curve will see better

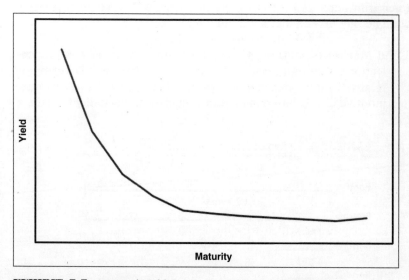

EXHIBIT 5.5 Inverted Yield Curve

EXHIBIT 5.6   Representation of Bullet Strategy

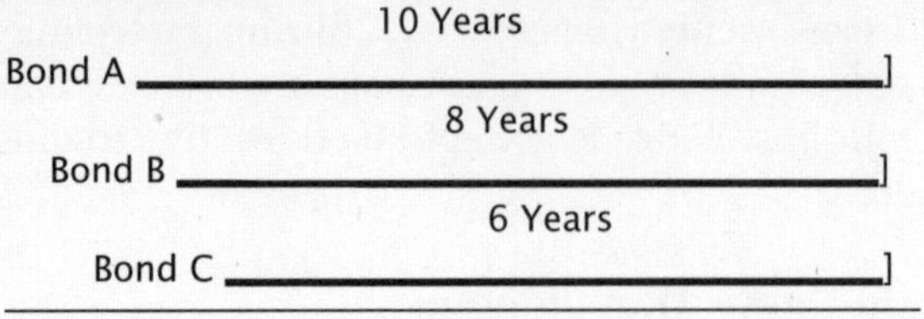

```
                        10 Years
        Bond A _____]
                         8 Years
         Bond B _____]
                          6 Years
            Bond C _____]
```

results from the barbell; in a climate where the yield curve is steepening upward, short-term yields are dropping while long-term yields are gaining, which means that your barbell structure—heavy on short- *and* long-term maturities—is getting crushed as you lose both ways.

Bullets   The purpose of the bullet strategy is to target a fixed point on the yield curve with the selected maturities/durations. Often, the strategy is implemented by purchasing the bonds at staggered intervals, which allows you to manage interest rate risk; for example, targeting a 10-year maturity by purchasing a 10-year, an 8-year two years later, and a 6-year two years after that (see Exhibit 5.6).

Barbells   With the barbell strategy, you buy long-term and short-term bonds, but not intermediate-term maturities. Your long-term barbell "end" means that you have secured competitive long-term rates, while the short-term maturities give you the flexibility to move out into something else if the bond market takes a hit (see Exhibit 5.7).

> **Bond Market Selection:** Along with currency management, the selection of the best-performing markets in an effort to overweight relative to the index can be a profitable strategy. This is as much intuitive as it is based in empirical evidence; the ability to achieve

EXHIBIT 5.7   Representation of Barbell Strategy

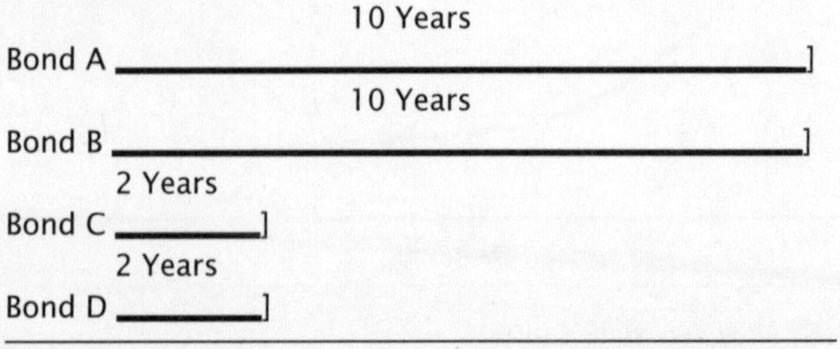

```
                        10 Years
        Bond A _____]
                        10 Years
        Bond B _____]
                2 Years
        Bond C _____]
                2 Years
        Bond D _____]
```

excess returns is going to be greatest in those areas where there is the most room to do so. The ability to access virtually any functional investment market, on a country basis, gives you a tremendous opportunity to add value to your fund.

Sector Rotation: Sector rotation can certainly serve as another source of alpha, although we are inclined to attribute to the strategy a lower weighting as far as its contribution toward realizing excess returns. The fact is that the significant differences that persist among countries and regions will always, in our opinion, trump the significance of sectors, for as long as those differences exist. When we talk about bond sectors, traditionally, we speak in terms of type, quality, and call feature, although a second, applicable definition of bond sectors is the industries that you target with fixed-income investing (industrials, utilities, financials, etc.). As for the former, the growth of the investable universe worldwide has caused a substantial growth in sectors available; for example, the corporate bond market has grown significantly since the advent of the European Monetary Union (EMU). This increased availability has caused a natural increase in opportunity to maximize returns. Your sector analysis has to include close attention to issues that can have great influence, like matters of leverage and liquidity. A sector that is highly leveraged and has poor liquidity in a poor economic environment is a cue that it may be a good candidate to see greater defaults.

Extra-Index Trading: Investing in markets outside of a given index has the potential to significantly elevate returns. Exhibit 5.8 represents the returns for the 10-year period from September 1993 to September 2003 for the J.P. Morgan Global Government Bond Index, ex-U.S., as well as a blend of the J.P. Morgan EMBI, EMBI+, and EMBI Global Indexes, characterized here as the EMD Index.

The significantly superior returns of the emerging markets debt index (blend) clearly shows that investing in emerging markets debt during these

EXHIBIT 5.8	Returns for J.P. Morgan Global Government Bond Index (ex-U.S.) and blend of J.P. Morgan EMBI, EMBI+, and EMBI Global Indexes, 09/1993 to 09/2003	
	1993–1998	**1993–2003**
J.P. Morgan GG Bond	4.63%	6.25%
EMD Index	16.86%	11.89%

Source: Morgan Stanley Investment Management.

time periods would have allowed the investment-grade government debt investor to enjoy excess returns. In order to determine which outside markets are most appropriate for a value-added effort, you have to begin by isolating all of them on the basis of the old-fashioned analysis that we mentioned earlier, which starts with a global look and that gets you to a more regional range of countries to consider. From there, you determine which specific markets are most favorable for a bond allocation, and go from there.

Your strategy as a fund manager in applying this excess return mechanism is to engage in top-down analysis of both the markets in which you are considering investing *away* from the benchmark, as well as the markets in the benchmark you are considering underweighting as a function of the application. Do not forget, as well, that you must establish currency trends for the related currencies on both sides of the equation in order to, first, confirm that the strategy should be applied here, but also to determine if you need to hedge at any level your out-of-index transactions.

CHAPTER 6

Making the Buck in Currency Trading

FOREX BACKGROUND

We will never forget our first experience with currency trading. We had been managing investment portfolios for roughly 15 years, and had traded more than a billion dollars of investable assets. Our portfolios bore good results as we managed to successfully match our wits against the unpredictability and intricacies of the global capital markets. We were not initially planning to take our client account dollars and trade currencies, but we thought we would take some of our personal dollars and do some trading. The experience was eye-opening. Understand, many of the fundamental factors that affect global stock markets are the same fundamental factors that affect the global currency markets. As well, many of the same technical patterns and indicators we use to trade stocks are also applicable to the currency world. However, the *speed* at which you can make or lose money in the currency markets makes this a completely different animal. Much of this volatility can be explained by the use of leverage we find in trading these currencies. Nonetheless, you want to be sure to put on your seatbelt before trading currencies. Harkening back to our initial experience, in our first five days of trading, we were up 40 percent. We thought we could do no wrong. In the next 48 hours, however, we lost 60 percent of our money. Trading in the foreign currency market is not for the faint of heart, and the undisciplined traders will quickly be dispatched to the woodshed. Later in the chapter, we go into greater detail with regard to trading strategies, risks, and the importance of investment discipline. For now, let us get our feet wet by looking more generally at the foreign exchange market.

Foreign currency trading is exciting for all of us because it gives an investor the opportunity to trade in the world's largest and most liquid market, the foreign currency market. An unbelievable $3.2 trillion changes hands on a daily basis and the foreign currency market moves exceptionally fast, with prices changing by the second. Outside of some indirect foreign central bank interference, no single event or institution can rule this market. It is truly "unmanipulatable" because of its sheer size, which assures investors that they are getting a fair shake.

The first question we need to answer is, "What is the Forex market?" The foreign exchange market (or Forex) is one of the largest and most liquid financial markets in the world. It includes trading among large banks, central banks, corporations, governments, and traders like you and us. The foreign exchange market that we see today started evolving during the 1970s when, from all over the world, countries gradually switched to a floating exchange rate away from their fixed rates, as per the Bretton Woods system. As a refresher, the Bretton Woods Accord of 1944 was established to stabilize the global economy after World War II and is generally accepted as the original beginning of the foreign exchange market. It created the concept of trading currencies against each other and the International Monetary Fund (IMF). Currencies from around the world were fixed to the U.S. dollar, which in turn was fixed to gold prices in hopes of bringing stability to global foreign currency events. Central banks were allowed to revalue their currency in the face of certain "imbalances," but other than that, the currencies all traded in a tight range. Eventually, the Accord failed, but it served its purpose to bring stability to the global currency markets while it was in effect.

The purpose of the Forex market is to facilitate trade and investment. The need for a foreign exchange market arises because of the presence of multiple international currencies such as the U.S. dollar, the euro, and so forth, and the need to trade in such currencies. Let us say that you are a Dutch company that wants to buy Levis from Levi Strauss in the United States. Can you take your euros, fly to San Francisco (Levi Strauss's headquarters), and buy jeans? Of course not; you would have to convert your euros to dollars and then make your purchase. Now, take our simple example and multiply it exponentially across the world. How many companies and governments conduct business across borders every single day? The number is staggering, which is why the Forex market is so important not only to traders, but to businesses, as well.

The average daily volume in the global foreign exchange and related markets is continuously growing. Daily turnover was reported by the Bank-for International Settlements to be more than $3.2 trillion in April 2007. Since then, the market has continued to grow. According to Euromoney's annual FX Poll, volumes grew an additional 41 percent between 2007 and 2008. Much of this growth can probably be attributable to the growing interest and access to the currency markets that traders have now found. Keep in mind that most small investors did not even have access to this market as recently as 10 years ago.

Unlike most stock markets, where all participants have access to the same prices, the Forex market is carved up into levels of access. At the top is the *interbank market,* which is made up of the largest investment banking firms. Within the interbank market, the spreads are razor sharp and usually unavailable to players outside the inner circle. If an institution can guarantee large numbers of transactions for large amounts of money, they can demand a smaller difference between the bid and ask price, or an improved spread. The levels of access that makes up the foreign exchange market is determined by the amount of money with which an entity is trading. The top-tier interbank market accounts for 53 percent of all transactions. After that, we find smaller investment banks, followed by large multinational corporations (which need to hedge risk and pay employees in different countries) and large hedge funds. In Exhibit 6.1, you can see a list of the top currency traders from around the world.

One of the unique features of the Forex market is that there is no unified or centrally cleared marketplace to conduct trading, and there is little cross-border regulation. In all honesty, because of the size of the Forex market, it almost regulates itself through highly fluid supply and demand. In place of a formalized market, we see a number of interconnected

EXHIBIT 6.1	Top 10 Currency Traders, Percent of Overall Volume, May 2008	
Rank	**Name**	**Volume**
1	Deutsche Bank	21.70%
2	UBS AG	15.80%
3	Barclays Capital	9.12%
4	Citi	7.49%
5	Royal Bank of Scotland	7.30%
6	J.P. Morgan	4.19%
7	HSBC	4.10%
8	Lehman Brothers	3.58%
9	Goldman Sachs	3.47%
10	Morgan Stanley	2.86%

Source: EuroMoney FX Survey, FX Poll 2009 (www.euromoney.com).

marketplaces, where different currencies and currency-based instruments are traded. What this implies is that there is no *single* exchange rate, but rather a *number* of different rates or prices, depending on which bank or market maker is trading. In reality, the large majority of rates are close to one another, as otherwise they could be exploited by arbitrage in some form or fashion. Due to London's dominance in the market, a particular currency's quoted price is usually the London market price. The main trading center for Forex is London, but New York and Tokyo are also important centers. Also, unlike most markets, currency trading takes place constantly throughout the day; when the Asian trading session ends, the European session begins, followed by the North American session and then back to the Asian session (excluding weekends).

Fluctuations in exchange rates are usually caused by typical economic indicators; factors like GDP growth, inflation, interest rate changes, and other macroeconomic conditions make one country's currency more or less valuable than others. In the end, investors are continuously attempting to gauge both *from* where and *to* where the flow of money will be traveling, as well as which economy will (or will not) benefit from major macroeconomic changes.

RISKS

The risks associated with currency plays are real, to be sure. That said, they are also manageable, assuming you both seek to learn as much about your "enemy" as you can, and you adhere to a strict discipline, the active investor's greatest safety net.

Trading Risk Management

Before we get too much into the technical side of currency trading, let us talk about risk. As you see in Chapter 9 on portfolio management, our belief is that risk, not returns, is the most important part of investing. Returns are the "end all" goal to investing, but risk management is what controls your returns on the downside and prevents you from experiencing catastrophic losses in your portfolio. For example, let us say you have $10,000 in a new currency trading account and you decide to make 10 trades of $1,000 each to get started. You place your trades and leave your positions for a month. When you revisit your account, you see that you had eight winning trades where you netted 5 percent gains on each trade—but the two losing trades lost 50 percent of their value, and so at the end of the month you were left with $9,400. You hit 80 percent of your trades, but *lost* money. If you had controlled your risk and used downside protection (like simple stop losses), you would have made a respectable profit during your month. As it stands, your lack of risk protection cost you quite a bit of money.

What would you say if we told you that you can make great profits in the currency market while only hitting 60 percent of your trades? You would be surprised, right? That statement is actually quite valid, but you have to be a disciplined trader and you have to incorporate functional risk protection in your portfolio to make it so in *your* case. Peter Lynch once said, "In this business if you're good, you're right six times out of ten. You're never going to be right nine times out of ten." Peter Lynch managed stocks, but he firmly understood the concept of risk management and what it takes to be a successful trader, in general. Before you make one currency trade, or even one paper trade, we would encourage you to highly define your investment discipline. Do not decide that your gut instincts alone will be sufficient to make you money in the currency market. It is precisely this sort of "belief system" that represents the kiss of death to traders and why they fail much more often than they should. Sean Casterline actually has pretty good instincts, and yet he was eviscerated the first time he traded currencies. To be a successful currency trader, you need to develop your sense of discipline in such a way that it becomes mechanical and otherwise devoid of any emotional influence. To do this, begin asking yourself some basic questions: Are you going to be a long-term trader, a short-term trader, or a scalper (taking a few pips and running)? You can be some combination of these three if you wish, but define your standard as clearly as you can prior to trading. In answering that question, you may find the answer to others; for example, are you going to use a 7 percent, 10 percent, 15 percent, and so forth, stop loss across the board? In reality, your stop loss levels may be something you tweak as you get into the flow of trading. Do not go into trading without some preestablished levels. We cannot tell you how many times we have seen new traders initiate a transaction and watch it go down 10 percent, only to double-down and lose more after that. Know your downside and establish a limit. As we move forward in the chapter, we show you on our exhibits how to define your stop levels. For now, it is enough to know you need to protect your downside. Currency trades, even more than stocks, are much like buses; there is always another one coming, so there is positively no excuse for marrying a trade.

How about this: When do you sell a position when it has made money for you? This is another common mistake traders make. They watch a profitable trade become a loss. If your discipline is to use 5 percent trailing stops, then use them; if you are going to automatically sell any position that gains 20 percent, then sell there—but do not go into currency trading without knowing exactly where your "out" is. Again, you can always adjust these levels and triggers—the point is to have them.

We talked about stop loss orders in particular, but we have yet to define the array of transactional-specific orders available to the currency trader, so let us mention them briefly.

Market Orders: A market order is an order to trade immediately, buying and selling the currency for the best-available price. If you are buying the currency, you will pay according to the ask price; if you sell the currency, the price will be set near the bid price. Because of the highly fluctuating nature of the Forex market, the price at which the market order will be executed is not necessarily the last traded price. The bid and ask prices can deviate considerably, depending on the stability of the currency.

Limit Orders: *Buy* limit orders are marked below the current price in an effort to buy the currency lower than the current price. On the other side, *sell* limit orders are placed above the present currency price to make sure you sell the currency above the market level. In a limit order, the trader specifies the price at which to buy/sell the currency pair, as well as the duration of time for which the order is to remain open.

There are two types of time durations for a limit order; GTC (Good 'til canceled) or GFD (Good for the day). The GFD order expires at the end of the trading day if it is not executed, while the GTC order stays open until canceled by the trader.

When you trade with stop loss and limit orders at the same time, an OCO (order cancels other) order should be placed as well. This means the moment the market triggers either the stop order or the limit order, it cancels the opposite order. By using an OCO order, you are not left exposed with an open order after either of the others is filled.

Stop Orders: Stop orders are placed like limit orders at a predetermined price, but they turn into market orders when the market reaches the triggering price. A stop loss order is a type of limit order that serves as a protection mechanism against a large drop in currency price. If the currency price falls beneath the price you set, it is automatically sold at market. For example, if you bought the EUR/USD currency pair at the exchange rate of USD $1.32, you may decide to put a stop loss at 7 percent, or at a price of $1.23. If your trade went against you and the EUR/USD pair fell to $1.23, your position would be sold at market. This protects your downside and does not require you to constantly monitor your positions.

Trailing Stop Orders: A trailing stop is actually a stop-loss order set at a percentage level below or above the current market price. The trailing stop price adjusts itself higher or lower as the price changes. The trailing stop order can be also placed as a trailing stop limit order, or a trailing stop market order. The advantage of a trailing stop is that the order automatically "trails" the rate if the position moves in your favor, offering the potential for greater gains while still guarding against price declines.

UNIQUE GLOBAL RISKS TO CURRENCIES

By definition, every astute investor is also a risk manager. He or she must constantly appraise the potential upside of a transaction against its potential downside, taking necessary precautions to preserve principal while attempting to take advantage of opportunities for growth. As is the case with other common forms of investing like stocks, bonds, real estate, bank deposits, antiques, and precious metals, currency trading has some inherent risks and rewards. Many of the broader global economic influences were covered more fully in our equities chapter, but note some of the risks more specific to global currencies that are outlined in the following sections.

Leverage Risk

When you are trading currencies, you are using leverage to make a profit. Defined, leverage is the use of loaned money to increase the potential return of your trade. The reason you need to use leverage in this market is because profits are made at exchange-rate differences that are only fractions of a cent, so you must trade with larger sums of money to make the small movements worth trading. Although trading hundreds of thousands of dollars may sound exhilarating, when you trade at these high volumes, even a small mistake can wipe out all you have in your account, so remain aware of leverage's awesome power.

News Risk

This is a relatively straightforward risk, but one for which most people fail to prepare, and if you see yourself as a long-term trader in currencies, this one is particularly important for you. For eons, investors have bought stocks and bonds in their portfolios and left them until they retired. That works in some markets, although we are not really believers in the "buy and hold" approach to investment management. In currency trading, "buy and hold" becomes "buy and forget about it," as this approach is the easiest way to lose everything you have, due in no small way to remaining ignorant of the shifting winds in national and world politics. Movements in currencies are sensitive to changes within broad national economies and associated changes within governments and government policies, and the news of these changes can flip your trade quickly. Accordingly, if you are going to invest in currencies, be sure to have some way of monitoring breaking news stories, even if all you do is keep one eye to a financial news network like CNBC throughout the day.

By the way, there is an interesting twist to "news risk," and it has to do with a certain kind of risk that *does not* exist when you learn of some key, helpful information in the course of being a currency trader. Let us say that your biggest Japanese client, who also happens to golf with Masaaki Shirakawa, the Governor of the Bank of Japan (BOJ), told you at lunch one day that the BOJ is planning to lower rates at its next meeting; you could go right ahead and short as much yen as you like. No one will ever prosecute you for insider trading should your bet pay off, because there is no such thing as insider trading in the Forex market. In fact, many European economic statistics, such as German employment figures, are often leaked days prior to their official announcement. This kind of information can be helpful to you, and it is the sort of information for which you should be constantly watching.

Interest Rate Risk

A change in interest rates by a country's central bank can dramatically affect your currency position. For example, every time the European Central Bank decides to raise or lower interest rates, the value of the euro will be affected. Generally, when a central bank announces an increase in interest rates, it drives up the value of their currency. This happens because the higher rates increase demand for the currency. If the European Central Bank recently raised its rates to 3.25 percent and the Reserve Bank of Australia has its benchmark rate set at 2.50 percent, whose currency do you think should be stronger? The euro would be stronger because investors around the world are seeking the highest rates available. In this simple example, the euro would be the stronger currency and would appreciate further against the Aussie dollar because the European Central Bank raised rates. Also, keep in mind that investors will primarily trade *in anticipation* of what rates are going to do. Therefore, if European rates were at 3.25 percent but investors felt the central bank was going to lower by 50 basis points in the next six months, you would most certainly see the euro decline much sooner than at the time of the actual announcements of lower rates; also, a decrease in interest rates will likely result in the selling of the euro, so its value will drop in value on that basis.

Counterparty Risk

Whenever you enter into a currency transaction, there are two parties involved: a buyer and a seller. The person or entity with which you are trading is called the counterparty. As such, you always face *counterparty risk*, or the risk that the person/entity on the other side of your trade will not fulfill his obligation.

You can avoid this hazard by resolving to trade only with known companies that have excellent credit ratings and clean backgrounds. You need to fully investigate any entity with which you intend to work by researching as to whether any problems have been reported, such as insolvency or questions of ethical conduct. A good place to begin your research is the Commodity Futures Trading Commission (www.cft.gov). Commodity trading is crazy enough without having to worry about whether you will get paid on your trades.

GENERAL TERMINOLOGY/TYPES OF TRADERS

We looked at the background of the Forex market and also defined some of the risks against which you have to guard, so let us now start working into some of the terminology involved in trading currencies. First, we define the types of traders/trading strategies that exist in the realm. From there, we go over some trading terminology. If you have traded in other capital markets, you may be tempted to jump forward to some of the analysis, but we would caution you not to do that. The currency market has a terminology all its own, and you do not want to try and pick it up as you trade along.

First, one of the most confusing aspects of currency trading is that there seems to be no single definition of "trader." As you probably know from investing in other capital markets, traders come in all forms. You may have yet to decide the *type* of trader you are going to be in the Forex market, so let us discuss the general categories of trading available to you and go from there; remember, discipline is *everything* when trading the Forex market.

> *Scalping*: This is a trading strategy in which a currency pair is bought and held for a short period of time in an effort to make a profit. It generally involves trading huge sums through the use of leverage and taking small/quick profits. A minute change in a currency equals a respectable profit. A scalper makes dozens, if not hundreds, of trades per session.

Day Trading: Day traders are just that; traders who are in a trade for no longer than a single day. They may hold a trade for minutes or hours, but, by the end of the session, they have unwound their positions and look to fight the next day.

Momentum Trading: Momentum traders look to find stocks that are moving significantly in one direction on high volume and try to jump on board to ride the momentum train to a desired profit. Momentum traders do not try to get in at the bottom to find a reversal, and they do not try to get out at the top of a trend; rather, they attempt to take advantage of the middle portion of the trend once it gains steam.

Swing Trading: Swing trading sits in the middle of the continuum between day trading to trend trading. Currency day traders hold a pair anywhere from a few seconds to a few hours, but never more than a day. A trend trader examines the long-term fundamental trends of a country and holds the currency pair for a few months, quarters, or years. Swing traders typically attempt to identify pivot points (stocks pivoting from downtrends to uptrends, and vice versa) or they will trade price patterns/formation such as channels, triangles, head-and-shoulders tops/bottoms and pennants. You can see a six-month chart with swing trade pivot points in Exhibit 6.2.

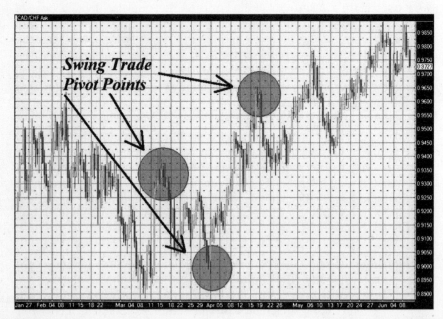

EXHIBIT 6.2   Swing Trade Pivot Points
Source: Fxaccucharts.com.

Fundamental Trading: Fundamentalists trade currencies based on fundamental news and analysis, which examines factors like corporate events, government actions, or general global economic announcements. Instead of analyzing charts, they analyze fundamental data from around the world.

Trend Trading: The trend trader is a longer-term trader who is looking to capitalize on extended trends in a country or countries. The trend trader will be in a trade for months, quarters, or years. As long as the long-term trend or theme is in place, the trend trader will remain in his or her position. For example, from late 2001 through most of 2008, the Canadian dollar was strengthening in comparison to the U.S. dollar; you can see the respective movements represented in Exhibit 6.3. The commodities boom was providing fuel to the Canadian economy and, by consequence, to the Canadian dollar. If you were a trend trader in this pair during this time frame, you would have been short the USD/CAD pair for quite a few years and made a ton of money. As a side note, the shaded area shows you where the trend finally turned in favor of the U.S. dollar.

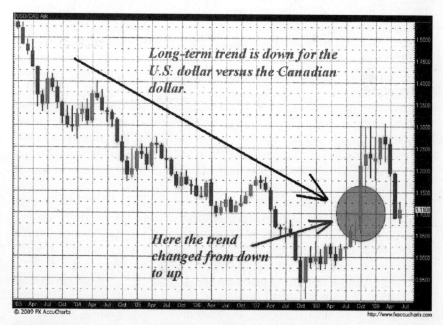

EXHIBIT 6.3 Chart of USD/CAD Pair Movement, 2003 to Mid-2009
Source: Fxaccucharts.com.

Keep in mind that you may not fit perfectly into one trading category. You may decide to be a fundamental trader who times entries and exits by looking at charts, or you may be a scalper who trades only on quick vibrations made via fundamental announcements. The point is that you need to discern what type of trader you are going to be before entering the currency markets, as these markets are way too volatile to attempt to "learn on the fly"; you could easily run out of money before you develop your discipline, and then it will not really matter.

THE LEXICON OF CURRENCY TRADING

Let us look at some critical terminology germane to currency trading. You may recognize some of it, but these markets have their own way of doing things, so pay attention to the details.

PIPS

To begin with, currencies are measured in something called "pips." A pip is a small measure of change in a currency pair. It can be measured in terms of the quote or in terms of the underlying currency. The pip is a standardized unit and is the least amount by which a currency quote can change, which is usually $0.0001 for U.S.-dollar related pairs (more commonly referred to as 1/100th of 1 percent). Remember, when you are trading currencies, you are using a heavy amount of leverage, so it takes only small movements to make money.

Assume that we have a USD/EUR (U.S. dollar to euro) direct quote of 0.8745; what this quote means is that for a US$1, you can buy 0.8745 euros. If there was a one-pip increase in this quote (to 0.8746), the value of the U.S. dollar would rise relative to the euro, as US$1 would allow you to buy slightly more euros. Said another way, the dollar has *strengthened* against the euro.

When a trader executes a trade on the Forex market, he or she is buying or selling currency in units commonly referred to as *lots*. There are two main types of lots that traders will buy and sell. A $100,000 unit is called a *regular lot* and a $10,000 unit is called a *mini lot*. When you buy and sell a regular lot, you get paid $10 a pip versus $1 a pip on the mini lot.

As an example, let us say that your hedge fund was interested in trading the GBP/USD combo (British pounds to U.S. dollars). If you were buying one currency lot on the combo, the current exchange rate sits at $1.524 dollars for every British pound. If the currency moved in your favor and ran to $1.528, at which point you decided to lock off your profit, you would be locking in a profit of 40 pips. To equate the pips to monetary value, you need to remember that 1 pip equals approximately $10 on a $100,000 transaction or $1 on a mini-lot transaction. If we made 40 pips, that equates to 40 pips multiplied by $10, which equals $400 on a $100,000 account or $40 on a $10,000 account.

With most companies, the average minimum deposit for trading with leverage is 1 percent, which means that for every $100,000 lot you trade, you must have $1,000 in your margin trading account. For mini lots, you need a minimum of $100 in your margin trading account on deposit.

Pairs

In any transaction, you have a buyer and a seller. Currencies work primarily the same way and always trade in pairs, which means that when a trader makes a currency trade, he is always long one currency and short the other. For example, if your hedge fund sells one standard lot of NZD/JPY, it would have, in essence, exchanged New Zealand dollars for yen and would now be "short" New Zealand dollars and "long" Japanese yen.

There are dealers who will trade exotic currencies like the Cambodian Riel or the Indonesian Rupiah, but the majority of trading occurs in the seven most liquid pairs in the world.

The four major pairs are:

1. EUR/USD (European euro/U.S. dollar)
2. USD/JPY (U.S. dollar/Japanese yen)
3. GBP/USD (British pound/U.S. dollar)
4. USD/CHF (U.S. dollar/Swiss franc)

The three commodity pairs are:

1. AUD/USD (Australian dollar/U.S. dollar)
2. USD/CAD (U.S. dollar/Canadian dollar)
3. NZD/USD (New Zealand dollar/U.S. dollar)

These currency pairs, along with their variety of combinations, account for more than 95 percent of all speculative trading in the Forex market. Moreover, the Forex market offers a small number of trading instruments, with only 18 pairs and crosses actively traded. It is a much more concentrated market than the equity or bond markets of the world, which makes it much more manageable for your hedge fund. We recommend that you fine-tune your trading and become an expert on a small number of pairs.

The Carry Trade

The *carry trade* relies on the reality that every currency in the world has an interest rate attached to it. The idea behind the carry is straightforward: the trader goes long the currency with a high interest rate, and finances that purchase with a currency with a low interest rate. In 2005, one of the best pairings was the NZD/JPY cross. The New Zealand economy, spurred by huge commodity demand from China and a hot housing market, saw its rates rise to 7.25 percent and stay there for an extended period of time. Meanwhile, Japanese rates remained mired at 0 percent. If your hedge fund went long the NZD/JPY pair, it would have harvested 725 basis points in yield from the rates in New Zealand. At 10:1 leverage, the carry trade in NZD/JPY would have produced a 72.5 percent annual return from interest rate differentials alone, without factoring in any contribution from capital appreciation. However, before you rush out and buy the next high-yield pair, be aware that when the carry trade unwinds itself, the declines can be rapid and severe. Think of it like stretching a rubber band and that rubber band eventually snapping. This process is known as carry trade liquidation and occurs when traders decide that the carry has run its course. With every trader seeking to exit his or her position at once, bids disappear and the profits from interest rate differentials are not nearly enough to offset the capital losses. *The best time to position in the carry is at the beginning of the rate-tightening cycle, allowing the trader to ride the move as interest rate differentials increase.*

CHOOSING A BROKER

There are thousands of companies through which you can trade. All you have to do is run a Google search for "Forex Trading" and you will come up with umpteen pages full of brokers ready to deliver your pot of gold. As with anything else like this, however, you want to tread carefully.

Most of these brokers will offer you commission-free trades, but remember that *nothing* comes for free. The way most brokers make money is based on the spread between the bid and ask price. Thus, when you are searching for a broker, always look for tight spreads to save money on your true underlying trading costs.

Most importantly, you need to find an established and reputable broker with whom to work. In some unusual cases, you will find some brokers who are not regulated at all. Stay away from them. Know that any outfit can hold itself out as a Forex broker without becoming registered with the regulatory agencies; make sure *your* broker is registered by using the National Futures Association's Background Affiliation Status Information Center at www.nfa.futures.org/basicnet.

Following are a few of the firms on which we have done research and/or actually used, and believe to be reputable outfits. Be sure to look at more than a few to find out which one fits your style; for example, you may prefer the charting software of one over another, or you may find tighter spreads from one site to the next.

Interactive Brokers (www.InteractiveBrokers.com): To us, Interactive Brokers is the most valuable company in this group because they give you so much flexibility. You can trade stocks, bonds, currencies, and options all from one single account. Most brokers do not allow you this flexibility. Also, the company is publicly traded. As a disclaimer, we do have an advisory relationship with the company. The minimum account size is usually a bit higher at $10,000 for most individuals. That minimum drops to $4,000 for IRAs and $3,000 for individuals aged 21 or younger.

Forex.com (www.Forex.com): Forex.com is a division of GAIN Capital Group. The firm is well capitalized and has a great web presence. Chinese, English, and Spanish are all available languages at Forex.com, and you can open a mini account with as little as US$250.

FX Solutions (www.FxSol.com): FX Solutions promotes their proprietary Global Trading Systems (GTS). It is a price discovery and delivery system that they feel gives retail traders equality with the professional world of interbank traders. The company has been recognized as one of America's fastest-growing private companies by *Inc.* magazine for three consecutive years. Languages available are Chinese, English, and Spanish. You can open an account with as little as $250. As a disclaimer, the authors and associated persons have personal currency trading accounts with FX Solutions.

Global Forex Trading or *GFT* (www.GFTForex.com): GFT has been around since 1997 and has a unique proprietary trading platform called DealBook 360. GFT offers the platform in English, Chinese, French, German, Japanese, Korean, Polish, Portuguese, and Spanish. You only need $250 to open an account.

Discipline

It is time to start progressing into the analysis side of this chapter. In our chapter on equities, we went over a lot of global macro and country fundamental analysis. That type of analysis is applicable in this area if you want to trade currencies simply off of fundamental information. However, as illustrated in the equity section, we believe that you should use both fundamental *and* technical analysis in your currency trading. Since we have already covered country analysis as part of our equity chapter, the bulk of this chapter is driven from the technical side. We want you to understand how to effectively read charts and comprehend those indicators that have the most value in the currency-trading world.

The first thing we want to discuss is your discipline. The currency markets move like lightning, and if you do not have your discipline set in stone, you can find yourself in a lot of trouble. Have you ever noticed that the kids who have been disciplined throughout their young lives are the ones who act the best in public? Have you ever noticed that the best hitters in baseball are the ones that are disciplined enough to wait on, and hit, the curveball? Have you ever noticed that the best quarterbacks in the NFL are the players who are disciplined enough to stand in the pocket and get slaughtered by a blitzing linebacker as they deliver the touchdown pass? It is no coincidence that discipline is the common denominator of success in a wide variety of life's facets and pursuits—and currency trading is as much the constructive beneficiary of discipline as anything else.

Tom Naylor once said, "The bigger the real-life problems, the greater the tendency for the discipline to retreat into a reassuring fantasy-land of abstract theory and technical manipulation." Now, be honest with us here; does this sound like most investors when the markets start to get hairy? You become dazed and confused and try to justify holding onto that "piece of garbage" currency trade until you are down 50 percent. The discipline you thought you possessed retreated into some hole far, far away. Making sell decisions is the single hardest thing to do in investing, and that is why you need a discipline. A discipline can completely remove the emotion from your day-to-day investing, and, by doing so, essentially makes the decisions for you; it makes your investing mechanical, which means, in terms of trading, to be completely void of human emotion.

An adherence to disciplined investing does not mean you cannot buy speculative issues; it is, in fact, an adherence to disciplined investing that serves as the reason why you *can* buy more speculative issues. If your discipline is "buy and hold," then buy and hold and do not second-guess that decision when the pair is going against you; if your discipline is to use 10 pip stop loss orders, then use 10 pip stop loss orders across the board and do not make exceptions; if your investing discipline calls for picking trades out of the formations in the stars then, darn it, trade pairs that call to you from the heavens. In reality, your discipline, and your comfort level with that discipline, will take awhile to surface. Ultimately, one's investing style manifests itself through one's personality and risk tolerance. Ascertain a discipline that makes you comfortable and allows you to sleep through the night, fully adopt it, and live it. One caveat: Remember that more volatile markets lend themselves less to success through the use of disciplines that are characterized by more passivity, so keep that in mind.

Support and Resistance

Levels of support and resistance are easy to understand and fairly simple to identify, but do not overlook their importance. In our experience, trading simple support and resistance lines can be the most effective strategy, particularly when applied to currency trading. Support and resistance represent key areas on a chart where currency forces of supply and demand come together. Prices themselves are driven by supply, which pushes prices down, and demand, which pushes the currency pair higher. As demand for a currency increases, the price of that currency advances. Similarly, as supply increases, prices decline.

Support can be defined as the price level for a currency pair at which demand is thought to be strong enough to prevent the price from declining further. In other words, buyers see value and support the pair at that price. Logic dictates that as the price falls toward a support area and the currency gets cheaper, buyers become more inclined to buy and sellers become less of a mind to sell. By the time the price reaches this support area, demand overcomes supply and prevents the price from declining below the support level.

On the other side of the coin, we find resistance. Resistance is the pair area at which selling is thought to be strong enough to prevent the price from rising further. You can think of it as a ceiling. As the pair advances toward a resistance level, sellers become more apt to sell and buyers become less inclined to buy. By the time the pair reaches the resistance level, supply overcomes demand and prevents the price from rising above this ceiling.

Let us take a look at a few examples. Exhibit 6.4 shows a weekly chart for the EUR/AUD pair. As you can see, the euro was stuck in a range for almost two years versus the Australian dollar. Every time the pair came up toward the 1.725 area, investors sold the pair and sent it back down. This area of resistance was indicative of oversupply. At the time, investors believed the euro was becoming overvalued versus the Aussie dollar, so the sellers came in and traders were more than likely shorting the pair. Moving forward, something changed; the European economies became more valuable than the Australian economy, and the pair broke resistance in a big way (shaded circle). Notice the "moon shot" that took place

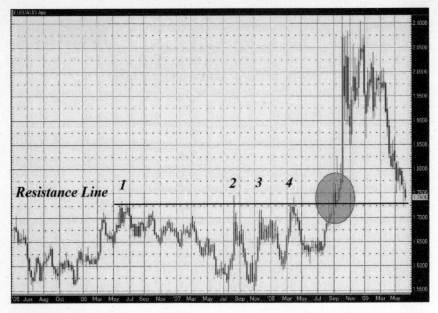

EXHIBIT 6.4   Chart of EUR/AUD Pair Movement, Mid-2005 to Mid-2009
Source: Fxaccucharts.com.

after the breakout. If you bought the pair on this breaking of resistance, you realized a handsome profit. Be sure to notice that the pair hits this resistance line four times prior to breakout. The more times a pair sets up that line of support or resistance, the more significant that level becomes. Therefore, when it is finally broken, the move that follows can be significant.

Exhibit 6.5 shows an hourly chart for the U.S. dollar versus the Japanese yen (USD/JPY) and a good look at a support level. Again, what you are seeing is really an exhibit of supply and demand. The dollar had been strong against the yen rising from 96.70 to more than 98.90. However, the pair went into a consolidation, which showed support at the horizontal line on the exhibit. The pair bounced off this line of support four times because buyers saw value in the pair at this level and bid the pair up. Once the pair broke support to the downside (circle), there was a massive unwinding of currency shares and the shorts forced the pair down. One of the early giveaways was the fact that each time the pair bounced off support, it went on to set a new "lower high." That lower high was telling you there were more sellers in the pair than buyers. The trading was foreshadowing a break to the downside, and that support more than likely was not going to hold. The pair came back up after the breakdown and retested

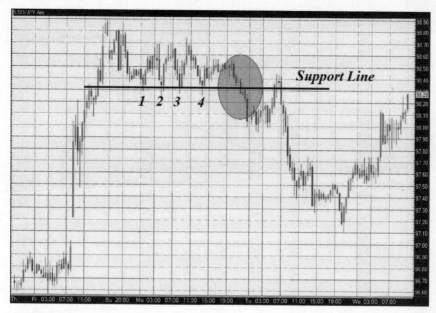

EXHIBIT 6.5 Hourly Movement Chart of USD/JPY Pair Movement
Source: Fxaccucharts.com.

this line of support. Once support is broken, it becomes resistance. In this case, the pair was rejected at this previous support line before suffering a big fall.

Let us take a look at one last example that may throw a curve into your thoughts about support and resistance. Exhibit 6.6 is a daily chart for the U.S. dollar versus the Canadian dollar (USD/CAD). What we want to show you here is that you will often see support and resistance lines come into play via ascending or descending lines, and not horizontal ones. For about a year, the U.S. dollar appreciated against the Canadian dollar. You can see it represented on the exhibit by an ascending trendline of support. The trendline was set up four times, as referenced by the numbers. Eventually, the pair topped and broke below the support line (circle). One of the most important things you need to glean from this exhibit is the retest of the ascending line of support (arrow). Remember, once a line of support is broken, it then becomes resistance (and vice versa). In this case, once the pair broke the support line, it successfully retested resistance (which *was* support) at the down arrow. If you were looking for a point to short the pair, this was it. From this area, you had a very reasonable downside you could use as the basis for a buy stop-loss. As you can see, the pair suffered significantly after the breakdown.

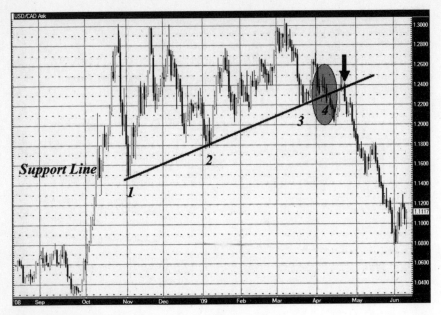

EXHIBIT 6.6   Daily Chart of USD/CAD Pair Movement
Source: Fxaccucharts.com.

TRENDLINES AND CHANNELS

Trends and trend identifiers are the essential components of technical anaylsis, and the successful Forex trader will seek to become as well-versed as possible in their recognition. To that end, what follows is a discussion of both trendlines, as well as the channels that suggest longer-term trends in movement.

Trendlines

We touched on trend analysis in our equity chapter but we want to revisit the topic here because it is equally important in currency trading. Learning how to identify the trend should be the first order of business for any investor. It stands to reason that if you are invested in a currency pair that is trending in the wrong direction, your chances of success decrease dramatically.

The best tools for uncovering the trend are called, oddly enough, *trend-lines*. An evaluation of any chart will quickly reveal that prices usually move in trends; a series of ascending "bottoms" in a rising market can be joined together by a straight line, and the "tops" off a descending series of rally peaks can be joined the same way. These lines, known as trendlines, are simple but useful mechanisms by which to discover currency rotations. In fact, the careful use of trendlines represents the foundation of our currency investment analysis. Note that a proper trendline has to connect two or more peaks or troughs; too frequently, we see people constructing lines that only touch one point. This is a fundamentally important flaw of which to take notice, because whenever you draw or interpret a trendline, you cannot forget that a true trendline is a graphic way of representing the underlying trend; consequently, if it only touches one point, it is not a true trendline.

Let us take a look at a few examples. Exhibit 6.7 is a weekly chart for the euro versus U.S. dollar pair (EUR/USD). From 2006 through mid-2008, the euro had been appreciating versus the U.S. dollar. It made sense at the time, as the U.S. economy was slipping into recession but the rest of the world was still unconvinced that the weakness would spread to them. The upward-pushing trendline was hit five times, as indicated by the five arrows. Toward the middle of 2008, the pair extended *away* from the line, but a massive Moving Average Convergence/Divergence (MACD) sell signal (bottom indicator) foretold of gray clouds on the horizon. The red-shaded circle shows you where the trend was formally broken and a massive

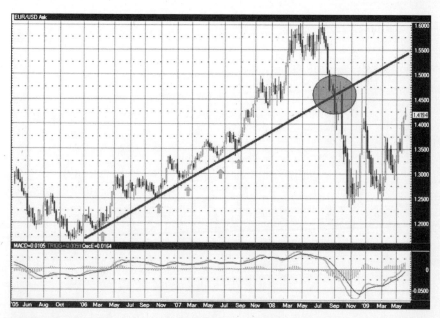

EXHIBIT 6.7 Weekly Chart of EUR/USD Pair Movement, Mid-2005 to Mid-2009
Source: Fxaccucharts.com.

sell-off ensued. Notice how the EUR/USD pair retested the trendline after it was broken; you can see this in the shaded circle. Remember, former support becomes resistance, and vice versa. When this upward-trending line of support was broken, it became resistance. If we were long on the pair when the trendline was broken, we would have sold it on the retest back toward 1.465 rather than on the initial downdraft.

Exhibit 6.8 gives us a look at how the trend can change from negative to positive for a currency pair. You see a chart for the British pound versus the U.S. dollar (GBP/USD). The downward-sloping trendline was set up nicely on four different occasions, as indicated by the negative arrows. The circle on the lower right side of the exhibit shows where the trend was broken, and the trend for the pair changed from negative to positive at that time. As we saw earlier, the trendline was broken and then that line of resistance was again tested as support. You can see this point indicated by the upward arrow. If you were considering buying into the pair, you would buy it on the retest of this line of support, which was previously resistance. Notice how the MACD at the bottom was showing a series of higher highs and higher lows, even as the pair was setting lower highs and lower lows. This was a good early indication that the trend was about to change and the British pound was getting to take over a leadership role over the U.S. dollar.

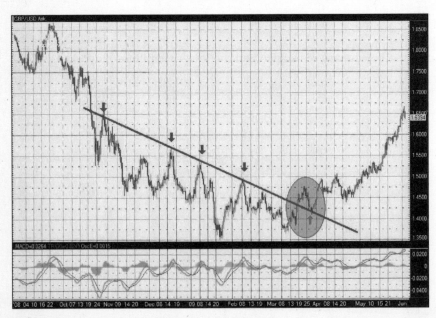

EXHIBIT 6.8   Chart of GBP/USD Pair Movement
Source: Fxaccucharts.com.

As traders, it is imperative that we always have an opinion of the macro currency trends. It is not to say that you are always going to be correct. However, if you attempt to fight the trend by picking pairs before laying the groundwork of trend analysis, you will continually find yourself on the short end of the stick. This is not to say that identifying the trend is always easy. After years of research, however, we can tell you that the great investors of our time all had one thing in common: they were masters at identifying the trend. On that note, remember that you can mine for trendlines in daily, weekly, or minute charts; trendlines remain highly useful without regard to your analytical time horizon.

Channels

There is no individual component that is more important to the technical analyst than the identification of trends. One of the technical formations that can help you identify the overall trend on a short- or intermediate-term basis is the *channel*. When prices trend between two parallel trendlines, this is referred to as a channel. You can envision the formation as a simple channel of water where water flows from one bank to the other, but always in the primary direction. As you can see in Exhibit 6.9, the channel can be horizontal, descending, or ascending in structure.

Price channels by themselves do not give us a whole lot of information about a potential trend change and thus, viewed in a vacuum, cannot be considered a continuation *or* reversal pattern; it could be either. The upper trendlines mark resistance and the lower trendlines mark support, so channels with negative slopes are considered bearish and those with positive slopes are primarily considered bullish. That said, these rules should be viewed more as guidelines and not "set in stone" commandments. For example, a descending channel that is broken to the upside can be indicative of a bullish event (a "bullish channel" will refer to a channel with positive slope and a "bearish channel" to a channel with negative slope). Let us take a closer look at some of the characteristics of a price channel:

> ***Primary trendline***: It takes at least two points to form the main trendline. This line sets the tone for the trend and the slope. For a bullish price channel, the main trendline extends upward. As with any uptrend, the trendline is a series of higher highs and higher

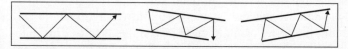

EXHIBIT 6.9 Illustration of Channels

lows, so this line is simply drawn as a connection of the higher lows. At least two points are required to draw it. For a bearish price channel, the main trendline extends down across the lower highs that define the downtrend.

Channel line: This is the line drawn parallel to the main trendline that defines the "other bank" of our river. Ideally, the channel line will be based off of two reaction highs or lows. However, after the main trendline has been established, some analysts draw the parallel channel line using only one reaction high or low. The channel line marks support in a bearish price channel and resistance in a bullish price channel.

Bullish price channel: As long as prices continue to advance and trade within the ascending channel, the trend is considered bullish. The first warning of a trend change occurs when prices fall short of channel line resistance. A subsequent break below the main trendline support would provide further indication of a trend change and, depending on the time frame, it could be a significant shift. A break above channel line resistance would be bullish and indicate an acceleration of the advance.

Bearish price channel: As long as prices decline and are confined within the channel, the trend is considered bearish. Our preliminary warning of a trend change occurs when prices fail to reach channel line support. A subsequent break above resistance of the main trendline would provide confirmation of a trend change. A break below channel line support would be bearish and indicate an acceleration of the decline.

As a hedge fund trader who has identified a bullish price channel, you more than likely look to buy when prices reach primary trendline support. Conversely, some traders look to sell, or short, when prices reach primary trendline resistance in a bearish price channel. As with most price patterns, other aspects of technical analysis should be used to confirm signals. If you use indicators like On Balance Volume (OBV) and MACDs, you can often confirm the breakdown from the internal side prior to confirming the price breakdown. Because technical analysis is just as much art as it is science, there is room for flexibility.

Let us take a look at a few real-life examples. Our first example in Exhibit 6.10 shows a daily chart for the GBP/JPY pair. What we see on the first part of the exhibit, on the left-hand side, is a serious depreciation of the British pound versus the Japanese yen. However, about midway through the exhibit, the trend changes and our channel begins. The channel is marked on both sides by rising trendlines. The lower line is support and the upper line is resistance. As hedge fund managers, our first instinct

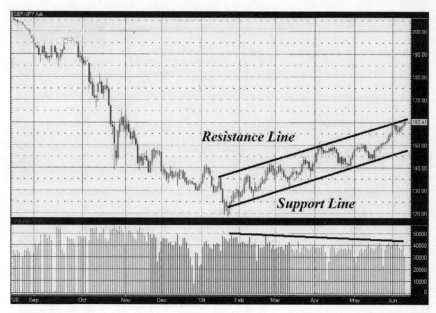

EXHIBIT 6.10 Chart of GBP/JPY Pair Movement
Source: Fxaccucharts.com.

would be to buy the pair any time it hits the support line and short the pair any time it hits the resistance line. If you do this, you can use a reasonable stop-loss just above or below your trade in order to control your downside if the pair breaks the channel. Further, take a look at the volume levels in Exhibit 6.10. As you see, the volume in the pair is declining as the pair trades higher. This does not bode well for the pound. As we told you earlier, the channel can be a continuation or a reversal pattern. In this case, while the pound is strengthening in a bullish channel pattern in the short term, our data also reveals that it is rising on thinning volume after a monstrous sell-off. The pattern appears to be more of a bearish formation, overall, which means the channel will eventually break to the downside; the bears are simply taking a rest before sending the pound back down.

Exhibit 6.11 shows an hourly chart for the NZD/CAD (New Zealand dollar/Canadian dollar) pair. This particular channel is a horizontal channel. Again, the easiest way to trade it would be to short off of resistance and go long off of support, and you can place your stop-losses just above or below those lines. You also want to pay attention to the MACD indicator at the bottom of the exhibit. The MACD gave buy signals on two separate occasions when the pair was coming off the support line. In this case,

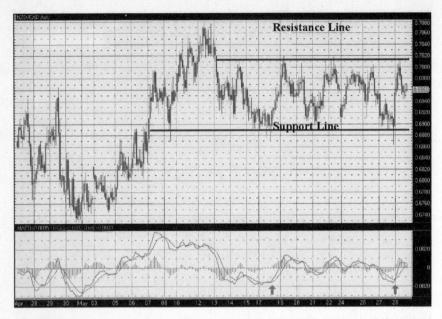

EXHIBIT 6.11 Hourly Chart of NZD/CAD Pair Movement Exhibiting Horizontal Channel
Source: Fxaccucharts.com.

using MACDs along with the channel formation proves to be a very potent combination.

If you look at a hundred exhibits, you will find a hundred channels. You can find channels in daily, weekly, and minute exhibits alike. The key to trading channels is fitting them into your particular discipline and getting a feel for many of the internal indicators that are useful complementary tools to the pattern (i.e., Volume, On-Balance Volume, MACDs). As with any type of technical formation, the channel is not foolproof, but it is one of the more dependable patterns you find in trading currencies today simply because it takes you back to the initial rules of support and resistance.

PRICE PATTERNS—HEAD AND SHOULDERS, TRIANGLES, DOUBLE-TOPS, AND DOUBLE-BOTTOMS, CUP-AND-HANDLE

The use of well-known price patterns in technical analysis is one of the investment manager's best weapons. In terms of currency trading, their utilization is a natural element of managing especially volatile trades.

Here, we look closer at the key patterns with which you should become familiar.

Head and Shoulders

There are two versions of the formation and both can be found at market extremes. The top formation occurs at market peaks and inverse the head and shoulder formations at bottoms and, as you can imagine, they are most widely known as a trend reversal formation. Visually, the pattern contains three successive peaks with the middle peak (head) being the highest and the two outside peaks (shoulders) being low and roughly equal. The reaction lows of each peak can be connected to form what is called the "neckline."

As its name implies, the head and shoulders pattern is made up of a left shoulder, head, right shoulder, and neckline. As with most technical formations, the pattern itself is more than just a price formation. It is a psychological shift in investor sentiment that involves volume, the breakout, price target, and support turned resistance. Let us break the formation down into its component parts and then put them together with a few examples.

Prior Trend: It is important to establish the existence of a prior uptrend (or downtrend for an inverse head and shoulders pattern) for this to be a reversal pattern. Without a prior trend to reverse, there cannot be a head-and-shoulders pattern, or any reversal pattern for that matter. A true reversal pattern forms because the mentality regarding a particular pair has shifted. The pattern is simply the hard data to show you the shift, but the formation is driven by investors' mental perceptions and their accumulation or distribution of a currency pair.

Left Shoulder: While in an uptrend, the left shoulder forms a peak that marks the high point of the current trend. After making this peak, a decline ensues to complete the formation of the first shoulder. The low of the decline usually remains above the trendline, keeping the uptrend intact. The left shoulder is important because it is what assists in defining the neckline. With an inverse head-and-shoulders pattern, we see the exact opposite action. Instead of setting a new high, the issue would have set a new low to start the formation on the left shoulder.

Head: From the low of the left shoulder, an advance begins that exceeds the previous high and marks the top of the head. After peaking, the low of the subsequent decline marks the second point of the neckline. The low of the decline usually breaks the uptrend line, putting the uptrend in jeopardy. As we know from our technical analysis 101 classes, an uptrend is defined as a series of higher highs and higher lows (and vice-versa for a downtrend). At this point in the formation, we truly do not know that the formation is taking shape. We simply see an uptrend. However, the head of the formation will end up being the exhaustive phase of the pattern. For an inverse head-and-shoulders pattern we have the exact opposite action. The head is setting a new low, which makes it appear as if the downtrend is still intact.

Right Shoulder: The advance from the low of the head forms the right shoulder. This peak is lower than the head (a lower high) and usually in line with the high of the left shoulder. While symmetry is preferred, sometimes the shoulders can be out of whack. As with most technical formations, perfection is rarely found. In the end, however, the right shoulder should definitely be below the head and really should not retest that high in any manner. The decline from the peak of the right shoulder will confirm and define the neckline. For an inverted head-and-shoulders formation, we get the exact opposite action. The right shoulder will be a movement off the neckline that takes the pair to a shallower low than the head. Again, this gives us an early signal that the downtrend may be over.

Neckline: The neckline forms by connecting the low points of the right side of the right and left shoulders with the low on the head. Depending on the relationship between these lows, the neckline can slope up, slope down, or be horizontal. Further, the slope of the neckline will affect the pattern's degree of bearishness: a downward slope is more bearish than an upward slope. Sometimes more than one low point can be used to form the neckline.

Volume: As the head-and-shoulders pattern unfolds, volume plays a *critical* role in confirmation. As with most technical patterns, if you have "head-and-shoulders" on the brain, you can convince yourself you see them everywhere. However, to have success trading this pattern, you need the volume to fall into place in the *correct areas*. Ideally, but not always, volume during the advance of the left shoulder should be higher than during the advance of the head, and the volume on both the first shoulder and the head should be relatively heavy. This is the exhaustive phase of the pattern. The warning sign to notice arises when volume increases on the decline from the peak of the head (the volume on the right shoulder should be very thin on the way up and increasing on the way down). With an inverted head-and-shoulders pattern, we see the exact *opposite* action with our volume: Volume should be very heavy on the first shoulder and the head (on the way down). This is the exhaustion selling that is shoving the weak hands out of the issue. The volume should be thinner on the left side of the right shoulder with increasing volume to the buy side as the pair progresses back toward the neckline.

Neckline Break: The head-and-shoulders (or inverse head-and-shoulders pattern) is not complete and the trend is not reversed until neckline support (or resistance) is broken. Ideally, this should also occur in a convincing manner with an expansion in volume. Many technicians use two to three times the average daily volume as a benchmark for volume on the day the pair breaks the neckline. As well, some traders will not trade a pattern until the pair has closed at least 3 percent below the neckline. That is not something to which we adhere, but it is worth mentioning as quite a few traders use this benchmark.

Support-Turned-Resistance: Once a support line is broken, it becomes resistance and vice versa. Once the neckline is broken in this pattern, it is common for this same support level to turn into resistance (or vice versa for a reverse head-and-shoulders pattern). Sometimes, but certainly not always, the pair will return to the support break and offer a second chance to trade the formation.

Price Target: After breaking neckline support (resistance), the projected price decline (advance) is found by measuring the distance from the neckline to the depth of the head. This distance is then subtracted from (or added to) the neckline to reach a price target. Currencies often reverse violently after they achieve their target; this occurs because technical traders all see the price target being met and close their positions. You want to be aware of your target at all times and lock in your profit when the goal is achieved if you're trading the pattern.

Let us take a look at what a reverse head-and-shoulders pattern looks like in terms of a currency pair. In Exhibit 6.12, you can see a chart for the New Zealand dollar/U.S. dollar pair. The recession that gripped the world in 2008 caused a huge flow into the U.S. dollar in a move that was driven by a flight to quality and safety. However, when the global economies began to firm, investors went back into the higher-growth countries, and that is what you see evidenced in Exhibit 6.12. The NZD reversed its downtrend against the dollar through a textbook reverse head-and-shoulders pattern. You can see all the elements detailed for you in the exhibit; the shoulders, the neckline, the head, and the important measuring implication. There are a couple of critical points on which to focus. First, notice that the pair first broke out and then retested. This is important because, more often than

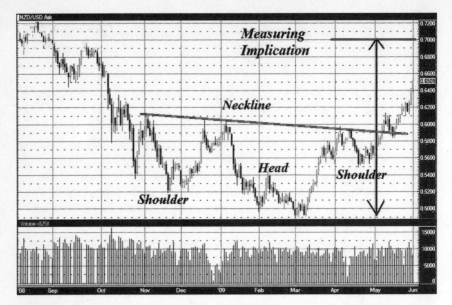

EXHIBIT 6.12 Chart of NZD/USD Pair that Reflects a Head-and-Shoulders Price Pattern
Source: Fxaccucharts.com.

not, these pairs will *retest* their breakout and the retest is typically where we like to get in. If the pair retests and holds that line of support, which previously served as resistance, we place our trades. Second, you notice that this particular trade shows a measuring implication toward .700. If we are in this particular trade, we would place a sell limit order at .700 or just below. When the pair gets to this level, we will automatically be sold out of the position with a nice profit.

The head-and-shoulders pattern is one of the most dependable reversal formations you will find in the currency markets. It is important to remember that it occurs at market extremes and usually marks a major trend reversal when complete. As well, you will find this pattern on weekly, daily, and intraday exhibits, so it is ideal for any type of trader. The formation is one of my favorites to trade because of its constancy, but also because of the measuring implications. A set target and clearly defined exit point gives the trader an edge because the pair will not tie up your capital for extended periods of time; the pattern gives you a reliable exit strategy. For what more could a trader ask?

Triangles

As volatile as currency trading is, pairs do not go straight up and straight down. Typically, during any trend, there are times of indecision for a currency pair, a time of consolidation before the next push or reversal. One of the technical formations we tend to see frequently in the currency markets are called triangles, and there are three varieties of this formation: ascending triangles, descending triangles, and symmetrical triangles.

The ascending triangle is typically a bullish formation that forms during an uptrend as a continuation pattern. There are instances when ascending triangles form as reversal patterns at the end of a downtrend, but that occurs less frequently. Regardless of where they form, ascending triangles are bullish patterns that indicate accumulation. On the ascending triangle, the horizontal line represents overhead supply that prevents the security from moving past a certain level. It is as if a large sell order has been placed at this level and it is taking a number of weeks or months to execute, thus preventing the price from rising further. Even though the price cannot rise past this level, the reaction lows continue to rise. It is these higher lows that indicate increased buying weight and give the ascending triangle its positive bias.

Exhibit 6.13 shows an example of an ascending triangle that formed on an intraday chart for the British pound versus the Japanese yen (GBP/JPY). The pound was on a nice run versus the yen, but it got extended, which led to a consolidation in the pair. As you can see, the triangle was formed by

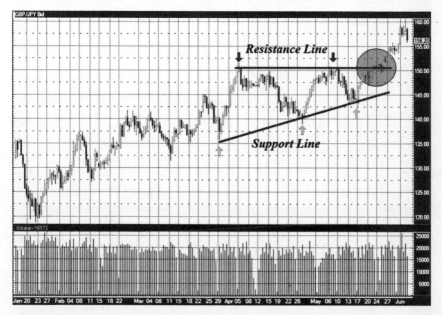

EXHIBIT 6.13 Chart of GBP/JPY Pair that Reflects an Ascending Triangle Formation
Source: Fxaccucharts.com.

a series of higher lows on the bottom (indicated by the upward-pointing arrows) and a horizontal line of resistance (downward-pointing arrows). Once the pair broke from this pattern, the pound continued on its upward trek. In reality, the triangle was simply a breather for the currency, but the demand pressure remained intact.

The descending triangle is typically thought of as a bearish formation and can usually be seen near the top of a market or pair move. There are times when the triangle will break out of its formation on the descending resistance side, which would be bullish, but typically when you see the descending triangle, it is an ominous sign. This type of triangle is distinguishable by the declining level of overhead resistance that accompanies the pattern. It is a negative trait that mirrors a series of lower highs and lower lows that you would see in a negative trend line.

Exhibit 6.14 is an hourly chart for the British pound versus the Australian dollar (GBP/AUD). It is not real easy to see from the exhibit, but the pound was in a serious downdraft versus the Aussie dollar for some time. However, that trend reversed and the pound began to strengthen in a two-wave movement to the upside. That up move was all but put to sleep when we began to see the ominous clouds of a descending triangle on the

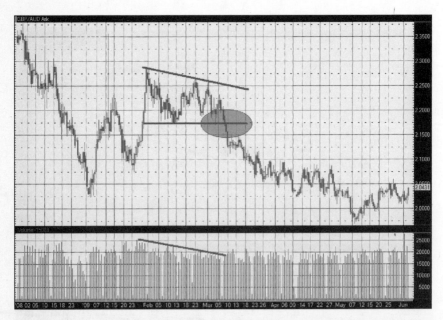

EXHIBIT 6.14 Chart of GBP/AUD Pair that Reflects the Descending Triangle Formation
Source: Fxaccucharts.com.

horizon. The shaded circle indicates where the pattern was broken and the macro downtrend was resumed. Finally, notice the descending line of volume indicated on the bottom of the exhibit. In most triangle formations, you will see the volume decline until the breakout occurs. This is just another confirmatory indication that the pattern is only temporary before the trend continues or reverses.

The symmetrical triangle (also referred to as a coil) usually forms during a trend as a continuation pattern. In other words, if the pair is in an uptrend and then enters into a symmetrical triangle, the chances are strong that the overall trend will continue when the pattern is broken. The pattern contains at least two lower highs and two higher lows. When these points are connected, the lines converge as they are extended and the symmetrical triangle takes shape. You could also think of it as a contracting wedge, wide at the beginning and narrowing during the formation.

Exhibit 6.15 is a weekly chart for the euro versus Australian dollar pair (EUR/AUD). It is unusual, but in this instance, the symmetrical triangle actually reversed the overall trend. We wanted to put this exhibit in the book because it is important for you to realize that although each triangle has a typical tendency, the tendencies are not set in stone. In fact, triangles are

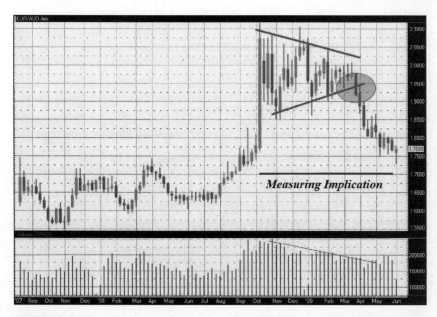

EXHIBIT 6.15 Chart of EUR/AUD Pair that Reflects a Symmetrical Triangle Formation
Source: Fxaccucharts.com.

nothing more than lines of resistance and support. Therefore, whichever side is broken is the relevant direction to trade. In this case, the euro had experienced significant appreciation against the Aussie dollar prior to the formation, but that all changed when the symmetrical triangle was broken to the downside (shaded circle). One other point we would mention is that all three triangles have measuring implications that project how far the pair should run or fall after it has moved out of the pattern. The measuring implication is simply the width of the triangle at its widest point. In the case of this example, the top of the triangle is around 2.10 and the bottom is around 1.85, which translates to a target of 0.25 to the downside (2.10–1.85). You measure the fall from the point the pattern was broken. In this case, the pattern broke around 1.95. The measuring implication is 1.70 (1.95–.25).

Exhibit 6.16 is the more common look we get from the symmetrical triangle. The exhibit is a daily chart for British pound versus the Swiss franc (GBF/CIIF). The pound had been depreciating against the franc, but about midway through the exhibit that picture changed: The pound bottomed and made a significant move, but it got extended and entered a consolidation stage that took the form of a symmetrical triangle. The shaded circle shows the point at which the pair broke out of the triangle. The breakout

EXHIBIT 6.16 Chart of GBP/CHF Pair that Reflects the Symmetrical Triangle Formation
Source: Fxaccucharts.com.

signaled that the British pound was ready to resume its march of appreciation against the franc.

Double-Tops and Bottoms

Have you ever looked at a plummeting currency pair and thought, "It has to be close to a bottom?" One of the time-honored challenges perpetually faced by investors is learning how to discern whether the peaks and valleys that characterize a currency's lows and highs represent real turning points, or are instead just temporary "breathers" that will eventually lead to additional movement in the previous direction. Believe it or not, there is a common technical formation that can give you the answer to that question. In reference to a currency hitting a low, it is called a "double-bottom." In the case of a currency or pair near a top, it is called a "double-top." The patterns are mirror images of one another, and even though they occur in different ways, they are both characterized by the same features.

A double-top begins when a pair attempts to break out above a recent peak, but fails. As you know, previous highs serve as points of resistance, so the pair must break through that earlier high in order for the upward trend to remain intact. If a pair does not immediately get through previous resistance, it does *not* automatically signal the formation of a double-top (and thus a reversal of trend). For confirmation, the correction valley between the two peaks, or support, must be broken to the downside. On the flip side of the coin, a double-bottom occurs when a pair attempts to break below a recent low, but holds that previous level of support for a second time. Once again, for confirmation, the correction peak between the two highs must be broken to the upside for confirmation.

Although there can be exceptions, these formations usually mark an intermediate- or long-term change in trend. In just about any market, you will see formations that look like a double-top or double-bottom, *but until the key support or resistance is broken, a reversal cannot be confirmed.* To help clarify, we will look at the key points in the formations and then walk through a few examples. Keep in mind that the defining characteristics are the same for both patterns; their *appearance* is such that one is a true mirror image of the other.

- **The Prior Trend:** A reversal pattern obviously would not be a reversal pattern if there was not anything to turn around. Thus, there must be an existing trend to reverse. In the case of the double-bottom, a significant downtrend of several months, if not years, should be in place for the currency pair. Likewise, with respect to a double-top, a major uptrend must have taken place.

- **Advance from Peak or Trough:** There should be clear evidence that volume and buying pressure are accelerating during the second half of the formation. Often you will see exhaustive buying/selling pressure as the top or bottom starts forming.
- **Support or Resistance Break:** Even after trading down to support (or up to resistance), the double-bottom/double-top and trend reversal are still not complete. Breaking support/resistance from the lowest/highest point between the peaks/troughs completes the formation. This, too, should occur with an increase in volume.
- **Support-Turned-Resistance, and Resistance-Turned-Support:** Broken support/resistance becomes potential resistance/support, and there is sometimes a test of this newfound level with the first correction. Such a test can offer a second chance to close a short position or initiate a long.
- **The Price Target:** The distance from the support/resistance break to peak/trough lows can be subtracted/added from/to the support/resistance break to estimate a target. This would imply that the bigger the formation is, the larger the potential advance.

Now that we have defined the pattern, let us take a look at a few examples. Exhibit 6.17 is an intraday chart for the British pound versus

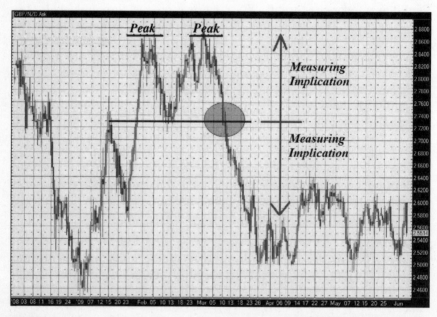

EXHIBIT 6.17 Chart of GBP/NZD Pair that Reflects a Double-Top Formation
Source: Fxaccucharts.com.

the New Zealand dollar (GBP/NZD) and it is a good example of a double-top. You can see that, prior to the top forming, the pair was in a nice uptrend and the pound was appreciating strongly against the New Zealand dollar. The first peak set a new high so the uptrend was still intact. The pair then pulled back to the trough and made another run at new highs. However, that run was stopped dead in its tracks and the second peak was formed. If you were long the pair, you then start to become a bit concerned. That said, this second peak is not the sell signal. In reality, the pair may have simply formed a channel before breaking higher. The sell signal, or short signal, came when the pair broke through the previous trough, which is shown by the shaded circle. As an investor, you also have an idea where the pair is headed because the measuring implication tells you the pair should fall the equivalent distance of the peak to trough. You can see on the exhibit what the distance should be. If you were short the pair, you would have looked to cover your position, or at least attach a trailing stop, when the pair entered into the area of the bottom arrow.

Exhibit 6.18 shows a real good example of a double bottom. It is a weekly exhibit for the Australian dollar versus the Japanese yen (AUD/JPY), and as you can see, the Aussie dollar was in a ferocious

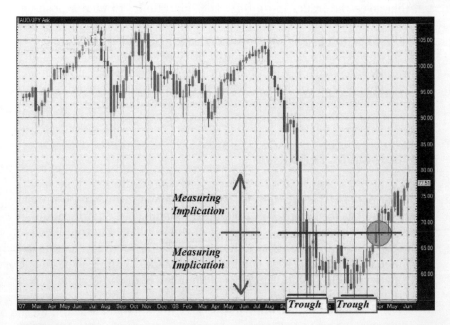

EXHIBIT 6.18 Chart of AUD/JPY Pair that Reflects a Double-Bottom Formation
Source: Fxaccucharts.com.

downtrend versus the yen for almost three months. This was a quick down-draft that cut the Aussie dollar value over 40 percent (did we mention the currency market is volatile?). The downtrend appeared to be intact, until the second leg of the trough held its ground and showed respect to the previous level of support. From there, you can see the pair broke to the upside. The double-bottom was confirmed when the pair broke back above the middle peak (of the "W"), which is indicated by the shaded circle. Once again, the pattern itself is telling you how far the pair should run to the upside by the depth of the formation itself. If you were long the pair off this pattern, you would want to sell the pair, or put in a trailing stop, when the price hit the top of the arrow on the left. This is the measuring implication. Notice that the pair broke out and then came back down to retest that breakout a few weeks later. This is common with this pattern and gives the trader an edge because he doesn't have to chase the breakout. He can be patient and wait for the retest to enter his position.

It is important to remember that these two formations are intermediate to long-term reversal patterns that will not form in a few days, or a few time periods in the case of an intraday pattern. Bottoms usually take longer than tops to form, and patience is highly recommended. Further, because they show major reversals, the breaks will typically be retested and this gives the trader more than one opportunity to take a position. Keep an eye on many of your other indicators, like the MACD, as the second part of the formation is materializing. Often these indicators will show buying pressure before the actual price action falls into place (very important). In closing, we will tell you that the double-tops and double-bottoms are some of the more reliable patterns we see. They often occur on longer-term exhibits and seem to give a more dependable reading than most patterns.

Cup-and-Handle Formation

As the name logically implies, there are two visually distinct sections of this particular pattern; the *cup* and the *handle*. The cup forms after a normal advance and has the same look as a typical rounding bottom formation. In reality, the cup looks like an ordinary bowl you would find in your kitchen. As the cup comes to completion, a short-term trading range develops on the right-hand side and this range comprises the handle. A subsequent breakout from the handle's range signals a continuation of the prior advance and thus completes the formation.

As with most technical formations, it is not simply a visual pattern for which we are looking. There are several qualifiers that go along with the cup-and-handle pattern, and traders should be sure that each of the qualifiers has been met before throwing their hats in the ring and trading on the signals. There is an old German proverb that says, "Ordung ist das halbe Leben" or "Order is half to life." Order and discipline are the absolutes for successful traders, so be sure to confirm all the signals line up for this pattern. Here are the confirmatory points for the pattern:

Cup: The cup should be "U" shaped and resemble a mixing bowl or rounding bottom formation. Often you will see "V" shaped bottoms in the market, but these are considered too sharp of a reversal to qualify. The softer "U" shape confirms that the trend is changing with a strong line of support at the bottom of the cup. The ideal pattern will give equal highs on both sides of the cup, but this is more of an "ideal" situation than it is a set-in-stone feature of the rule.

Handle: Typically, the high on the right side of the cup will match the high level set on the left side. After the high forms on the right side of the cup, there is a pullback that defines the handle. Often this handle will come in the form of another technical pattern. In fact, we would even go so far as to say that most formations will have a handle that is defined, in a smaller time frame, by a technical pattern. In the past, we have seen handles that took the shape of a channel, symmetrical triangle, or a short double-bottom. In essence, the handle represents the final consolidation before the big breakout and can retrace up to one-third of the cup's advance during its pull down. The smaller the retracement is, the more bullish the formation and significant the breakout.

Duration: The cup can extend from one to six months and often longer on weekly charts. The handle can be from one week to many weeks but ideally completes within one to four weeks. Keep in mind that the handle is a short-term phenomenon. It is basically formed because the pair has come up to resistance at the top of the cup and, as we often see when pairs approach resistance, weak-handed investors who bought near those old highs are clearing out their positions simply thankful that they were able to get their money back.

Volume: In an ideal volume, both ends of the cup should show heavy volume and the action that forms the cup in the middle section should see thin volume. The heavy volume on the right side will be the volume that breaks the pair out of the handle. Further, volume should be decreasing as the handle is being formed. The last thing you want to see is a pair hitting resistance and then pulling back on heavy volume. This type of action would invalidate the pattern.

Target: As we mentioned earlier, one of the best parts about the formations is that they give a trader a defined upside projection. The projected advance after breakout can be estimated by measuring the distance from the right peak to the bottom of the cup. You simply add the difference of these two numbers to the top of the cup and this tells you how far the issue should travel after the break.

Let us take a look at an example. Exhibit 6.19 shows a chart for the British pound versus the U.S. dollar (GBP/USD). On the exhibit, you can easily see the horizontal line of support that defines the top of the formation and the long rounding bottom that embodies the cup-and-handle. On the right side, you will see a shaded circle that defines the handle. In this case, the handle is forming in the fashion of a symmetrical triangle, and the target for the formation is measured as the depth of the cup from the horizontal line of resistance down to the rounding bottom. The formation will be validated when the handle is broken. This break should also be accompanied by heavy volume. We will give you an even better breakdown of this particular exhibit at the end of the chapter when we run through our *drilldown approach.*

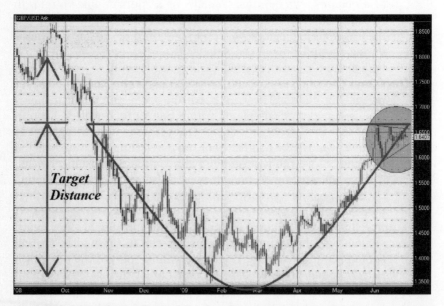

EXHIBIT 6.19 Chart of GBP/USD Pair that Reflects a Classic Cup-and-Handle Formation
Source: Fxaccucharts.com.

In the end, the cup-and-handle formation is not something you see often. Additionally, it has been our experience that the most reliable examples of these patterns are those seen on weekly exhibits, rather than on daily exhibits. That said, it is an ideal pattern, as is does not just tell you when to get in—it also tells you when to exit.

CONFIRMATORY INDICATORS—MACDs, MOVING AVERAGES, FIBONACCI

We believe that every investor, whether institutional or individual, should have some type of technical education. It is not enough to simply analyze companies and countries; you need to be able to analyze and interpret charts. The indicators we are covering in this section are ones that should be used in conjunction with other indicators or even patterns to get a true feel for what is going on with that particular country. Let's take a look at them individually.

MACD

The Moving Average Convergence/Divergence indicator, or MACD, was developed by Gerald Appel, and is one of the simplest and most dependable indicators available to all types of traders. We like to use MACD on more of a short-term basis and prefer it to help us time our entries. The indicator uses moving averages, which are essentially lagging indicators, to include some trend-following characteristics. These lagging indicators are converted into a real-time momentum oscillator by subtracting the longer moving average from the shorter moving average. The result is a line that oscillates above and below zero, without any upper or lower limits. Like many indicators we use, it is a centered oscillator, meaning that it will always gravitate toward the centerline when the trend is reversing. An example of a MACD indicator can be seen in Exhibit 6.20 for the USD/CAD pair on an hour chart. The MACD is at the bottom of the candlestick exhibit and is actually showing you both examples of how the MACD can be represented. The histogram portion gravitates above and below the zero line and looks like small mountains on the exhibit. Your buy-and-sell signals occur each time the histogram crosses zero. However, some signals are more powerful than others. The two oscillating lines are the second representation and are showing the difference between the MACD (12-period Exponential Moving Averages minus 26-period EMA) and the MACD Signal Line (9-period EMA of the MACD). Notice that each time the two lines

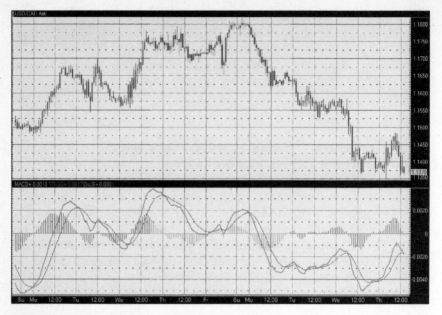

EXHIBIT 6.20   Chart of USD/CAD Pair that Reflects the MACD Indicators
Source: Fxaccucharts.com.

cross, the histogram crosses the zero line. Thus, both indications give you the same signals.

The two exponential moving averages will tend to cross over each other from time to time, signaling buy and sell action. When the crossover occurs, whether indicating a buy signal or a sell signal, knowing where it happens *in relationship to the centerline* is going to determine just how powerful the movement is going to be. If a cross occurs while the two lines are far away from the centerline, it is a more powerful signal. A *positive* MACD indicates that the 12-day EMA is trading above the 26-day EMA; a *negative* MACD indicates that the 12-day EMA is trading below the 26-day EMA. If MACD is positive and rising, then the gap between the 12-day EMA and the 26-day EMA is broadening. The interpretation is that the rate-of-change of the faster moving average is higher than the rate-of-change for the slower moving average. Positive momentum is escalating, and this would be considered bullish. If MACD is negative and declining further, then the negative opening between the faster-moving and slower-moving averages is getting bigger. Downward momentum is snowballing, and this would be considered bearish for the currency. *MACD centerline crossovers* occur when the faster moving average crosses the slower moving average.

There are three common methods for making investment decisions with the MACD:

1. ***Crossovers***: As we mentioned earlier, when the MACD falls below the signal line, it is a cue to sell; when the MACD rises above the signal line, it is the time to buy. The further away it is from the 0 line at which the cross occurs, the more powerful the signal.

2. ***Divergences***: When a security or index diverges from the MACD indicator, it often signals the end of the current trend. This type of signal works well in congruence with technical price patterns on currency pairs.

3. ***Overbought/Oversold***: When the MACD rises dramatically (i.e., the shorter-term moving average gets extended away from longer-term moving average), it is a signal the security is overbought and will soon return to normal levels.

Let us take a look at a few examples. Exhibit 6.21 is a daily look at the EUR/CHF (Euro/Swiss franc) pair and it gives us an example of how *crossovers* look and react. The buy signals are indicated with green arrows,

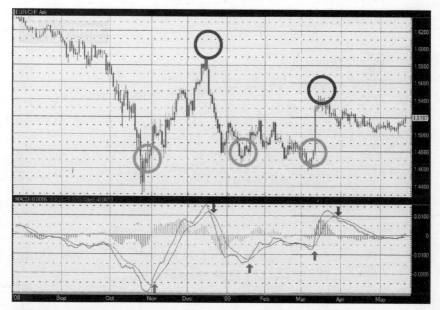

EXHIBIT 6.21   Chart of EUR/CHF Pair that Reflects Crossover Behavior
Source: Fxaccucharts.com.

while the sell indications are indicated with red arrows. Remember, the farther the two lines cross away from the zero line, the more significant or powerful the signal itself is.

Exhibit 6.22 shows a good example of how a *divergence* looks using a MACD indicator. This daily exhibit for the GBP/USD shows that the price chart for the pair was declining, but the MACD indicator at the bottom was diverging from this price decline and showing a series of higher highs and higher lows. In this case, the MACD was telling traders that a reversal was coming, and it most certainly did.

Frequently, you will see an important divergence show itself when a pair is trading within a technical pattern, or when the pair is in the process of putting in a double-bottom (or top) in Exhibit 6.23. As it pertains to a double-bottom, the second leg on the price chart will hit a new low, but the MACD reading will *not* hit a new low. This can be a great sign the double-bottom has legs to the upside and can be trusted for a trade; the same scenario can also be seen with double-tops. Along those lines, the MACD can be used for pure trading (i.e., trading just the signals themselves), but you can become a more effective investor/trader if you use indicators like the MACD as confirmatory indicators for a pattern. Take a look at the next exhibit. Exhibit 6.23 shows a double-bottom pattern for the AUD/JPY. The

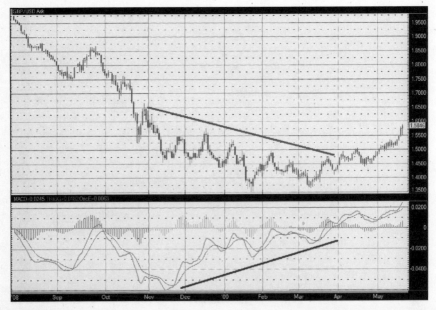

EXHIBIT 6.22   Chart of GBP/USD Pair that Reflects Divergence
Source: FX AccuCharts, 2009.

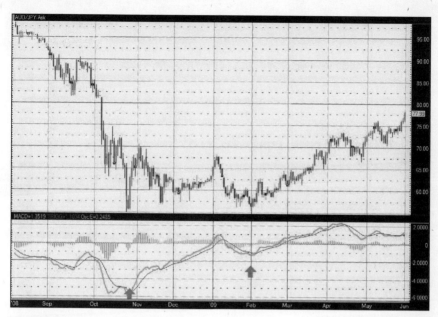

EXHIBIT 6.23 Chart of AUD/JPY Pair that Reflects a Double-Bottom Pattern against a Rising MACD Line
Source: Fxaccucharts.com.

two arrows on the MACD indicator point to the fact that the MACD line was moving higher, even as the pair hit a new low in forming the pattern. Again, the MACD was telling a story even before the pattern itself unfolded.

Now let us take a look at what an *overbought* or *oversold* MACD reading looks like. In Exhibit 6.24, you see a daily chart for the EUR/GBP pair. Of particular interest is the cross that occurred in December 2008, which is circled both on the chart and on the MACD indicator. What you are seeing is that the MACD got significantly overbought as the euro strengthened against the British pound. Like a rubber band snapping back, the MACD saw a steep decline back toward the zero line as the upward move digested itself and profit-takers swept in. The depth of the move on the MACD line is significant and when the MACD becomes significantly overbought or oversold, the snap back in the other direction can be meaningful and fast.

Moving Averages

Moving averages come in various forms and fashions and there are different ways to use moving averages, but their core purpose is to help us track

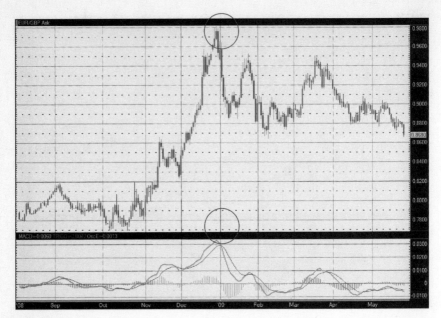

EXHIBIT 6.24 Chart of EUR/GBP Pair that Reflects a MACD Indicator of "Overbought"
Source: Fxaccucharts.com.

the trends of currencies by smoothing out the day-to-day price fluctuations, or "noise."

By identifying trends, moving averages allow us to make those trends work in our favor and increase the number of winning trades. The two averages we primarily use are the 50-day and the 200-day moving average. The 50-day moving average tells us what the short-term trend for the currency pair is doing, while the 200-day moving average shows us how the long-term trend looks.

Let us take a look at an example. Exhibit 6.25 is a chart of the Australian dollar versus the Japanese yen. The red smoothed line that is closest to the price bars is the 50-day moving average. The blue smooth line represents the 200-day moving average. The exhibit is showing us that, for most of 2008, the AUD was depreciating against the JPY. However, in early 2009, for the first time in almost a year, the short-term average began to flatten out and the trend began to change; then, it turned positive. Additionally, when the short-term moving average turned higher, it flattened out the longer-term moving average.

Another thing we want to point out is that pair prices can be reactive to these moving averages. In other words, the short- and long-term moving

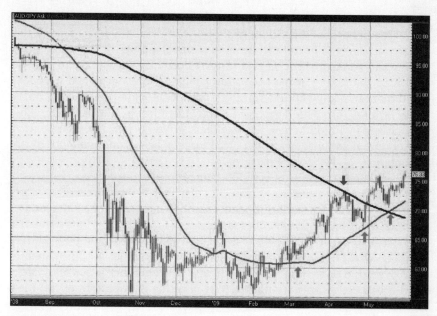

EXHIBIT 6.25   Chart of AUD/JPY Pair that Reflects Short- and Long-Term Moving Average Activity
Source: Fxaccucharts.com.

averages are good support and resistance lines to monitor when you are trading. On the exhibit, you can see three instances (upward arrows) where the pair found support at the short-term moving average. If you felt the AUD was going to continue appreciating against the JPY, you could have used any of these three points for entry. Also, the downward arrow on the exhibit shows how the pair found significant resistance at the long-term moving average. It was a significant move when the price finally pierced above the 200-day moving average.

Keep in mind that moving averages are not, by themselves, an end-all in currency trading analysis. However, they are a good "add-on" indicator to the rest of your research. The best part about moving averages is that they are simple to use and interpret and they give you an overall feel about the general direction of the pair.

Fibonacci

There are actually two specific indicators that we want to discuss as they relate to the Fibonacci theories, in general: Fibonacci Retracement Levels and Fibonacci Fans. Both indicators tell you much of the same story and, like the MACD, most currency trading software programs make both indicators readily available for their traders.

If we believe a currency pair is in a sustained up- or downtrend and we want to enter or short on a short-term corrective phase, the next issue relates to the timing of the trade. After making long, sustained moves in one direction, many markets retrace a part of the move before continuing in the primary direction. Fibonacci retracement levels and Fibonacci fans, popularized by Ralph Nelson Elliot (Elliott Wave Theory), are used to forecast potential support levels and price targets, based on the height of the overall move and any wave patterns.

Fibonacci himself was actually named Leonardo de Pisa. He was a 13th-century Italian mathematician who discovered the unique number sequence that bears his name. Fibonacci numbers are a sequence of numbers in which each successive number is the sum of the two previous numbers: 1, 1, 2, 3, 5, 8, 13, 21, 34, 55, 89, 144, 233, and so on. These numbers interrelate in a variety of ways. For example, any given number is approximately 1.618 times the preceding number and any given number is approximately 0.618 times the following number. You find this is important as we look through the actual retracement percentages.

The number 1.618 is commonly referred to as the Golden Mean. The real value of this number series is that it, according to R. Fischer, is "the most important mathematical presentation of natural phenomena ever discovered." Understand, we are not talking simply about investing; we are talking about everything in nature. It keeps popping up in everything from the proportions of the Egyptian pyramids, to the number of florets in flower heads, to the double helix of the DNA molecule, to the logarithmic spiral of the nautilus shell. The frequency with which it appears throughout so many seemingly unrelated aspects of life is actually quite sobering—and prompts even the most casual of observers to believe there is more than coincidence at play here.

Fibonacci Retracement Levels   The retracement indicator itself is a multiline indicator that helps determine subsequent areas of support or resistance as a correction to the primary trend. These are zones in which a rise in prices may stall, or where a price decline may be stopped. Fibonacci retracement lines are displayed by drawing a trendline between two extreme points (high and low). Trendlines are then drawn from the first extreme point so they pass through Fibonacci levels of 23.6 percent, 38.2 percent, 50.0 percent, and 61.8 percent. As the theory goes, as a currency pair rises from trough to peak, when it does begin to correct, it should find support as it drops 23.6 percent, 38.2 percent, 50 percent, and 61.8 percent of that primary move. As a simple example, if a pair increased from 1.50

to 2.00 and then slipped back 50 percent, this *retracement* would take it to 1.75 before it continued upward again.

Let us take a look at how we can use retracement levels in our trading. In Exhibit 6.26 you see a daily chart for the British pound versus the Japanese yen (GBP/JPY). We shortened up the exhibit a bit to make the retracement levels clearer, so you cannot see that the pound was in a long-term decline versus the yen leading up to this exhibit. What you are seeing here is the first up-leg of the new trend. The numbers one and two on the exhibit indicate the trough and peak of the new uptrend on which we drew our Fibonacci retracement levels. At this point, many hedge fund managers may have thought that this rally from point one to point two was simply a bear market rally, and that the pair was due to fall down to new lows; you, however, thought differently, and believed the pound was in a new bull market versus the yen, and so wanted to take a long position in the pound. Where do you enter? After drawing your Fibonacci retracement levels on the exhibit, you can clearly see multiple areas of support that would give you good areas of entry. In my experience, the 23.6 percent and the 38.2 percent levels will be the areas that will hold the best if, in fact, the trend is still intact. In this case, the upward-pointing arrow shows the

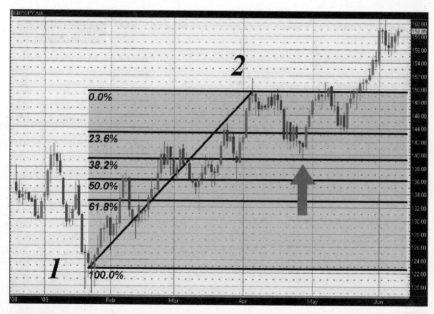

EXHIBIT 6.26 Chart that reflects GBP/JPY Pair that Reflects the Use of Retracement Levels
Source: Fxaccucharts.com.

point where the pair held support and began to once again march higher. This was the ideal entry point for your purchase.

Let us take a look at another example, this time of a pair in a downtrend. Exhibit 6.27 is for the euro versus the New Zealand dollar, and as you can see from the exhibit, the euro had been in a significant decline versus the New Zealand currency. However, pairs do not trade in one direction forever, and this pair subsequently started a counter trend move by trading higher. The peak-to-trough trend we are measuring against is again labeled from point one to point two. The pair began to move higher but you, as a savvy hedge fund manager, believed the primary downtrend was still intact and, for this reason, you were looking for a place to go short. The answer became clear when you attached your Fibonnaci retracement levels. The down arrow shows where the counter trend rally ran out of steam and the primary downtrend reasserted itself; this was the ideal point to enter a short position.

Now that we have the concept down, let us take a look at an example. Exhibit 6.28 is a weekly chart for the New Zealand dollar versus the U.S. dollar (NZD/USD). The pair had been trending lower for most of 2008 as the NZD depreciated against the USD. Then, the trend changed. As astute hedge fund managers, we want to know how significant this reversal was

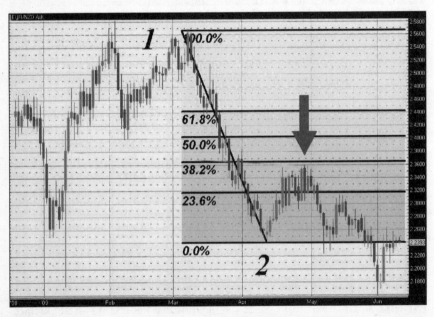

EXHIBIT 6.27 Chart of EUR/NZD Pair that Reflects the Use of Retracement Levels
Source: Fxaccucharts.com.

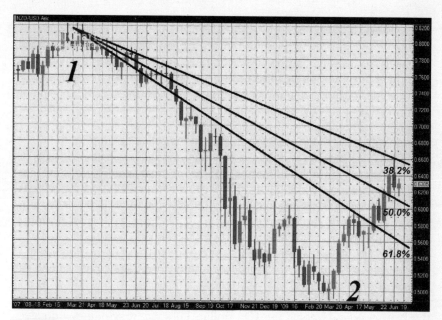

EXHIBIT 6.28 Chart of NZD/USD Pair that Reflects the Use of Retracement Levels
Source: Fxaccucharts.com.

and where our lines of resistance would lie. The Fibonnaci Fan tool told us the story. As you can see from the exhibit, the pair initially found a great deal of resistance at the 61.8 percent line. However, when it broke through that line, it quickly ran to the 50 percent line and broke through *it*. Notice what happened when the pair hit the 38.2 percent line: it found a ton of overhead supply and was sold off. If you were looking to buy the pair, you could now look at the 50 percent line as a line of support for entry. Also, notice the pair formed a nice reverse head and shoulders when putting in this bottom. We have not drawn the neckline, as we want you to see it for yourself, but you will notice that the neckline comes across and crosses on the right shoulder, very close to the 61.8 percent line. In this cast, you had several confirmatory patterns/indicators that foreshadowed higher prices for the pair.

Often, investors get a little jumpy with the markets. They see a specific currency or pair making a big move and feel they have to be part of what is going on. These Fibonacci studies are not intended to provide the exact point for the entry and exit of a currency pair. However, they are useful for estimating *areas* of support and resistance that can be used as entry and exit points.

THE DRILLDOWN APPROACH

The majority of this chapter has been designated to spotting trends, patterns, and turning points within the currency market, in general, as well as on behalf of individual pairs. For the most part, these are the principal tools in your *currency* toolbox. However, we now want to shift our focus a bit and engage in more of a philosophical conversation, one that centers on helping you to deliver returns in a more complete fashion.

If you are a day trader in the currency markets, you are focusing on intraday charts to make money. If you are a swing trader, you are most likely focusing on the daily pair charts. However, we would tend to argue that it is the exhibits above and below your current focus that are the most important to your trading, regardless of style. In other words, if we are swing trading a pair, it is important that the weekly chart be in our favor. As well, after we have identified a positive weekly and daily scenario, it is crucial that we continue to drill down into our intraday charts to find the ideal entry point.

Let us take a look at an example. Exhibit 6.29 is a weekly chart for the British pound versus the U.S. dollar. Personally, we fancy ourselves as longer-term traders in currencies, so we are showing you this example

EXHIBIT 6.29 Weekly Chart of GBP/USD that Reflects a Cup-and-Handle Formation
Source: Fxaccucharts.com.

from the vantage point of a longer-term position trader. We will day trade on occasion, but our principal style is to get into a trade to which we can commit for some weeks or months and thus take bigger chunks of change out of the trade. As you can see from the exhibit, the global economic melt-down that encompassed 2008 led to a flight to quality and a run into the U.S. dollar. The pound suffered significantly against the U.S. dollar during this time frame. However, in early 2009, that changed. As you can see from the exhibit, the pound put in a rounded bottom that led to a cup-and-handle formation. I liked the look of the weekly chart so I next dialed my analysis down to the daily chart.

Exhibit 6.30 shows us a better view of what the pattern looks like. The long rounded line shows us the formation of the cup. This reversal pattern took seven months to form, which makes sense because the decline of the pair was so drastic. Notice that the handle has been forming on the right side, which is marked by the shaded area.

One more tool at which we want you to look in this case is the Fibonacci retracement levels. We have attached the retracement tool in Exhibit 6.31, and we ran it from the bottom of the cup to the horizontal re-sistance line. Notice that after the pair began to form the handle, the initial corrective phase took it down to the 23.6 percent retracement level. The

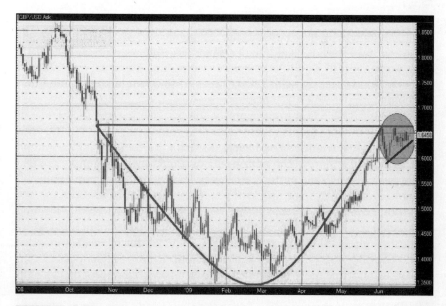

EXHIBIT 6.30 Daily Chart of GBP/USD Pair that Reflects a Cup-and-Handle Formation
Source: Fxaccucharts.com.

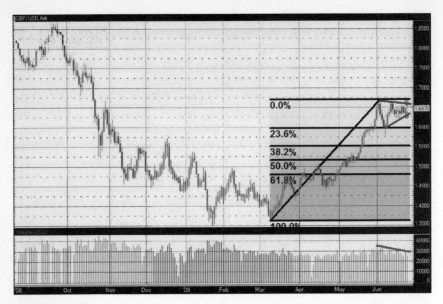

EXHIBIT 6.31   Daily Chart of GBP/USD Pair that Reflects Fibonacci Retracement Levels
Source: Fxaccucharts.com.

pair immediately bounced off this line. Coincidence? We think not. At this point, we have both a weekly and daily chart that we like, and the daily chart has a pattern we are comfortable in trading. Now, we need only to properly time our entry, which forces us to drill down further to the intraday chart.

Exhibit 6.32 is a four-hour chart for the pair. Notice that the handle of the longer-term cup-and-handle formation is coming to fruition in the form of a symmetrical triangle. You have a declining level of resistance and inclining level of support. The pattern is confirmed by the thinning volume as we push through the pattern. At this point, we note two potentially actionable events. If the pair breaks through the shaded circle at the top, we would buy the break, or maybe the retest; if the pattern breaks through the shaded circle on the bottom of the pattern, the pair would most likely retest the horizontal line of support at 1.58, and so this is another area we would consider entry if the pair is able to hold that area of support.

Let us take one more example. In this scenario, our approach can help keep you out of a bad trade. Exhibit 6.33 shows you an intraday look at the U.S. dollar versus the Canadian dollar (USD/CAD). At first glance, the pair is behaving well. We see a strong line of support (bottom horizontal line), followed by a break of resistance at the line above it and a subsequent

EXHIBIT 6.32 Four-Hour Chart of GBP/USD Pair that Reflects Potential Action Cues
Source: Fxaccucharts.com.

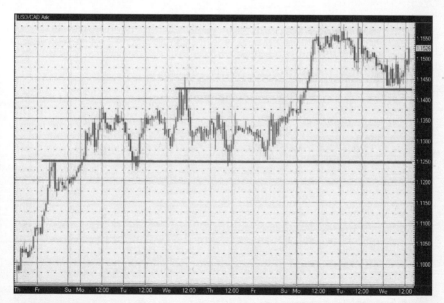

EXHIBIT 6.33 Intraday Chart of USD/CAD Pair before Enhanced Analysis (below)
Source: Fxaccucharts.com.

successful retest of that breakout. On the surface, this looks like a decent setup. If this was the exhibit on which we were basing our trade, we would have to think that things look good. However, what you do not see right now is the bigger picture, which is something on which you must always keep your focus, as well.

Exhibit 6.34 shows the next level up from the preceding intraday chart. In essence, we are drilling *up* in this case. What we can easily see on the daily exhibit is a pair that has been in a steep decline, and for which the primary trend is still most definitely down. Additionally, the pair is currently sitting right at a significant line of resistance that would be a formidable line to break through. Our belief, then, that the intraday chart looks strong is *misleading*, because the pair is already in a danger zone in terms of the bigger picture. If you enter this pair on the long side, you stand a good chance of being reversed very quickly. In fact, after looking at the daily chart, we would be more inclined to fade this rally and short the pair, even if it was only for a day trade. You see the significant overhead resistance you are facing, so, instead of day trading long, wait for the pair to show strength and go short.

When it comes to currencies, we remain utterly convinced that your ultimate effectiveness at making money relies on your willingness to adhere to a comprehensive trading system. The inherent volatility in the

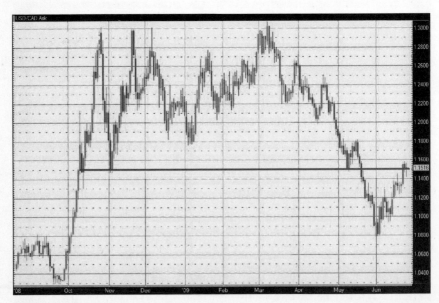

EXHIBIT 6.34   Daily Chart of USD/CAD Pair after "Drill-Up"
Source: Fxaccucharts.com.

currency market simply does not allow for you to engage it any other way. As you make currencies a significant component of your overall hedge fund, should you choose to do so, you will find that technical analysis is about the best friend you will ever have to the end of regularly making money from your efforts. Your use of other investable instruments will also benefit from this kind of analysis, but when it comes to the currency market, its implementation is really nothing short of essential. As we pointed out at the beginning of this chapter, despite our collective experience and success at managing money in equities, our first venture into currency trading introduced us, first-hand, to the awesome power of the Forex, as well as the ability of that power to cut both ways in a personal trading environment. To that end, your best weapon, both offensively and defensively, is an intensively managed trading system.

CHAPTER 7

Accessing Foreign Real Estate

U p until the last few years, investment professionals did not spend much time considering the implementation of significant amounts of foreign real estate into their portfolios; until the implosion of the domestic real estate market, along with the historical relative inaccessibility of real estate in foreign countries, there was little reason to seriously consider "going global." The United States was motoring along quite nicely, and the perceived challenges of investing globally, particularly directly, seemed to substantially outweigh the benefits, considering that was what is available in the United States.

That perception has been radically altered by the great economic meltdown of 2008, and while U.S. real estate has the potential to remain every bit the beneficial investment opportunity it has always been, it is time for the skilled hedge fund–minded investor to look with great scrutiny at opportunities available overseas. One of the enablers of effective global real estate investment has been the Internet, which has allowed for a more prompt and effective flow of information. Additionally, many nations have actively sought to relax once-stringent rules regarding the purchase of real estate by non-nationals.

One of the reasons we like going global with real estate has to do with the demonstrated low correlation that exists among real estate markets on a worldwide basis, and there are numerous pieces of information that attest to that lack of relationship. For example, the data in Exhibit 7.1 was the correlations between real estate markets on behalf of a variety of highly developed nations.

EXHIBIT 7.1 Correlation of Real Estate Stocks by Country or Region

Country/ Region	United States	Canada	UK	Europe	Australia	Hong Kong	Japan
U.S.	1.00	.37	.33	.36	.26	.23	.16
Canada	.37	1.00	.22	.37	.16	.15	.22
UK	.33	.22	1.00	.71	.27	.30	.25
Europe	.36	.37	.71	1.00	.31	.45	.15
Australia	.26	.16	.27	.31	1.00	.24	.12
Hong Kong	.23	.15	.30	.45	.24	1.00	.10
Japan	.16	.22	.25	.15	.12	.10	1.00

Based on monthly returns in local currencies from 01/1990 through 12/2006.
Source: CSIM Real Estate Research; FTSE EPRA/NAREIT Global Real Estate Index global, regional, and country series.

Outside of the matter of low correlation, we see that real estate, as an asset class, presents the same opportunities for diversification and opportunity as do negotiable securities. As for *opportunity*, roughly two-thirds of the real estate we consider as good for investment exists outside of the United States at present. That said, the ratio has not changed in recent years, but has been like this for decades, and is roughly the same ratio as that which exists on behalf of the global securities markets. What *has* changed, however, is the *accessibility* of these properties. The accessibility obstacle has been lessened on two fronts. First, there is the matter of basic exchange of information; the global use of the Internet has largely conquered that problem. Additionally, investors have had to deal with proprietary national laws prohibiting foreigners from owning real estate directly; that is changing. A variety of global markets, once off-limits to foreign investors, has opened up widely in the last 10 to 15 years. Nations such as South Korea and Turkey, once prohibited to access U.S. investors' markets, are now quite receptive. There are plenty of other countries like these, but, admittedly, there are also others like China that have greatly *restricted* the ability of individual investors to functionally purchase real estate for investment purposes exclusively. Nevertheless, access is broadly increasing, to be sure.

Diversification remains one of the strongest reasons to take your real estate investing global. In this day and age, diversification remains a hotly debated issue, as the interconnective nature of relationships between global markets has made the assumption of a guarantee of diversification through international investing a "no brainer" *no longer*. There is plenty of data available that shows a negative correlation among many markets, but it is reasonable to assume that such diversification may become less evident on a widespread basis as global markets continue in their tendency to move more or less in lockstep with one another. The beneficial assumption that we can fairly make, however, is that *foreign* real estate, as with the domestic brand, is local. Just as there is really no such thing as a national real estate market in the United States, so it is that real estate as a market will tend to fluctuate in any other given nation depending on which specific region of the country you are focusing. It makes sense that the behavior of the United States to other developed markets is going to be more highly correlated than the United States to emerging or frontier markets, but one of the great things about real estate as an asset is that there is some correlative disparity even among developed nations that persists.

The issue of diversification and correlation for global investors is particularly acute when comparing asset classes. Although there is ample opportunity for growth in nondomestic stocks, for example, it is getting tougher to establish a reliable noncorrelative relationship between U.S. and foreign stocks. Not that one cannot be found, to be sure—just that it is not as easy as it once was. The simple reality is that the matter of correlation when it comes to stocks seems to have adopted a component of psychological simpatico—as we know, when Wall Street catches a cold, there is plenty of sneezing done on the Hang Seng and FTSE. The data in Exhibit 7.2 seems to bear out that, long term, correlations between popular global stock indexes are much greater than they are when measured against global *real estate* equities, in particular.

For real estate investors, the benefit of localized differences in markets adds a level of diversification that is just not present in other asset classes; to wit, stocks on the NYSE are not also influenced by the market behavior of investors trading on the El Paso, Texas Stock Exchange, as there *is* no such exchange. However, real estate market activity is directly influenced

EXHIBIT 7.2 Correlation of Major Indexes from June 1993 through June 2008

	S&P 500	Russell 2000	MSCI EAFE	LB Aggregate	FTSE EPRA/ NAREIT
S&P 500	1.00	.72	.72	.03	.53
Russell 2000	.72	1.00	.65	−.07	.58
MSCI EAFE	.72	.65	1.00	−.06	.64
LB Aggregate	.03	−.07	−.06	1.00	.13
FTSE EPRA/NAREIT	.53	.58	.64	.13	1.00

Source: FactSet (www.factset.com) and Northern Trust (www.northerntrust.com). Major indexes cited: S&P 500, Russell 2000 (U.S. Small Cap) MSCI EAFE (Foreign Stocks), LB Aggregate (U.S. Bonds), and FTSE EPRA/NAREIT (Global Real Estate Equities).

at every level—globally, by continent/region, by country—all the way down to the local municipality. An easy illustration can be found in the United States residential market: While the general real estate market has been soft in the United States since the onset of the Great Recession, there are plenty of areas that have fared much worse (and better) than others. For example, Amarillo, Texas saw a 3 percent increase in its median home prices from June 2008 to June 2009, during a period when median home prices nationally declined 15 percent. More tellingly, monthly sales volume of residential properties was up 4 percent in Amarillo over the same period, while it was down 11 percent for the entire state of Texas. The complex, multilayered nature of the downturn in U.S. residential real estate in 2007 to the present is such that there are strong negative influences on all housing markets throughout the country, but those that are facing much less of a headwind, like Amarillo, are doing so for solid fundamental reasons that are relevant for real estate investors the world over: first and foremost, low unemployment; Amarillo benefits from an unemployment rate that, at this writing, is the lowest in Texas—Amarillo is characterized by a strong presence in Texas mainstay industries like oil and cattle (roughly 25 percent of the U.S. beef supply is processed in and around Amarillo), but also benefits from the presence of employers like Bell Helicopter and the Pantex plant, which is the nation's *only* facility for the assembly and disassembly of nuclear weapons, and is charged with overseeing the safety and security of the U.S.'s entire nuclear weapons stockpile. Amarillo's single-largest employer is multinational giant Tyson Foods, and there are assorted other recognizable names in the area, including Owens-Corning.

Additionally, Amarillo enjoys the same low interest rates that the rest of the United States is seeing at this writing, as well as housing prices that have generally remained *within* the stratosphere while others moved up, up, and away. It is these factors, in combination, that have allowed for a resiliency in the Amarillo market when so many others in the United States have fallen off a cliff. The point is that real estate truly is a local market, and while top-down analysis is an excellent way to begin its evaluation, it is a market where the analysis you perform at the most local levels can reveal trends that actually buck those occurring regionally and nationally. The reality is that the local nature of real estate investment is such that it will tend to weigh down any measurable inclination toward higher correlation—in the end, the reason one wants to live or work in Mumbai, India, for example, is largely going to be unique to Mumbai, and therefore that space, be it residential or commercial, is not easily substituted with similar real property in Minneapolis, Minnesota. The bottom line is that while there certainly remain opportunities for real diversification in negotiable securities, there is little question that it is in real estate as an asset class that the best opportunities persist for more intricate levels of investment disassociation.

There remains a variety of other relevant and quite current reasons why one should examine real estate investing outside of the United States; let us look at the state of the U.S. economy, as a whole.

The real estate crash and associated credit crisis that is plaguing the United States—and will likely do so for years to come—has had a significant impact on the future of real estate values in the United States. A combination of greed and social engineering on the part of U.S. financial institutions and government conspired to cause an obscene overheating of real estate values from 2001 through 2006. Lower underwriting standards, prompted largely by well-intentioned policy decisions designed to make the dream of home ownership a reality for more Americans, led to a simple, mad increase in the volume of transactions—with little attention paid to the endgame.

With the universal acceptance of higher debt-to-income ratios, along with loan-to-value ratios of 100 percent becoming standard, all available to borrowers with credit scores as low as 580, we had a formula for disaster, and so it was that one was visited on us. The resulting implosion has caused prices to drop in an unprecedented fashion, and has cruelly subordinated the investment profiles of those U.S. real property investors who are now left to wait for market improvement; it may be a long wait. Speculation now is that it may take another 20 years for real estate values to return to their highs of 2006 and 2007 in some places in America, which means that the newer real estate investor has to consider if there are not better alternatives waiting for him outside of the United States in markets that are clearly more responsive.

Let us continue our discussion of the motivating factors and associated risks with accumulating a global real estate presence.

Real estate has become a highly revered asset class in the minds of many. Talk to many investors, and quite a few will mention the tangible nature and usefulness of real estate as an investable asset class; we have a professional acquaintance who invests in nothing but real estate with a substantial portfolio, and does so because, as he puts it, "it's the only asset you can actually use." The aforementioned propensity of real estate to remain fairly well detached from negotiable securities in terms of correlation has been a historically strong draw, as well. The relatively stable returns are popular, too, and real estate returns in the United States from the last quarter-century of the previous century averaged roughly 5 percent per year. In Exhibit 7.3, you see data that illustrates the high return and competitive dividend yield realized by global real estate securities in comparison to three popular global equity indexes.

In addition to the benefits associated with terrific diversification at a multitude of levels, a portfolio that includes a diversified presence of

EXHIBIT 7.3	Performance of Global Real Estate Against Major World Stock Indexes from June 1993 through June 2008		
	Return	**Standard Deviation**	**Dividend Yield**
FTSE EPRA/NAREIT Global	10.98%	15.24%	4.76%
S&P 500	9.22%	13.95%	2.26%
Russell 2000	8.92%	17.95%	1.49%
MSCI EAFE	7.21%	14.34%	3.60%

Each of the figures is quoted on an annualized basis.
Source: FTSE EPRA/NAREIT, S&P, Russell, MSCI, FactSet (www.factset.com), Northern Trust (www.northerntrust.com).

properties across a variety of local economies throughout the world helps to stabilize that portfolio. Total returns in real estate investment are principally determined by the income seen from rent revenue and associated operating fees. This income, comprised of the totality of the yields derived from positions held in a variety of markets, is made more stable as a result of that yield composition. Essentially, then, you see a global real estate portfolio provide a hedge at two levels: first, within real estate itself as an asset class, with the gathering of the penetrated markets serving to buttress the total return, and then more generally, in terms of stabilizing the overall portfolio, with a reliable income stream in a class with low correlation to the other major asset classes that compose your hedge fund.

The large and expanding size of the total investable universe of global real estate is another benefit, as it, in turn, provides tremendous opportunities for primarily domestic investors. The trend toward a more favorable outlook about investing, generally, along with a trend toward more personal property ownership by nationals and foreigners in more countries in recent years has gone a long way to expanding the overall investable universe of real estate. Not only is the accessibility of direct real estate investment much more prevalent (Japan, for example, has been in the midst of slowly but surely loosening its tight, nationalistic grip on its real property for some years now), but the number of countries that have allowed for the *securitization* of real estate has risen dramatically in recent years. There are now well over 20 countries with REIT-type legislation, whereas until 2000, there were just eight. Of the developed markets, it is estimated that about 15 percent of their total capitalization of all material asset classes is accorded to real estate. It is the securitization of real estate that has so vastly expanded the asset class's investability size, and that trend will only continue based on the more favorable acceptance of capitalistic practices throughout the world, complemented by more and more nations seeking to adopt REIT-like legislation.

CURRENCY AND TAX IMPLICATIONS

Although the increased securitization of real estate has brought greater liquidity and flexibility to the asset class, exposure generally remains a constant. Accordingly, it is this tendency to longer-term exposure, particularly for more direct investors, that largely mitigates the attention we pay to specifically dealing with currency risk; in other words, because *time* is probably the best single hedge, overall, against many (but not all) of the more usual risks of international investing, and because it is the anticipated long-term performance of the asset that we believe is the most compelling factor to consider, we do not weight the matter of currency risk highly with regard to this asset class. Still, we accept that investment styles and strategies differ, and so some of you may want to actively hedge your real estate bet. Although we think the best hedge is to have multiple market exposures, which in turn gives you currency hedges by way of a cross-section of national currencies, or perhaps to engage in a practice as simple as using the income from a property in the target country to pay the interest on a loan you have against the property from that same country (thereby reducing the amount of income that must be considered in terms of currency risk), you can look to the oft-used options and currency contracts. We tend to like options in this case, because forwards do not really give you the ability to benefit by favorable movements (although, overall, they can be the most effective tools for flat-out lowering volatility). With call options, you make money when the exchange rate moves higher than the strike price, which means you can buy the foreign currency at the lower price; as for put options in this case, they are beneficial when the rate drops below the strike price, which allows you to sell at the higher rate. Unlike forwards, you do not have to exercise the option unless it makes sense. Again, we do not think you have too much to worry about here if you have multiple property market exposures over the long term, but options are perhaps a decent way to go if your particular global real estate strategy requires some hedging.

Efforts at tax minimization can be tricky when it comes to global real estate holdings owned directly. The central problem is that modifications in tax regimes are not keeping up with the speed at which the investment structures themselves are being augmented and liberalized. More countries are beginning to change laws so as to encourage foreign investment, and the European Union has asked its members to work on standardizing their tax structures, but that is clearly a work in progress. In terms of your direct real estate investments, depending on the anticipated level of exposure and the result of your cost-benefit analysis, you may wish to structure an offshore trust or company through which to make your purchases.

Many countries have no legal basis to tax the underlying assets of a foreign company, so you could conceivably set up an offshore company in another tax-friendly nation, and use it to hold your assets. Note that you will want to properly vet your plan with an appropriate expert, to be sure it will fly; there was a big case some years back involving a U.S. firm buying and selling a large piece of South Korean real estate through a Malaysian holding company, which was established by the firm for the express purpose, apparently, of taking advantage of a beneficial tax treaty between the two Asian countries. In the end, South Korea was less than pleased, and the Americans ended up getting pounded for a huge fine. Granted, we are talking about a high-profile deal that registered in the hundreds of millions of U.S. dollars, but the principle of cultural and legal awareness still applies, even at your level. Do your due diligence with the help of an appropriately qualified attorney.

In the end, a target country's tax regime needs to be thoroughly reviewed, and in the process you may find some beneficial mechanisms contained within. For example, although France's capital gains rate is 33.3 percent for non-EU residents (compared to 16 percent for EU residents), if you hold the acquired property for at least 15 years, no capital gains tax is due. The bottom line is that if you are seeking to buy directly in a given country, you will want to be clear on your tax responsibilities and calculate those against anticipated rent revenues (if applicable), as well as have clear knowledge as your capital gains liabilities when it comes time to sell.

GLOBAL REAL ESTATE INVESTMENT MECHANISMS

Once you decide to include real estate as a part of your overall portfolio, you are next left to consider the multitude of fashions by which to do so. One of the biggest struggles for prospective real estate investors is trying to determine the best way to hold the asset class. Because real estate is broadly securitized, the full range of options is open to the investor, from individual real estate stocks on through (mutual funds, closed/open-end funds, etc.). For the purposes of this book, we decided to focus on those mechanisms that are somewhat unique to the real estate market, and also offer more targeted opportunities to the global investor.

Clearly, the biggest advantage to real estate securities is the fact that you can access the market with a much more modest investment (typically) than that which is required to make a direct investment in real estate, and certainly with regard to commercial property. For example, with just a few thousand dollars, you can bring a global real estate allocation to your portfolio through the use of some well-chosen REITs and/or REIT ETFs.

Our discussion, then, will center on explanations of, and thoughts about, indirect ownership through global/international/foreign REITs and associated REIT ETFs, somewhat direct ownership through limited partnerships and private placements, and direct ownership of residential properties. Note that in the area of direct ownership, we are limiting our discussion to residential properties, for two reasons. From an asset allocation standpoint, securitized real estate does not own detached single-family resident housing, so purchasing real estate directly in foreign countries is really your only option to gaining a material interest in it. Also, the ability to functionally acquire and manage commercial property in foreign markets falls far outside the scope of the vast majority of individual investors; plus, when you can ably penetrate *that* market with liquidity and agility as you can with REITs and their associated derivatives, it makes little sense to do it directly in your capacity as a personal fund manager.

Real Estate Investment Trusts (REITs)

From the standpoints of diversification, investment viability, and opportunity, it is our belief that the single best mechanism to use in an effort to gain an interest in global commercial property markets is the Real Estate Investment Trust, or REIT. REITs in their natural form are highly useful tools, and when you consider that REIT derivatives exist in the form of other securities (like mutual funds and ETFs), there is probably no better way to access these markets. On that note, let us begin our discussion by touching on some REIT basics; we realize this may be a bit of old information for more investment-savvy readers, and we are not going to bury you with unimportant details, but let us do a quick review.

REITs are exchange-listed companies that invest in various components of commercial real estate. While there is some diversity and subcategorization as to all the different ways the companies invest, REITs come in three broad forms: equity, mortgage, and hybrid. The purpose of equity REITs is to invest in commercial, income-producing property. That said, equity REITs do not simply invest in the property; they also manage and operate the acquired properties to the fullest extent. In fact, one of the features of REITs that sets them apart from other real estate companies is that they have to acquire the properties with the intent to own and operate them for the long term, rather than buy and then sell them once the development phase is complete. The central beneficial feature of the REIT mechanism is the potential for high current income; prospective growth, while certainly a component of REITs, is more secondary (partly because they pay out basically all of their profit; there is nothing available to reinvest in any definable sort of way, as is usually done within a typical company structure).

Mortgage REITs loan money; that is their purpose. They loan money to developers, owners, and operators of commercial real estate, although mortgage REITs nowadays loan only against existing properties. Mortgage REITs typically originate the loans, but they can also purchase secondary mortgages. Either way, the income from these REITs is derived from the totality of interest and fees, minus expenses. As for hybrid REITs, they are companies that have a hand in each pot; they simultaneously own and operate property, *and* loan money, which means the income is derived both from rent revenue and interest income.

Like any bona fide company, REITs have boards of directors or trustees. The board is elected by shareholders, and the board members, in turn, choose the folks who perform the management functions. It is the board that determines the specific investments made by the REIT. On that note, you want to carefully consider the performance of the REIT's board and management team in particular respects before you invest. For example, how ably is management reinvesting cash flow? Is the REIT successful at acquiring properties for which the rent levels are below market? Does management have a sound and transparent strategy for addressing tough markets and thinking creatively to enhance upsides and limit downsides? Track records are, of course, important, as are the credentials of board members and appointed managers. In your due diligence, you want to see records of success at every level, particularly during markets that were historically bad.

The aforementioned high current income comes courtesy of an IRS requirement that the entities pay out nearly all of *their* income. In the United States, in order for a company to qualify as a REIT (which is technically a tax designation), it must distribute at least 90 percent of its income to investors. That said, because REITs can deduct dividend payments to shareholders, they usually pay out *100 percent* of their taxable income. It should be noted, however, that foreign REITs have disparate distribution rules. For example, while the distribution rules of Hong Kong REITs are similar to U.S. REITs, Spain has no distribution requirement, at present. Still, most REITs pay out most of their income, so beneficial dividend payments remain a core advantage of REITs, regardless of in which country they are domiciled.

As with certain other types of collectives, REITs can trade at premiums or discounts to Net Asset Value (NAV). Under normal market conditions, REITs sell at slight premiums to NAV, but you want to keep your eye on those that are available for discounts—*maybe*. The reality is that there has been a split for some time between REIT investors as to the relevance of NAV in determining the true value of REIT stocks, and in the end, you as a fund manager will have to decide where you fall in the debate as to how you will evaluate prospective REIT selections for your portfolio. Let us look at the two sides.

Establishment of a REIT's Intrinsic Value   Where you fall in the consideration of NAV depends largely on which you believe is the more important element of a REIT: the buildings or the management. To some, the real value of a REIT lies principally with its assets, the bricks and mortar structures that fundamentally live exclusively in the real estate market, separate from the securities markets; to others, the value is in the management, and the proponents of that idea point to the fact that REITs are real companies, "living" corporate entities that are constantly making business decisions on behalf of shareholders. The anti-NAV crowd (that is not a completely fair characterization, but it suits the purpose of ease with respect to this discussion) likes to point out that other companies, like Caterpillar, for example, do not have *their* value assessed on the basis of the simple liquidation value of its hard assets, like facilities, inventory, and so on. The problem with *that* view, in our opinion, is that it does not allow for the central asset-based difference between REITs and other companies: namely, where it is the symbiotic totality of the hard assets of other kinds of companies that make for the finished products, the core assets of REITs really *are* the finished products.

The value of what a REIT owns is basically calculated by dividing the REIT's projected net operating income (NOI) by the capitalization rate. Cap rate is itself a function of NOI, and is defined as:

$$\text{Capitalization Rate} = \frac{\text{Annual Net Operating Income}}{\text{Cost/Value}}$$

Cap rate represents the ratio between NOI and capital cost of the asset, and is used to measure the value of income-producing real estate investments. In terms of valuing a REIT, the cap rate is going to be derived from the properties that compose the entire portfolio. On a singular basis, it is used to determine asset value on the basis of a year of expected income. The higher the cap rate, the lower the NAV, and vice versa (simple example: $100,000 divided by 8 percent = $1,250,000; $100,000 divided by 10 percent = $1,000,000). The key to NAV, then, lies in the cap rates.

The pro-NAV camp is generally strongest, and has perhaps some preponderance of the evidence to back it up. For example, three Columbia University professors, William Gentry, Charles Jones, and Christopher Mayer, published a paper titled *REIT Reversion: Stock Price Adjustments to Fundamental Value* in 2003 (updated in 2004) that contends that trading REITs solely on the basis of NAV, meaning buying when stock prices are at discounts and shorting when they are at premiums, will be more than sufficient to invest successfully (you can review the scholarship yourself at www.greenstreetadvisors.com/Journal_of_Finance_REIT_Reversion.pdf).

The anti-NAV camp believes that consideration of NAV alone is woefully insufficient, and that management supplies great value through its operational applications, like decisions to buy, sell, and so forth. In their world, the valuations of discounted cash flow (DCF) are king. DCF is a forward-looking metric that proponents of its use feel reflects the fluid, transient nature of a business; NAV, they claim, simply pins valuation on a present-moment snapshot of underlying asset value. There is, for example, proof of REITs that have bucked the system and continue to see a substantial rise in stock shares, all the while trading at huge premiums to NAV. How is that explained? Management at these REITs would tell you that the answer is, well, *management*.

Ultimately, you will have to decide for yourself how you choose to value your prospective REIT investments, because there is, admittedly, some evidence that supports both sides of the debate. To our way of thinking, the compelling reality of principally considering NAV, by virtue of the investment record realized by doing so, means that if someone put guns to our heads and forced us to choose a valuation method, we would opt for NAV. The truth, too, about NAV is that it is not fair to completely characterize it as having no future value benefit, because the calculations used to compute NAV *have* to look to the future to some extent, anyway.

When considering the methods of analyzing REITs, in terms of broad principles of investment analysis, the top-down and bottom-up methodologies about which we spoke in Chapter 4 each have merit, but again, out of deference to our global interests, we have to prioritize the top-down approach. Looking at REITs from the top down, you have to consider the macroeconomic factors that will affect commercial real estate, such as the economic profiles of regions, countries, and local markets: What are the levels and trends of unemployment and interest rates? How about demographics—in what direction is the population flowing, and what are the age breakdowns? In short, all of the standard considerations we give to any foreign industry and company, as well as to foreign real estate, more generally, are those we evaluate for the benefit of our REIT. Certainly you will analyze the individual REIT at the company level for its investment viability, but there is little point in doing that until you have accurately assessed the condition, and more importantly, the *trend*, of the regional, national, and local real estate markets in which you are planning to invest, which is why you really have to begin from the broadest and widest position and work from there to narrow your field of consideration. When you *do* arrive at the point where you have to look at the intrinsic company and its components, you will perform all of the usual functions: evaluate the ability of management to realize growth from efforts at enhancing rental income and funds from operations (FFO), as well as paying attention to how leverage is used; in that regard, you could look simply at debt-to-equity ratios, but perhaps a better leverage consideration is something just a bit more nuanced, like the relative weightings of fixed rate and floating rate debt in consideration of the level and trend of interest rates at a given time. The point is that the REIT itself certainly matters, but not as much as the overriding factors of country and regional market fundamentals (as well as technical trends).

In the end, the analysis of REITs puts you in the position of having to evaluate an asset class that is principally real estate, but also has strong relationships to equities and fixed-income markets. Accordingly, the use of fundamental analysis of real estate can also be complemented by the application of technical analysis to the REITs share movements, and so your use of both in making portfolio decisions is important.

When researching a prospective REIT investment, you will want to examine the portfolio of properties with an eye to evaluating the strength of the commercial real estate market in the prospective target areas. First, begin by visiting the REIT company websites to see the precise makeup of the portfolio, and do your research to evaluate both the current strength of the real property market, as well as the trend of values into the future. Again, this research is no different from the kind you would be doing if you were considering the direct purchase of a commercial property, and while it might seem a bit laborious, it is well worth the effort in what have become highly complex markets. Beyond all of that, you should take advantage of all of the wonderful free information the Internet has to offer, as well as some of the information that *costs*, depending on how serious you are. We are big believers in evaluating commercial real estate opportunities in part by looking at what some of the most substantial players have to offer, and they offer plenty. For example, we love the information we grab from the site of Cushman and Wakefield (www.cushwake.com). Cushman and Wakefield is a commercial real estate firm that offers a wide range of services, and their web site has a Knowledge Center that we happen to like. There is plenty of excellent free research on the site, including their terrific *MarketBeat* reports, and if you *really* want to step up to the plate, $625 (at this writing) will buy you the current edition (published annually) of their *International Investment Atlas*; the Atlas is an outstanding compilation of high-level research on a wide variety of developed and emerging markets. The Atlas is loaded with quantitative research and terrific analysis with just about everything you need to expertly research some of the most investable and otherwise viable real estate markets. Of course, there are other firms that do what Cushman does, and these days, quality investment research and the Internet go hand-in-hand. A Google search for "global real estate research" will return results that should provide you with a wealth of information.

As a REIT investor, you want to fully acquaint yourself with the many excellent resources of the online presence of the National Association of Real Estate Investment Trusts (www.reit.com). The site has too many great features to mention all of them here, but among them is the now-digital edition of *Real Estate Portfolio* magazine, complete with back-issue access; of particular interest in the magazine is the *International Forum*, for which you can find archives articles directly at www.nareit.com/portfoliomag/ menu/international_menu.shtml. The site also includes useful industry data, to include the up-to-date and historical returns of the FTSE EPRA/NAREIT Global Real Estate Index, broken down by component regions (Americas, Asia/Pacific, Europe, and Middle East/Africa). There are plenty of other quality resources available to REIT investors, but we can tell you that the NAREIT site is at the top of our list.

REIT Derivatives In addition to existing as negotiable securities in their own right, REITs serve as the components of other types of collectives, like open-end mutual funds, closed-end funds, and ETFs. Having discussed REITs to the extent we have, separate discussions of each of the other REIT derivatives would be a bit of overkill, in our opinion. The central understanding of the REIT and its valuation underpinnings will get you to where you need to be, regardless of how the REIT is packaged. That said, given their growing universe and effectiveness as relatively unmanaged instruments, let us say just a few words about REIT ETFs.

As is the case with the typical ETF, REIT ETFs are exchange-traded funds that happen to hold REIT stocks in such a way as to track a particular index. Among the more commonly tracked are the well-known FTSE NAREIT and FTSE EPRA/NAREIT Indexes, such as the Mortgage REITs Index and Developed Asia Index. There are not a bunch of these right now—in fact, just a small handful—but you can expect the availability to grow as interest in both ETFs and REITs continues to expand.

One thing to note about REIT ETFs is that the tax efficiency that so typically characterizes the ETF is lost with the REIT component; the distributions that have to be paid out to the investor in the standard REIT must still be paid out to the REIT ETF investor. In fact, REIT ETFs are commonly known as "dividend ETFs."

The reason you might opt for a REIT ETF as opposed to a REIT itself is for the normal reasons you look to an ETF as rather than an individual stock; investment fluidity and full trading mechanism through a basket of REITs. Nothing really changes there. Still, we see no reason why deciding between a REIT and REIT ETF has to be an "either/or" proposition, as both mechanisms have their places.

Here are the International/Global REIT ETFs accessible on U.S. exchanges:

Name: iShares FTSE EPRA/NAREIT Developed Asia Index Fund
Ticker: IFAS
Exchange: NASDAQ
Style: Tracks the FTSE EPRA/NAREIT Developed Asia Index, which measures the performance of companies that own, develop, and operate within the parameters of the broad Asian real estate market.
Name: iShares FTSE EPRA/NAREIT Developed Europe Index Fund
Ticker: IFEU
Exchange: NASDAQ
Style: Tracks the FTSE EPRA/NAREIT Developed Europe Index, which measures the performance of companies that own, develop, and operate within the parameters of the broad European real estate market.
Name: iShares FTSE EPRA/NAREIT Developed Real Estate ex-U.S. Index Fund
Ticker: IFGL
Exchange: NASDAQ
Style: Tracks the FTSE EPRA/NAREIT Global Real Estate ex-U.S. Index, which measures the performance of companies that own, develop, and operate within the Canadian, European, and Asian real estate markets.
Name: First Trust FTSE EPRA/NAREIT Developed Market Real Estate Index
Ticker: FFR
Exchange: NYSE Arca
Style: Tracks the FTSE EPRA/NAREIT Global Real Estate Index. The fund may invest at least 90 percent of its assets in common stocks that make up the Index, or in ADRs, GDRs, and EDRs.

And here are the International/Global REIT ETFs available on foreign exchanges:

Name: iShares FTSE EPRA/NAREIT Asia Property Yield USD
Ticker/Exchange:
- IASP.L / London Stock Exchange
- IDAR.L / London Stock Exchange
- IASP.AS / Euronext Amsterdam

- .VLIAS / Paris Stock Exchange
- IASP.MI / Milan Stock Exchange

Name: iShares FTSE/EPRA European Property EUR
Ticker/Exchange:

- IPRP.L / London Stock Exchange
- IPRP.AS / Euronext Amsterdam
- .VLIPO / Paris Stock Exchange
- IPRP.MI / Milan Stock Exchange

Name: iShares FTSE EPRA/NAREIT Developed Markets Property Yield USD
Ticker/Exchange:

- IWDP.L / London Stock Exchange
- IDWP.L / London Stock Exchange
- IDWP.AS / Euronext Amsterdam
- .VLWDP / Paris Stock Exchange
- IWDP.MI / Milan Stock Exchange

Name: iShares FTSE EPRA/NAREIT UK Property CHF
Ticker/Exchange:

- IUKP.L / London Stock Exchange
- IUKP.MI / Milan Stock Exchange

Name: Claymore Global Real Estate ETF
Ticker/Exchange:

- CGR.TO / Toronto Stock Exchange
- CGRa.TO / Toronto Stock Exchange

There is no resource specifically dedicated to REIT ETFs on which we normally rely, which is to be expected because they are just now gathering steam as a form of security. Additionally, the elemental research really takes place at the REIT level, anyway. Still, Morningstar (www.morningstar.com) and ETFConnect (www.etfconnect.com) are excellent resources. We happen to prefer Morningstar in some respects, particularly because they go deeper in listing the component REIT holdings of the ETFs.

Foreign REITs In the end, this book is about investing in other countries, and so we want you to be aware of the fact that the REIT universe continues to grow in no small way due to the expansion of the REIT system *globally*. As we mentioned earlier, the number of countries adopting REIT-like structures has increased quite substantially since 2000. Also, as greater numbers of nations grow more comfortable with a style of economics that allows for the securitization of real property, you will see even more of them. The reality is that the global increase in wealth is one factor, as many of these dollars are looking for more opportunities to grow. Additionally, as populations in many areas continue to be defined by demographical age

EXHIBIT 7.4 Countries with Functional Publicly Traded REIT Markets

Country	Number of REITs
Australia	64
Belgium	14
Bulgaria	N/A*
Canada	33
France	48
Germany	2
Hong Kong	7
Italy	N/A*
Japan	42
Malaysia	13
Netherlands	8
New Zealand	8
Singapore	20
South Africa	6
South Korea	6
Taiwan	N/A*
Turkey	13
United Kingdom	19
United States	148

*Countries with newer REIT markets for which readily accessible information is not regularly forthcoming at this time.

increases, and as life expectancies also inch upward, this population segment is going to want to have access to more choices among yield-oriented investments.

Exhibit 7.4 shows a list of the countries that have functional REIT structures. By that, we mean countries that have publicly traded REITs for which there is accessible information, to one degree or another. This issue can be a little tricky, because there are several countries that have, to one degree or another, REITs or REIT-like entities domiciled, but not all of them are readily accessible by the investment community. We have tried to limit this list to those that are accessible.

Exhibit 7.5 shows rankings of the top 10 REIT markets by country, evaluated over two periods: (1) a three-year period from June 2005 through June 2008, and (2) a one-year period from June 2007 through June 2008. You will surely notice that the United States is notably absent from the top spots of both lists; also, the lists are dominated by developed market nations, which may seem counterintuitive for those who recognize that emerging and frontier market nations, generally, represent the best investment opportunities. The problem in that regard is that the securitization of real estate is a function of the sophisticated development of

EXHIBIT 7.5 REIT Markets	

Top 10 REIT Markets, Ranked by Total Return, for the Three-Year Period 6/30/2005 to 6/30/2008

Country	Return
South Korea	13.46%
Canada	8.80%
France	8.23%
South Africa	7.79%
Singapore	6.81%
New Zealand	4.89%
Belgium	2.89%
Turkey	2.32%
Netherlands	1.78%
United States	−1.82%

Top 10 REIT Markets, Ranked by Total Return, for the One-Year Period 6/30/2007 to 6/30/2008

Country	Return
South Korea	5.17%
Malaysia	−2.68%
Belgium	−8.50%
Hong Kong	−8.86%
Canada	−9.86%
New Zealand	−18.38%
Netherlands	−20.37%
Turkey	−21.04%
South Africa	−21.63%
United States	−21.94%

Source (both sets of statistics): Ernst and Young, Global REIT Investment Trust Report 2008 (www.ey.com/realestate).

financial structures and modern economic outlooks, and emerging and frontier markets generally do not fit that profile. That said, you will notice the presence of South Africa, Turkey, and Malaysia on the lists, emerging markets all.

LIMITED PARTNERSHIPS AND PRIVATE PLACEMENTS

In the world of securitized real estate, some opportunities come available through smaller, more targeted types of offerings than REITs and other collectives transacted more broadly throughout the general public. There are all sorts of clever legal entities available through which capital-raising ventures can be structured, but most are variations of the limited partnership (LP) and the private placement (PP). Generally speaking, these entities are used by companies seeking to raise capital with some combination of greater control and less regulatory hassle than that afforded by other forms of securitized real estate. These kind of entities are essentially a hybrid of security and direct ownership, because they offer the advantage of owning an interest in real property that you do not have to manage (like a REIT), but they are also illiquid in the way that direct ownership of property is illiquid. Given this illiquidity and, by consequence, the greater overall risk, the only reason you would move forward with an investment in either, assuming you meet the qualifications in the first place, is because the general partner or company has assembled what appears to be such a compelling opportunity for prospective return that you are willing to assume the risks. Please note that we have decided against an attempt to present any sort of specific list of global LP or PP opportunities here; because LPs and PPs are formed irregularly, we are not in a position to provide a list of global or foreign opportunities in either. The other problem we have is that although some current opportunities are indeed known to us, the nature of these investments is such that we are less than comfortable even *suggesting* possible sources of LPs or PPs, for fear that someone may construe the mentions as a recommendation. That said, we believe it is useful to discuss the entities more fully, as your global real estate needs may ultimately be met in part through these sorts of vehicles.

Limited Partnerships

There are a variety of legal entities and capitalization programs that allow for smaller collectives of investors to profit (hopefully) from more targeted sorts of real estate ownership that essentially sits only a half-notch above owning the real property directly. Although the benefits of these kinds of investments to the investor include not having to deal with the day-to-day management and operations of the venture, that may well be the only noticeable difference. The aspects of direct real estate investment that make it most unenjoyable—the relatively high cost of entry (particularly in the case of private placements), the lack of liquidity, and the long-term commitment of principal—are present in more private offerings. The upside is that a smaller pool of investors, combined with the broad, discretionary, and expert management of the commercial portfolio, means that the potential return can be much better than that which one might see from a typical REIT or other collective investment scheme.

The limited partnership (LP) option gives the commercial developer the means to do what she needs to using money that is not her own.

Limited partnerships were in much wider use domestically 20-odd years ago when they enjoyed more favorable tax treatment than they do presently, but they still exist and do so for the benefit of the right investor. The investor in a limited partnership (a limited partner) is ideally seeking to derive three benefits from his investment: significant income, a share of the appreciation realized from the eventual sale of the properties owned by the partnership, and, if available, some useful tax benefits. Although some readers may be intimately familiar with LPs, here is a quick overview for those who are not.

A limited partnership is a type of investment to most of us, but it is technically a legal entity. In a *general* partnership, the owners (partners) share in the profits and losses that accrue on behalf of the specific venture for which the partnership was organized. The use of the general partnership entity is often found to be distasteful by those who do not like the "jointly and severally" feature that characterizes the partners' liability. Under "joint and several" liability, someone who has a claim against the partnership can ultimately collect from any partner, as partners' personal assets are on the hook to pay any claims.

The attraction of the *limited* partnership, as an entity, to investors is that their liability is limited; the risk to a limited partner extends only to the limit of his investment. In an LP, there have to be at least *two* general partners, and these general partners decide on what the partnership will buy and how the properties are to be managed. It is the limited partners who provide the bulk of the capital.

Traditional limited partnerships can be excellent investments, but they have risks associated with them that cannot be ignored. The most famous risk of a LP is that it is illiquid. The number of properties that make up the portfolio is typically small and quite targeted in terms of commercial purpose. Limited partnerships are sold in units to subscribers, and the subscribers (investors) have to pass a process of accreditation, which basically proves (to the extent realistically possible) that an investor cannot only part with his investment for up to many years, but can survive the loss of the principal investment altogether.

One of the other features of a real estate limited partnership that makes them unappealing to many is the length of time for which your investment is tied up, referred to earlier. The illiquidity of LP investments is generally without exception. That is, the investment monies are used to buy commercial properties, and other than one of the properties becoming subject to liquidation, there is no ready cash available to pay an investor seeking an early exit. This is why the matter of accreditation is so important. An LP investor may lose complete access to his principal for many years. Real estate LPs are structured with a variety of term lengths, but most have life spans of between 3 and 10 years. It is, unquestionably, a commitment to invest in one.

Another feature of LPs that many dislike is the lack of transparency. In a real estate LP, we can tell you quite honestly that the feeling of general partners is as follows: "Thank you very much for your investment. Now, please go away." This is not because they all of a sudden do not like you now that they have your money (unlike your deadbeat brother-in-law), but rather because limited partners work best as *silent* partners. It is the general partners who decide when to sell the properties in the portfolio, as well as at what price. Beyond the fact that partnerships, in general, have disparate investment terms, individual limited partnership investments themselves generally do not have set life spans; rather, the prospectus will indicate a prospective or estimated term of the investment—say from five to seven years. The purpose of using a window is ideally for the benefit of general and limited partners alike: If the prospectus dictated that the partnership had to terminate exactly six years after the close of the offering, while an investor might feel better at the outset that he knew, in advance, when the investment would end, the problem is that if real estate values are down at that time, a required dissolution would be bad news for everybody. A *range* of years gives the general partners the flexibility of deciding when it makes the most sense to liquidate the properties, but still establishes a general time frame that all investors can use to estimate the return of their principal investments, plus any appreciation.

The benefits of investing in real estate via limited partnerships are essentially the same as investing in real estate in any fashion. You are looking to receive income during the holding period, and receive a nice chunk of appreciation when the properties are liquidated. The appeal of some limited partnerships historically has been enhanced through the additional feature of *tax credits*, which, unlike tax deductions, represent a dollar-for-dollar reduction in your liability. These, however, are available principally for domestic partnerships, of course, and revolve around the partnership's inclusion of low-income housing or historic housing properties in its portfolio. These are generally not features you would expect to find in a global real estate limited partnership, so such especially generous tax benefits would not normally be a feature of a global LP investment.

Anyone seeking a partnership investment should absolutely focus on general partners that have an excellent track record assembling, managing, administering, and liquidating these investments (at their natural conclusion). Again, the basic idea behind the partnership is that it allows one to derive high current income from the rents and mortgage interest during the years your money is tied up, and then rewards you with the return of both your principal as well as a share of the appreciation. These goals cannot always be met successfully by neophytes at this game, so you want to be aware of that before you invest. Again, any partnership you are considering should be able to provide you with a solid list of previous partnership investments they have overseen with excellent results. The longer the list, the better; not only does that demonstrate a high degree of experience in this field, it shows that the general partners have the acumen to be successful throughout several market cycles, which is no mean feat.

A Word About Master Limited Partnerships

Although LP investors know going in that they are entering something long term and illiquid, human nature, being what it is, does not prevent limited partners from looking for a way out before the investment has run its course. The formation of the master limited partnership (MLP) was designed to deal with that issue head on. MLPs are, simply, exchange-traded limited partnerships. There is not an abundance of them that are set up as real estate partnerships, currently, on domestic exchanges. That said, there is one, actually an LLC, which trades on the NYSE and has exposure to both domestic commercial real estate as well as to that in 15 foreign countries. We will go back just slightly on our earlier decision to avoid even mentioning an LP or private placement (PP) investment, because this is one that as a MLP is highly liquid; it is W.P. Carey and Co. LLC, and it trades on the NYSE under the symbol WPC. That said, its mention here is purely illustrative in intent. Note that we do not have an investment interest in Carey at this writing, nor are we contemplating one. Also, Carey is not a foreign MLP, but could be considered a U.S.-domiciled global real estate MLP because of its foreign holdings.

For more information on MLPs, you can refer to the National Association of Publicly Traded Partnerships; the web site is www.naptp.org. Note that the NAPTP has information only on MLPs traded on U.S. markets.

Private Placements

A private placement involves the sale of securities to a limited number of investors who meet certain eligibility criteria. There is no strict definition of a private placement, but rather the structure is known to be one through its characterization by certain features. Chief among those is that PPs are exempt from SEC registration, as well as the standard reporting requirements. In exchange for the privilege of sidestepping registration and disclosure demands, PPs cannot sell shares through public offerings, or any sort of public solicitations or advertising. Additionally, while private placements need not meet standard regulatory requirements, that does not mean they can do anything they want. They must still abide by all applicable state laws, and the break they get on disclosure does not give them a license to defraud; PPs must strictly comply with the applicable antifraud rules found in securities laws, and must make the disclosures necessary to prospective investors to ensure they have enough information to make a knowledgeable decision about the investment.

The private placement can be a great tool for companies seeking an investor-funded capital base but who are not prepared or otherwise unsuited to make an initial public offering (IPO). For some companies, the IPO is not conducive to a business created specifically for a targeted purpose with a finite life span. The private placement, having been relieved of many onerous administrative requirements, allows an entity to raise money relatively quickly and with less hassle, and the entity can exercise a great deal of discretion in how invested money is applied to assets. Additionally, many entities opt for PPs because they have a great deal of control over the investment infrastructure and capital-raising process. For example, PPs can be selective about the investors and how much they are permitted to invest. On that note, the investors themselves have to be more sophisticated and meet certain requirements; let us take a look at those.

In order to invest in a private placement, investors must meet strict suitability requirements, and for good reason. Private placements are highly illiquid and ask for use of principal for several years; additionally, private placements are often characterized by higher risk levels, in large part precisely *because* of the illiquidity and extended investment commitment, but also because, by definition, the investor is helping to capitalize a new company and/or more speculative venture. Rules 505 and 506 of Regulation D of the Securities Act of 1933 allow for a company to sell its own securities to an unlimited number of what are called "accredited investors." You can refer to the Act's Rule 501 (of Regulation D) yourself for the legal specifics, but basically, to qualify as an accredited individual investor, one must have, at a minimum, one of the following (remember, these are U.S. rules only):

- A net worth (or joint net worth, with a spouse) that exceeds $1 million at the time of the purchase of the PP shares. The net worth calculation can be inclusive of residence equity, furnishings, and automobiles.
- A level of income such that he has earned more than $20,000 in each of the previous two years; if an investor (or investors) wants to be qualified on the basis of joint income, that income threshold rises to an excess of $300,000 in each of the previous two years. In both cases, the standard further demands that the same level of income must be expected to be realized in the current year, as well.

There are a variety of other qualifying entities that can purchase shares in a PP, but these criteria are most relevant for individuals. Minimum investments in private placements will vary, but few will be interested in dealing with individuals seeking to invest less than $100,000; that said, we are familiar with some that have had minimum investment requirements of around $50,000.

It should be noted that if you come across a global real estate private placement that you find intriguing, and you do not meet the standard for accreditation, there is still hope—maybe. Per Rules 505 and 506 of Regulation D, private placements are permitted to raise capital from up to 35 unaccredited investors, but that does not mean they have to, and many do not want to bother with unaccrediteds. The upside to the unaccrediteds is that smaller operations, those that find it easier to make lower offering minimums and do not have the pool of accrediteds for which they were hoping, have another route by which to see capital. The downsides, at least for the PP, can be acutely troublesome; first off, when PPs make the offering available to unaccrediteds, the disclosure rules change, and some of the hassles the company was seeking to sidestep in the first place return to their doorstep. Another problem is that unaccredited investors, by virtue of that very status, tend to be folks who cannot ultimately withstand the inherent constraints of the investment (like the illiquidity and term-length features) as well as they claimed they could at the outset. This is significant, and as a result, many PPs do not bother with unaccrediteds. On that note, we would suggest you avoid them yourself if you are unaccredited, unless you have the opportunity to access the investment for an unusually low minimum investment.

In order to invest in a PP, you must do it through a brokerage/ investment bank. The institution will have executed a selling agreement with the entity offering the PP, and the shares will be made available through the brokerage. The information basis for learning about the offering is the private placement memorandum, or PPM. The prospective investor reviews the PPM as a prospectus, and will usually (if he or she is smart) perform his or her own due diligence (something that is much easier to do nowadays, courtesy of the Internet). Should an investor decide to actually make an investment, he or she will fill out the subscription agreement through the brokerage.

For the right person, private placements can be excellent ways to penetrate the global real estate markets. The people behind many global real estate private placements have cultivated long-standing relationships that allow for the acquisition of excellent commercial properties in specific regions of the globe. As a matter of fact, the volatility of the stock market over the last several years has prompted some well-known regional developers to consider swapping out their planned IPOs in consideration of private placements. There are a variety of firms that serve as the connection between investment property and the capital needed to maximize its value. We are disinclined here, as you know, to provide any specific names, as the nature of PPs is such that we prefer that readers locate them on their own, but they are quite available; for example, there is one of which we are aware that is touting returns of 40 percent–plus over the course of about 18 months, investing in property in Peru (again, disclosure: we have no investment interest in it, nor have any plans to gain one). The key to remember is that you want to invest in a PP where management, as with the limited partnership, is highly experienced and has a great track record with similar offerings.

DIRECT PURCHASE OF REAL ESTATE

We made a decision right off the bat to focus on the purchase of residential real estate in our discussion of direct investment. For most people seeking to build a personal hedge fund, the manageability of assets has to be a large consideration, and the ability of an individual to functionally invest directly in commercial properties is limited without an abundance of time and a substantial amount of financial resources. We understand that a few readers may have the capability and interest to invest in foreign commercial real estate, but our research among prospective readers before we began this project indicated a great deal of interest in learning how to enter the residential markets, with much less interest indicated in how to penetrate the commercial side directly. The reality is that the diversification you seek by accessing real estate markets with low correlation to U.S. markets can be realized perfectly well through the acquisition of residential real estate.

Another issue concerns what appears to be a pending stagnation in the commercial property market in some foreign markets, one that is following the same malaise in the residential market but from which it may be more difficult to free oneself; indeed, the consensus is that we may well be looking at a new round of bank difficulties and failures as the commercial market continues to deteriorate globally, and so for the near-to-mid term, it is probably wise for the individual investor to access that market through more liquid means, or at least through means that involve the use of investment management that has assembled a strong basis for why a partnership or placement has selected the properties it has chosen. That said, should you insist on investing directly in commercial property, you will find that the same resources we cite in this section will also be able to assist you with the purchase of same. However, it is our opinion that the use of collectives, partnerships, and private placements is probably a better way to invest in foreign commercial property and still keep your sanity. Believe us, purchasing and managing a portfolio of foreign-based residential properties will be challenging enough in and of itself.

At the outset, you have to focus on your market as you decide where, and in what, to invest. For example, most countries will have local markets that cater principally to tourists, while others cater mostly to locals. Do you want to purchase a property in or near a resort location of a given country so that you may enjoy rental income from vacationers, or are you more interested in penetrating a local industrial market and renting to residents there? Part of that decision-making process may involve your consideration of whether you ever see yourself living in the property one day; for example, if you like Bulgaria as a real estate market, you may consider an apartment along the Black Sea coast, where you can rent to tourists with an eye to using it yourself one day. Alternatively, you may be intrigued by Japan's low correlation to U.S. markets and decide to invest there, but wish to take advantage of Tokyo's density and improving rental market (many of Japan's youth prefer renting). In the end, you may find yourself with a portfolio that includes some of each type of property.

Those who seek to purchase real estate directly have to deal with a variety of considerations not faced by those who invest through securities: foreign countries represent a variety of challenges for U.S. investors, including those related to the aforementioned issues of taxes and currency, as well as wrestling with unusual legal requirements. The matter of addressing common leasing concerns (to include the lease itself) is much more significant with a tenant who is not only off-site but off-*country*. More obvious problems associated with language differences and time zones round out a general list of obstacles that can make foreign investment in real estate potentially difficult for the average person. That said, it is difficult to ignore the tremendous opportunities that exist, especially in light of a U.S. market that is expected to be beaten down for years to come.

There are several considerations you must weigh as you look to investing directly in real property outside of the United States. Although we highly advise that you look to experienced professionals, you should become familiar on your own with the major issues associated with these transactions.

TRANSACTIONAL CONSIDERATIONS

Purchasing real estate is always a sober task (or should be, at any rate). That said, the complexities of the transaction can be magnified greatly when you seek to buy property directly in a foreign country. Let us take a closer look at some of the more pronounced aspects of the overall transaction so that you may note details of which you should be particularly aware.

Legal Representation

It is basically this simple—get a lawyer. In all of our collective years involved in real estate transactions, both personally and as industry professionals, we have always been amazed at the number of people who are content to engage the process without legal representation. Although the odds may be in your favor that you will be able to consummate such a deal in the United States without regret if you are *sans* attorney, that is by no means an assurance, and when it comes to buying and selling outside of the United States, the odds decrease significantly. Not only should you always have representation when buying in less mature markets, even transactions in developed markets should not be handled without an attorney that *you* retain and who works only on your behalf in the deal. Even if the nature of a market is such that both the use of a real estate agent and the acceptance of title insurance are standard (which is by no means the case in every market), the retention of an attorney to oversee the entire transaction is worth every penny. Generally, you want to use someone who lives and works in your target country, and preferably in the same specific area in which you plan to make your purchase. He or she should have an established, verifiable history of working with U.S. citizens in the acquisition of real estate in that country. Additionally, the person should speak English well. Your attorney should also be expected to ride shotgun on every part of the transaction, to include the matter of the mortgage; this is especially true if you secure the mortgage from a bank from within the country in which you are purchasing. Loan documents are challenging enough when they are written in English, by and for Americans, on behalf of U.S. property; change all of that, and you now have something infinitely trickier with which to deal. If you feel safe in scrimping on representation in the good 'ole USA, shelve that feeling of safety when you venture overseas.

Increased Costs

One of the issues to consider is the total cost associated with getting a deal done. We are not discussing mere property price here, but rather the total cost of the transaction. If you have completed real estate transactions stateside (which we heartily recommend before you decide to complete them elsewhere), then you are familiar with the HUD-1 settlement statement that outlines the charges associated with the transaction. When transacting real estate outside the United States, there are other things to watch for. Some countries will assess fees with which we are not familiar here in the United States, and will assess taxes that you normally do not encounter in the states. Remember that your tax obligations generally go up when investing in overseas properties, as you now are beholden to two masters: Uncle Sam, and the home country of your target investment.

Geopolitical and Economic Issues

When you invest in property within the United States, you have to pay some attention to the changing winds of local and state governments, as well as any changes that may occur at the federal level. That said, the United States is stable and predictable, in comparison to the rest of the world. The same cannot be said of other countries. Although there is always the issue of political risk, for example, when investing overseas, that risk is much more pronounced when you own an investment that you cannot simply sell on an exchange with the click of a mouse. The appeal of investing in emerging markets countries is sometimes much easier to appreciate when you are doing it with a *mutual fund* as opposed to buying a piece of property. In both cases, the opportunities may be substantial, but the risk to the real estate investor will be greater. Do not rely on what you think you know about a country. Become a student of the countries in which you are considering investing, and understand their histories as well as their current political climates. Granted, there are issues with which you can receive assistance from the professionals who specialize in these different areas, but again, do not leave this work entirely up to them. The reality is that once you consummate the transaction, your real estate professional is out of the picture, and it will be up to you to continue to monitor the political and economic movements to determine the ongoing viability of your portfolio's investments.

Although you are certainly free to invest in less stable countries, as you desire, remember that truly unstable countries are not likely be worth the risk. It is not out of the realm of possibility for the governments of such countries to use their version of what we call eminent domain to appropriate property as they see fit. Additionally, significantly less developed countries tend to have stronger streaks of xenophobia, as their lack of development gives them little basis for having enjoyed long-standing relationships with "outsiders." The simple reality is that for all of the reasons that you appreciate having negotiable securities as a mechanism by which to invest in less mature markets, those are the same reasons on which you rely for deciding against anchoring yourself to those countries more permanently by purchasing real estate in them. That said, we would advise you to avoid discarding the baby with the bathwater. There are actually smaller, less sophisticated markets that do not present the difficulties of others, and we have sampled a few of those here.

It is important to learn the intricacies of your prospective deal, and part of that involves becoming a good student of the country in which you are seeking to buy. First off, become familiar with the language. You need not become a fluent speaker, but learning the language to a functional level will accomplish two things. First, it will show a respect for the country and the people not often evidenced by Americans abroad. Your effort at ingratiating yourself to the locals will engender more good feelings, and consequently a greater interest in helping you as the need for such assistance arises. Second, learning the language will be highly useful to you as you practically apply your real estate investment efforts. On that note, it is especially helpful to master *tense*—as in past, present, and future tense. There are many components at play throughout an ongoing real estate transaction, and it is so important to always be aware of where you are on the timeline.

Remember to school yourself in the area of both national and local customs and processes. We all take for granted such things in this country, because they come naturally to us. You will not enjoy that luxury when looking to buy in foreign countries, and you must endeavor to get yourself educated. Again, this becomes more important as you look to less-developed countries for investment. Many such countries fall outside of what would be considered the Western culture that tends to bind many nations in one way or another, but many other nations, particularly those that fall into the emerging category, may have cultures, day-to-day rituals, and ways of doing business that fall far outside of that to which you are familiar.

You need to perform your due diligence on the *local* economy, as well. It is not enough to get a read that a particular country offers a great deal of real estate potential, at present; you want to be particularly aware of what is going on in local regions and communities. Even during the United States' most recent real estate boom, there were plenty of areas throughout the country that were hardly worthy of your investment dollars, and conversely, the collapse has seen pockets of tremendous resiliency, even relative prosperity, like in previously referenced Amarillo, Texas.

All of this said, we believe that an excellent way to buy property overseas is through firms that specialize in doing just that on behalf of foreign investors. There are actually plenty of such firms that have sprouted up for the benefit of developed markets, with smaller numbers of similar firms available to assist with transactions in less sophisticated places. Using firms like these does not preclude you from the need to become well acquainted with the local market and all phases of the transaction on your own, but the simple reality is that it is often worth the money to retain a firm that will hold your hand. Many such firms will basically do everything for you, from helping you find a place to guide you through to closing. Japan, for example, is a market that we particularly like for such services, because even though Japan is a developed market, and therefore one that many might instinctively feel is safe for foreign investors, the difficulty associated with locating financing for a Japanese property is, by itself, a large enough issue to warrant having some help.

Financing Considerations and Title Insurance

One of the biggest impediments to successful direct investment in foreign real estate has traditionally been the matter of financing. Until recently, many parts of the world limited transactions to a "cash-only" basis because traditional financing mechanisms had yet to catch up with the more sophisticated considerations associated with transborder real estate investing. Additionally, historical demand was low, so there was little impetus for the structure to change.

Take Costa Rica, for example. Costa Rica has long been considered an ideal portfolio addition for U.S. investors because of the ability to purchase both an investment and an ideal piece of property to which one might consider retiring. Unfortunately, the area offered limited ability to foreign investors to arrange financing until recently. Now, several national and international banks have initiated nonresident financing opportunities for people who seek to buy, and even the well-known Stewart Title has opened doors to a title office in Tamarindo, Guanacaste, so that U.S. investors can purchase real estate in the country with the same degree of confidence with which they can purchase property domestically. Banks like HSBC and Scotiabank have good programs for financing there, and will write loans for as much as 85 percent of the purchase price, but more local institutions generally limit their lending to those seeking to buy a primary residence and live in the country full-time.

Other than more evolved national and international banks, the other real source of money is private money, and that generally means mortgage brokers. Mortgage brokers have received a bad name in the United States in the wake of the subprime mortgage crisis, but that portrayal has been a bit unfair, in our opinion. The truth is that mortgage brokers exist primarily to represent unique borrowers, unique lending programs, and other types of unique situations, and anyone who does not fit into any of these categories probably does not need a mortgage broker, anyway. The number of international mortgage brokers is growing all of the time, and these can be excellent sources of money for nonresident transactions. You need to do some careful research as you look for financing; if you perform a Google search for "international mortgage brokers," you will find several that proclaim far-reaching access to loan monies for properties available around the globe. That said, the international real estate market is constantly in flux in every facet, and you want to be sure you perform the necessary due diligence in this part of the transaction.

In the end, a motivated mortgage broker with good international connections can be an excellent asset to your wealth-building team as you proceed down this road. A good mortgage broker, even if he or she does not have established relationships in a particular area of the world, will not be shy about pursuing them and finding an excellent opportunity for you. You should note that the documentation requirements for obtaining a loan to buy a foreign property, whether through an institution in the home country or through an international mortgage broker, are basically the same. You should expect to produce the following:

- Copy of passport and proof of permanent address (such as a copy of a utility bill)
- Certificate of marital status (marriage license or divorce decree), if applicable
- Several pay stubs dated within the last 90 days, with one of those dated as recently as possible; our suggestion is that you simply begin keeping your pay stubs in a file, beginning from the 90 days (more or less) before the date you plan to make application
- Bank statements from the previous three to six months (be prepared to go back as far as six months). Also, you may be asked for a letter of reference from your bank
- W-2s or other applicable year-end tax summary documents from employer(s)

Note that self-employed applicants will be required to supply copies of their most recent tax returns (instead of pay stubs and W-2s), and should be prepared to provide a year-to-date profit and loss statement, as well.

Title insurance is a staple of developed markets, but not as prevalent in less mature markets. The good news is that the situation is changing rapidly, as younger countries seeking more foreign money realize that they have to modernize the appropriate structures and practices so that investors will feel better about spending their capital. We suggest that you purchase title insurance whenever you buy a piece of property, and whenever possible, utilize the most recognizable names in the business. For example, companies like Stewart Title (www.stewart.com) and First American Corporation (www.firstam.com) are quickly increasing their presence throughout the global real property marketplace. Note that these title companies offer the opportunity to enjoy additional peace of mind by helping you navigate through foreign transactions in their entirety; they are excellent resources for many phases of the transaction, and can provide you with many different services along the way.

SAMPLE COUNTRIES IN WHICH TO TARGET YOUR ACQUISITIONS

Viability is a major issue when considering where to make a direct real estate investment outside of the United States. Although it is theoretically possible to purchase real estate directly in a large number of countries throughout the world, the geographical, cultural, economic, legal, and/or sociopolitical structures of many countries and regions will make such an effort prohibitive, for all practical purposes. That said, we wanted to give you an overview of many countries that *are* reasonable possibilities for you to consider for real property investment. Our selection of countries may strike some as a bit arbitrary, but we wanted to sample all major regions of the globe, and also present a breadth of selection that includes developed, emerging, frontier, and unrated markets and provide some good, useful information on behalf of those that seem worthy of reasonable consideration in your quest to establish a truly global real estate investment portfolio. Additionally, we want to pay particular attention to markets that have some worthwhile combination of accessibility, stability, and opportunity. At the time of writing of this book, the Great Recession had gripped much of the world, and property values were down in many areas. However, even when near-term opportunities become less attractive, the markets outlined here should provide some reasonable longer-term opportunities once we have moved fully beyond this historic moment in time.

North America

Clearly, Canada and Mexico are the most accessible foreign countries for most Americans. What follows is a look at the pros, cons, and key details associated with buying property in each.

Canada Canada may not be what many have in mind when considering a "foreign" real estate investment, but foreign it is. It is the second-largest country in the world and contains what, to many, is some of the planet's most beautiful geography. The most significant feature of Canada that adds to the perception that it is just "America *light*" is that the vast majority of the population lives within 100 miles of the U.S. border (which admittedly raises the issue of how economically diverse it is from the United States). The country is made up of a variety of ethnicities and cultures, and the county is bilingual (English and French), although you would be hard-pressed to find a place where you could not get by in English.

Canada's form of government is a constitutional monarchy, which is a system where the monarch's role as head of state is largely ceremonial, and the head of government is actually the prime minister (PM). In the case of Canada, the sovereign monarch is the reigning monarch of the United Kingdom, who, at this writing, is Queen Elizabeth II. Because the Queen does not live in Canada, there is an appointed Governor General who represents her interests in Canada, although the appointed governor's selection is made largely on the prime minister's say-so. Although the prime minister is technically appointed by the Governor General, the PM is normally the leader of whatever political party has the most seats in the House of Commons; practically, it is Canada's bicameral legislature, made up of the House of Commons and Senate that makes things happen. In Canada, it is the party with the majority of seats in the House of Commons that wields the most power, so it is that status to which you want to pay attention as a prospective property owner in the country. For example, at this writing, that is the Conservative Party, which is generally more supportive of free market principles than the other relevant parties.

Economically, Canada has much to recommend. It is, for starters, one of the wealthiest nations in the world, and has seen its economy grow steadily, overall, for the last 20 years. Unemployment is actually in check at this time, which speaks well of its resiliency during the Great Recession. Significantly, the expectation is that Canada's debt-to-GDP ratio will be dropping to about 20 percent during 2009, which, remarkably, will put it at much less than half of the anticipated average for all G-8 member nations.

Attractiveness to Investors Canada is fundamentally much like the United States when it comes to matters of money and finance. It is a wealthy nation and operates as a free market economy, in essence. It is often derided by Americans as "socialist," but in truth is subject in many areas to only a little more government influence than that seen in the United States. It is an easy place for foreigners to buy property, because there are really no restrictions in that regard. Additionally, the housing market is generally strong in Canada, fueled in no small way by a steady influx of immigrants who are generally welcome there. On that note, the rental market in Canada is especially strong in some areas, particularly around principal cities. Tenant rights are strong in Canada; in particular, the rent rates in Prince Edward Islands are actually determined by a government agency, the Office of the Director of Residential Rental Property.

One of the biggest attractions of Canada, more generally, is its multilevel compatibility with the United States. The general commonality of culture, language, geographical proximity, combined with Canada's increasing free market approach to business, makes it a foreign country that is not terribly foreign to U.S. investors. The previously referenced low unemployment level (about 7 percent nationally as of early 2009), propensity for economic growth, and low debt levels is a good formula for further enhancement of opportunity in the years to come. Part of Canada's economic strength lies with its reserves of natural resources; Canada is an exporter of energy products, which is unusual for a developed nation, and can lay claim to having the second-largest oil reserves in the world, behind only Saudi Arabia. Canada is a leading supplier of agricultural products, and is also the world's largest producer of zinc and uranium.

For real estate investors in particular, the Canadian market is a good consideration. First, as an overall destination, Canada's strong economy and desire to grow economically, combined with its developed status, means that a U.S. investor can feel good about plunging cash into the market directly. One of the biggest advantages is that Canada does not have a culture of making risky loans, which means that the subprime crisis that slaughtered the U.S. residential market did not have an opportunity to take root in Canada; by consequence, Canadian banks also have money to lend. Canada did experience a slowdown in 2008, but saw sales rise again substantially through the first half of 2009.

Notes on the Buying Process   The process to transact real estate in Canada is about as similar to what one might find in the United States as you will find anywhere. Unlike many countries you might consider, the real estate agent culture in Canada is actually quite strong, and agents are regulated and operate in much the same way as they do in the United States. Accordingly, you may not feel as compelled to retain a Canadian attorney to help escort the process along on your behalf, but we would suggest it, nevertheless. Additionally, there is really no restriction on foreign ownership of real estate in Canada. As for title insurance, it is regarded in much the same way it is in the United States in terms of usage. Again, there is little difference between the way real estate is transacted in the United States and in Canada.

For More Info

- www.crea.ca – The official web site of the Canadian Real Estate Association.

Mexico   Americans are every bit as familiar with their neighbor to the south as they are to their neighbor to the north. As a government, Mexico is ruled by a constitutional republic, and is composed of 31 states and a

Federal District, not unlike the structure of the United States. Since the 1994 economic crisis, the policy leaders in Mexico have aggressively sought to improve their standing in the economic community. Mexico has sought closer ties with the United States and Europe, and has worked hard to improve industrialization and infrastructure. Mexico does have a substantial dependence on the U.S. economy, which, as with Canada, raises potential issues of "faux diversification." Mexico is chiefly export-based as an economy, with more than 9 percent of its trade falling under free trade agreements (notably NAFTA). Indeed, roughly half of its exports and imports involve Canada and the United States, which, again, is something to note in terms of your quest for diversification.

As we noted earlier, Mexico's form of government is a federal constitutional republic; Mexico's constitution dictates that the government shall be divided into three branches, not unlike the United States: the legislative, executive, and judicial branches. The legislative branch is a standard bicameral congress, comprised of a Senate and Chamber of Deputies, which are both broadly similar to their respective counterparts in the United States. The executive branch is represented by the president. In Mexico, the judicial branch is represented by the Supreme Court of Justice, made up of 11 judges appointed by the president. Although Mexico has a long tradition of left-leaning government, and an Institutional Revolutionary Party (known by other names earlier in the twentieth century) candidate had been president for about 70 straight years through the year 2000, Vicente Fox and Felipe Calderon, both of the center-right National Action Party, have held the presidency since the turn of the millennium. Although the presence of, and sympathy for, the PRI (Institutional Revolutionary Party) remains strong in Mexico, there is an indication that Mexicans are increasingly interested in a further embrace of free market policies.

Mexico may be an emerging market (as designated by MSCI Barra), but is the 11th-largest economy in the world (as measured by GDP in terms of purchasing power parity) and sports a solidly upper-middle income profile in many respects. The rate of poverty, once substantial, has been declining steadily since 2000. That said, Mexico still must deal with the matter of inequitable income distribution, as the upper one-third of earners account for more than half of all the income.

Although there is a lot to recommend Mexico, it is also characterized by an unfortunate crime rate, particularly with respect to violent crime. Overall, crime affects 12 out of every 1,000 people in the country. The homicide rate is about 12 per 100,000 inhabitants, and Mexico's drug cartels are particularly problematic; overall, the cartels can lay claim to having about as many members as the Mexican army. The current president, Felipe Calderon, seems dedicated to gaining the upper hand, and has not been shy about dispatching the military to cities that have proven especially troublesome. It is anticipated that this sort of dedication to finally solving the problem may improve the climate for citizen and tourist alike.

Attractiveness to Investors   Mexico has a free market economy, which is always good news to Americans seeking to make fortunes elsewhere. The private sector is now playing more of a role in business than ever before, egged on by administrations that have sought to increase competition in a variety of industries, including telecommunications, electricity, and natural gas distribution, to name a few. In the end, the overwhelming desire by Mexico *for* Mexico to continue to attain a higher status in the global world is something that is appealing to its foreign investors. Mexico is in a phase of internal *über*-development, which can mean a lot to your real property investment if it is in a region of the country that is earmarked for substantial growth.

Despite the unfortunate crime problem and the matter of unequal income distribution, Mexico continues to develop its economic resources. The trend toward broad private ownership has seen a marked increase in competition among a variety of important services, like the enhancement and management of railroads and airport services, among many others. Mexico is actually, now, the largest manufacturer of automobiles in North America, and the country's greatest source of income from foreign countries is oil. You may remember from our discussion earlier in the book that some include Mexico in the prospective future economic powerhouse of BRIC, thus making it "BRIMC." Back in 2001, Mexico was not considered for inclusion as a component, but is looked to now because the country exhibits many of the same characteristics as the original four, including GDP growth of about 5 percent per annum (although at this writing the figure is weaker because of the acute effects of the global meltdown). The bottom line is that the anticipated consumer market is expected to be tremendous, given Mexico's continued trend of lowering poverty, improving infrastructure, and a host of other enhancements designed to strengthen the economic power of the consuming public.

For the real estate investor in particular, Mexico, long a popular destination market for retirees and those looking for a second home, presents an appealing opportunity, even in the face of high-profile crime problems. The Great Recession and upsurge in crime has weighed down purchase activity, but prices remain a tremendous value. Given the government's serious attempts at dealing with the crime problem, as well as the nation's consideration of direct real estate ownership by foreigners, the beneficial results of such activity could create a tremendous wealth opportunity for the investor who looks to the market in the near term. Beyond that time frame, the enhanced economic picture of Mexico, overall, suggests it to be a great market for foreign real estate investment for years to come.

Notes on the Buying Process   As with many countries in Central and South America, Mexico has a tradition of real estate transactions where a single attorney—a *notario*—acts as the centerpiece to the transaction. In Mexico, the notario is a public official who is also a licensed attorney. It is actually a respected position in the country. It is the job of the notario to essentially walk the process through to its conclusion once the contract is executed.

There remains a strong tradition in Mexico of buyers and sellers negotiating directly, but real estate agents are being used more frequently these days as time and technology continues to move forward. You may well want to use the services of a real estate agent; that is up to you. You should know, however, that to ensure the deal goes smoothly, you want to retain your own counsel in addition to the notario, who is theoretically an impartial party but is chosen by the seller. Our advice is that because real estate agents are poorly regulated (compared to those in the United States), that you use an agent to help *find* a property, if you wish, but that you rely on an English-speaking Mexican attorney to represent your interests.

Once you make an offer and it is accepted, you will have your attorney memorialize the offer in writing with a contract. Once accepted in writing, you have to put down about 10 percent of the purchase price as an earnest money deposit. Our advice is that you retain the services of a U.S.-based title company to hold the money. You have to be careful here, because escrow is still a sketchy matter in Mexico. You should not give your deposit directly to the seller under any circumstances, or even to the real estate agent (if you use one). You can either give it to the counsel you choose to retain (you want to be sure you are happy with his escrow arrangements), or, again, give it to a U.S.-based title company to hold.

Once the terms of the contract are met, there is a closing. You should know that the deal is not really done until the notario registers your deed at the Public Registry of Property. We would advise you to follow up on this, because there are plenty of stories afoot about notaries who do not quite finish the job. You might want to take your closing documents (including your deed, which you receive at the closing) to the registry office to be sure the registration was handled properly; if not, get a hold of the notario right away.

There is really no limitation on foreign individuals and businesses owning property in Mexico, and such ownership may take place in a variety of manners. That said, there *is* a restriction on foreigners owning land within 50 kilometers of the coast and within 100 kilometers from international borders. In order to gain these properties, you have to do so through a bank trust called a *fideicomiso*. The fideicomiso gives you the same rights as a Mexican citizen, but it is actually the bank that holds title. Any of the Mexican banks can set up a fideicomiso for you, but if you need this structure as a function of your transaction, it is another reason why you would do well to retain a lawyer on your behalf to oversee the whole process.

As for the matter of title insurance, get some. As with many countries (other than the United States), there does not exist a strong tradition of using title insurance—but get it anyway. Although it is part of the notario's job to perform a title search, do not take any chances. We would suggest using a well-known U.S.-based title insurance company like First American (www.firstam.com), one that also has a strong, global presence. Whichever company you select may well be your choice to hold your deposit, as well.

For More Info

- www.ampidf.com.mx – This is the Spanish-language site for the Mexican Association of Real Estate Professionals.

Central/South America

Central and South America present a variety of enticing possibilities to real estate investors from around the world. Here, we focus on Costa Rica and Nicaragua, two countries that, while different in many ways, each offer the global real estate investor the key benefits associated with owning property in this region.

Costa Rica   Costa Rica, with its long tradition of democracy, remains one of the most stable countries in a region characterized by some measure of historical *instability*; Costa Rica has no army, with only a civil guard in existence to ensure the safety of citizens. It stands to reason that the country sees no reason for much of a militaristic outlook, as the place is composed mostly of coastline—a beach nation, if you will; hardly the sort of place that would prompt many to walk around in a perpetual state of anger.

Costa Rica has, quite amazingly, managed to avoid much of the political upheaval that has plagued Latin America through the years. The country has a firm constitutional history, and prides itself on its many decades of pure democracy. The democratic structure in Costa Rica is familiar to Americans, with the same general three branches of government in place in the United States: legislative, executive, and judicial.

Costa Rica boasts of a literacy rate well over 90 percent, and has one of the world's highest life expectancies at birth—higher, even, than that found in the United States. The public education system is regarded as excellent, and Costa Rica is known as a place where government-sponsored health care is part of the landscape.

Costa Rica is basically tropical in climate, with a dry season that goes from December to April, and a rainy season that runs from May to November. Adding to the climate and the beaches is Costa Rica's notably high regard for conservation efforts. On that note, Costa Rica currently ranks first in Latin America and fifth in the world on the Environmental Performance Index, which is an index created jointly by departments at Yale and Columbia universities and is designed to measure the effectiveness of a country's environmental policies. Additionally, in 2007, Costa Rica announced an ambitious goal of becoming the world's first carbon-neutral (achieving net zero carbon emissions) country by the year 2021. Although well-known for its beaches and world-class surfing opportunities, Costa Rica also has a wide variety of topography that includes jungles, mountains, valleys, and volcanoes. The aforementioned aggressive approach to conservation ensures that the wide variety of species that inhabit the countryside will likely all be present long after we are gone.

Attractiveness to Investors   Costa Rica's appeal as a Latin American country with a long history of economic stability is strong, and said stability is of paramount importance whenever you seek to direct purchase real estate outside of your home country; most individual investors managing personal portfolios simply do not have the resources to ably withstand a direct investment disaster. The country's three biggest industries are tourism, agriculture, and electronics, and Costa Rica has the second-largest GDP in South America. Additionally, the country is in the midst of a pronounced expansion in high-tech, with companies like Intel happy to take advantage of the tax exemptions currently being offered to corporations. Costa Rica recently signed off on CAFTA, the Central American Free Trade Agreement, which is expected to lead to a doubling of exports, with the United States and China expected to be the nation's principal buyers of goods.

Another positive feature for investors is that Costa Rica's emphasis on improved infrastructure has opened up accessibility to several less expensive parts of the country. The Guanacaste Gold Coast is one of the tourism jewels of the country, and it is an excellent location for investors seeking to enter the vacation tourist market, but other investors seeking to find potentially greater value in off-tourist property markets will appreciate the effort at infrastructure improvements. The roadway and airport upgrades, as they continue, will allow for even greater accessibility.

Many years ago, Costa Rica was looked at as a great place to grab some investment real estate by value-oriented foreigners, but that perception changed for a while as costs began to creep up and dealing with the government became more difficult. That said, things are back to an "improvement phase": Prices have stabilized, and the government is trying to do its part by being a little easier to work with, to include making the title search process better and more streamlined.

English is spoken throughout Costa Rica, which means that although you are heartily encouraged to sharpen your Spanish, you find that you can get by pretty well in English.

Notes on the Buying Process   As with many countries outside the United States, attorneys are a big part of real estate transactions here. In Costa Rica, an attorney will prep the sales agreement, which is actually a public deed that is then filed with the National Property Registry (along with proof that the transfer tax and stamp taxes have been paid). Once the transfer deed passes muster, the buyer is now the owner; if there are problems with the transfer deed, the document is returned to the notary and will have to be corrected. The whole process can take about 30 days, which is actually fairly quick for a country in this part of the world.

There are few restrictions in terms of in what manner property can be titled, and there are essentially no restrictions on foreign ownership of property. As stated earlier, the matter of title insurance is becoming better and more accepted, but you want to be sure that the attorney you retain performs a thorough title search. As always, we advise against using an attorney recommended by the seller.

For More Info

- www.camaracbr.or.cr – The official web site of the Costa Rican Real Estate Association.
- www.amcham.co.cr – The Costa Rican–American Chamber of Commerce.
- www.arcr.net – The web site of the Association of Residents of Costa Rica, a great organization that exists to help expatriates and others seeking to live and work in Costa Rica.

Nicaragua   Nicaragua is a representative democratic republic in Central America, with Costa Rica its neighbor to the south. It is actually the *largest* country in Central America, with an area of about 200,000 square miles, which makes it roughly equivalent to the state of New York in area. As with Costa Rica, there is heavy emphasis on conservation, and about 20 percent of the land mass is protected in the form of national parks and a variety of nature and biological reserves.

Nicaragua is composed of three principal geographical regions: the Pacific Lowlands, the Amerrique Mountains (aka North Central Highlands), and the Mosquito Coast (or Atlantic Lowlands). The Pacific Lowlands region is the most populous of the three with more than half of the nation's population residing there. The geography consists of everything from beaches to volcanoes. The North Central Highland region represents a cooler climate, and as such is characterized by a fair amount of agricultural activity. The region of the Atlantic Lowlands is where you can find Nicaragua's rain forests, and the Bosawas Biosphere Reserve, at about 12,000 square miles, is the largest rain forest north of the Amazon.

Like a lot of its neighbors, Nicaragua is in the process of trying to attract foreign dollars and simultaneously improve economy and infrastructure. Nicaragua's principal industry is agriculture, but construction, mining, and general commerce are in phases of expansion right now. Although agriculture makes up roughly 60 percent of total exports, its contribution to GDP is well behind that of the service and industrial sectors.

In Nicaragua, Spanish is the official language, but again, English is prevalent, as well. Education is free and compulsory, but a literacy rate at well below 80 percent speaks to the inaccessibility to the system for much of the population (it is the second-poorest country in the Western Hemisphere).

Attractiveness to Investors   First and foremost, because Nicaragua is now working hard to become more attractive to foreign investment overall, its mindset to that end is probably the most important feature. One of the features of Nicaragua that makes it such a great place to invest is that it is still unfairly tainted by the upheaval from decades past. When you say "Nicaragua" to most people, they immediately envision a third-world country in the midst of a civil war, and a country that is on the verge of becoming a communist state. That is simply not the case. Granted, the poverty and literacy rates we spoke about previously suggest that this is not yet a fully developed nation, but it is by no means in turmoil; additionally, it is precisely some of these less appealing features that have helped to keep real estate values attractive for quite a while now.

Nicaragua remains in the midst of an aggressive effort at overall improvement that has seen such developments as the recent consummation of a deal with the Nicaraguan government by a U.S.-based company to run Puerto Cabezas, which is the country's closest developed port to the United States; the U.S.-based company plans to spend upward of $100 million on improvements, and the end result will be a dramatic improvement of the productivity and overall efficiency of the port. Tourism is a major emphasis of the country now, and Nicaragua now has its first office of tourism in the United States (in Miami).

The price of real estate right now in Nicaragua is competitive both in terms of vacation rentals for tourists, as well as for homes and commercial property for the benefit of local individuals and businesses. Tourists and expatriates will look to Nicaragua as a place where their dollars can go further—a couple can enjoy a great dinner, including booze, for less than $20. As for the locals and businesses, the emphasis on activity will raise the income of workers and present more opportunities for businesses, making Nicaragua a great place for direct investment.

Notes on the Buying Process   In Nicaragua, real estate agents are gaining traction as sources for property searches, but the actual transaction process itself takes place rather simply among three parties: buyer, seller, and notary. It should be noted that in Nicaragua, a notary is an attorney, and, in fact, the notary position in Nicaragua is the highest level of attorney qualification to be attained. You will agree to the purchase price directly with the seller, and the notary then prepares the *promesa*, or promise to sell. The promesa is signed by all three parties. Once fully executed, the notary prepares a *testimonio*, which is a copy of the promesa, and records it in the public record; this is to let other prospective buyers know that the property is under contract.

Once the promesa conditions have been met, the notary prepares a deed that is, once again, executed by all three parties. Again, a testimonio is drawn up, which is taken to the property registry. After the testimonio is registered, an appraisal is done. After the transfer taxes have been paid, the testimonio is recorded in the public registry office.

In Nicaragua, title can be held in a variety of manners, and there are no restrictions on foreign ownership of real estate. Remember that as an emerging market country, the matter of gaining clear title is not quite as straightforward and as reliable as it is in the United States and elsewhere. You are strongly urged to retain counsel in Nicaragua, and use someone who is well versed in this area.

For More Info

- www.canibir/es/index.php – This is a Spanish-language web site for the Nicaraguan Chamber of Real Estate Brokers.
- www.intur.gob.ni – This is a Spanish-language web site for Nicaragua's government tourism agency.
- www.visitanicaragua.com – A Nicaraguan tourism site with an English-language option.

Europe

For many, the prospect of owning property in Europe is nothing short of a dream, but the reality is that there can be excellent investment benefits realized, as well. We've chosen here to focus our look at Europe—specifically

France, Spain, and Bulgaria, three countries that can represent great opportunity for the attentive value investor.

France   To this day, France remains one of the world's most idealized and romanticized countries. Its long history and popular traditions make it one of the centerpieces of world history and culture.

The government of France is a republic with an outstanding record of democratic rule. As for political leanings, the politics of France are rather neatly divided between the socialists and the conservatives. It is the largest member country of the European Union, that alliance of economic and political powers developed largely to defuse the sort of nationalism that had been blamed for causing problems on the continent in the prior decades and centuries.

As an economy, France is a highly developed nation, with the fifth-largest GDP in the world. Although a country with a strong tradition of private enterprise, France also has a long tradition of government oversight and intervention in business. That said, although the French government remains involved in the industries of transportation, electronics, and telecommunications, it is gradually *lessening* its interventionist role as time goes on; the government is selling off interests in key industries, and companies like Air France and France Telecom are the direct beneficiaries of such a change in course. France also enjoys the title of the most independent country in the West in terms of energy reliance, which is directly related to France's aggressive development of nuclear power.

As a tourist destination, nothing compares to France. France is consistently ranked as the number one tourist destination in the world, which is not difficult to understand, given the country's appealing geography and cultural attractions.

Attractiveness to Investors   As with all countries at which we look, we want to find those that, first and foremost, have a generally welcoming attitude when it comes to foreign investment. France, although somewhat constraining historically, is doing much better these days in terms of becoming more inviting to business. There has been a concerted effort by the government to attract investment by promoting an extensive program of incentives. There is a variety of subsidies available at national, regional, and local levels for the effort of attracting jobs to poorer areas of the country, and the eligibility requirements for securing grants and subsidies are the same for both nationals and foreign investors. There is also a wonderful set of tax breaks available to businesses that set up shop in designated areas throughout France. It is largely due to this strong pro-business climate that an environment is expected to be fostered where real estate values stand an excellent chance to appreciate over time.

Surprisingly, given the country's attractiveness on so many levels, the price of real estate is currently reasonable. As with any country, you are not going to find many bargains in downtown Paris, but that is to be expected. That said, it is not at all unusual to secure a great deal in the country's less fashionable areas, so take note.

It is important to note that foreign investment in commercial real estate has grown substantially in recent years, which is no surprise; France's recent embrace of a pro-business outlook has engendered a great market for commercial investment, and that will most certainly continue. Additionally, the interest of foreign nationals in French property has always been relatively high, anyway, and there are no signs of that trend abating.

Notes on the Buying Process   In France, the transaction process is handled by a *notaire*, who is essentially a certified real estate attorney that acts in the public interest (a notaire is a public official). It is the notaire's job to walk the process through. Real estate brokers can certainly be used to locate properties, but it is the notaire who really gets the deal done. It should be noted that although a given notaire is supposed to be an impartial party to the transaction, and many notaries are used simultaneously by both buyer and seller, it is advisable that you retain our own. This is really no different from prosecuting a real estate transaction anywhere else, where each side has representation. The seller typically appoints the notaire, and you can use the seller's, or retain your own. If you decide to get your own, the protocol is that the two notaries split the work and the fees. The fee for the notaire is usually about 6 percent of the purchase price, and that is in addition to other fees and commissions, so keep that in mind.

The negotiation as to price is usually handled directly between the buyer and seller. Once a price is agreed to, the notaire gets started. The notaire will draw up a contract, called a *compromise de vente*. Once a buyer and seller execute the compromise, the buyer makes a deposit of about 10 percent, which is held in escrow by the seller's notaire. When the contract is signed, the buyer has seven days to back out of the deal with no explanation and no penalty. As soon as the terms of the contract are met (searches, examinations, etc.), it is time for a closing. The notaire actually reads aloud the final deed of sale, and then both parties sign.

Title to property purchased in France may be held in a variety of manners. Title insurance companies like First American (www.firstam.com) have created policies that specialize in insuring individuals and businesses buying foreign property. It is a good idea to get a title policy from a reputable company whenever possible, but the importance of clear title is why it is a good idea to retain your own notaire—they handle your title search, as well.

For More Info

- www.franceguide.cm – The official web site of the French Tourist Office.
- http://en.century21.fr – Century 21's English-language site for their presence in France.

Spain   As with France, Spain is a country rich in tradition and culture. Functionally, the government of Spain is a parliamentary democracy. Interestingly, Spain is actually highly decentralized; this came about as a function of the passing of the constitution in 1978 (following the death of Franco), when it was deemed that Spain would be composed of 17 autonomous communities, as well as two autonomous cities. The Spanish Constitution, appearing a little contradictory, recognizes the rights of regions and nationalities to self-govern, but also pronounces the indivisibility of the nation of Spain. The effort at decentralization of what we in the United States would think of as states' rights; these autonomous communities and cities are themselves responsible for the procuring and management of policies, infrastructure, and administration of education, health care, social services, and a host of other services. In fact, the central government of Spain is responsible for less than 20 percent of public spending.

The economy of Spain is one of the largest in both Europe and the world, and was growing noticeably well as late as 2007, when the Great Recession reared its ugly head. The global real estate contraction we have all come to know has hit Spain rather hard, as construction had come to represent about 20 percent of GDP. That said, it is worth noting that the banking crisis that has so ill-affected many U.S. financial institutions did not hit Spanish institutions nearly as much, as the approach to financing and regulatory matters has historically been much more conservative in Spain.

Attractiveness to Investors   At this writing, Spain, like much of the rest of the developed world, is wrestling with a pointed economic slowdown. It was during Q3/2008 that Spain's GDP officially contracted for the first time in 15 years, and the International Monetary Fund estimated further, significant contractions for 2009 *and* 2010. 2011 is the soonest that most are expecting evidence of a recovery to any appreciable degree.

That said, the news is not all bad, especially when you look at Spain as a longer-term play. As Spanish homeowners participated in and thus further fueled the country's housing bubble during the early to mid-twenty-first century, the level of household debt basically tripled during those years, and the ultimately unsustainable levels, followed by the big burst, has created opportunities for real estate investors not seen in many, many years. It is Spain's extended vision of economic growth and investment potential on which prospective real property purchasers should focus. In short, Spain is working hard to make itself more attractive to foreign investment; in 2007, Spain significantly lowered the capital gains rate for nonresidents who sell property—from 35 percent all the way down to 18 percent. More generally, there are many reasons to be more optimistic about Spain longer term. As we said previously, it is one of the largest economies in the world (eighth, according to IMF) and is the sixth-largest recipient of foreign direct investment in the world. Spain also has an especially highly skilled labor force; Spain ranks fourth in the world in the number of people who possess some amount of a postsecondary school scientific or technical education, and in comparison to the other countries that compose the top three (Germany, France, and the United Kingdom), has the lowest population, which means the percentage of higher-educated citizens is higher. Among the most important features is Spain's excellent positioning as a centerpiece of international trade; its geopolitical positioning gives it a leg up in transacting with markets in southern Europe, as well as those in Latin America, with which it has an obvious kinship. Beyond that, its transportation infrastructure is excellent; domestically, it has benefited by the second largest EU highway network (7,100) miles, and both domestic and international transportation is enhanced by 44 seaports located both Atlantic-side and Mediterranean-side, and Spain is home to 47 airports and 250 airlines at last count.

As a real estate investor in particular, although Spain may be in choppy waters at this writing, its long-term potential remains excellent. It is important to note, too, that Spain is regarded as having a modest population, overall, with the interior of the country providing the best investment opportunities (coastal areas are actually quite packed now), and the aforementioned excellent infrastructure means that travel will not be an issue for tourists and residents seeking to rent a place to live.

Notes on the Buying Process   Spain is a country like many others where the use of a real estate agent has become slightly less than a novelty only fairly recently. Americans are used to agents serving as the most important human components to the transaction in the United States; in Spain, it is the lawyer. Still, an agent is an excellent resource for property searches.

Note that in order to buy property in Spain, you need a *Numero de Identificacion de Extranjero*, or NIE number. This number is issued by the National Police of Spain. Although Spanish law dictates that you must apply for the number in person, it is possible to have it handled through a representative in Spain by way of a power of attorney. There are a number of places that can handle that for you, and a quick Internet search reveals the most current vendors of that service.

Once you have the NIE number, you are free to transact. Again, it is imperative to utilize the services of an English-speaking, Spanish attorney (or "solicitor") to oversee your interests. Once you sign the "reservation agreement," you will normally pay a percent or two to the seller as deposit, who will, in turn, remove the listing, which gives your attorney the ability to perform what is basically a title search but which is known as a "land registry check." Once the check comes back okay, the official contract is signed, and you will make a deposit of about 10 percent at that time. Once the contract terms are met, to include the securing of financing, as applicable, the deal is consummated at the public notary's office.

There are essentially no limitations as to the type of entity that may own property in Spain. As for title *insurance*, like in many other countries, it is a relatively new concept. Firms like Stewart Title (www.stewart.com) are gaining ground as providers of title insurance and escrow services in foreign countries, and we heartily suggest you make use of resources like this when your search for a property in Spain picks up steam.

For More Info

- www.spainexpat.com – A decent information site for expats who seek to make Spain a home.
- www.remax.es – RE/MAX Spain's official site; available in English.

Bulgaria   Bulgaria, known officially as the Republic of Bulgaria, has one of the richer organized traditions and histories in Europe, dating back to the seventh century, although that which is known as modern-day Bulgaria is home to Varna Necropolis, a burial site dating all the way back to the fifth millennium BC. Present-day Bulgaria is structured as a parliamentary democracy within the confines of a constitutional republic. The president of Bulgaria, who acts in the capacity of head of state, is elected by popular vote for a five-year term, and can be reelected once for another five-year term. The head of government is the *premier*, who is elected by the legislature. Bulgaria is presently divided into 28 provinces, and the 240 members of the National Assembly are also elected by popular vote for four-year terms. The key point for investors is that it is a country that abandoned its communist ties after the "Autumn of Nations" revolutions of 1989 and moved rather emphatically to an embrace of democracy and capitalism.

Bulgaria has been a member of the European Union since 2007, although it remains one of its *poorest* members. The principal industries within the country are services, agriculture, and industry, and Bulgaria is the source of a lot of raw materials production. Interestingly, Bulgaria's GDP growth, which was about 6 percent in 2008 and expected to be somewhere between 4 percent and 5 percent in 2009, is remarkably high, considering the far-reaching effects of the Great Recession on nearly the entire world.

There has been a significant increase in the purchase of Bulgarian land by foreigners, but investor confidence has to some degree been hampered by a substantial amount of corruption. Oddly, Bulgarian officials have been reluctant to effectively deal with the corruption problem in any meaningful way, and the result has been a wave of *emigration* from the country (which has only exacerbated Bulgaria's decades-old problem of negative population growth). That said, officially, Bulgaria remains committed to satisfying the standards of both the IMF and the EU (the EU has actually frozen funds earmarked as aid—about $350 million—until it gets its act together and gets the problem of corruption under control).

Attractiveness to Investors   Despite some of the problems with which it is wrestling currently, such as the aforementioned corruption, there is much to find attractive about Bulgaria in terms of its resource as an investment-friendly economy. Indeed, while Bulgaria is still in the throes of coming to full compliance with EU standards, it is reasonable to consider Bulgaria quite heavily right now before that eventuality comes to pass.

One of the key considerations for investment remains geographical proximity to current and prospective economic allies, as well as the maturity of infrastructure, and the inherent association between the two. The natural geography of Bulgaria is diverse, as is its climate; it runs the gamut from mountains to beaches, from valleys to plains. More importantly, it has free trade agreements with markets that in their totality represent about 1 billion people, and has long-served as an economically central location for the benefit of the European, Asian, and African continents. As for infrastructure, the system of roadways throughout the country is consistently improving, with key routes planned between major cities and existing thoroughfares; as it stands, several of the links to the Trans-European Motorway either sit, or *will* sit, within Bulgaria's boundaries. There is also a modestly sized, but clearly growing, network of railways, shipping ports, and airports; Bulgaria has six international airports, and there are elaborate plans to expand and modernize several of them.

For real property investors in particular, Bulgaria offers intriguing possibilities. By U.S. standards, real estate is inexpensive there, which coincides with the low cost of living. There is much potential for future price appreciation based on some of the broader economic factors referenced earlier, but the record of ROI in real estate has consistently been above 10 percent per annum for some time now. Mortgage loans in Bulgaria represent about 5 percent of the total credit supply, where in most developed economies the number is closer to 20 percent. It is Bulgaria's popularity with lower-income tourists, which, in part, sustains the demand for affordable rental property. That said, Bulgaria has not been spared the effects of the global financial crisis, and property values—still strong through most of 2008—started to slip noticeably going into 2009. Investors with solid financial resources can now take advantage of this contraction in a number of areas, including along Bulgaria's much-coveted Black Sea coastal region. In short, Bulgaria is a good spot to look for both near-term and longer-term reasons; great deals for the foreseeable future, within a country with excellent prospects over the mid to long term.

Notes on the Buying Process   Right off the bat, it is important to note that in Bulgaria, foreigners may not buy property with land unless they do so in the form of a Bulgarian registered company (this requirement is slated to exist until 2014). Accordingly, many investors have sought to purchase apartments/condos, which has dovetailed nicely with the desire of many to own along the Black Sea coast. This means that if you seek to buy property with land, you will need to set up the registered entity. It is not that difficult to do, and there are a number of places that will take care of the setup for you, which you can locate through a simple Internet search. Basically, you can set up what you know in the United States as an LLC. You should know, though, that the entity has to be capitalized to the tune of 5,000 Bulgarian leva, which is around $3,800 at this writing. This means that you have to set up a bank account in association with the entity. You can search the Internet specifically for this service, and many companies that assist with the process now exist—one Google search for "set up a Bulgarian registered company" will give you an array of companies from which to choose. While all of this may seem like more trouble than it's worth, consider what the effect will be on prices once this restriction is removed—and it is not that big of a deal *now*. You need not set up the registered company prior to making your offer, but it needs to be done once the offer is accepted. At that time, you make a deposit (about 10 percent) that is usually made to the lawyer you retain to hold in escrow. At that point, the process to meet the terms of the contract in earnest begins, and the deal is consummated on the basis of a notarized deed once the terms are met.

As stated, foreign individuals can buy only apartments, at present, while property with land has to be transacted by foreigners through a Bulgarian registered company. As for title insurance, the relative immaturity of the Bulgarian legal system, combined with the improving-but-still-unfortunate culture of corruption, demands that you purchase title insurance. Well-known title insurers like First American (www.firstam.com) have an established presence in Bulgaria, and can also be great references for other services you may need during the course of your property search and overall transaction. Also, you should note that in terms of the overall transaction, Bulgarian Properties Ltd. (www.bulgarianproperties.com)

provides a comprehensive service that takes you from A to Z in buying in Bulgaria, and there are several other companies just like it; a quick Internet search will help you get started.

For More Info

- www.century21.bg – The Century 21 site for their presence in Bulgaria; there is a button for English language translation.
- Also, we would direct you to the previously referenced link for Bulgarian Properties Ltd.

Asia/Pacific

Our look here at the Asia/Pacific region focuses on Australia and Japan, two nations from this growing economic powerhouse of a region that present global real estate investors with very different ways to which to gain access to it.

Australia   Australia remains one of the more fantastical locations in the world in the minds of many. Australia's world-famous coastline, to include the Great Barrier Reef, is an epic draw for visitors from around the world. Additionally, Australia's rich and diverse geographical profile is made up of mountains, rain forests, plenty of woodlands and grasslands, as well as its famous desert region known as the Outback. In association with its amazing geography, Australia is characterized by an environment that is quite unique. Australia is one of the world's 18 *megadiverse* countries, as determined by the United Nations' World Conservation Monitoring Center, which means that it is regarded, by virtue of the number of species that can be found there, as extremely biodiverse. Uniquely, Australia is the only place in the world that is regarded simultaneously as officially being a continent, a country, and an island. Australia is rich in natural resources, and an important component to its economy is the export of agricultural and mineral products, as well as energy-related resources like natural gas and coal.

Australia's governmental structure is a constitutional monarchy in association with a parliamentary democracy. The parliament has two houses, a House of Representatives and a Senate. The head of Australia's government is the prime minister, and he or she is actually selected by the House. Australia is divided up into six states as well as two territories, and the states enjoy a fair amount of self-governance.

Australia is one of the world's developed markets, and its economy is generally quite free-market oriented. Indeed, Australia ranks third, behind only Hong Kong and Singapore (and *ahead* of the United States), in the 2009 Index of Economic Freedom (the Index is created on the basis of 10 measurements of economic freedom devised jointly by the Heritage Foundation and the *Wall Street Journal*). The services sector of the Australian economy is its biggest, representing 68 percent of GDP, but the nation's agricultural and mining sectors, while representing only about 4 percent and 5 percent of GDP, respectively, account for almost 60 percent of the country's exports.

Attractiveness to Investors   As with all of the countries profiled here, we see both a broader attractiveness to investors in Australia as well as more real estate–specific opportunities. As to the former, it is worth noting that Australia receives a substantial inflow of FDI (foreign direct investment) in comparison to the other developed countries of the world. According to the 2008 World Investment Report of the United Nations Conference on Trade and Development (UNCTAD), Australia's ratio of inward FDI to GDP is about 35 percent, where the same ratio on behalf of other developed nations is about 27 percent. The EU is the largest source of FDI by region, and the four biggest source investors of FDI in 2008 were the United States, United Kingdom, Japan, and the Netherlands.

For investments of any kind, a stable political and business structure is important, and Australia certainly has both. Australia has low levels of corruption, as well as a modern and transparent judicial system.

Significantly, Australia is well positioned to benefit from the rapidly growing economies of Asia. China and Japan are, at present, Australia's top two-way trading partners, and its overall positioning with Asia means that its sea and air freight services are both direct and regular, and travel times are much less than those between Asia and other highly developed economies.

Australia's ranking on the human development index (HDI) is currently third in the world, its life expectancy is currently fifth-highest, has highly livable cities, and the third-lowest cost of living in the developed world (source: IMD World Competitiveness Yearbook 2008).

For real estate investors in particular, Australia is attractive for numerous reasons. Once again, we refer to Australia's highly stable and transparent government and business environments, but beyond that, Australia is expected to see growth and stability in its real property markets in the coming years. China is particularly interested in real estate investment in Australia on the basis of its perception that Australia is a safe place to invest. Property values were not destroyed in the Great Recession, and foreign investors accounted for about 12 percent of total real property transactions in the first half of 2009. At this writing, both Sydney and Melbourne are going through a noticeable period of population growth, and rental vacancies are near zero. It is generally believed that Australia's residential housing market will lead the recovery, and at this writing most of the country seems to believe the worst is over.

It is this kind of resiliency that investors seek both now as well as into the future. Short-term bargains are nice, but more important are fundamental reasons to like the opportunity long term, which Australia provides.

Notes on the Buying Process   Foreign residents are welcomed and encouraged to buy property in Australia, but before you make a serious effort to buy property, you must secure permission to do so from Australia's Foreign Investment Review Board, or FIRB (www.firb.gov.au). The role of the board is to examine requests by foreign nationals to make investments in Australia, with an eye to ensuring that both the investor and investment is in keeping with Australia's national interests. Because the approval process can take about three months, and most people do not want to bother initiating a serious property search *before* securing approval (buying without an approval can result in a forced sale), they make application about three months before they plan to start searching in earnest.

The use of real estate agents in Australia is customary these days, so buying property in Australia feels more like a U.S. transaction than it does in other foreign countries. Once an offer is accepted, the buyer makes a "holding" deposit of 10 percent, and the contract for sale is drawn up. Once the contract is completed and signed, the deposit becomes irrevocable. From here, the terms of the contract are fulfilled (securing of financing, verifying clear title, etc.), and there is a closing. By the way, an excellent site for locating both property in Australia, as well as an agent, is that of the REA Group (www.realestate.com.au).

There is essentially no restriction on the manner in which title can be held in Australia. As for title insurance, the major worldwide carriers (Stewart Title, First American) have an organic presence in the country, and we suggest that you always purchase title insurance whenever you make a purchase.

For More Info

- www.remax.com.au – RE/MAX Australia's online presence.
- Also, we would suggest the previously referenced REA Group site for further information.

Japan   At roughly 146,000 square miles in total area, Japan ranks 61st in geographical size of all the countries of the world, but make no mistake: Japan is an absolute giant in so many other ways. Japan, by all measurements, can lay claim to having the second-largest economy in the world as measured by nominal GDP, and has the third-largest economy as measured by purchasing power parity (source: 2008 CIA World Factbook). Japan is one of the world's largest importers *and* exporters, and is the only Asian member of the G-8. As for demographics, Japan is the 10th-most populous country in the world (at a little over 127 million people), with one of the highest life expectancies; Japan is currently ranked eighth on the basis of the Human Development Index (HDI). The list goes on and on but the point is obvious: Japan is a powerhouse in just about every measurable aspect of modern human existence.

As for the structure of government in Japan, it is a constitutional monarchy with a parliamentary government. The government is a democracy, and is composed of a House of Representatives as well as a House of Councillors; the relationship between the two is not wholly unlike that of the two houses of Congress in the United States. The members of the two houses in Japan are elected by popular vote, and the prime minister, who is Japan's head of government, is appointed by the emperor (mostly a ceremonial position now) after designation by parliament.

Geographically, Japan is highly diverse, but only about 20 percent of the country, overall, is habitable. As a result, most of the population lives in the coastal regions, and with the 10th-largest population living on the 61st-largest in area, and only about 20 percent of *that* able to sustain habitation, the population density is simply incredible. As it is, Greater Tokyo is the largest city in the world by population, with more than 30 million residents.

The economy of Japan represents, perhaps, its greatest strength. As stated earlier, it is the second-largest in the world, and while it has had a history of overheating, with, by consequence, several years of stagnant growth returns, the amazing resiliency and dedication to achievement of the people ensures it is always a "player" on the world economic stage.

Attractiveness to Investors   Japan's long-standing tradition of dedication to the highest standards of business culture and productivity make it naturally attractive to foreign investment. FDI has been steadily increasing in Japan for years now, and despite the onset of the global recession, saw an increase of FDI to about $180 billion by the end of 2008. Although FDI represented only about 3.6 percent of GDP at the end of 2008 (compared to much higher rates in other developed markets; 48.6 percent in the United Kingdom, 24 percent in Germany, and 37 percent in France), Japan adopted 91 new policies through its Program for Acceleration of Foreign Direct Investment in Japan in an effort to substantially increase FDI in the country.

As you would expect, infrastructure is highly advanced. Japan has made a concerted effort to increase the amount of money spent on road development in recent years, while the rail system is itself highly advanced and a fundamental means of travel throughout the country. Japan also has a large number of airports, as well as seaports. As for education, the Japanese are an exceedingly well-educated citizenry, with nearly 80 percent of high school graduates attending some form of postsecondary school institution. The culture of competitiveness that characterizes many other facets of Japanese life, including business, is quite prevalent in its schools. On that note, two of the top five leading institutions of higher education as of 2008 can be found in Japan: Tokyo and Waseda universities.

Overall, Japan presents a powerful presence as both a highly developed market, strategically located to benefit within the global business community, as well as a single-minded, aggressive top-to-bottom posture for achieving continued economic growth for years to come.

As for those seeking specifically to buy real estate, the nature of the Japanese economy and business climate, combined with the rate at which Japan's property market is recovering from the Great Recession, should present pleasing opportunities to investors. Japan, along with Australia, has seen the settling of the market, to include the restructuring of debt, occur more quickly than it has in many other markets. Price corrections have been substantial in the Japanese market, and yet Japan remains the world's second-largest economy. As with many markets, the opportunity to flip or otherwise transact in and out more quickly on a property may be more limited—the key to profiting in Japan is through current yield opportunities combined with *long-term* growth potential. All areas of Japanese real estate should present good opportunities for some time, to include vacant land, where developers are under particular stress and will remain so for the foreseeable future. The Tokyo market, at this writing, is seeing a lot of interest from foreign investors. The scarcity of land in Tokyo in particular, and in Japan more generally, is a good long-term consideration for investors, so it is important to give great weight to penetrating the market during the sorts of economic dips we see at this writing. In fact, buying raw land is one of the more popular routes to take for investors, because the persistent threat of earthquakes in Japan is a nonissue for owners of raw land. Additionally, one of the key benefits of real estate investment in Japan is the market's historically low correlation with the U.S. real estate market, a feature that has persisted despite the tendency of most developed markets to track each other with greater frequency throughout equity classes.

Notes on the Buying Process Let us mention up front that if you need financing to buy a property in Japan, your options will be limited. The vast majority of in-country banks and financial institutions will not lend to nonresidents of Japan, although the absolute standard of having to have permanent residency has relaxed a little. A few banks, like HSBC (www.hsbc.co.jp), will make loans to nonpermanent residents who have a valid Alien

Resident Card. Because the "rules" on foreigners obtaining a mortgage are a bit in flux, you will have to determine the latest status of that issue when you get ready to buy. An all-cash transaction is going to be your most direct route here, but financing is by no means out of the question. You will, however, likely have to work hard to find it.

As for the process of purchasing a property, it is similar to that in the United States. A property is selected, a contract is negotiated, deposit paid (about 10 percent), and once the terms of the contract are met, the closing takes place. The key is that in Japan you are strongly advised not to go it alone to save a few bucks. We do not advise that anyway, regardless of the foreign country you are targeting, but Japan's strong reluctance to give up land to foreigners (despite what the government says) means that you want some help. Companies that specialize in assisting foreign buyers with transactions are springing up all of the time. Two used quite often are Ken Corporation (www.kencorp.com) and MKC Properties (www.mkc-properties.com). As most foreigners seek *rental* property in Japan, you find that both companies are geared to that market, but both also specialize in purchases.

There are not any noticeable limitations on how title can be held when buying property in Japan. As always, title insurance is recommended, and as a developed market, the acceptance of title insurance is an ingrained part of the Japanese real estate culture. Companies like Stewart Title (www.stewart.com) and First American (www.firstam.com) are excellent resources for both title insurance in Japan, as well as serving as assisting you with the overall transaction process.

For More Info

- www.century21.jp – The site for the Japanese presence of Century 21. There is an English-language translation button at the bottom of the home page.
- Also, we would direct you to the previously mentioned sites of Ken Corporation and MKC Properties for more information.

Africa

Africa continues, overall, to see a tangible increase in its long-term economic prospects. One of the individual nations in the region best-situated to provide significant, beneficial impact to real estate investors is South Africa.

South Africa South Africa, known formally as the Republic of South Africa, is an emerging market nation that is increasingly well positioned to realize substantial economic growth and stability in the coming years. That South Africa enjoys that posture at all is somewhat of a minor miracle, given the well-known internal strife that unfortunately characterized the nation for so many years (and which still rears its head on a not entirely infrequent basis). South Africa is now, overall, regarded quite universally as the most economically viable African nation outside of North Africa, and of all the nations on the continent (53), only Egypt, Morocco, and South Africa qualify as emerging markets per MSCI Barra (2009); none qualifies as a developed market.

The form of government in South Africa is a constitutional democracy, where aspects of both presidential and parliamentary systems are significant and relevant. There are three branches of government, not unlike the United States: a legislative branch that is composed of a parliament that is made up of two separate bodies (aka "bicameral"), the National Assembly and the National Council of Provinces (very similar to the House of Representatives and Senate in the United States); the executive branch, which is the president (he is elected from parliament); and the judiciary, which is made up of the Constitutional Court, the Supreme Court of Appeal, and the High Court. What makes South Africa unique from many other nations is that each branch of government, as well as those that are more provincial and even local, are as much separate and distinct as they are interdependent. The point is to satisfy the South African Constitution's intent that the country is run as much as possible on the basis of cooperative governance. For countries in sub-Saharan Africa, South Africa's effort at fair, effective, and yet benevolent governance is actually quite successful; per the Ibrahim Index of African Governance, which is an index designed to monitor and rate the quality of governance throughout sub-Saharan Africa, South Africa ranked fifth-highest in the individual category of Rule of Law, Transparency, and Corruption, third-highest in the category of Human Development, and second-highest in the category of Sustainable Economic Opportunity.

Attractiveness to Investors For businesses and individuals seeking a country in which to invest that presents some greater-than-average risk (in some respects), with the potential of a substantial upside, South Africa is an excellent option. We believe that the average investor seeking a direct ownership real estate play in a foreign country might want to stay with more developed markets, but those inclined to something just a bit chancier might be okay with South Africa. Perhaps the biggest downside remains the crime problem, a persistent issue in the country and one for which the solution has so far proven elusive. South Africa has, for years, remained near the top of lists of nations ranked as those with the worst crime problem, and even by the measure of the Ibrahim Index, only five countries in sub-Saharan Africa rated worse than South Africa in the category of Safety and Security.

On the upside, the overall economy, while far from perfect, is a work in progress that seems headed in the right direction. It is the most developed of the sub-Saharan economies, with rather advanced key sectors such as communications, energy, and transport. The financial sector is highly developed, as well, and is best represented by the success of the JSE Limited, which is presently the 16th-largest stock exchange in the world and which has designs on serving as the first pan-African exchange on the continent. Of GDP measured in terms of purchasing power parity, South Africa is currently ranked 25th of all the countries in the world (per the 2008 CIA World Factbook).

For real property investors in particular, South Africa's signals seem to be pretty solid. In the short-to-near term, the country, although hit hard by the global recession, has seen signs of stabilization; there was actually an increase of 1.2 percent in South Africa's average property prices from June 2008 to June 2009 (source: Ooba), with some predicting property price increases of up to 60 percent through 2012. The best deals will likely be in medium-priced homes for the foreseeable future, which is in keeping with price trends in many markets. Sub-Saharan Africa is attracting some serious interest from outside developers, including Dubai's Kensington Real Estate, and another, Dubai World Africa, has actually made its home in Cape Town. These and other developers are expected to pour a wave of money into Africa in the coming years, and the interest of developers such as these are good cues for individual investors seeking opportunity. South Africa is already attracting its share of foreign investors who are targeting both the more fashionable Western Cape and poorer Eastern Cape, where cheaper prices present the prospect of greater accessibility to investors.

Notes on the Buying Process   Because South Africa is eager to grow and ideally serve as the benchmark sub-Saharan African country in the global marketplace, it welcomes foreign investment of all types. There is a lot of foreign national ownership of South Africa real estate, and there are no restrictions on foreign nationals when it comes to buying property in South Africa. Just as importantly, there are no restrictions on nonresidents obtaining a mortgage from within the country, but it should be noted that South African financial institutions normally do not loan more than 50 percent of the purchase price to nonresidents. The real estate agent component is actually well established in South Africa, but you will also want to retain an attorney to oversee your interests. As for the agency issue, it is worth noting that RE/MAX (www.remax.com) an agency well-known to U.S. residents, has a substantial presence throughout South Africa. It is a familiar process, composed essentially of search, contract deposit, followed by the satisfaction of terms, and then a closing. You should expect the entire process, from property selection to closing, to take between six and eight weeks.

Title may be held in a variety of manners by foreign investors, and with regard to title insurance, well-known First American (www.firstam.com) has experience providing title services in South Africa.

For More Info

- www.century21.co.za – The online presence of Century 21 in South Africa.
- Also, we would direct your attention to the previously referenced RE/MAX site for more information.

CHAPTER 8

Derivative Use for Offense and Defense

M any people are tempted to turn and run when they hear the word "derivatives." One of the most famous quotes about derivatives in recent years comes from Warren Buffett, when he said that, "Derivatives are financial weapons of mass destruction," and when the Oracle of Omaha speaks, investors listen. That said, what we intend to show you in this chapter is that derivatives can be used in a conservative fashion to hedge certain risks, which is how most hedge fund managers employ derivatives. Like many things in life, derivatives are neither good nor bad in and of themselves, but it is how they are used that determines their legacy in one's portfolio; on that note, we are reminded of the words of Sir Josiah Stamp, president of the Bank of England in the 1920s, who said, "It is easy to dodge our responsibilities, but we cannot dodge the consequences of dodging our responsibilities." As that quote relates to derivatives, it tells us that you can be as aggressive and as speculative as you want to be, but like John Meriwether and Long-Term Capital Management learned in 1998, you will eventually pay the consequences of not using derivatives in responsible fashion.

Okay, so what are derivatives? Many of us first encountered derivatives in mathematics courses; in calculus, derivatives are a measurement of how a function changes when the values of its inputs change, and the definition as it pertains to the capital markets is essentially the same. Derivatives are financial instruments, the prices of which are derived from the value of something else, which is usually called "the underlying." The underlying on which a derivative is based can be the price of an asset, like stocks, commodities, or residential mortgages, or even an index, like interest rates, exchange rates, stock market indexes, consumer price index (CPI), or other similar sorts of benchmarks; *credit* derivatives, the most famous kind in these days following the implosion of global financial markets in 2008, are based on loans, bonds, or other forms of credit. The principal types of derivatives are forwards, futures, options, and swaps.

Derivatives can be used to mitigate the risk of economic loss arising from changes in the value of the underlying security. This activity is known as hedging. For example, if you held a position in the stock of Nestlé and felt its longer-term prospects were strong, but that short-term inventory problems would force the stock down in the coming quarters, you may decide to buy *put* options to protect your position as Nestlé went through a corrective phase. Alternatively, derivatives can be used by investors to take a risk and make a profit if the value of the underlying security moves the way they expect. This form of derivatives use is much more aggressive and is known as *speculation*. It may suit the palate of some investors to go out on a limb in such a fashion, but the majority of this chapter is going to be geared toward how to use derivative instruments to shore up your portfolio, and not for the purpose of speculation.

We will be chiefly speaking of options and futures. We thought about including a section for swaps but decided that the swaps market is not as readily accessible to investors and is, for the most part, institutionalized. When we started out to write this book, we wanted to strive for something you could use and practically apply in creating your own hedge-type portfolio. Most people do not have access to the swaps market, so we do not waste your time by making you read something that would prove to be of little practical value.

OPTIONS

Many investors do not know that options are a form of derivative, but they are probably the most utilized type of derivative in the market today. An option is a contract between a buyer and a seller that gives the buyer the right, but not necessarily the obligation, to buy or sell a particular asset (usually equities) at a later day at an agreed price. In return for granting the option, the seller collects a *premium* from the buyer.

As a general overview, a *call* option gives the buyer the right to buy the underlying asset, while a *put* option gives the buyer of the option the right to sell the underlying asset. If the buyer chooses to exercise this right, the seller is obliged to sell or buy the asset at the agreed price. The buyer may also choose not to exercise the right and let it expire. The underlying asset can be a piece of property, shares of stock, an index, or some other security, like a futures contract. For example, buying a call option on Allied Irish Banks provides the purchaser the right to buy 100 shares of the bank at a set price (the *strike price*) at some time on or before expiration. Buying a put option on Allied Irish Banks would grant the right to sell 100 shares, on or before expiration, at the strike price. Upon the option holder's choice to exercise, the party who sold, or *wrote*, the option, must fulfill the terms of the contract. Thus, if you sold a call option and the receiving part wanted to exercise the option to buy the underlying shares, you would have to provide those shares at the strike price. If you owned them, you can take them out of your own inventory; if you do not own them, you would be forced to buy them in the open market, regardless of price.

Terms and Concepts

Before we dig in, let us go over some key terms and concepts that will always have relevance in any meaningful discussion of derivatives. Your useful familiarity with these ideas is something that falls both outside of, as well as within, the scope of this chapter's contents. It is imperative that you develop a solid foundation of understanding as you proceed into the world of derivatives.

Pricing: Options trade under the same bid/ask format as equities. However, you need to be careful about using market orders with options because they can trade at larger spreads, much like thinly traded stocks. It is not to say you should not use market orders; it is simply to say that you should not use them blindly. Always check the bid/ask spread prior to placing an order. Additionally, each options contract represents the purchase or sale of 100 shares of the underlying stock; if you see a quote for $3.50 and you buy one contract, your out-of-pocket expense would be $350—you have to use a multiplier of 100 when calculating the contracts.

Reality: When you buy a call option, one of three things can happen: the stock can go up, it can move sideways, or it can go down. If the stock goes up, your call option would likely appreciate; if the stock goes sideways or down, you would likely lose money. The reality of options is that you stand a 67 percent chance of losing money. It can be an aggressive game, to say the least. The majority of options, from the institutional side, are bought for hedging existing positions, but the hedge fund manager is not as concerned with making money as he or she is with protecting an existing position. Therefore, whether he or she makes money on the option is not always the most relevant issue.

Options Clearing Corporation (OCC): The Options Clearing Corporation (OCC), founded in 1973, is the world's largest equity derivatives clearing organization, as well as a clearing firm in commodity futures, commodity options, and security futures. By acting as guarantor, the clearing organization ensures that the obligations of the contracts they clear are fulfilled.

OCC operates under the jurisdiction of both the Securities and Exchange Commission (SEC) and the Commodity Futures Trading Commission (CFTC). Under its SEC jurisdiction, OCC clears transactions for put and call options on common stock and other equity issues, stock indexes, foreign currencies, interest rate composites, and single-stock futures.

Strike Price: The strike price, also known as the "exercise price," is the value at which a specific options contract can be exercised. Strike prices are fixed in the contract. For call options, the strike price is the price at which the security can be bought, up to the expiration date. For put options, the strike price is the price at which shares can be sold. Let us say you owned the Canadian doughnut company Tim Hortons Inc. in your hedge fund and it was currently trading at $25.50. If you wanted to hedge your position, you may consider a January 2010 $25 strike put option. This $25 strike price tells you that you can sell the stock for $25 any time between now and the third Friday of January 2010.

Time Value versus Intrinsic (or Price) Value: There are two components to the price of any option: the time value component and the intrinsic, or price, value component. If you own a $25 strike call option on Rogers Communications Inc. and the stock is trading at $27, you are said to be "in the money" on your call option because you can convert the option and buy the stock at a lower price than that at which it is currently trading in the open market. If the option price itself was $3.50, $2 of that price is the actual value the option gives you because of the strike relation to the open market price; this is the *intrinsic value*, while the remainder of $1.50 is the *time value* portion of the price. As the option gets closer to expiration, the time value of the option declines to zero because you have less and less time for that stock to get into, or *stay* in, the money. Therefore, when you are trading options, you have to consider both components before making a trade. If you bought a put option at $3.50 and it ran up to $7.50, with $4 of that representing intrinsic value, you may consider selling the option even if you think the stock may fall a little more because you know that, as time marches on, you will be eroding the time value component of the option. It will always go toward zero as the option runs its course.

Call Options: A call option is a financial contract between two parties, the buyer and the seller. Specifically, it is the option to buy shares of stock at a specified time in the future at a specified price. The buyer of the option has the *right*, but not the *obligation*, to buy an agreed quantity of a particular stock, commodity, or index. The option spells out the expiration date and price. The seller, or writer, is obligated to sell the commodity or financial instrument should the buyer so decide to convert the option. The buyer pays a fee, called a premium, when he purchases the option.

The buyer of a call option wants the price of the underlying instrument to rise in the future; the seller expects that it will not, or is willing to give up some of the upside from a price rise in return for the premium. Call options are most profitable for the buyer when the underlying instrument is appreciating. The call buyer believes it is likely that the price of the underlying asset will rise by the exercise date. The risk is limited to the premium that the buyer paid. In other words, if we buy a call option on Brazilian Petrobras and pay $3.50 for it, that is all the skin we have in the game. If the stock goes down, our option can become worthless, but we cannot, as the buyer, lose more than the amount of our initial investment.

The seller, or writer, of the call does not believe the price of the underlying security is likely to rise. The writer sells the call to collect the premium. For example, if you owned a stock in your hedge fund and felt that it was probably going to be moving sideways for some months, you may write a call against your position to gain the premium while the stock treads water. This is called *covered* call writing, as you actually own the stock in your portfolio. We show you some practical applications later in the chapter. If you are wrong about the anticipated movement and the stock actually moves solidly higher, the buyer may take it away from you, but you would keep the premium. That said, if the stock goes from $50 to $75 after you wrote your call, you just lost $25 of potential gains on the position, so there can be a large opportunity cost associated with losing a stock like this. The total loss for the call writer who is *naked* (i.e., you do not actually own the stock on which you are writing calls) can be very large. If you write one covered call against a stock at $15 and it goes to $25, you are obligated to provide 100 shares of stock to the buyer of the call option, which means, in that case, that you would have to buy the stock in the open market and give those shares to the buyer. Hypothetically, your risk is limitless.

Call options can be purchased on many financial instruments besides stock; options can be purchased on futures and interest rates, as well as on commodities like silver and crude oil.

Put Options: A put option is a financial contract between two parties. The buyer essentially acquires a short position offering the right, but not obligation, to sell the underlying instrument at an agreed-upon price, the strike price. If the buyer exercises the right granted by the option, the seller has the obligation to purchase the underlying at the strike price. In exchange for having this option, the buyer pays the writer a fee, or option premium.

The put *buyer* believes that the price of the underlying asset will fall by the exercise date, or hopes to protect a long position in the asset (hedging).

The advantage of buying a put over short selling the asset is that the risk is limited to only the premium. The profit, for a put buyer, is limited to the strike price less the underlying's spot price. In other words, if you bought a put on a stock with a $25 strike price, it can go only to zero, so your maximum profit is $25 of price.

The put *writer* does not believe the price of the underlying security is likely to fall. The writer sells the put to collect the premium. The total loss for the put writer is limited to the strike price *less* the market price and premium already received. Similar to what we saw with the call option, a naked put (also called an *uncovered put*) is a put option where the option writer does not have a position in the underlying stock or instrument.

If the market price of the underlying stock is below the strike price of the option when expiration arrives, the option owner can exercise the put option and force the writer to buy the underlying stock at the strike price. That allows the exerciser to profit from the difference between the market price of the stock and the option's strike price. However, if the market price is above the strike price when expiration day arrives, the option expires worthless and the writer profits by keeping the premium collected when he sold the option.

The potential loss on a naked put for the seller can be substantial. If the stock falls all the way to zero (i.e., the company goes into bankruptcy), the loss is equal to the strike price minus the premium received. The potential upside is only the premium received when selling the option. If the stock price is above the strike price at expiration, then the option seller keeps the premium and the option expires worthless.

LEAPS (Long-Term Equity Anticipation Securities): LEAPS are simply options contracts with expiration dates that are longer than one year. Structurally, LEAPS are no different from short-term options, but the later expiration dates offer the opportunity for long-term investors to gain exposure to prolonged price changes without needing to use shorter-term option contracts.

LEAPS are an excellent way for a hedge fund manager to gain exposure to a prolonged trend in a given security without having to roll several short-term contracts together and without having to tie up substantial funds. These long-term options can be purchased not only for individual stocks, but also for equity indexes. Let us say you are a hedge fund manager and you are expecting a substantial chunk of cash into your fund next year, but you feel the market is primed to make a substantial move before then. You could go out and buy LEAPS calls on the S&P 500 to take advantage of the rise you are expecting without having to lay out a substantial sum of money. As you see in the next section, you can also accomplish this with futures.

PRIMARY STRATEGIES

What follows is a look at the principal option strategies to which the global portfolio manager will regularly look in order to enhance his positions. Here we highlight straddles, straps and strips, strangles, and that old favorite, covered call writing.

Straddles

A straddle is the simultaneous purchase (or sale) of a call and a put option with the same underlying asset, strike price, and expiration date. A long straddle requires the purchase of the put and the call, while a short straddle sells both contracts. The long straddle takes positions in both a call and a put, giving the investor a combination that will appreciate in value whether stock prices *rise or fall* in the future. Thus, the buyer is confident his underlying stock is going to be volatile and make a big swing in one direction or the other. Buying two options increases the initial cost (i.e., to profit from this investment, stock price movements must be more pronounced than if the investor had predicted changes in a single direction). In this sense, a straddle is a volatility play. The buyer expects the price of the stock to move strongly one way or the other, while the seller hopes for lower than normal volatility so he can simply collect the premiums.

Let us take a look at how you might use this strategy in your hedge fund. Say that one of the positions in your fund is Anglogold Ashanti (AU) out of South Africa; take a look at Exhibit 8.1 so you can follow our reasoning. AU, and the rest of the gold bugs, sold off hard during 2008. World economies were slowing, and deflation was gripping the world. An inflationary environment is where gold stocks usually flourish, so the deflationary environment hurt the group. That said, from October 2008 to December 2008, you saw AU begin to reverse to the upside via a double-bottom formation, so you began to build a position. You were correct, as usual, because you read this book, and you built a nice profit in the stock. However, as you can see from the three arrows on the right side of the chart, the stock began to lose momentum and entered into a sideways trading range. You are confident the stock will reemerge from its consolidation slumber, but it has already made a big move, so you are not sure it will not jerk lower before it goes higher. How can you take advantage of the big volatility you see coming? You buy a straddle. You go to www.CBOE.com to get your free options quotes and find that the January 2010 $35 strike call options cost $5.80, and that the equivalent puts cost $3.30. You would pay $9.10 to build your straddle. If the stock breaks from this range, in either direction, you will make money on your straddle. For example, if AU were to break higher

EXHIBIT 8.1   Chart of Anglogold Ashanti (AU) that Illustrates a Straddle Opportunity in the Position
Source: StockCharts.com.

and trade up to $45, your call options would probably be worth about $12. You would lose all your money in the put but your overall position cost you $9.10 to buy, so your profit would be about 33 percent. If the stock stays in this range until January 2010, your straddle will have failed and you would most likely lose most of the money you put into the position. Keep in mind that you do not have to own the stock to buy a straddle like this. We simply used a long position in this case to show you how you can add incremental profit to positions you may have in your portfolio.

Let us take a look at another example. Your hedge fund owns Turkcell (TKC) out of Turkey; see Exhibit 8.2. The company has made a substantial move and you are glad to own the stock, but it has moved ahead of itself via its recent parabolic move to the upside, and you feel it is time for the stock to consolidate. You still think TKC is worth holding and that it will trade higher in the long term, but suspect that in the short to intermediate term, it will likely just trade sideways. Therefore, to add value to your portfolio, you decide to write a straddle and take the income. You again go to www.CBOE.com to get your free options quotes, and you find that the January 2010 $17.50 call option is trading around $3.50 and the equivalent put is trading $1.10. You write a straddle and take in $4.60 per contract. If you write 10 contracts, you would take in $4,600 (10 contracts × 100 shares multiplier × $4.60) for your hedge fund. If TKC stays in a range, as you

EXHIBIT 8.2   Chart of Turkcell (TKC) that Illustrates a Straddle Opportunity in the
Position
Source: StockCharts.com.

expect, both contracts will expire and you will have bettered your fund by
the premiums you were able to collect. In other words, your stock did nothing for four months, but you still made money on it by writing a straddle.

Straps and Strips

The long straddle position assumes that the investor has no intuition about
the likely direction of future stock price movements. A slight adjustment of
this format is the overweighting of either the put or call position to stress
a directional belief, while maintaining a contract that would profit from
a price movement just in case the stock goes the other way. A long *strap*
position is the purchase of two calls and one put with the same strike price,
suggesting that an investor thinks stock prices are more likely to increase.
An investor with a more bearish view could generate a long *strip* position
by purchasing two puts and only one call.

If you go back to our Anglogold Ashanti (AU) chart in Exhibit 8.1, it
would not be unreasonable to assume that this stock would break to the
high side, not the down side, when it emerges from its consolidation. The
primary trend is up, and if nothing fundamentally changed in the group or
the global economies, we as hedge fund managers may decide to enter into
a long strap position as opposed to a straddle. This strap position would

give us more "bang for our buck" if we are correct and AU breaks out of its consolidation and trades higher.

Strangles

Like the straddle, a strangle is the synchronized purchase or sale of a call and a put on the same underlying security with the identical expiration date, but unlike the straddle, the options used in the strangle do not have the same exercise price. Instead, they are chosen so that both are out of the money. By purchasing two out-of-the-money contracts, the investor reduces the original straddle position's cost. Offsetting this reduced cost, though, is that stock prices will have to change in either direction by a greater amount before the strange becomes profitable. Consequently, the strangle can be viewed as having a more modest risk-reward structure than the straddle.

Imagine you owned Reed Intl (RUK) out of England. You can see Exhibit 8.3. RUK has been trading in a range of support and resistance from $26 to $33. To employ the strangle option strategy, you would enter into two option positions, one call and one put. Say the call is a strike of $32.50, which is out of the money as the stock currently trades at $29. We paid $1.75 for the call contract and are buying 10 contracts, or a total of $1,750

EXHIBIT 8.3 Chart of Reed Intl (RUK) that Reflects a Strangle Opportunity in the Position
Source: StockCharts.com.

for the position ($1.75 × 100 × 10). The put is a strike of $25 and is also out of the money. We paid $1.35 for each put, or $1,350 for our 10 contracts. If the price of the stock stays between $25 and $32.50 over the life of the option, the loss to you would be $3,100, which is the amount you paid for the 10 contracts of each option type. Your hedge fund will make money if the price of the stock starts to move outside of the range. Say that the price of the stock ends up at $38. The put option will expire worthless and the loss will be the premium you paid on the put. The call option, however, has gained considerable value, as it is worth $6,500 (we are approximating), so the total gain to your hedge fund is $3,400 ($6,500–$3,100).

Covered Call Writing

This is one of the strategies we use quite a bit in our managed accounts. A covered call is a financial market transaction in which your hedge fund would sell call options on stocks that you own in your portfolio. If you were to buy the underlying stock at the same time as you sell the call, the strategy is called a "buy-write" strategy. There are actually mutual funds and ETFs that are geared toward buy-write strategies.

The long position in the underlying instrument is said to provide the "cover," as the share can be delivered to the buyer of the call if he decides to exercise it. Writing a call generates income, in the form of the premium paid by the option buyer. If the stock price remains stable or declines, the writer will be able to keep this income as a profit and also keep his equity position intact. This "protection" has a potential disadvantage because the option writer may be forced to sell his stock below market price should it trade substantially higher and the buyer of the call decides to exercise his right to buy the stock at the lower strike price.

Let us take a look at an example. See Exhibit 8.4 for a Chinese company that you own in your hedge fund called Sinopec Shanghai Petrochemical (SHI). Like the rest of the world, the company went through a nasty correction in 2008, but then found its footing in 2009. You see two areas circled on the chart. As we have discussed a number of times, stocks do not go straight up and then straight down. They go up, they consolidate, and then move higher again or reverse course. That said, if you saw SHI make a big move and thought it was time to take a breather, why would you not write a covered call against the position? SHI itself is consolidating and will not make you any money, but you can write the call, take the premium, and make money on your overall position even at a time when the stock is stalled out. In our example, there were two chances to make money. If we owned 1,000 shares of SHI and wrote three-month calls in the time frames circled on the chart, we may have taken in $5,300 ($2,800 + $2,500) in premiums during a time frame where our $30,000-ish position

EXHIBIT 8.4 Chart of Shanghai Petrochemical (SHI) that Reflects a Covered Call Opportunity
Source: StockCharts.com.

in SHI was doing nothing. We just added 17 percent to our total return in SHI. Both of these consolidations were three months or longer. The downside to this strategy potentially comes about if SHI were to see a sharp run-up after we wrote our calls; we could end up losing the stock if the buyer exercises the option and he gets to buy it from us at a lower price than for what it is trading in the open market. Still, if the stock began to move against us, we could also buy the option back, or after the buyer took our stock, we could wait for SHI to correct and simply buy it back for the portfolio.

Another strategy you can employ with covered calls is simply writing calls against a position to buffer an oncoming correction. Let us say that your hedge fund owned 1,000 shares of German software company SAP AG (SAP) during the time frame. You really like the stock over the long term but became concerned when the stock gapped down through the horizontal line of support. What can you do? Well, *one* thing you can do is write

EXHIBIT 8.5 Chart of SAP AG (SAP) that Reflects a Covered Call "Cushion" Opportunity
Source: StockCharts.com.

a covered call against your position to help buffer the fall. As you can see in Exhibit 8.5, you may have written 10 calls against your shares and received $2,400 in premium (10 × 100 × $2.40). The stock proceeded to fall another 28 percent, but your total portfolio loss would have only been about 23 percent because you took a 5 percent premium when you wrote your covered calls. In this case, we are buffering a potential loss in our holding and getting to keep our position.

PORTFOLIO INSURANCE

Portfolio insurance is just what it sounds like it is; we are hedging a stock, or our entire portfolio, against a downside risk. In this case, we are buying protective put options to help us hedge that threat.

Let us take a look at an example to see how this might work. Exhibit 8.6 shows Deutsche Telecom (DT), which you owned in your hedge fund. DT was on a nice uptrend, as you can see from the clear series of higher highs and higher lows. However, at the circled portion, DT broke down and officially changed trend. To protect yourself, you could go out and buy a put option. If we bought a January 2009 $15 put option, it would have cost us roughly $1 per contract. It is relatively cheap because we are buying the

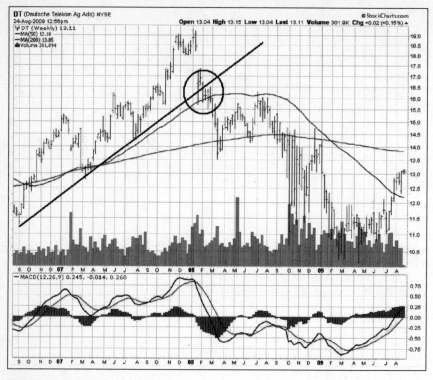

EXHIBIT 8.6 Chart of Deutsche Telekom (DT) that Illustrates the Option-as-Portfolio Insurance Opportunity
Source: StockCharts.com.

contracts out of the money, which was a judgment call. If we owned 1,000 shares, our total out-of-pocket expense would have been roughly $1,000. DT subsequently fell from $17 to about $10.50. Because we held a $15 strike put option, we would have the right to sell the stock at $15, so we did not eat the last $4.50 of the fall. The fall alone would have cost our hedge fund about $5,000, so the hedge worked out well.

Let us look at one more example related to hedging our portfolio, as a whole. If you ran a million-dollar hedge fund and believed we were headed into a bear market, what do you do? You could certainly sell all the stocks, but then you would pay taxes on any gains and transaction costs; you could also buy put options for all your positions, but that would be costly. Because you are a savvy hedge fund manager (and you read this book), you would hopefully come to the conclusion that you do need a way to hedge your entire portfolio, but also that you have to make it happen in a cost-manageable sort of way. In this case, a good choice would be to go out and buy put options on the iShares MSCI EAFE (EFA) ETF; in other words, you buy put options on an index that most closely resembles what you are holding. If we are holding $1 million worth of stocks from around the world, the MSCI EAFE is a good benchmark; if you are holding all Japanese stocks, you would buy put options on the Nikkei index.

See Exhibit 8.7 for the EFA. On the exhibit, you can clearly recognize, by the circle, that the market broke a crucial line of support. You have decided to buy put options on the EFA, but how many should you buy? The answer is easy. You simply divide the portfolio size by the strike price. Thus, our million-dollar hedge fund divided by $62.50 (circled support) comes out to 160 contracts. If the contracts each cost us $1.10, the total cost to hedge our portfolio would be around $17,600. Said differently, we are spending 1.76 percent ($17,600/$1,000,000) of our portfolio to fully hedge a million dollars worth of stock.

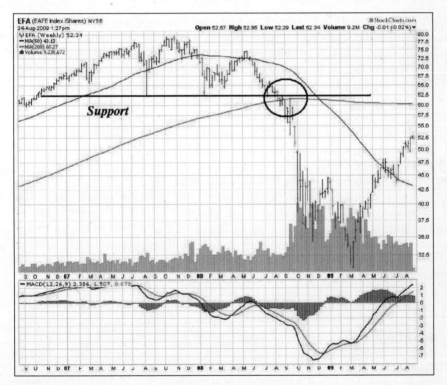

EXHIBIT 8.7 Chart of iShares MSCI EAFE (EFA) that Reflects a Put Option Protection Opportunity
Source: StockCharts.com.

Converting Short-Term Capital Gains

A good strategy to minimize the recognition of short-term capital gains is to consider selling call options against the underlying stock position, rather than selling the underlying stock and incurring capital gains. For example, suppose you were not as bullish on Honda Motor Co (HMC), but you bought it nine months ago at $18 and it is currently trading around $33. You would like to reduce your position, but you do not want to get hit with short-term capital gains. You could write a nine-month call option with a $35 strike and receive a $4 premium to buffer your position until your capital gains situation passes from short- to long-term capital gains. The solution is to sell a *qualified call* option, which is one that is either at the money or out of the money, as you do not want to run the risk of getting the option converted against you before your tax liability goes from short to long.

Tax Loss Harvesting

You may want to sell a stock at a capital loss to offset realized gains in your portfolio, but once the stock is sold, you cannot repurchase that stock for 31 days (without triggering a wash sale). Additionally, you may really like the sector, or the markets in general, but want to lock in these tax losses. Selling a put option is an efficient way to reestablish exposure to such stocks sold at a loss. The put sale offers two important advantages: first, as long as the put is not deep in the money, it does not violate the wash-sale rule; and second, transaction costs are low because the put and stock sale tend to counteract each other; if the put is exercised, the stock position is reestablished.

Let us say you bought Embraer Empresa (ERJ) at $50 and you are at a loss. You can sell the underlying stock and lock in your tax loss, while simultaneously selling a nine-month put option on ERJ with a strike of $55 and receiving a premium of $4.75. As long as the stock trades below $55, you will more than likely end up essentially repurchasing the stock at $50.25. In other words, you gave up $0.25 on the stock in order to lock in a tax loss that may have saved you thousands of dollars in taxes.

FUTURES

Suppose you lived in Mexico and raised pigs on a huge farm, and we are (Sean and Bob) corn farmers in Indiana and do nothing but grow corn. For years, we have all done business together. Sean and Bob grow the corn, sell it to you, and you feed it to your pigs for more than a year. We all agree to use the spot price for corn on an agreed-upon date each year to set our price and each year our cycle begins again. One year, we farmers decide that we should attempt to set our prices a year in advance so we do not have to worry about prices for the coming year. Both sides agree that this type of contract would allow us to budget better and have more visibility in our fiscal year. Further, we decide that $4.50 per bushel is a fair price and agree to lock our prices for next year's crop. We have entered into a forward contract.

As the year goes on, both sides realize this contract may not work in the favor of either of us. What happens if a worldwide corn shortage forces prices to $8 per bushel? At that point, we farmers may be leaving $3.50 per bushel on the table. What happens if a bumper crop drives prices down to $3.75 per bushel? You would likely want to buy at that lower price. Neither of us would have the right to get out of the contract. Additionally, what if we sell our corn farm? Would the new owner feel obligated to stick to the contract? Who knows?

A forward contract is the basis for a futures contract. It involves two parties agreeing to exchange a good, currency, or other tradable asset at a future date and at a previously set price. However, the biggest drawback of a forward contract is that it is not liquid. It is a contract that is typically entered into by two parties without the ability to back away from the contract. Futures contracts were devised to solve these problems, while retaining most of the major benefits of the forward contract. A futures contract is simply a forward contract with a few new bells and whistles added in.

Futures traders are traditionally categorized in one of two groups: *hedgers* and *speculators*. Hedgers have an interest in, or otherwise own, the underlying asset, which could include an intangible such as an index or interest rate. This group uses futures in an effort to "hedge out" the risk of price changes. Do not get too stuck on the term "hedgers" in this section, as these are not hedge fund managers; these are typically companies attempting to hedge a risk in the futures market. For example, Tropicana may hedge the potential for a catastrophic event in the orange market by using orange juice futures. Or, Lufthansa Air may hedge rising oil prices by buying oil futures to lock in their price for some years to come. On the other hand, speculators seek to make a profit by predicting market moves and opening a contract related to the asset "on paper." They have no intention of actually taking or delivering the underlying asset. In other words, the investor is seeking exposure to the asset in a long future or the opposite effect via a short future contract. In other cases, some speculators build financial models and attempt to use arbitrage to profit from market inconsistencies. For example, if your hedge fund developed a model and it showed a specific correlation between the Canadian dollar and oil prices, and this relationship got out of whack, you may go long the Canadian dollar and short oil futures in an arbitrage play to make money on the pair until the relationship came back into order.

An example that has both hedge and speculative notions involves a separately managed account whose investment objective is to track the performance of a stock index. The portfolio manager often "equitizes" fund deposits in an easy and cost-effective manner by investing in S&P 500 stock index futures. This gains the portfolio exposure to the index, which is consistent with the fund or account investment objective, without having to buy an appropriate proportion of each of the individual 500 companies. This also preserves balanced diversification and maintains a higher degree of the percent of assets invested in the market. When it is economically feasible, the portfolio manager can close the contract and make purchases of each individual stock.

Terms and Concepts

Most unique markets have unique verbiage that go along with them, and the futures market is no different; let us go over a few important terms and concepts to get you comfortable with how things work prior to moving forward.

Shorts and Longs: Any futures contract is for a specific grade, quantity, and delivery month. For example, the futures contract for corn on the CBOT (Chicago Board of Trade) calls for 5,000 bushels of No. 2 yellow corn. All of these contracts are standardized contracts that can be broken by either party simply with an offsetting futures market transaction. In the futures market, there is a short position for every long position. Therefore, if one side is making money, the other is symmetrically losing money.

If two parties enter into a forward contract, no money is exchanged. It may be exchanged at the end of the contract, but not at the beginning. With futures contracts, you have to put up what is known as "margin money" when entering into a contract. This is not a down payment, but a good faith estimate to demonstrate you intend to pay for the commodity in full when it is delivered.

Cash versus Futures: The *cash* or *spot* price is the price at which that particular commodity is trading at in the marketplace today, right now. The *futures* price responds to changes in the cash price and to traders' expectations. The futures price is just that, the price that investors expect will be in place at some predefined date in the future. For example, if it were March and spot wheat prices were currently at $5.25 per bushel with the overall price trend moving lower, investors may expect that trend to continue and the December futures price may be trading at $4.99 per bushel. You can see an example for December 2009 wheat in Exhibit 8.8.

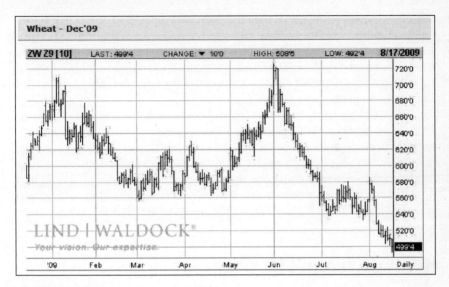

EXHIBIT 8.8 Wheat, December 2009
Source: Lind-Waldock.com.

Futures prices will closely mimic the movements of the cash market, but the futures prices that are most affected by a change in the cash price are those of the nearest expiration month, because those prices will soon be the same as the cash price. Distant futures months are less responsive, because the day-to-day noise or gyrations of these markets tend to flatten out as you push the contract *further* out.

Clearinghouse: Each futures exchange has its own clearinghouse, and all the members are required to clear their trades through the clearinghouse at the end of each trading session and to deposit with the clearinghouse a sum of money sufficient to cover the member's debit balance. For example, if a member broker reports to the clearinghouse, at the end of the day, a total purchase of 100,000 bushels of May corn and total sales of 50,000 bushels of May corn, he would be net long 50,000 bushels of May corn. Assuming that this is the broker's only position in futures and that the clearinghouse margin is six cents per bushel, this would mean the broker would be required to have $3,000 on deposit with the clearinghouse. Because all members are required to clear their trades through the clearinghouse and must maintain sufficient funds to cover their debit balances, the clearinghouse is responsible to all members for the fulfillment of the contracts.

Commodity Futures Trading Commission (CFTC): All futures transactions in the United States are regulated by the Commodity Futures

Trading Commission (CFTC), an independent agency of the U.S. government. The commission has the right to hand out fines and other punishments to individuals or companies who break any rules. Although, by law, the commission regulates all transactions, each exchange can have its own rules, and under contract can fine companies for different things, or extend the fine handed down by the CFTC.

The CFTC publishes weekly reports containing the details of the open interest of market participants for each market segment that has more than 20 participants. These reports are released every Friday (including data from the previous Tuesday), and contain data on open interest split by reportable and nonreportable open interest as well as commercial and noncommercial open interest. This type of report is referred to as the *Commitments of Traders Report*, aka COT-Report or simply COTR.

WHAT TO TRADE AND WHERE

There are a wide variety of futures markets in today's marketplace. Many are commodities futures and many surround financial instruments like currencies and indexes. For ease of discussion, it is best to group them as follows in Exhibit 8.9.

The preceding list is not complete, but it gives you an idea of the broad array of futures contracts you can trade; the point is that if you are a hedge fund manager who has invested in a broad portfolio of stocks, commodities, or bonds, you have a way to hedge your portfolio to short- and intermediate-term fluctuations. Additionally, if you are more aggressively

EXHIBIT 8.9 Principal Categories of Futures

Category	
Grains	Wheat, corn, oats, soybeans.
Meats	Live cattle, feeder cattle, hogs, pork bellies.
Metals	Platinum, silver, high-grade copper, gold.
Foods and Fibers	Coffee, cocoa, sugar, cotton, orange juice.
Interest Rates	T-bonds, t-bills, Eurodollars, LIBOR.
Foreign Currency	Swiss franc, Euro, Mexican peso, Australian dollar, Japanese yen.
Index	S&P 500 index, NASDAQ 100, Goldman Sachs Commodity index.
Energy	Crude oil, heating oil No. 2, unleaded gas, natural gas.
Wood	Lumber

Source: Lind-Waldock.com.

inclined, you might even trade baskets of futures as the primary positions in your hedge fund.

Pricing: Let us make a special mention regarding the pricing of futures. It is imperative that prior to investing in any futures contract, you understand the multiplier component to that contract. For example, if you want to trade cattle futures, each cattle future does not represent one cow or one pound of cows; it represents 40,000 pounds of cattle, and each quote is based on cents per pound. Thus, a price quote of 85.87 would mean 85.87 cents per pound of cattle. If you are long one futures contract and the contract goes up 2.08 cents that day, you made $1,120 during that session ($.0208 × 40,000 pounds). Futures prices for all meat futures are expressed in cents per pound. The futures prices for all grains are priced in cents per bushel. Metal futures are not uniform, as gold, palladium, and silver trade in troy ounce contracts, whereas other metals like copper trade in pounds. The multiplier for indexes trades under a different circumstance entirely, with the S&P 500 trading at a $500-times-index multiplier. With most quoting resources, like the listings in the *Wall Street Journal*, you are provided with guidance as to what multiplier you need to recognize, but suffice it to say, you may or may not be trading the pure quantity of what you believe you are.

At this point, you may understand *what* to trade, but you also need to understand with *whom* to trade. Most investors simply seek out the lowest commissions. However, buyer beware; the lowest-price provider probably will not give you much more than a low commission, whereas many of the larger companies will provide you with low commissions *and* a substantial amount of charting and research tools and resources. As a hedge fund manager, the key is to weigh the research against the low trading costs and find the firm that fits your needs somewhere in between. Several of the brokers in the following list have also been mentioned in other areas of the book, as they provide access to multiple investment instruments (i.e., stocks, currencies, futures, bonds).

- **Interactive Brokers, www.interactivebrokers.com:** You will probably notice that we also mentioned IB in our section on currency trading. Further, as a disclaimer, note that our investment management company has a relationship with Interactive Brokers. The reason we favor IB is because you can trade just about anything you want on their platform. You can build a true hedge fund, one that includes currencies, equities, futures, options, bonds, and so on. IB is a publicly traded company that trades on the NASDAQ under the symbol "IBKR."
- **Tradestation Securities, www.tradestation.com:** The positives for Tradestation are similar to those of Interactive Brokers. The company gives you a single platform on which you can trade a bevy of different

types of investments. Tradestation is a publicly traded company that trades on the NASDAQ under the symbol "TRAD."

- **Lind Waldock, www.lind-waldock.com:** Lind Waldock is a firm that specializes in futures trading, which may make it more suitable for those of you who want to focus on futures speculation and not hedging. The company has been around for more than four decades, and even offers managed accounts on behalf of futures-centered investors.

PRACTICAL APPLICATION OF FUTURES USE IN YOUR HEDGE FUND

We now need to spend some time examining the practical applications of futures in your hedge fund. Earlier, we mentioned that you can use futures in your portfolio either to *speculate*, or to *hedge* certain risks. Let us look more closely at the implementation of each approach.

Speculation

There are two ways you can analyze the world—at least the *investment* world: technically, and fundamentally. We have been over this ad nauseam, but it really hammers home the point that regardless of that in which you are investing (i.e., stocks, currencies, futures, bonds), there are two primary ways to analyze the investment. Some would argue that *quantitative analysis* is a third school of investment analysis, but, for ease of discussion, we will lump the quants into the fundamental side. Fundamental analysis is, of course, the methodology of looking at the numbers, from top to bottom; technical analysis principally involves analyzing chart patterns for the purpose of determining future price action.

The fundamental side of the equation is simple. If you look at Chapter 3 on equity, you will find our methods for analyzing global economies and individual countries. As an example, let us say that you have analyzed the Japanese economy and feel that the Nikkei 225 is ahead of itself and is significantly overvalued as compared to the rest of the world. Exhibit 8.10 is for the Nikkei 225 (dollar) September 2009 futures contract. You would short the contract as a speculative bet against the Japanese average. If you wanted to be a bit more conservative on that bet, you could push your contract out to December 2009 or March 2010 to give yourself more time.

You can see another representation of this type of speculative trade in Exhibit 8.11. Perhaps your friend's uncle's cousin's nephew—twice removed—who happens to be a Russian farmer, (oops, we mean your *research*) tells you that Russia is facing a major food shortage and the price

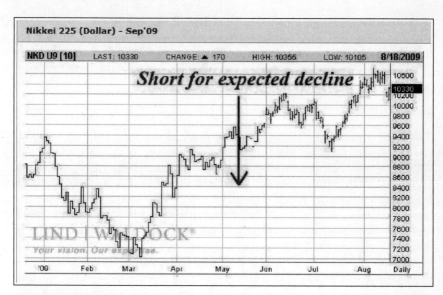

EXHIBIT 8.10 Nikkei 225 (Dollar) Sept 2009
Source: Lind-Waldock.com.

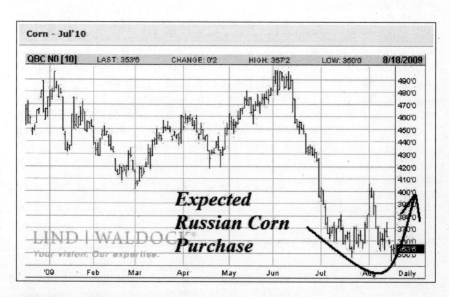

EXHIBIT 8.11 Chart Illustrating Potential Opportunity in Going Long Corn
Futures
Source: Lind-Waldock.com.

of that shortage does not seem to be reflected in grain prices. In this case, you may want to go long corn futures simply from the information you have discovered. In this case, we pushed out the future contract we chose to July 2010 to give ourselves more room for this long-term trend to gain traction.

Hedge

The more regular use of futures in your portfolio is going to be on behalf of the purpose of hedging. For the sake of discussion, let us say that it is late 2007 once again. You are managing your hedge fund of international stocks, and you feel that the excessive bubble in the housing market is about to burst and cause a worldwide financial crisis. To extend the example, let us say you have held most of the stocks in your portfolio for many years, and have huge capital gains built into the portfolio. You now see the dark clouds on the horizon, but you do not want to take a huge tax hit by just selling the stocks. What do you do? You remember what we taught you in this book and you hedge your intermediate downside market exposure using futures. By hedging your portfolio through the shorting of futures, you are able to hold the stocks in which you continue to believe, avoid a huge taxable event, and protect your portfolio from the oncoming storm: win, win, and win.

Maintaining our scenario example, let us take a practical look at how this might work. Exhibit 8.12 is your hedge fund that we discussed. It is a bit simplistic in terms of the number of stocks, but is still a good working model. If you were sitting with these stocks in December 2007 and felt the global markets were getting ready to fall off a cliff, you have three options: hold the positions through the storm, sell your positions and donate roughly $80,000 to the government in taxes (while also risking the chance you are wrong and the market continues to go up), or maintain the stocks and hedge your position by shorting futures contracts.

EXHIBIT 8.12 Sample Portfolio Comprised of CRH PLC (CRH), Sybase (SY), and KB Financial Group (KB)

Name	Symbol	Country	Purchase Value	Current Value	Unrealized Gain
CRH PLC	CRH	Ireland	$100,000	$230,000	$130,000
Sybase Inc	SY	United States	$100,000	$320,000	$220,000
KB Fincl Group	KB	South Korea	$100,000	$260,000	$160,000
Cash			$150,000	$150,000	$ 0
		Total	$960,000	$510,000

Source: www.investorspassport.com.

Let us assume that you decided to hedge your position with futures. This leaves you to answer the question of how many contracts to short. The MSCI EAFE Index futures trade in "E-mini" form, which simply means they trade with a multiplier of 50 instead of the 500 multiplier for the regular S&P 500 futures. This is good for our hedge fund, because the position will cost less out of pocket. With the MSCI EAFE index around 2,200 in December 2007, the *value* of one September 2008 contract is (50 × 2200) $110,000. The *price you actually pay* for each contract is $2,200 per contract. Remember, it has a 50 multiplier, which is where you get the bang for your buck. The portfolio value is $960,000, but only $810,000 of that value is in equities. Therefore, the simple way to find the number of contracts we need to buy in order to cover our stock holdings is to divide $810,000 by $110,000, which gives us eight contracts. The actual number is 7.36, but you cannot buy partial contracts, and if we want to be fully covered in the portfolio, you would need to buy eight contracts. However, that contract calculation is not entirely correct, because the simple calculation is not accounting for the risk to our portfolio. If our portfolio is significantly more aggressive than the MSCI EAFE Index, then we could end up losing far more on our portfolio than our hedge will protect. Accordingly, the more accurate way to calculate the number of contracts needed is noted here:

$$\frac{V_P}{V_F} B_P = \text{Number of Contracts}$$

where: V_P = Value of the portfolio
V_F = Value of the futures contract
B_P = Beta of the portfolio

If the beta of our portfolio was 1.20, we would need to buy nine contracts (($810,000/$110000) × 1.20 = 8.83), not the original eight we had calculated earlier.

You can see our new hedged portfolio in Exhibit 8.13.

Let us fast forward to September 2008. The MSCI EAFE Index has fallen almost 40 percent from its 2007 highs. Let us look at the likely consequences realized from each of our three possible choices: if you sold, you were correct, but you donated a chunk of your money to the government for taxes (to say nothing of the transaction costs incurred by selling) and you are now left with the unenviable position of trying to figure out when to get back in; if you held the portfolio through the storm, the value dropped substantially, and you lost plenty of sleep in addition to all of the dough that sailed away; if you hedged your portfolio, you lost money in your stocks, but you made a pile of money in your hedge. If we decided to close our

			Purchase	**Current**	**Unrealized**
EXHIBIT 8.13 Sample Portfolio Comprised of CRH PLC (CRH), Sybas (SY), and KB Financial (KB), Now Hedged					
Name	**Symbol**	**Country**	**Value**	**Value**	**Gain**
CRH PLC	CRH	Ireland	$100,000	$230,000	$130,000
Sybase Inc	SY	United States	$100,000	$320,000	$220,000
KB Fincl Group	KB	South Korea	$100,000	$260,000	$160,000
Cash			$150,000	$150,000	$ 0
MSCI EAFE E-min Short Futures Position (8 Sept 08 Contracts)			($990,000)	($990,000)	

Source: www.investorspassport.com.

hedge with the future contract trading at 1,400, we would have made a whopping 36 percent gain on our overall hedge transaction (the percentage difference between 2,200 and 1,400). Said differently, we would have realized a $360,000 gain on our hedge (800-point contract price difference × 50 multiplier × 9 contracts). The $810,000 equity portion of our portfolio fell about $350,000 ($810,000 × 36% × 1.2 [beta]), so our hedge worked out perfectly. If we had bought only eight contracts, we would have come up short, as our hedge would have netted us only about $311,000.

Futures can also be utilized in fixed-income management as a hedging tool, as we know. An example of this might be the fixed-income manager who is managing a bond portfolio against a global bond benchmark, and currently has a duration equal to 95 percent of the benchmark duration. Perhaps the manager's opinion has recently changed on interest rates, and he wants to move to a new target duration of 105 percent of the benchmark, in an effort to take advantage of what he believes will be a global reduction in interest rates.

The most efficient way to implement this change is to use futures. Futures incur lower transaction costs than if we tried to trade actual bonds to adjust our portfolio and much less "curve" risk. This strategy is particularly appropriate in global fixed-income portfolios. Domestically, cash plus futures in the right proportions is equal to a synthetic bond, while in terms of foreign markets, domestic cash plus foreign futures is equal to a *currency-hedged* synthetic bond. If you need to lengthen duration, take your cash and buy foreign futures. The automatic result is a currency-hedged synthetic bond.

Most people who have never used futures and who are familiar with them only from what they have heard on the news in recent years are understandably skittish about their application in any way. That is unfortunate, because futures are a powerful, useful tool that can bring as much strength and safety to a portfolio as they can destructive effects. Certainly they can be used for speculation, and are indeed used that way often. However, using them as a defensive hedge mechanism for your fund is a whole different ball of wax. As you can see from the preceding example, using futures as a hedging tool is simply a way to help insure your portfolio, and given the multifaceted construction of your fund, with multiple lines of instruments and asset classes, the ability to include an insurance policy, of sorts, really becomes more a necessity than a luxury.

CHAPTER 9

Portfolio Management Applications

D onald Trump recently related an amusing anecdote that illustrates the sometimes-silly ends to which many will go in the search to "get rich." He said, "A friend called me up the other day and talked about investing in a dot-com that sells lobsters. Internet lobsters. Where will this end? The next day he sent me a huge package of lobsters on ice. How low can you stoop?" Besides serving as a funny little tale, the story speaks volumes about the dot-com bubble and the mistaken emphasis that investors sometimes place purely on chasing returns. Don't get us wrong; we're all in this game to make a buck. Everyone wants to beat the market, and we would all like to pick the next Microsoft. As a result, it is not surprising that we find ourselves focusing the bulk of our energy and efforts on accumulation-centered philosophies and strategies, and so little on portfolio management. What most people do not realize in time is that portfolio management is *critical* to the success you experience in the global markets. Granted, it is far more interesting to read about explosive growth in emerging market countries than it is to talk about the steps involved in creating a portfolio or in executing trades. Still, the portfolio management process does not seem to get enough attention, and expertly understanding it is vital for a hedge fund manager.

Portfolio management involves the art and science of making decisions about investment mix/policy, matching investments to objectives, setting up a suitable asset allocation and balancing risk against performance. It all, admittedly, sounds boring, but the reality is that, as a hedge fund–type management component, its practical application is essential. For example, let us say you are managing a portfolio full of international stocks, but you fail to monitor the risk levels within your portfolio. If the global equity markets tank, like they began to in 2008, you could drop significantly more than the index (the MSCI EAFE), because international stocks as a group tend to be riskier. If the market goes down 30 percent and your risk levels are above the market, you could drop 40 percent to 50 percent. If you were a prudent manager and monitored your risk levels, you may have had the foresight to adjust your holdings to a more moderate level or even raise your cash levels. That move alone could save you 10 percent to 20 percent in investment performance, if not more.

Let us take it one more step. If you are managing a long/short portfolio and you were prudent in managing both your risk as well as the risk of the market, you may have had the foresight to go short and even make money in a declining market. The point is that the days of buying a bunch of stocks and holding them for eternity is gone. In this day and age, it is important to be a good stock picker, but just as important to exercise prudent portfolio management. Although this may not prove to be the most exciting portion of the book, it is as important as any other chapter.

We break the chapter down into three primary areas. The first part of the investment process involves understanding the needs, the tax status, and the *risk preferences* of your hedge fund. For an individual investor constructing his or her own portfolio, this may seem like it would prove to be a simpler task than it might for the professional fund manager, but understanding one's own ability and willingness to take on risk is as important a first step for you as it is for the paid portfolio manager.

The second part of the process is the actual construction of the portfolio. The most important decision lies in how to *allocate* the portfolio across different asset classes (i.e., stocks, bonds, cash, and real estate). This asset allocation decision can also be simultaneously framed in terms of domestic assets versus foreign assets, and the factors driving *this* determination. An additional component is the asset selection choice, where individual assets are picked within each asset class to make up the portfolio. In practical terms, this is the step where the stocks that make up the equity component, the bonds that make up the fixed-income component, and the real assets that make up the real asset component, are picked.

The third part of the process, and often the most painful one for professional hedge fund managers, is the *performance evaluation*. The point, after all, of your efforts is to make the most money you can, given the risk constraints under which you have decided you can operate. Investors are not forgiving of failure and are unwilling to accept even the best of excuses, and thus loyalty to money managers is not a commonly found trait.

RISK

Risk is an element that many growth-oriented equity investors rarely consider seriously (if they are honest), but it is also the one factor that, when left unmonitored, can ruin a portfolio for years—even for a lifetime. You do not need to look much past John Meriwether and the collapse of the massive hedge fund Long-Term Capital Management (LTCM) hedge fund for evidence of this; established in 1994 and roaring out of the gate with annualized rates of return of about 40 percent per year for the first several years, LTCM was effectively destroyed in 1998 when, in a period of just a few months, it lost almost $5 billion on the heels of the Russian financial crisis. When you throw in the additional myriad of risks that accompany international investing, the threat levels in your portfolio are something you need to understand fully and, more importantly, manage effectively.

Investment or portfolio risk can be categorized in terms of two main categories, according to the two sources of investment return: macro factors and micro factors. The macro factors are all-encompassing aspects, such as the national economy. The micro factors are localized factors, like the company itself.

The risks associated with macro factors are called *systematic risk*. Interest rates, recessions, and wars all represent sources of systematic risk because they affect the entire world market and cannot be avoided through diversification. Systematic risk can be mitigated only through hedging, because returns depend in a systematic and associated way on that factor. If the economy does well, returns on assets are likely to do well, too.

Micro risks are factors associated with a particular company and are called *unsystematic risks*. For example, news that is specific to a small number of stocks, such as a sudden strike by employees of Toyota, is considered to be unsystematic risk. In this area, investment returns are uniquely determined by the firm's underlying earning power, such as its turnover of assets, operating margin, and return on equity. The amount of this type of unsystematic risk can be reduced through appropriate diversification.

There are a few risks to international investors that are not considered systematic or unsystematic risks, and we will break them down a bit later. For now, let us look more closely at the risks that we face in our everyday work: systematic risk and unsystematic risk.

Systematic Risk

There are three interrelated systematic risk factors that are common to all assets. As we mentioned before, these are risks that cannot be mitigated simply through diversification. You can be fully diversified in your portfolio, but still lack the ability to withstand the effects on the global equity markets when a terrorist attack or a natural disaster occurs; for that sort of insulation, you need to address the three principal manifestations of systematic risk: inflation risk, interest rate risk, and market risk.

Inflation risk is the chance that returns will be better or worse than expected because of changes in the levels of inflation. This type of risk is also known as *purchasing power risk*. Inflation erodes the true value of any asset and therefore erodes your purchasing power. Remember that systematic risks are interrelated, which is something we touched on in Chapter 2 on intermarket analysis. If inflation is rising and moving above our expectations, interest rates will have to rise to combat that inflation. Rising interest rates tend to curb economic growth and thus slow earnings. Slower earnings translate to lower equity markets. Remember, as well, the inverse relationship between bond prices and interest rates; when rates move up, bond prices typically fall.

Inflation is the macroeconomic component that national governments typically work hardest at controlling, because it can prove so devastating to a country's economy if it remains unchecked. One of the worst cases of inflation in history was seen in Hungary after World War II. In 1944, the country's highest currency denomination was 1,000 pengo (the existing currency at the time). By the end of 1945, it was 10,000,000 pengo and by mid-1946 it had rocketed to *100,000,000,000,000,000,000* pengo. A special currency, the adopengo, or tax pengo, was created for tax and postal payments. The value of the adopengo was adjusted each day and those changes were made public by radio announcement. In January 1946 one adopengo equaled one pengo. By late July, one adopengo equaled 2,000,000,000,000,000,000,000 pengo. When the pengo was replaced in August 1946 with a new currency, the total value of *all* Hungarian banknotes in circulation amounted to one-thousandth of one U.S. dollar.

Interest rate risk is the possibility that returns will be better or worse than we are anticipating because of changes in the level of interest rates. As mentioned before, the prices of most investable assets tend to rise as interest rates fall, and vice versa. Investors tend to think of interest rates only in the context of bonds, but rates affect all investable assets, including equities, money markets, and real estate.

It is important to note that the *trend* of interest rates is as significant as the *level* of rates, and that in certain instances, markets may even react in an opposite fashion to what you would think normally happens when interest rates shift. For example, in most bear markets, you find that policy makers around the world are lowering interest rates in an effort to spur economic growth. However, in the bear market that began in 2007, we saw interest rates going down and most categories of bonds also heading lower. You can see that in Exhibit 9.1, which shows the movements of interest rates and corporate bonds during the Great Recession. Corporate bonds, municipal bonds, and high-yield bonds *all* found themselves getting pounded during this time frame. This movement is uncharacteristic of the typical relationship we see between bonds and rates. However, remember that this bear market was caused by a credit crunch, which led to banking failures and significantly reduced liquidity, which are elements that create a bad environment for bonds. In the spring of 2009, a number of analyst reports advised us to "beware the global bond markets," as they would falter further when the global economies strengthened and rates began to rise. We thought that was hogwash because bonds did not rise when rates were falling as the turmoil around the world was building. This was an unusual circumstance. In the end, we felt bonds would actually rise when interest rates began to rise because higher rates would evoke confidence in the economy and in most segments of the bond market. As your own hedge fund manager, you have to be able to recognize when the normal market relationships are not holding true to course and react accordingly. In this particular instance, we were actually buying bonds for our managed

EXHIBIT 9.1 Chart Illustrating the Uncharacteristic Movement of Bonds and Rates Together
Source: StockCharts.com.

accounts even though rates were most likely going to be rising in the coming months and quarters. Keep in mind, if managing investment portfolios was easy, everyone would be a millionaire.

Market risk is the chance that market influences will alter anticipated returns of investments in ways that were not expected. You do not have to look much past the bear market that latched its teeth onto both the global equity and fixed-income markets in 2008 to see how unexpected turns can materialize in capital markets. As a function of the flight to quality that characterizes typical bear markets, many areas of the global fixed-income market will normally flourish; however, in 2008, the *unexpected* occurred and hedge fund managers had to face the reality that the global bond markets were also ravaged by the same bear market that overtook stocks.

In the equities market, the returns on individual stocks are influenced by the price movements of the marketplace in which they are traded, a movement guided as much by their sensitivity to the overall direction of the market as by the near-term behavior of the sectors in which they trade. The fixed-income market will always be affected by the general economy, but more so by interest rates and perceived risk levels of the underlying companies, municipalities, or governments. As we saw in Chapter 2 on intermarket analysis, these markets are intertwined and can be influenced by many of the same economic factors.

Unsystematic Risk   This is company- or industry-specific risk that is inherent in each investment. The amount of unsystematic risk can be reduced through appropriate diversification. An example of this type of risk may be news that oil workers in Brazil are going on strike. This risk is generally relevant to a small number of stocks.

Unsystematic risk consists of two primary components: credit (or company) risk, and sector (or industry) risk.

Credit or company risk – Credit risk consists, more elementally, of a company's business and fiscal risks; business risk is the risk inherent in the environment of the business and/or the industry in which it operates, while financial risk is the risk that arises from using financial leverage. For example, many electric power companies are considered to have lower business risk because their demand is typically predictable. However, they are also an industry with high debt levels, which tends to increase their unique risk.

Sector or industry risk – Sector risk is the risk of doing better or worse than anticipated as a consequence of investing in one sector of the economy instead of another. It is obvious that if you are using a sector rotation strategy and you are wrong on your choices, you will most likely underperform the global equity markets. That said, one of the main determinants of your ultimate performance will be your ability to find your way into the right sectors at the right time. This type of risk can easily be reduced by diversifying it away, but you will find that most hedge fund managers do not really attempt to mitigate this risk through diversification. They will instead seek to *maximize* this risk in an effort to earn superior returns; they increase this area of risk by making sector bets and, if they are correct, will beat their benchmarks and attract more capital.

Additional International Risks   There will always be certain risks that are unique to transborder investing, risks that are unpredictable at times and typically cannot be diversified away; in the case of *currency risk*, you can manage that by hedging yourself to protect your position, but there is not really a single, acute mechanism that allows you to mitigate the unpredictable nature of *political risk*.

Political risk is the chance that returns will be affected by the policies and stability of the nations in which you are investing. The danger of debt negation (or failure to meet debt service), expropriation of assets, differences in taxes, restrictions on repatriating funds and prevention against exchanging foreign currency are typical investment-specific manifestations of more general political risks. On the surface, these risks do not seem likely to affect your portfolio, but rest assured that the only predictable aspect of the governments that oversee many of the emerging and frontier markets in which you will seek to invest is their unpredictable nature.

Currency (exchange) risk describes the risk that returns will be affected by changes in rates of exchange because investments have been made in foreign markets whose principal is not denominated in domestic currency. Concerns regarding currency risk have long been an impediment to global investing because fluctuations in relative foreign exchange values tend to accentuate return *and* risk in domestic currency terms. For example, if you were to go direct and buy an Australian government bond in your hedge fund and the Aussie dollar appreciates significantly against the U.S. dollar, you may make 5 percent interest on your bond, but lose 20 percent of your principal when you attempt to convert your Aussie dollars to U.S. dollars at the end of the bond term. The same type of risk is evident in the context of corporate earnings. How many times have you seen multinational companies mention a currency effect on their earnings from quarter to quarter? In the 2008–2009 climate of a super-weak dollar, many U.S.-based multinationals have actually been saved precisely by the beneficial currency influences from their overseas revenue.

Dealing with currency risk is an important issue for global investors, and the particulars of hedging decisions are probably some of the most intensely scrutinized considerations for hedge fund managers. Although longer holding periods can cancel out adverse currency returns, you should not ignore the substantial risk of unfavorable short-term currency movements; it is safe to say that once you cross borders, a new level of risk is introduced.

MEASURING RISK

Have you ever been to a dinner or party and overheard some lug nut sitting there bragging about how he killed the markets last year? We have, and it is the main reason we rarely tell people what we do for a living. What the lug nut will not tell you is that he probably lost a fortune the year *before*, and may well do the same next year. Many so-called investors are actually people who spend the majority of their time blindly chasing admittedly appealing sectors and markets, but do so without the smart controls that consequently put them in the position of living and dying by the same sword. If 50 percent of your portfolio was invested in Taiwanese semiconductor manufacturers from 1995 to 2000, you made a killing, but you took a *ton* of risk doing it. From 2000 to 2003, you lost it all and then some. As a hedge fund manager, if you are able to understand, measure, and adjust the risk levels in your portfolio, you can use this portfolio management skill to dial the risk up when you think the global economies will grow and dial the risk down when you think the "bear dance" is coming. In reality, you do not have to be a superior stock picker if you can manage market risk and adjust the risks in your portfolio at the appropriate times. Let us take a look at some of the risk measures you can use to gauge the threat level in your hedge fund.

Standard Deviation: In the investment world, standard deviation is a representation of the risk associated with a given security or the risk of a portfolio of securities. As we have discussed, risk is an important factor in determining how to efficiently manage a basket of investments because it determines the variation in returns on the asset or portfolio and gives you, as a hedge fund manager, a mathematical basis for investment decisions. The overall concept states that as risk increases, the expected return on the asset or portfolio will increase as a result of the risk premium. Said differently, investors should expect a higher return on an investment when that particular investment carries a higher level of risk, or uncertainty of return. It stands to reason that if you buy an emerging markets ETF like the Ishares MSCI Emerging Markets ETF (EEM) you are taking on much more risk and volatility than if you bought the broad-based Ishares MSCI EAFE Index Fund ETF (EFA). However, because economies and markets are receptive to international equities, you should also expect to reap the rewards of much higher returns because of this assumption of risk. Standard deviation provides a quantified estimate of the uncertainty of future returns for these types of investments.

Let us look at an example. Assume an investor sought to choose between two coal-mining stocks. Yanzou Coal Mining (YZC), a Chinese coal producer, posted an average rate of return over the past 10 years of 10 percent, with a standard deviation of 20 percent. Arch Coal (ACI), over the same period, had average returns of 12 percent, but a higher standard deviation of 30 percent. On the basis of risk and return, you may decide that Yanzhou Coal Mining is the safer choice, because Arch Coal's additional return is not worth the additional level of standard deviation. In this example, Yanzhou Coal Mining is expected to earn about 10 percent, plus or minus 20 percent, which tells us that an investor in Yanzhou can expect a rate of return during any given year to fall in the range of 30 percent to −10 percent in returns. As a portfolio manager looking at these two stocks, you need to weigh the overall risk-versus-return benefit that each of these two stocks might add to your portfolio. If you think that the coal industry is on the cusp of a raging bull market, Arch Coal would give you more bang for your buck and would more than likely be the better choice; if you feel coal is a good place to be, but your overall portfolio risk is already high, you may choose the more conservative route with Yanzhou Coal.

The calculation for the standard deviation of an investment is relatively straightforward and can be performed by following a few simple steps. First, calculate the average return of a security for your given time period to generate an expected return on the asset. For each period, subtracting the expected return from the actual return results in the *variance*. Next, we square the variance in each period to find the effect of the result on the overall risk of the asset. *The larger the variance in a period, the greater risk the security carries.* Taking the average of the squared variances results in the measurement of overall units of risk associated with the asset. Finding the square root of this variance results in the standard deviation of the investment tool in question. In Exhibit 9.2, you see a 10-day standard deviation calculation for Turkcell (TKC).

Sum of Deviation Squared = 21.14
Deviation Squared/10 = 2.11
Standard Deviation (Sq. root) = 1.45

One thing to mention is that, in this calculation, we are using historical or known prices. In many standard deviation calculations you find on the Web, they are using expected returns for the future and not historical prices from the past. Thus, from site to site, you may find the standard deviation numbers to be different. We prefer to look at the level and the trend of risk by using historical prices for our calculations. We just do not believe that investors or academics are able to accurately predict an expected range of returns for stocks. That said, whether your source is using historical numbers or expected returns, the overall trend and relative

EXHIBIT 9.2	10-Day Standard Deviation Calculation for Turkcell (TKC)		
Close	**10-day Mean**	**Deviation**	**Deviation Squared**
$15.00	$17.36	2.36	5.550736
$14.75	$17.36	2.61	6.791236
$16.50	$17.36	0.86	0.732736
$18.50	$17.36	−1.14	1.308736
$17.88	$17.36	−0.52	0.269361
$17.00	$17.36	0.36	0.126736
$18.00	$17.36	−0.64	0.414736
$18.75	$17.36	−1.39	1.943236
$19.25	$17.36	−1.89	3.587236
$18.00	$17.36	−0.64	0.414736

Source: www.investorspassport.com.

placing among industry peers should give you about the same amount of information for your investment decisions.

The calculation for the standard deviation is pretty painless. However, when you are analyzing hundreds of stocks, these calculations can be daunting. As well, the standard deviation of returns will change on a continuous basis. Therefore, we typically rely on a few sources for finding the standard deviations of our investments.

Yahoo Finance: We really like this resource more for ETFs and mutual funds. If you go to www.YahooFinance.com and put in the symbol for any ETF or mutual fund, you will see a listing down the left side for different information categories. If you click on the link for "Risk" halfway down that list, you can get a plethora of information on both returns and risk of the funds. Further, the site gives you an extra benefit, as it shows the standard deviation for the industry group as well as the investment itself. Therefore, you can compare the investment to the industry with relative ease. We talk about performance measurement later in the chapter, but this is also a good place to find information on ETF and mutual fund returns. This is also a good resource for finding statistics on beta and R-squared, which are two more of our risk concepts.

www.StockCharts.com: This is a great site for charting, regardless of the type of investing you are doing. You can use this site to research the standard deviations for stocks, ETFs, and mutual funds.

If you go to the site, you can pull up a SharpChart for any stock by simply putting in the symbol. When the chart comes up on the next page, you have the ability to manipulate the indicators you want to see, as well as the chart itself. We typically use a three-year weekly chart because we are trying to get a picture of the longer-term trend. Once you have the chart

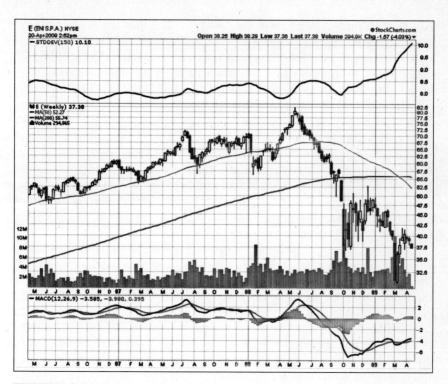

EXHIBIT 9.3 Three-Year Chart for Eni S.P.A. (E), Including Standard Deviation
Source: www.StockCharts.com.

up, scroll down to the bottom left of the page and look for a subgroup titled "Indicators." In the indicators area, you have the ability via drop-down
menus to manipulate the types of indicators you have on your chart. Drop
down one of the boxes and pull up "Std. Deviation." The parameters field
will match the time frame on the chart. Therefore, if you put "10" into that
area, you will be looking at the average standard deviation for 10 weeks.
Typically, we use 150 (for 150 weeks) in the parameters area to match the
length on the chart. Again, what we are looking at is the longer-term trend
of volatility, and thus risk, so we prefer to have a smoother trend line for
the standard deviation. The shorter your time frame, the more volatile the
output chart will be.

Exhibit 9.3 is a chart for Eni S. P. A. (E), an Italian oil and gas concern. The exhibit is a weekly three-year chart for the company, and we
have manipulated the standard deviation for a 150-week period. Note that
the standard deviation trend is just above the price chart. One of the first
things that jump out at you is the fact that the company has seen a big

rise in its volatility measure in the last year. This has happened because of the dynamic drops in the stock price. Remember, standard deviation is measuring the distance the return is varied away from its expected or average price. Therefore, when there is a huge swing either way, the level of volatility increases. Another thought to consider is that Eni S P A has seen its standard deviation stay around that 8 percent to 8.5 percent range for almost three years prior to the recent global meltdown. I would expect that, as the global economies firmed, Eni S P A would return to its normal standard deviation of closer to 8.5 percent and not stay toward the 10 percent figure to which it jumped. Again, the trend of the standard deviation is every bit as important as the actual number itself. If you went to a given web site and simply found that the company had a standard deviation of 10 percent, you are doing no more than taking a snapshot and not truly considering the company's volatility in a more normalized trend.

One last aspect of standard deviation that we need to discuss is the standard deviation of your *portfolio as a whole*. With many risk measures, the risk of the portfolio is simply the weighted average of the factors for the individual positions that make up the group. Our next indicator, beta, can be calculated this way. However, establishing the risk of a portfolio as calculated by standard deviation is a more complex matter, because the rates of return in the portfolio are of the individual assets and those assets are not likely to move together perfectly. Assuming they do not, the risk of the combined set of assets cannot be estimated by simply averaging their individual standard deviations. Not only must the risk of the individual assets be incorporated into the analysis, but the extent of the co-movement of those assets must also be accounted for. There are a number of programs on the Internet, as well as embedded into portfolio management sites, that will calculate this portfolio number for you, so we do not go into the manual calculations here. The process can be a bit daunting, and not something you find most people doing on a regular basis when you can easily access the tools on the Internet. The point, however, is that you cannot simply average the standard deviations of the positions in your portfolio to gain an accurate measure of your overall risk.

Beta: Beta is another risk or volatility measure we use in analyzing stocks and it is a bit friendlier in its application to our portfolios. It is calculated using regression analysis, but we do not go into the details of how to calculate it because beta figures are readily available on almost every major financial site on the planet. You can think of beta as the tendency of a stock's or bond's returns to respond to swings in the "benchmark" market. For most calculations on the Internet, the benchmark will be the S&P 500, although betas calculated using the MSCI EAFE can also be found on the Internet and they would probably be more relevant to you as an international hedge fund manager.

This may be a bit of "Investing 101" for some of you, but we mention it anyway. A beta of one indicates that the underlying security's price move will move step for step with the market itself. A beta of less than one means that the security will be less volatile than the market and should rise or fall less than the index. Finally, a beta of greater than one indicates that the security's price will be more volatile than the index. For example, if a stock's beta is 1.5, you can expect it to be 50 percent more volatile than the underlying benchmark. If the market goes up 12 percent, the stock should go up 50 percent more than the index and thus rise 18 percent. This also works to the downside so if the index were to drop 12 percent, you can expect the stock to drop by 18 percent.

Higher-beta stocks signify greater volatility and are therefore considered to be riskier. That said, they are, in turn, supposed to provide a potential for higher returns. The global technology industry is a good place to find high-beta stocks. Low-beta stocks offer less risk but also lower returns in a good market. Utility stocks are typically low-beta offerings. Betas can be zero, and as such, some zero-beta securities are essentially risk-free, such as Treasury bonds. However, it is not safe to *assume* that because a beta is zero, the asset is risk-free. A beta can be zero simply because there is *no correlation between that item and the market*. An example might be the betting on a rugby game; the correlation with the market will be zero, but it is certainly not a risk-free endeavor.

A negative beta simply means that the stock is inversely correlated with the market. Many precious metals and precious metal–related stocks are beta-negative, as their value tends to increase when the general market is down and vice versa.

The nice thing about using beta as a risk measure is that you can easily calculate it for your entire portfolio in an effort to see how much risk you have intertwined in your holdings. The beta of a portfolio is the weighted sum of the individual asset betas. You can easily put this data into an Excel spreadsheet and keep a running estimate for risk.

Let us say that our portfolio consisted of the following in Exhibit 9.4:

The beta for our portfolio can be calculated as:

$$\textbf{Beta} = \text{BHP portion} + \text{GRO portion} + \text{BBD portion} + \text{DEG portion}$$

$$+ \text{SAP portion} + \text{PG portion}$$

$$\textbf{Beta} = .19(1.45) + .12(1.84) + .15(1.60) + .18(.72) + .15(1.05) + .21(.54)$$

$$\textbf{Beta} = 1.14$$

Looking at our portfolio beta, we can assume that if the market goes up 10 percent, our hedge fund will go up about 11.40 percent and if the markets decline by 10 percent, our hedge fund will decline by 11.40 percent.

EXHIBIT 9.4   Sample Portfolio with Associated Beta Measurements

Name	Country	$'s Invested	% of Portfolio	Beta
BHP Billiton Ltd (BHP)	Australia	$19,000	19%	1.45
Agria Corp (GRO)	China	$12,000	12%	1.84
Banco Bradesco (BBD)	Brazil	$15,000	15%	1.60
Delhaize Group (DEG)	Belgium	$18,000	18%	0.72
SAP AG (SAP)	Germany	$15,000	15%	1.05
Procter & Gamble (PG)	United States	$21,000	21%	0.54
	Total	**$100,000**	**100%**	

Source: www.investorspassport.com.

If we believe that our beta was too high, we may consider selling Agria Corp (GRO) and replace it with Swiss-based Syngenta AG (SYT). Both companies work in the agricultural operations industry, but SYT has a beta of .92, which would drop our portfolio beta closer to 1. Keep in mind that SYT and GRO are not exact replacements for one another, as each do work on different sides of the agricultural industry. For our simple example, however, it makes the point.

Let me also say that, in our calculation, we used the beta for the companies as compared to the S&P 500, which is something with which some academics may have a problem. Personally, we do not. We realize that a beta gauged off the S&P 500 is going to be different from a beta pegged to the MSCI EAFE, but we are inclined to believe the difference would not be so drastic that it would defeat the usage of the betas as a whole, especially considering the high correlation of the developed markets that we discussed in Chapter 1. The fact is that beta figures calculated from the MSCI EAFE are not readily available on the Internet and until they are, we do not have a problem with using the S&P 500 as long as the aforementioned correlations remain in place (which they surely will for at least the foreseeable future).

Let us mention a key shortcoming associated with using beta: beta does not incorporate new information coming into the market. Consider the electrical utility company American Electric Power (AEP). In past years, AEP has been considered a defensive stock with a low beta. However, it then made the strategic decision to enter the merchant energy business and assumed high debt levels. From this point forward, the historical beta for AEP no longer captured the substantial risks the company took on. At the same time, many technology stocks, such as Google, are so new to the market that they have inadequate price history to establish a dependable beta.

One more thing: do not confuse beta with the diversification correlation discussed in Chapter 1. The correlation coefficient associated with measurement of diversification is measured on a scale of −1 to +1, while beta measurements frequently fall outside of that range; more importantly, diversification correlation is a measurement of *direction*, while beta is a measurement of both *direction* and *magnitude*, and thus serves in its totality as a measure of volatility.

ASSET ALLOCATION

Asset allocation describes an investment strategy that aims to balance risk and reward by apportioning a portfolio's assets according to that individual or institution's goals, risk tolerance, and investment horizon. The three principal asset classes to which we pay the most mind in this endeavor are equities, fixed-income instruments, and cash. Real estate is a fourth fundamental asset class that can have relevance here, but we want to, for the purposes of this discussion, focus primarily on those assets that will have near-universal applicability for the reader. Aside from real estate–based securities, movements in and out of real property interests are generally more cumbersome, which means that asset class does not lend itself to the nimble allocation movements we discuss here. Many readers may decide to include real estate as a part of their hedge fund, but others will decide against it, so we keep our discussion of asset allocation limited to the aforementioned instruments.

As all three of our main categories have different levels of risk and return, so it is that each will behave differently over time, depending on global economic and market conditions. In Exhibit 9.5, you find historical return numbers for each (1926–2006). In reality, if you are running only a long/short hedge fund, you probably will not be concerned with asset allocation, for the simple reason that you will be operating only within the realm of equity-based investments. However, if you seek to create a hedge fund based on diversification, maintaining the proper mix among stocks, bonds, and cash is important. Always keep in mind that asset allocation, if approached properly, remains a fluid process; you must remain prepared to lighten your equity weighting and take those dollars to the safety of bonds or cash if you believe the global equity markets are due to see a significant, near-term correction.

There is no simple blueprint that can find the right asset allocation for every investor. However, note that that asset allocation is one of the most important decisions that investors make; in other words, your selection of individual securities is *secondary* to the way you allocate your investment

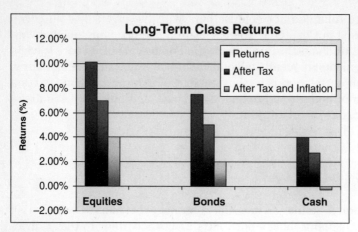

EXHIBIT 9.5   Time Period 1926–2006
Source: www.investorspassport.com.

in stocks, bonds, and cash. A fundamental justification for asset allocation is the notion that different asset classes offer returns that are not perfectly correlated. Therefore, proper diversification reduces the overall risk to the portfolio.

Strategic, Tactical, and Insured Asset Allocation

There are three primary types of asset allocation in which you should become versed: strategic asset allocation, tactical asset allocation, and insured asset allocation. Let us take this opportunity to discuss each.

Strategic asset allocation is a method that establishes and adheres to what is known as a "base policy mix." When a typical investor talks about his or her asset allocation, the investor is usually referring to his strategic allocation. This is a proportional combination of assets based on expected rates of return for each asset class. For example, if global equities have historically returned 11 percent per year and bonds have returned 6 percent per year, a mix of 50 percent stocks and 50 percent bonds would be expected to return 8.5 percent per year. As a hedge fund manager, you have to determine what constitutes both acceptable levels of risk as well as acceptable returns; it is these factors that will determine your asset allocation.

Tactical asset allocation is a dynamic strategy that actively adjusts a portfolio's strategic asset allocation based on the short- and intermediate-term market forecasts you make. Its goal is to take advantage of perceived inefficiencies in the relative prices of securities within different asset classes. As an example, in March 2003, the global equity markets were ascending out of a bear market. Let us say that your strategic asset allocation historically kept your portfolio with a mix of 60 percent equities, 30 percent bonds, and 10 percent cash. If you were able to identify this bear market low, your tactical asset allocation would direct you to adjust your long-term strategic asset allocation by potentially going 80 percent to equities, 15 percent to bonds, and 5 percent to cash. The objective for the tactical asset allocation is to systematically exploit inefficiencies or short-term imbalances in equilibrium values among different asset or sub-asset classes. Over time, strategic long-term target allocations are the most important determinants of total return for a broadly diversified portfolio, but tactical asset allocation can add value at the margin, if designed with the appropriate rigor to overcome the significant risk factors and obstacles unique to the strategy.

Your tactical asset allocation may also drive your decision to move from one level of risk in the portfolio to another. For example, let us say your strategic asset allocation currently stood at 70/20/10 (equities, bonds, cash), but you felt the global economies were going to strengthen in the coming quarters. Instead of taking a pure tactical approach and changing your 70/20/10 mix, you may decide to simply increase the *risk/return levels* within those categories. If you were holding positions in government bonds in the United States, the United Kingdom, and Germany as part of your fixed-income holdings, you may want to switch that portion of your portfolio over to the Powershares Emerging Markets Sovereign Debt ETF (PCY). The fund invests in U.S. dollar–denominated government bonds issued by approximately 22 emerging-market countries. In making this move, you would not be changing the strategic asset allocation you set up on behalf of your portfolio, but simply ratcheting up the risk/return level of the portfolio just a bit. Instead of investing in a government bond in the United States, the United Kingdom, and Germany, you are investing in government bonds in Russia, Indonesia, and Bulgaria with this move. Doing this would add more risk to the portfolio, but it would also drive your yields higher. As another example, if you were invested in the WisdomTree Small Japan ETF (DFJ) but saw some real signs that indicate the rate of economic growth in the Far East was going to slow, you may be inclined to reallocate those dollars to the WisdomTree Japan Total Dividend Fund (DXJ) in order to lower your risk. Again, you have not left the asset class; you simply changed the risk/return characteristics *within* that class.

Insured asset allocation is an allocation model that you typically find practiced with high net worth individuals who are looking to protect, in absolute terms, a certain portion of their wealth (this amount typically ranges between 75 percent and 100 percent of the portfolio). With an insured asset allocation, you establish a base portfolio value below which the portfolio should never be allowed to fall. As long as the portfolio achieves a return above its base, you will use active management in an attempt to increase the portfolio value as much as possible. If, however, the portfolio should ever drop to the minimum floor value, your primary weighting shifts to risk-free assets like Treasury bonds so that the base value remains uncompromised.

You can implement an insured asset allocation strategy either with a formula approach or with a portfolio insurance approach. The formula approach is a graduated strategy: as the portfolio value declines, you weight more heavily into risk-free assets so that when the portfolio reaches its base level, you are *entirely invested* in risk-free assets. With the portfolio insurance approach, you safeguard the base capital through the use of put options and/or futures contracts.

Insured asset allocation may be suitable for high net worth, risk-averse investors who desire a certain level of active portfolio management but appreciate the security of establishing a guaranteed floor below which the portfolio is not allowed to decline. For example, an investor who wishes to establish a minimum standard of living during retirement might find an insured asset allocation strategy ideally suited to his or her goals.

Because we are running an international hedge fund, one last consideration in our asset allocation decision has to be cultural influences. Non–U.S. investors make their asset allocation decisions, at least broadly, in much the same way we do in the United States, but because they face different social, economic, political, and tax environments, their specific allocation considerations will not be exactly the same as those of U.S. investors. The CFA Institute performed research in the early 1990s as part of their "Culture and Portfolio Mixes" studies, and what they determined was that in the United States, both foreign and domestic equities composed about 45 percent of invested assets for institutional dollars; from that same study, we learned that the percentage stood at about 72 percent for U.K. portfolios, while Germany and Japan saw their representative figures come in at around 11 percent and 24 percent, respectively.

Differences in the political and socioeconomic environments in each of these countries go a long way toward clearing up the variation in equity ownership levels. For example, of the countries we mentioned, the average age of the population was the highest in Germany and Japan, and lowest in the United Kingdom and United States; that fact goes a long way to explaining the lower equity weightings in Germany and Japan. In the United Kingdom, a government privatization program during the 1980s encouraged equity ownership among investors, while in Germany, government oversight prevents insurance companies from having more than 20 percent of their assets in equities—insurance companies are one of the largest institutional buyers of equities in the world, so this cap curbs the total equity weighting in this country. Additionally, both Germany and Japan have strong banking sectors that invest *privately* in firms, further limiting the capitalization of publicly traded securities in those countries. Since 1960, the United Kingdom's cost of living has risen at a rate more than four and a half times that of Germany, and this inflationary bias in the U.K. economy favors equities in its country's asset allocations. The analysis looks only at four countries, but the important point to take from this is that it behooves a hedge fund manager to, for the specific purpose of asset allocation, constantly monitor and fully understand the internal political and economic climates of the countries in which he is investing.

One final thought on asset allocation as it applies to the global markets pertains to the breakdown of assets within each of these classes. For the equity portion of the portfolio, you need to consider that the relative market value of a country's equities is their value as a percentage of the total value of all world equities. For example, the market value of U.S. equities is about 30 percent of the total value of all equities in the world, where the Japanese markets account for about 8 percent. If you are completely neutral on all the global equity markets, your portfolio would hold about 30 percent in U.S. equities and 8 percent in Japanese equities, along with the percentages for all the countries shown in Exhibit 9.6. However, if you were bullish on Japan and bearish on the United States, you may have 10 percent to 15 percent of your portfolio in Japanese stocks and only 15 percent to 20 percent of your portfolio in U.S. equities. That said, asset allocation decisions are not limited to general considerations of weightings in stocks, bonds, and cash; you must also make decisions *within* those classes in an effort to maximize your investment returns. Some may choose to make "bigger picture" decisions as to their asset allocations and then turn to index funds to help them keep their assets allocated correctly. For most, it is these deeper, more root-level allocation decisions that will keep you in a better position to realize quality returns. Note in Exhibit 9.7 a snapshot listing of the world equity market percentages, by country.

Studies on the factors that influence long-term investment performance have almost always arrived at the same, significant conclusion: 85 percent to 95 percent of overall investment returns arise from the first and second decisions that are made on the consideration of long-term asset allocation choice. This tells us that the chief determinant of investment returns, as well as sources of risk, lies with the asset allocation decision. As you approach the management of your hedge fund, you need to first come to the realization that while the actual research and investment selection may be the "sexiest" part of the process, it is in the area of portfolio management where you should principally concentrate before you invest the first dollar.

EXHIBIT 9.6 Percent of World Stock Market Cap by Country

Country	Jan. 04	Current	Country	Chg Since Jan. 04
United States	43.7%	29.9%	Saudi Arabia	877.5%
Japan	10.3%	8.2%	Egypt	561.6%
UK	7.8%	6.8%	Qatar	310.2%
China	1.7%	5.4%	Brazil	266.6%
France	4.6%	4.4%	UAE	241.0%
Hong Kong	2.4%	4.3%	China	218.7%
Canada	2.7%	3.7%	Russia	173.5%
Germany	3.5%	3.6%	India	123.7%
Brazil	0.8%	2.8%	Kuwait	111.0%
Australia	1.8%	2.6%	Argentina	85.2%
Switzerland	2.2%	2.2%	Hong Kong	81.6%
India	0.9%	2.1%	South Korea	67.8%
Italy	2.0%	1.8%	Mexico	65.9%
Spain	1.6%	1.8%	Israel	57.0%
South Korea	1.1%	1.8%	Singapore	55.7%
Russia	0.6%	1.8%	Australia	45.0%
Taiwan	1.4%	1.5%	Chile	41.2%
Argentina	0.6%	1.1%	Canada	36.4%
Sweden	1.0%	1.0%	South Africa	34.9%
Saudi Arabia	0.1%	0.9%	Spain	10.9%
Netherlands	1.2%	0.9%	Taiwan	6.1%
Singapore	0.6%	0.9%	Germany	3.2%
Mexico	0.5%	0.8%	Sweden	1.2%
South Africa	0.6%	0.8%	Switzerland	−0.2%
UAE	0.1%	0.4%	France	−4.8%
Kuwait	0.2%	0.4%	Italy	−10.7%
Chile	0.3%	0.4%	UK	−12.3%
Israel	0.2%	0.4%	Japan	−20.2%
Egypt	0.0%	0.2%	Netherlands	−25.2%
Qatar	0.1%	0.2%	United States	−31.6%

Source: www.seekingalpha.com.

PERFORMANCE EVALUATION

As a hedge fund manager, you should always be evaluating the performance of your portfolios. It can be costly and time-consuming to manage your investments and pick stocks, so it is important to ensure that the effort is worth the time and money you invest into it by also engaging in timely, effective performance evaluation. The key to proper performance measurement lies in understanding that it is not evaluated simply by matching your

		Average Annual	
EXHIBIT 9.7 Sample Portfolios with Associated Return and Beta Information for the Purpose of Computing Treynor Values			
Managers		**Return**	**Beta**
MSCI EAFE		10%	1
Our Portfolio		14%	1.05
Manager B		14%	1.15
Manager C		16%	1.22

Source: www.investorspassport.com.

performance against that of the EAFE and determining success or failure; performance evaluation without the consideration of risk is of little value to a hedge fund manager. It is not enough to say you have beaten the index if you have taken substantially more risk than the index in order to get the job done. Let us take a look at a few performance evaluation techniques you can use to analyze your portfolio.

Treynor Portfolio Performance Measure

This particular method of performance measurement, also known as the reward-to-volatility ratio, was developed by Jack Treynor in 1965. Treynor was the first to provide investors with a composite measure of portfolio performance that also included risk. Treynor's goal was to find a performance measure that could apply to all investors, regardless of their personal risk preferences. He suggested that there were really two components of risk: the risk produced by fluctuations in the market, as well as the risk arising from the fluctuations of individual securities.

The formula for the Treynor measure looks like this:

$$T_i = \frac{R_1 - RFR}{\beta_1}$$

where: $R_1 =$ the average rate of return for portfolio *1* during a specified period.

$RFR =$ the average rate of return on a risk-free investment during the same time period.

$B_1 =$ Beta = the portfolio's relative volatility

A larger Ti value indicates a larger slope and a better portfolio for all investors, regardless of their risk preferences. The numerator represents the risk premium and the denominator represents the risk of the portfolio; thus the value, T, represents the portfolio's *return per unit of systematic risk*. *All* risk-averse investors would want to maximize this value.

To better understand how this works, let us look at an illustration. Suppose that the 10-year annual return for the MSCI EAFE (market portfolio) is 10 percent, while the average annual return on Treasury bills (a good proxy for the risk-free rate globally) is 5 percent. We are evaluating our performance against two other managers with the following 10-year results in Exhibit 9.7:

Now, we can compute the Treynor value for each:

$$T(\text{MSCI EAFE}) = (.10 - .05)/1 = .05$$
$$T(\text{Our Portfolio}) = (.14 - .05)/1.02 = .0882$$
$$T(\text{manager B}) = (.14 - .05)/1.15 = .0783$$
$$T(\text{manager C}) = (.16 - .05)/1.28 = .0859$$

If we were evaluating the portfolio manager on performance alone, we may have inadvertently identified manager C as giving the best results simply because he had the highest return. However, when considering the *risks* that each manager took to attain his or her respective returns, our hedge fund demonstrated the better outcome. In this case, all three managers performed better than the aggregate market.

Because this measure accounts only for systematic risk, it assumes that the investor already has an effectively diversified portfolio and, therefore, unsystematic risk (also known as diversifiable risk) is not considered. As a result, this performance measure should really only be used by investors who hold diversified portfolios.

Sharpe Portfolio Performance Measure

The Sharpe ratio is almost identical to the Treynor measure. However, with the Sharpe measure, the risk gauge used is the standard deviation of the portfolio instead of beta. The Sharpe measure evaluates the portfolio manager on the basis of both rate of return and diversification. You see this as it considers total portfolio risk in the denominator. If we had a fully diversified portfolio, then both the Sharpe and Treynor measures should give us the same ranking. A poorly diversified portfolio could realize a higher ranking with the Treynor measure than with the Sharpe measure.

(You may recognize the Sharpe Ratio from our discussion of it when we were speaking about bond portfolio concepts, but we want to illustrate it again in terms of its role in overall portfolio management.)

	Sample Portfolios with Associated
EXHIBIT 9.8	Return and Standard Deviation Information for the Purpose of Computing Sharpe Ratios

Managers	Average Annual Return	Std Deviation
MSCI EAFE	10%	.18
Our Portfolio	14%	.11
Manager B	14%	.20
Manager C	16%	.22

Source: www.investorspassport.com.

The Sharpe ratio is defined as follows:

$$S_1 = \frac{R_1 - RFR}{SD_1}$$

Using our earlier example, and assuming that the MSCI EAFE had a standard deviation of 18 percent over a 10-year period and a risk-free rate of 5 percent, let us determine the Sharpe ratios for the following portfolio managers (see Exhibit 9.8):

$$S(\text{MSCI EAFE}) = (.10 - .05)/.18 = .278$$
$$S(\text{Our Portfolio}) = (.14 - .05)/.11 = .818$$
$$S(\text{manager B}) = (.14 - .05)/.20 = .450$$
$$S(\text{manager C}) = (.16 - .05)/.22 = .500$$

Once again, we find that the best portfolio is not necessarily the one with the highest return. Instead, it is the one with the most superior risk-adjusted return—which, in this case, was ours once again.

Unlike the Treynor measure, the Sharpe ratio evaluates the portfolio manager on the basis of both rate of return and diversification. Therefore, the Sharpe ratio is more appropriate for well-diversified portfolios because it more accurately takes into account the risks of the portfolio.

Jensen Portfolio Performance Measure

Named after its creator, Michael C. Jensen, the Jensen measure calculates the excess return that a portfolio generates over its expected return. This measure is also known as *alpha*. You will hear this term quite a bit within the hedge fund community, because, in the end, a hedge fund manager's

ability to deliver excess return is what this game is all about; that excess
return is called alpha. In our estimation, the calculation of alpha is the most
relevant performance measurement technique of the three, and the one you
will see most often quoted the most in investment circles.

The Jensen ratio measures how much of the portfolio's rate of return
is attributable to our ability to deliver above-average returns, adjusted for
market risk; the higher the ratio, the better the risk-adjusted returns. A
portfolio with a consistently positive excess return will have a positive alpha, while a portfolio with a consistently negative excess return will have a
negative alpha. A positive alpha of 1.0 means the fund has outperformed its
benchmark index by 1 percent. Correspondingly, a similar negative alpha
would indicate an underperformance of 1 percent.

The formula is broken down as follows:

Jensen's Alpha = Portfolio Return − Expected Portfolio Return
    (where Expected Return = Risk Free Rate of Return
    + Beta (Return of Market − Risk-Free Rate of Return)

If we again assume a risk-free rate of 5 percent and a market return of
10 percent, what is the alpha measurement for the funds in Exhibit 9.9?

The first thing we need to do is calculate our portfolios' *expected
returns*:

ER(Our Portfolio) = .05 + 1.05 (.10 − .05) = .1025 or 10.25% return
ER(B) = .05 + 1.15 (.10 − .05) = .1075 or 10.75% return
ER(C) = .05 + 1.22 (.10 − .05) = .1110 or 11.10% return

EXHIBIT 9.9	Sample Portfolios with Associated Return and Beta Information for the Purpose of Computing Alphas

Managers	Average Annual Return	Beta
Our Portfolio	14%	1.05
Manager B	14%	1.15
Manager C	16%	1.22

Source: www.investorspassport.com.

Then, we calculate the portfolios' alphas by subtracting the expected return of the portfolio from the actual return:

$$\text{Alpha Our Portfolio} = 14\% - 10.25\% = 3.75\%$$
$$\text{Alpha B} = 14\% - 10.75\% = 3.25\%$$
$$\text{Alpha C} = 16\% - 11.10\% = 4.90\%$$

Which manager performed the best? Manager C did so, on a risk-adjusted basis. Manager C added the most value to his investors' portfolios. Our portfolio performed better than portfolio B because, although manager B had the same annual return, it was expected that our portfolio would yield a lower return because the portfolio's beta was lower than that of portfolio B.

Both returns and risk for portfolios will vary by time period. The Jensen measure requires the use of a different risk-free rate of return for each time period in your analysis. So, if you wanted to assess the performance of a fund manager for a five-year period using annual intervals, you would have to examine the fund's annual returns *minus* the risk-free return for each year and relate the result to the yearly return on the market portfolio, minus the same risk-free rate. On the other hand, the Treynor and Sharpe ratios look at average returns for the *total period* under consideration for all variables in the formula. Like the Treynor measure, however, Jensen's alpha calculates risk premiums in terms of beta and therefore assumes the portfolio is already adequately diversified. Thus, the ratio is best applied with diversified portfolios.

Portfolio performance measures should always remain a key component of the investment decision process, notably so for you as you manage your hedge fund. These tools provide the necessary information for you to assess how effectively you are investing the money in your portfolio. Remember, portfolio returns are only part of the story, and they can be a very *misleading* part of the story. Without evaluating risk-adjusted returns, you cannot possibly see the whole investment picture, which may inadvertently lead to clouded investment decisions.

Index